Speaking to the Heart

Moments with Jesus

To Ralph and Karen
May God continue
to watch over
you and Bless
you Both
April Yarber

APRIL YARBER

Trilogy Christian Publishers
A Wholly Owned Subsidary of Trinity Broadcasting Network
2442 Michelle Drive
Tustin, CA 92780

For information, address Trilogy Christian Publishing
Rights Department, 2442 Michelle Drive, Tustin, Ca 92780.
Trilogy Christian Publishing/ TBN and colophon are trademarks of Trinity Broadcasting Network.

For information about special discounts for bulk purchases, please contact Trilogy Christian Publishing.

Manufactured in the United States of America

10 9 8 7 6 5 4 3 2 1

Library of Congress Cataloging-in-Publication Data is available.

ISBN 978-1-64088-427-4 (Print Book)
ISBN 978-1-64088-428-1 (ebook)

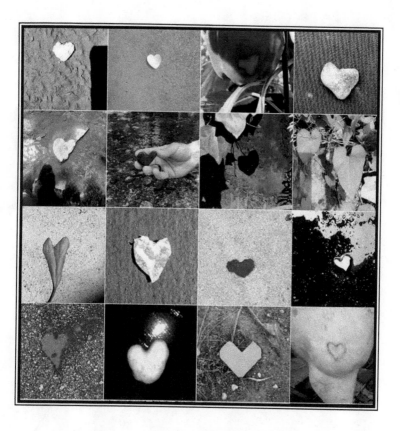

Having the eyes of your hearts enlight-
ened, that you may know what is the hope to
which he has called you, what are the riches
of his glorious inheritance in the saints.
—Ephesians 1:18 (ESV)

Dedication and Acknowledgments

Dedicated to the Lord for whom I write. I love you, Jesus, you are my Lord. Who leads, who gives, who loves, who forgives, and who fulfills your promises. You are who I thank for gifting this life to me, and all the people in it. I pray to you, Lord, that whoever reads this, please let it point them to you, bless them abundantly, and fill their hearts with all your joy and love. Stir in them a desire to know you more. I pray for them to know the fullness of God, amen.

This is dedicated to, my two beautiful daughters. Amanda and Autumn, if you dream it with God's good purpose you can achieve it. Follow your hearts, my girls, and let Jesus lead. Let him open his will for your lives. I love you both with my whole heart. Love, Mom.

Also, thank you to my babe, James, who gave me the encouragement to keep going. You were there during the tears I cried when I thought I could never accomplish the task of finishing what God was calling me to do. So thank you for always having faith in me. I love you, Mebe.

To my family, I love you all! All my sisters, my brother, aunts, uncles, and cousins, mwah!

To my father, who instilled in me that hard work is good and told me to try things because I would never know what good they would bring if I never took the chance. Thank you for all your years of hard work and providing for me. I love you, Dad.

To all my readers and supporters, to all who hear and are learning to hear God speaking to their hearts. A thank you and encouragement. He will meet you wherever you are.

Never give up, keep seeking Him and His truth and you will find Him when you seek Him with your whole heart.

To my mother, who grew in her faith and is always my rock. My own prayer warrior. I love you, Mom, and all your special ways.

To my stepfather, who always helped all my mom's children and grandchildren, as if we were his own. I have my career at the hospital because of your encouragement and support. Thank you for all the kindness you've shown. It hasn't gone unnoticed.

To my brother in Christ, Rick (Rico), thank you for always being an encourager. God definitely gifted you, and he surely blesses those around you who have been encouraged by you.

Thank you to all my work family, you all have been very supportive and helped me to keep on writing and pursuing this dream. Thank you for allowing me to share it with you before all the spell checks.

A special dedication to both my grandmothers who have passed away.

Grandma Hazel, your faith in the Lord was always something I admired. From you, I learned a tender heart and gentle nature and to trust the Lord without condition.

Grandma June, your strength of character and hope in the Lord gave me the ability to overcome what was hard in my youth.

From you, I learned strength and my worth... I love you both; see you again in heaven.

Let the words of my mouth and the
meditation of my heart be acceptable in your
sight, O Lord, my rock and my redeemer.
—Psalm 19:14 (ESV)

Preface

There is a purpose for this book, it is meant to encourage and to comfort my readers. It is meant to stir your spirit and to create in you a thirst for a stronger relationship with Jesus. It is my private treasured moments, my time spent with Jesus shared. It is not meant to replace the Holy Bible. Please read The Bible and always Seek HIM first. I have added Scripture throughout. There are 365 days of devotions one for every day of the year. I also included my prayer at the bottom of each page. There is one blank page before the start of the new year and one at the end of the year for you to write your prayer requests, reflections, and hopes for the upcoming year. This is my true labor of love. Just me working for the Lord. During my journey of writing, I have spent dedicated time with Jesus every day, and it has helped me personally grow in my faith and brought me closer to God the Father, whom I love. I am grateful to Him and all that he has helped me accomplish. All for His glory.

He answers our prayers not only in the way we would hope or presume, but Jesus has his own way of doing things and his are far better than ours or the way of this world. Before this journey, I asked him to help me read my Bible more and now for the last year, I have found myself mulling over scriptures and spending some much-needed time with him soaked in his word… He is just that way. I have never attempted to finish any good idea I have had, but this idea of writing the devotional was not my own. It was given to me by The Holy Spirit. And now I am close to completion. If I was writing for myself, I would have never accomplished it, God knows me full well. You will also notice I've have included some of the pictures of hearts that I have seen over the years. The title provided by Him as well. Speaking to the Heart—yes, makes sense to me. As that is what he does during our prayers and in our lives. He speaks to our hearts; it is only then our daily choice, to listen…

Seek God first and always follow your heart, he will lead you to some amazing places in the garden of your lives.

As always with love,
April<3

Monthly Prayers and Hopes
for the Upcoming Year

_____

_____

_____

_____

_____

_____

_____

_____

_____

_____

_____

_____

_____

_____

_____

_____

_____

_____

_____

_____

_____

_____

_____

_____

_____

January

And when your heart has wings you can fly!
Saw this heart on my lunch break walking at
work. God has a way of cheering us up when
we are feeling down and this day he cheered me
up by sending me a love that was soaring.

Bringing Light to the Darkness

Happy New Year's Day! My dear, beloved child, I have seen all that you have gone through in the past year. But you, my child, must keep your eyes fixed on the prize. Keep moving forward focusing on me, with your feet firmly planted on my good message. Keep balanced and remain rooted in me and my living word. Quench your thirst for me daily by reading my good book, the Holy Bible. Armor yourself daily with my verses and passages of Scriptures. Put on my whole armor each morning before you step out. You must remember that it is, I, your God, who has gone before you, and that with the strength of your faith, there is nothing to fear. As you will find victory rushing toward you, like healthy flowing rivers of abundance. There are streams in the desert, so hold fast to the Holy Spirit, the helper, who lives within you. Even when the lush gardens of abundance seem empty and barren, you must keep on. Keep working toward good goals and desiring to help others. As we bring an abundance of love that lasts, casting off shadows bringing the light of hope to the shadows, for this year and all the years to come. You shall stand brave as my child, as we will continue bringing light to the darkness.

> *Whoever believes in me, as the Scripture has said, 'Out of his heart will flow rivers of living water.'*
> (John 7:38, ESV)

> *You crown the year with your bounty: your wagon tracks overflow with abundance. The pastures of the wilderness over-*

flow, the hills gird themselves with joy, the meadows clothe themselves with flocks, the valley deck themselves with grain, they shout and sing together with joy.
(Psalm 65:11–13, ESV)

For nothing will be impossible with God.
(Luke 1:37, ESV)

And I will make them and the places all around my hill a blessing, and I will send down the showers in their season; they shall be showers of blessing.
(Ezekiel 34:36, ESV)

Prayer: Father God, thank you for this day, the first day of this beautiful new year. I pray that you walk with us all. Keeping us strong in our faith and bring to us an abundance of joy filled with your Presence and love. We can do all things through you, because of your strength. Please help us to maintain our goals as we keep working toward accomplishing them. In Jesus's name, I pray, giving thanks and praise for this good year to come. Amen.

January 1

As Life Unfolds

As your life unfolds, you will someday be gifted with the understanding of all I have done and am doing for you. I love you, my child, with an everlasting love that at this moment supersedes the thoughts of what your human mind can comprehend. Keep working toward the goals of my good nature. Take a breath of my sweetness all found with my love. Enjoying with a refreshed spirit the beauty in life. Remain hopeful and certain of what you have not seen, holding fast to the good promises I have given. As this is a gift of faith, and the light of a new understanding all found within my good purpose. There is victory, where there is love. Starting off in this new year, try not to doubt yourself, my child, as I call you to special tasks. I have given you this calling because I know your heart. I am your Lord and know what calling is prime for my children to succeed. Therefore, find no doubt in yourself, as I have no doubt in you and what I am calling you to do. Hear my words and put them into practice. Be happy and joyful finding the gift of my strength. Together we will walk into the glory of my good purposes, sharing with others, as your life unfolds.

For the word of God is alive and active. Sharper than any double-edged sword, it penetrates even to dividing souls and spirit, joints and marrow; it judges the thoughts of attitudes of the heart.
(Hebrews 4:12, NIV)

The unfolding of your words gives light; it imparts understanding to the simple.
(Psalm 119:130, ESV)

Therefore everyone who hears these words of mine and puts them into practice is like a wise man who built his house on the rock.
(Matthew 7:24, NIV)

Prayer: Father God, today I lift us all up to you and thank you for your plans for our lives. I know your ways are higher than ours and have faith in your good promises. I pray to remain joyful this day and pray to always be a blessing to others; I pray to remain faithful to your good purposes. Help direct our steps and lead us through this day full of love and happiness. In Jesus's name, I pray giving thanks, amen.

January 2

His Good Nature

Good morning, my beloved, today if the world brings you frustrations, just call on me to help you. Put away all the grumbling nature that many of my children have. If you do everything as if working for me, you will find satisfaction in the competition and joyful perseverance in the tasks. Let your light shine before others bringing to them an example of my good nature. Even in daily frustrations, you can be filled with my peace and the glory of love. Do not argue with others, but instead, show them what my kindness and understanding look like. Exemplifying the glory of your Lord. Let my examples shine through you being cheerful and present. Lacking nothing as I will provide all that you need. Shine brightly out casting any gray clouds, with the power of my Presence. I will shower you with my greatness and my Holiness and fill you with my good nature daily. Everything in my perfect time, as I am your Lord.

> *Do everything without grumbling or arguing, so that you may become blameless and pure, children of God without fault in a warped and crooked generation. Then you will shine among them like stars in the sky as you hold firmly to the word of life.*
> (Philippians 2:14–16, NIV)

> *And so I will show my greatness and my holiness, and I will make myself known in the sight of many nations. Then they will know that I am the Lord.*
> (Ezekiel 38:23, NIV)

I am the Lord; I have called you in righteousness; I will take you by the hand and keep you; I will give you as a covenant for the people, a light for the nations.
(Isaiah 42:6, ESV)

Prayer: Father God, thank you for this day and all that you bring. I pray to walk in the light of your good steps without complaining. I thank you for all my situations and give them to you. Your will, your way, because I know your timing is perfect, and thank you for the outcomes. In Jesus's name, I pray, lifting us all up to you Lord. I also pray for you to protect us and enshroud us. Filling us with the light of your love, amen.

January 3

Following the Light of the World

Oh, my precious child, another morning is here. Another day to shine the light I have placed within you and to follow me. You will hear me speaking to your heart. Sometimes in the still small voice, and others in a loud and thunderous roar... I will remind you, my beloved, you will never walk in darkness again, when you choose to follow me, as I am the light of the world. You can walk confidently through any circumstance, situation, or environment, knowing that I am with you. I am your Good Shepherd, no matter where we travel—you can trust me to lead you into my perfect will. If you let go and let me, I can lead you into the light of my plans for you. But you must first release all your own plans that you once held for yourself. Let go of yesterday's expectations, as I may be leading you somewhere new. Follow me, surrender to the natural flow of my most amazing current. Let your steps grow momentum. As you follow me and gain with each step more strength, peace, perseverance, and understanding. I am growing you up in love, my child. Growing you up in your faith. Stand up to the hurts and forgive. No more fear of darkness. I am your Lord. I AM the majestic...intensely, brilliant light that leads to life. Choose me, again and again, child. Loosen your grasp and give in, surrendering and following me, your Savoir, the light of the world.

For at one time you were in darkness,
but now you are light in the Lord. Walk as
children of light.
(Ephesians 5:8, ESV)

Again Jesus spoke to them saying, "I am the light of the world. Whoever follows me will not walk in darkness but will have the light of life."
(John 8:12, ESV)

This is the message we have heard from him and proclaim to you, that God is light, in him there is no darkness at all.
(1 John 1:5, ESV)

Prayer: Father God, thank you for this day. Make yours the loudest voice in my mind. Guide me into your will for my life. Make your paths known to me, my Lord, providing your most brilliant light. Please watch over all my family and friends. I praise you, Lord Jesus, and it is in your name I pray, amen.

January 4

The Wealth of Wisdom

Today when you arise, my child, be thankful for all that you have and for all that you've learned. As wisdom bestows well-being. When my children learn from past situations and mistakes it is good. As they are growing forward. Do not let your mind bring the past to you, day in and day out, or you may never leave there. Learn to let go of the past and embrace the present. Be hopeful for your future. I have plans for you, my child, not plans to harm you but to prosper you. Giving you hope and a bright outlook on what lies ahead. Keep hold of my promises and commit to my teaching. Holding my commands in your heart, for they will bring you peace and prosperity. My children who find wisdom are blessed, as wisdom is more precious than rubies. It is more profitable than silver and gold. Long life is in the hands of the child who holds onto wisdom and finds understanding in the lessons of life, which I teach. Practicing always the good ways of my teaching. As with each situation you journey through, you may gain peace and the steady learned wealth of wisdom.

Blessed is the one who finds wisdom, and the one who gets understanding, for the gain from her is better than gain from silver and her profit is better than gold. She is more precious than jewels, and nothing you desire can compare to her. Long life is in her right hand; in her left hand are riches and honor. Her ways are ways of pleasantness, and all her paths peace.
(Proverbs 3:13–18, ESV)

For the sake of Christ, then, I am content with weaknesses, insults, hardships persecutions, and calamities. For when I am weak, then I am strong.
(2 Corinthians 12:10, ESV)

Now that I am speaking of being in need, for I have learned in whatever situation I am to be content. I know how to be brought low, and I know how to abound. In any and every circumstance, I have learned the secret of facing plenty and hunger, abundance and need. I can do all things through him that strengthens me.
(Philippians 4:11–13, ESV)

Prayer: Father God, I pray to learn from all my situations, I pray to learn your good lessons and grow in strength and character. That you instill in me a love for my work and an appreciation of all that I have. I pray for all my family and friends your kindness in directing us to your paths and gentle easy nudges to move us along. I thank you, Father, in Jesus's name, I pray, amen.

*You make known to me the path of life;
in your presence there is fullness and joy; at
your right hand are pleasures forevermore.*
(Psalm 16:11, ESV)

January 5

Patient Endurance

Stay steadfast and endure with perseverance all the tests of life. Holding fast to all my teachings. Even during trials and storms of all sorts remain thankful and rejoice. As this is what it means to endure. When you feel you lack strength, seek me first to provide you with rest like a refreshing of your spirit. And once you have been properly rested you can go on. You can endure much more my child, as with me you can persevere. Do not focus on what you lack because it is in your weakness, that you are strong. It is suffering that produces endurance and endurance produces character and with character hope. As it brings forth strength and a steady forward movement of motion that in-turn reveals perseverance. Then through the journey, you will find if you keep moving along my good paths, you will claim victory. The victory brought forth by your faith in me. Stay in this good and present moment remaining faithful, rejoicing in hope and patient in affliction. With my Holy Spirit, you will experience a fullness of joy that is never-ending and free from change. A joy that is complete and everlasting. Just as I endured the cross, you will endure your trials. My children who keep holding tightly to me and display patient endurance to the end will be saved…

If we endure, we will also reign with him; if we deny him, he also will deny us.
(2 Timothy 2:12, ESV)

And we also thank God constantly for this, that when you received the word of God, which you heard from us, you accepted it not as the word of men but as

what it really is, the word of God, which is
at work in you.
(1 Thessalonians 2:13, ESV)

But the one who endures to the end
will be saved.
(Matthew 24:13, ESV)

Prayer: Father God, thank you for helping me to stay joyful in all the moments of my life. Thank you for helping me to have the strength to endure hardships and trials, and for giving me hope for my future and the future of my loved ones. I praise your name, Jesus, and pray that you will continue growing me up in my faith lovingly. Please watch over us all bringing rest when needed and refreshing our spirits with your love. In Jesus's name, I pray, amen.

January 6

Lessons to Teach

In the early dawn of the morning—thank me, amid the midday, praise me, in the dusk of the evening, find joy in me and love me during all times. There is serenity that I bring you, in the peaceful, calming, flow of a gentle easy day. During these times, I will call you to rest as there may be a business just over the horizon. But do not fear, bring your heart to me and know that I am Sovereign over your life. My will shall never lead you into trials you cannot overcome. I bring you to situations that I know you can manage. As concealed in some situations there may be lessons that are good for your teaching. Each circumstance or happenstance revealed in your life has meaning. There are no details that are left to chance. Even when you do not see the value of the lessons just yet, in time you will see. I love you my child and you must remember how I treasure your precious heart. Allow my good lessons to fulfill their purpose. I do not allow things to hurt you, but instead, they are meant to grow you and bring you closer to me. As these are the lessons, I will allow as they teach.

Train up a child in the way he should go; even when he is old he will not depart from it.
(Proverbs 22:6, ESV)

But the Helper, the Holy Spirit, whom the Father will send in my name, he will teach you all things and bring to your remembrance all that I have said to you.
(John 14:16, ESV)

But the anointing that you received from him abides in you, and you have no need that anyone should teach you. But as his anointing teaches you about everything, and is true, and is no lie-just as it has taught you, abide in him.
(1 John 2:27, ESV)

You call me Teacher and Lord, and you are right, for so I am.
(John 13:13, ESV)

Prayer: Father God, thank you for your good lessons. I pray to be open to learn all the ways of your teaching and remain joyful when I am tested. Please watch over all that I love. In Jesus's loving name, I pray, amen.

January 07

The Way-Maker

Remember always, my child, who you are... You are a child of God. You are chosen by me and called to certain tasks, because I know who you are and who I have created you to be. A bright light that shines in a darkened world, but you must hold tightly to your faith. Every one of my children has doubts from time to time, but you must seek me first and my good message. Holding fast to all that I am teaching you and being open to my corrections. Walk in the ways that I will show you. As I open the way before you with fearless intention, so that you will find no doubt in your steps while following me. Stay the course with me, my beloved. As I have much to show you. I AM the way-maker. No weapon formed against you shall prosper, as we stay moving forward in the light of my word, standing on the hope of my promises in the light of Salvation, and the Glory I bring. Where you see no way, I see my good path clearly. So do not let go of my truth, trust me. Hold onto my hand and I will lead, as I AM the way-maker.

> *Thus says the Lord, who makes a way in the sea, a path in the mighty waters, who brings forth chariot and horse, army and warrior; they lie down, they cannot rise, they are extinguished, quenched like a wick; "Remember not the former things, nor consider the things of old. Behold, I am doing a new thing; now it springs forth, do you not perceive it? I will make a way in the wilderness and rivers in the desert."*
> (Isaiah 43:16–19, ESV)

*And the Lord will guide you continu-
ally and satisfy your desire in scorched places
and make your bones strong; and you shall
be like a watered garden, like a spring of
water, whose waters do not fail.*
(Isaiah 58:11, ESV)

*I will instruct you and teach you in
the way you should go; I will counsel you
with my eye upon you. Be not like a horse
or a mule, without understanding, which
must be curbed with bit and bridle, or it
will not stay near you. Many are the sorrows of the wicked, but steadfast love surrounds the one who trusts the Lord.*
(Psalm 32:8–10, ESV)

Prayer: Father God, I thank you for this day and your leading. I pray that you watch over each of us Lord and that you enshroud us with your love protecting us as we venture out today and always. I give praise to you Lord for being the way maker. I know if I stay close to you and follow every-thing will be okay. Thank you, Jesus, and it is in your name I pray, amen.

Yes, way, Yahweh. He>i

January 8

The Course of Truth

Good morning, my sweet child. As you open your eyes, remain joyful in hope. As you walk the course of the day with me, stay peaceful. Be ready and willing to share my good news. Speaking with all who have questions for you about where your hope comes from, and about the light which shines in you. Show them the ways in which you follow me, always keeping my good examples. Speaking not only in truth but living it as well. With action and deed, be an example of my ways and my love. As you walk the course of my truth hold fast to your faith. Not longing to see what is ahead but finding peace and happiness in the presence of a good day. May you abound in hope and find the peace of believing. Keep reading and learning the Holy Bible, leaning on the Scriptures as they are my living words, providing food for your soul. May your heart always rejoice while walking in the course of my truth.

May the God of hope fill you with all joy and peace in believing, so that by the power of the Holy Spirit you may abound in hope.
(Romans 15:13, ESV)

But in your hearts honor Christ the Lord as holy, always being prepared to make defense to anyone who asks you for a reason for the hope that is in you; yet do it with gentleness and respect.
(1 Peter 3:15, ESV)

*For whatever was written in former
days was written for our instruction, that
through endurance and through the encouragement of Scriptures we might have hope.*
(Romans 15:4, ESV)

Prayer: Father God, keep me in your will. Direct my steps daily. I thank you for all the good gifts you give. I pray to be a blessing to others and that you strengthen us in our faith as we learn to walk the course of your truth. In Jesus's name, I give thanks and pray, amen.

January 9

Grow in Faith

Trust me, my child, always. Keep learning my ways and sharing my good news with others. Finding beauty in the light of my words and the spark of fire within your soul as you read Scriptures. Nothing shall be impossible for my children who believe. If it is my will, then it shall be. Spend time with me and let my presence create a stir within your heart. Growing you up in your faith. Find peace and joy, hopefulness, patience, and love all these good and perfect gifts that come from me. Listen to me with your heart wide open, while you spend time with me in prayer. I am never far from you; although it may feel that way at times. I am here with you and long for you to have the abundant life I have promised. In all your ways acknowledge me, my child, as I will lead you to the light of my will, making your paths straight. I have come so that you may have a full life, an abundant life, and eternal life. A life full of meaning and purpose. Standing strong in the face of adversity. Bring your faithfulness to the forefront of your life, fiercely and with all intensity to any and all challenges. The more time you spend with me the more your faith will continue to grow. Keep my words within your heart. Stay hopeful and in all your ways acknowledge me and you will find my good path and the good life I have planned for you.

My son, be attentive to my words; incline your ear to my sayings. Let them not escape from your sight; keep them within your heart.
(Proverbs 4:20–21, ESV)

But whoever listens to me will dwell secure and will be at ease, without dread of disaster.
(Proverbs 1:33, ESV)

Trust in the Lord with all your heart, and do not lean on your own understanding. In all your ways acknowledge him, and he will make your paths straight.
(Proverbs 3:5–6, ESV)

Prayer: Father God, I pray to you today Lord, lifting up, all that I love. Keep me moving forward on your paths. Your will, your way. Help me to remain hopeful and full of joy. I thank you for your grace and love. Watch over us always, Father. Lead us with kindness each day making our paths straight. Giving us the strength to be the people you have called us to be. In Jesus's name, I pray and give thanks, amen.

January 10

Safe in His Arms

Let me bring you peace my child and enshroud you with my love. Let me lighten the burdens that may start to weigh on your mind, slowing down all the commotion going on around you. Call out to me and I can slow even the busiest of days. Relax, sit, and take a deep breath, close your eyes and be still. Everything will be okay, just keep holding onto my promises and following my good ways. I am watching over you my child. So no need to fear. As fear creates worry, and worry leads to anxiety and anxiety turns into stress. No fear, no worry, no anxiety, no stress. I am your God, your Father, your protector. Your strength and shield. I am holding you. As you can find safety taking refuge under my wings. I will keep you safe with the cover of my Presence like a veil of light that surrounds you displacing the shadows of the day. I will uphold you and shelter you in my great hands and I shall bring you rest. I love you, my child.

> *Oh how abundant is your goodness, which you have stored up for those who fear you and worked for those who take refuge in you, in the sight of the children of mankind! In the cover of your presence you hide them from plots of men: you store them in your shelter from strife of tongues.*
> (Psalm 31:19–20, ESV)

> *The Lord is my strength and my shield; in him my heart trusts, and I am helped; my heart exults, and with my song I give thanks to him. The Lord is the strength*

of his people he is the saving refuge of his
anointed.
(Psalm 28:7–8, ESV)

And he said, "My presence will go
with you, and I will give you rest."
(Exodus 33:14, ESV)

Prayer: Father God, thank you for this day. Thank you for your protection and love. I pray today that you would be with us and watch over us. Help us to accomplish all the tasks of the day. Fill us with joy and bring a calm and easiness to this day. In Jesus's loving name I pray. Amen.

January 11

Wonderful Purpose

I am the resurrected King. Nothing is impossible for me or for my children who keep my commandments as they will find their place in my will. There is a good purpose that I have brought you to. Keep seeking me first and follow as that will lead you to the victory of the great and wonderful plans I have for your life. Do not give up my child, never giving in to the wicked ways of the world. Stay steadfast and faithful to me. Letting go of all the negativity that tries to invade your mind. You can accomplish the tasks that I have called you too. You can do all things with my strength and the light of my love as they will carry you through even on the darkest of days. I am never far off from you. As you draw near to me so shall I draw near to you. When you feel weak my child, my Spirit is still strong in you. Search yourself and find the strength that I have placed inside. It is my helper that will come upon you and will help you to fulfill the tasks that I have called you to. Just keep leaning on me, growing up in your faith and living in the light of my wonderful purpose.

Let us then with confidence draw near to the throne of grace, that we may receive mercy and find grace to help in time of need.
(Hebrews 4:16, ESV)

And without faith it is impossible to please him, for whoever would draw near to God must believe that he exists and that he rewards those who seek him.
(Hebrews 11:6, ESV)

The night is far gone; the day is at hand. So then let us cast off the works of darkness and put on the armor of light.
(Romans 13:12, ESV)

Prayer: Today I pray, Lord, for the confidence and strength I am needing to complete the tasks I'm called to do. I pray that you will be my strength when I am weak and give me rest when I am overwhelmed. I ask this for all my loved ones as well. And I give you thanks, Lord, for always filling my heart with your love. In Jesus's name, I pray, amen.

January 12

Growing the Distance

The shortest distance between two souls is my love. I love you, my child, and my heart sings when I see you making time to spend with me. When you put me first, you are displaying to me that I am truly entrusted with your life. Everything from the biggest of circumstances to the tiny small details of your life that you have given to me. This is what it means, my child, to be within my will. It is when you trust me with it all. And listen to me through my Spirit and my word. Align yourself daily with my will and soon you will become unstoppable. Nothing speaks more to the heart than the beauty of my love. My peaceful, gentle nature wrapped around you makes you free. When you are weak, it is then that you are strong. When you feel fear, your trust in me moves you forward, which displays that you are brave. You are capable of so much more than you realize. Keep growing with me and moving forward along my good paths. The more time you spend with me the more of your true self you will discover. With my love, you will find your truth. Even when the journey seems long in the physical realms—when you search your heart and find the embedded joy of my grace, I have placed inside learning to trust it then becomes for your soul a growing of faith. Your faith is the shortest distance to me. Keep seeking to grow closer to me my child, with your whole heart. In faith and trust, full of joy and love.

You will seek me and find me, when
you seek me with all your heart.
(Jeremiah 29:13, ESV)

And he said to him, "You shall love the Lord your God with your whole heart and with all your soul and with all your mind."
(Matthew 22:37, ESV)

I will praise you with an upright heart, when I learn your righteous rules.
(Psalm 119:7, ESV)

Prayer: Father God, create in me a clean heart. Take away my worldly desires and replace them with only the things you want for me in my life. Make your desires for me my own. I pray that your paths are the ones that I am walking on. Help me to stay true to your ways. I ask that you help all my family and friends grow closer to you. I ask this for myself as well. In Jesus's loving name, I pray, amen.

January 13

Fall into His Arms

Come to me, my child, fall into my arms. I know this world is not the easiest place. But in me, you can find your rest. You can feel the peace I bring to you, just embrace the nature of my goodness. I calm the winds and just like that, I can calm your spirit. The truth of purpose has shone its light within my mighty loving Spirit. As you and all my children share my good news, the message of redemption and salvation, I offer those who call me Lord. Casting off fear and stepping onto your faith each day. You never know what the day holds, but I do as I have gone before you. So in the knowledge of that, as you bring forward your faith you can stay hopeful staying confident as there is nothing to fear. You are forgiven, my child; you are made new and you are mine because you believe and have given your life to me. These trust ties we have can never be broken in the heart of my children who stay faithful to me. It is the true believers that honor me. They grow up in their faith and put their hope and trust in me even during trials. I know there have been times in your life where you may have been angry at me and I want you to know that you are forgiven for any harsh things you may have thought, said or done because you have come back to me feeling sorry in your heart and have asked for my forgiveness. I love you, my child, nothing you have done could ever separate you from my love. When you feel the weight begin, just fall into my arms my child and I will be your refuge filled with peace.

In peace I will both lie down and sleep; for you alone, O Lord, make me dwell in safety.

(Psalm 4:8, ESV)

The Lord is good. A stronghold in the day of trouble; he knows those who take refuge in him.
(Nahum 1:7, ESV)

For I am persuaded, that neither death, nor life, nor angels, nor principalities, nor power, nor things present, nor things to come. Nor height, nor depth, nor any other creature, shall be able to separate us from the love of God, which is in Jesus Christ our Lord.
(Romans 8:38–39, KJV)

Prayer: Father God, I thank you for this day and I thank you for your forgiveness. Forgiving me the times I have gotten angry or messed up in my actions and attitudes. Thank you for helping me to grow in my faith and for always loving me. I pray for all today Lord, that you keep us safe and fill us with your love. Amen.

January 14

Child of God

Dear sweet child, when the world comes and tries to steal your focus away from me, keep your eyes fixed on things above, holding fast to your faith and repeat these words, I am a child of God. When the night falls hard on you and your thoughts run wild. Call out to me so I may bring you rest and repeat these words; I am a child of God. When the obstacles of life stand in your way and seem bigger than any mountain that you alone can face, lean on me and repeat these words, "I am a child of God." When you can't see your way through a situation, cry out to me and let me restore your trust, then repeat these words, I am a child of God. When you feel like all hope is lost and you have no strength, hold onto me being filled with my strength and repeat these words, I am a child of God. Bring me all your hopes, fears, and dreams. You are my child, a child of God. Nothing is too hard for me as I am your God, your Creator, your Father, your Lord, your friend. I am the Messiah, I am the way, the truth, and the light of all life. No child of mine will ever walk in darkness again. Remember this most important truth about yourself You are a child of God, and all that I am becomes all that you are. Because you call me Lord. My strength becomes your strength. My peace becomes your peace. My gentleness is your gentleness. My love is your love. So do not fear and always remember who you are. You are who I call you to be, a child of mine. In truth, you are a wonderful child of God. Smile and be loved.

But to all who did receive him, who
believed in his name, he gave the right to
become children of God, who were born,

not of blood nor the will of flesh nor the will of man, but of God.
    (John 1:12–13, ESV)

See what kind of love the Father has given to us, that we should be called children of God; and so we are. The reason why the world does not know us is that it did not know him.
    (1 John 1:3, ESV)

Little children, you are from God and have overcome them, for he who is in you is greater than he who is in the world.
    (1 John 4:4, ESV)

Prayer: Father God, today and always I will follow you for I know I am a child of God. Today. Lord, I thank you for watching over all your children. In you we find our strength, we have hope and we believe. In Jesus's name, I pray and give thanks, amen.

January 15

Take It as It Comes

Take it as it comes today my child and do not get so caught up by troubles of the past. Do not get swept up by the worries of tomorrow. Just stay in the present of the day. For you cannot change the circumstances of yesterday, although you may have a lesson learned. Do not try to foresee the future as tomorrow has worries of its own. Just remember who is in control and delight yourself in the merriment of today. When you feel calm and clear-minded you do not always need to busy yourself, as the world would have you do. It is okay to rest and find relaxation in your thoughts and your activities or lack thereof. Allow yourself some time to refresh. My children in this age find themselves always busy. They burn the candle at both ends. Running themselves ragged. When you are overwhelmed and always busy, you can be making things harder on yourself. As it is said, those with tired minds tend to make poor decisions. All my children need to refresh and relax taking some much-needed time out to stay balanced and in tune. Once they get the rest they need and after prayer and supplication, they can come back to a situation and make a much better decision. Just let the day flow relax my child and take this as it comes...

So do not worry about tomorrow, for tomorrow will worry about itself. Each day has enough trouble of its own.
(Matthew 6:34, NIV)

In the day of prosperity be joyful, and in the day of adversity consider: God has made the one as well as the other, so that

man may not find out anything that will
be after him.
    (Ecclesiastes 7:14, ESV)

Yet you do not know what tomorrow
will bring. What is your life? For you are
a mist that appears for a little time then
vanishes.
    (James 4:14, ESV)

Prayer: Father God, thank you for this day. Help me to learn how to relax and slow down. I ask for rest. Please watch over all my family and friends and help us not to worry about tomorrow. Giving it all to you in Jesus's name, I pray, amen.

January 16

With You All Along

When you were born you had no idea of the life which was given. You can look back in reverence at the work of my great and mighty hands. I have been with you all along, my child, and I know you have been tested. But remain present with me in my Spirit, my faithful sweet child, as my light will always shine its way. I have walked with you in the garden of your life and rejoiced when you were happy. I have walked with you through the deserts of distress and have replenished your tired soul. I have cried with you my child, as when your heart breaks mine does too. I have never left your side since the first day you asked me into your heart. There have been times you strayed from me and tried to hide things from my Presence. But now you have grown and have come to see that there is nothing you can hide from me. You do not have to hide because you are forgiven, and you are loved eternally by me. There is nothing that can separate you from my love. I know every step you take. I help you when your world feels out of balance and place your feet on solid ground. There were many storms, delights, comforts, and trials that were used to get you to this place. To this loving place my child, here in the light of my love…and throughout this wondrous journey of your life, is where I have been with you all along.

Thus says the Lord, your Redeemer, who formed you in the womb: "I am the Lord, who made all things. Who alone stretched out to the heavens, who spread out the earth by myself?"
(Isaiah 44:24, ESV)

Do not be like them, for your Father knows what you need before you ask him.
(Matthew 6:8, ESV)

The Lord appeared to him from far away. I have loved you with an everlasting love; therefore I have continued my faithfulness to you.
(Jeremiah 31:3, ESV)

Prayer: Father God, thank you for always remaining present in my life. I ask that you lift me up Father each and every day and place me on the paths of only your calling. All for your glory as I continue to give my life to you. I pray for all my loved ones and thank you for watching over them. Fill us this day and all the days with the joy that is found in you. In Jesus's name, I pray, amen.

January 17

Simple Side of Life

As the sun rises, early in the morning, spend your time with me. As the day begins you can watch the glorious light shining through the clouds. Beautiful rays that beam down from the heavens over the solid canvas of the earth. Make this one of your to-dos at some point in your life take some time to watch the sunrise and take in my glory. Let yourself enjoy these treasures and enjoy the beauty of the day. Let your worries drift off into the farthest corners of your mind. Try this day my child to stay hopeful in all that you do. Laugh with good friends and enjoy the simple side of life. There are many sides to this world, but in this moment let your heart be light. Feel my Presence all around you as your heart is filled with love. You can find me every day, as I will meet you in your moments wherever you are. You can find me when you seek me with your whole heart. There are love songs all around you when you walk within the day. Listen to the birds as they sing my beautiful song. Watch them as they play flying high in the open expanse of the heavens. They are what I have created them to be. And I have blessed them. Just as you are who I have created you to be. And I am blessing you, each and every day. There is no weight that I cannot remove. Today I call you to the simple side of life. Rejoice, my child, rejoice.

The Lord preserves the simple; when I
was brought low, he saved me.
(Psalm 116:6, ESV)

Now there is great gain in godliness
with contentment, for we brought nothing

into the world, and we cannot take any-
thing out of the world. But if we have food
and clothing, with these we will be content.
(1 Timothy 6:6–8, ESV)

A joyful heart is good medicine, but a
crushed spirit dries up bones.
(Proverbs 17:22, ESV)

Prayer: Father God, thank you for all the beautiful nature that we get to enjoy. Thank you for the animals and all the natural gardens of life. I thank you for all the blessings in my life and the lives of those around me. I love you, Father. In Jesus's name, I pray and praise you, amen.

January 18

Delight in His Work

At the beginning of the morning, as the sun cast its light, I am with you. From the middle of the day to the dawn of night, I walk with you. In the darkest hours, I am holding you. I have fashioned you, my child, with the makings of a warrior that you shall bravely share my name. Being the light that I have called you to be. On your dimmest of days, you are more than a conqueror as my Holy Spirit strengthens you. Each one of my children has a job especially tasked out and assigned for them to do. I know what each one is capable of and where they will most excel and so I call them to it. At times they wander astray ignoring the urging of my Spirit. It is only when they accept the challenge and rise to the occasion choosing to serve me first, that they truly see the wondrous ways of my mighty plans in real time. Others experience it in hindsight as they can look back and recall in awe the work of my mighty hands. However, all my children will find delight in me, when they keep my good and righteous ways. Choosing to live in the Spirit rather than in the flesh. For your flesh may fail but the Holy Spirit reigns with victory in the lives of my faithful. In the lives of my children who delight themselves in my work.

Do your best to present yourself to God as one approved, a worker who has no need to be shamed, rightly handling the word of truth.
(2 Timothy 2:15, ESV)

Whatever you do, work heartily, as for the Lord, and not for men, knowing that

from the Lord you will receive the inheri-
tance as your reward. You are serving the
Lord Christ.
(Colossians 3:23–24, ESV)

Commit your work to the Lord, and
your plans will be established.
(Proverbs 16:3, ESV)

Prayer: Father God, thank you for the ability to work. Thank you for my selected skills and the innate abilities that you have given me. May you guide me always to use them in the areas that best serve you. I pray for all my loved ones that they may come to find (know, if they do not know) what you are calling them to do and walk in the ways that you are calling. May we all find your grace, peace, love, and mercy each and every day. In Jesus's name, I pray, amen.

January 19

Brilliant Light of Believers

The light of my Salvation shines bright within the hearts of all my children. The impossible becomes possible because they believe in me. This day, as all days, find your thankful, grateful attitude and loving spirit all wrapped within the strength of my love. Walk in the beauty of my nourished garden. Sharing my good news with all. Let my light shine brightly within you so that others may see the glory of salvation I bring. My children have wonderous natures and love to learn and grow. Learning from me their good Teacher, they walk in confidence and shine. There is light in this world! It is a great brilliant light, as all my followers gather in places to worship me. Surround yourselves, my children, with others who build you up. For at times they are the encouragers. They do not judge but lift your spirits to remind you of who you are. They truly love as I have called them to love. Reminding you and others that I am with you all the time. There are also times you are called to be an encourager, my child, and other times you are called to support, to comfort, and to show my love. For believers, it is my promised gift of life after the grave that creates a deep stir within the heart. There is hope when you think about my promise and the eternal life I give. Someday you may be welcomed into my kingdom and wrapped within my arms. Someday, child, but not this day. As this day, you have my wonderful purpose to live and to help share my good news with the world. As I call together all my children to worship. Creating the brilliant light of believers.

How then will they call on him in
whom they have not believed? And how

are they to believe in him of whom they have not heard? And how are they to hear without someone preaching? And how are they to preach unless they are sent? As it is written, "How beautiful are the feet of those who preach the good news!"
(Romans 10:14–15, ESV)

Just so, I tell you, there will be more joy in heaven over one sinner who repents than over ninety-nine righteous persons who need no repentance.
(Luke 15:7, ESV)

Fight the good fight of the faith. Take hold of eternal life to which you were called and about which you made good confession in the presence of many witnesses.
(1 Timothy 6:12, ESV)

Prayer: Father God, thank you for the encouragers that you place in our lives. Thank you for the tasks that you have given us to do, and the strength to be the children you've created us to be. I am thankful to be a member of the brilliant light of believers and pray to always know and follow the good paths of purpose that you lead me to. I pray for all of us, Lord lifting us high upon your shoulders for all the world to see. I am grateful and give you thanks, praise, and glory. In Jesus's name, I pray, amen.

January 20

Vast Glow of the Morning

A vast the glow of the morning hours as you rise you can bring your requests to me. There is no time that I am off limits. I am available to you whenever you require. Bring your prayers and supplications to me as often as you need. I want nothing but the best for you, my child. I want you to live an abundant life, where my joy rules in your heart. Seek first my kingdom and find your delight in me. When you find the true enjoyment in the Spirit then your fleshly desires will transform into something new and different. Your desires that were once of the flesh will fade, having found their new identity in the light and the glory of my Spirit and my love. These ways are righteous and fulfilling. These ways are loving and kind. You step out of the old casting off old wants and replacing them with new desires of the spiritual kind. This new thirst for me and my kingdom will bring you into the alignment of my will. What once made you temporarily happy in the natural will fade away being replaced with the true joy. That of which is eternal, full of love, and found in me. Happy, yes, I want you to be happy and joyful, full of merriment and delight. I want for you a life full of abundance of goodness, of gentleness, and of love. I want for you a successful life in the walk to which I'm calling. There are so many things that I want for you my child, so we shall start in relation together. Always finding joy a vast the glow of the morning. Beginning with morning prayer.

Rejoice always, pray without ceasing,
give thanks in all circumstances; for this is
the will of God in Christ Jesus for you.
(1 Thessalonians 5:16–18, ESV)

Let me hear in the morning of your steadfast love, for in you I trust. Make me know the way I should go, for to you I lift up my soul.

(Psalm 143:8, ESV)

And rising very early in the morning, while it was still dark, he departed and went out to a desolate place, and there he prayed.

(Mark 1:35, ESV)

Prayer: Father God, thank you for this beautiful day. I pray today that you continue to watch over myself and all my loved ones I pray that you fill us with your wants and desires for our lives and lead us on the paths of your calling so that we may walk in confidence in your will. I pray that you fill our hearts with joy and happiness today. In Jesus's name, I pray, amen.

January 21

Detailed Little Blessings

Be thankful for all you have. There are tiny little-detailed blessings that most of the time my children tend to overlook. But if they stopped and quieted down their minds, they would be able to see and appreciate all the delicate intricacies that take place to enable them these very little, but, miraculous blessings. When you come to me with an open heart in thankfulness you will begin to notice all the blessings that I bring more and more. My heart sings when you are attentive to all the wondrous details and truly open your eyes, as then you will be enlightened to see the true craftsmanship of my great and mighty hands in your life. There is sweetness in honesty in the relationship we formed from the first time you opened up to me in prayer. Declaring to the world that you are my child and I am your God. Knowing there is nothing that can separate you from my love. Sharing everything with me. Making our relationship grow and all the more impenetrable to the distractions of the day... The love ties that we have can never be broken. Let them always find their strength within the honor of my promises and the faithfulness of your heart. Your heart will begin to flourish among all the detailed little blessings experienced within the fullness and the beauty of my love.

And from his fullness we have all received, grace upon grace.
(John 1:16, ESV)

But, as it is written, "What no eye has seen, nor ear heard, nor the heart of man

imagined, what God has prepared for those
who love him."
(1 Corinthians 2:9, ESV)

And he rained down on them manna
to eat and gave them the grain of Heaven.
(Psalm 78:24, ESV)

Prayer: Father God, thank you for all the aspects of my life. Thank you for all the little details that bring your blessings to the forefront of my life. Thank you for being present with me through it all. I pray today Lord that I will continue and grow in my faith and feel deep joy being led by your Spirit. Watch over all of my loved ones and guard our hearts and our minds. Let them also experience the fullness of your love. In Jesus's name, I pray giving thanks, amen.

January 22

Finding Warmth

May the warmth of the sun surround you just like the light of my love. When you stand in the shadows of life just beyond the light, your soul may grow cold. Please, my child, find the light to which you are called and walk in it. Stand in the warmth of my Presence and let my Spirit lead. Try not to let the world and its heaviness and business weigh and drag you down. Make me the focal point of your life every day and I will keep you balanced and proportioned. Try not to stand off to the side as life passes you by. Go out and enjoy this world that I've created. Explore and experience what you have yet to see. There is more beauty in the world all nature filled with wondrous and mysterious things. There are blessings that culminate together and show the strength of their shape in my truth. Life is a gift and it is meant for you to live, not just an existence to make it through. I want you to get involved in living, get involved in conversation, and be the light that I have created you to be. Do not let fear stop you or let the world turn your tender heart to stone. Stay strongly soaked in my Presence and find the true warmth of your heart and the bright glow of your life. Finding warmth each day within your moments spent with others and your time spent with me…

Two are better than one, because they have a good reward for their toil. For if they fall, one will lift up his fellow. But woe to him who is alone when he falls and has not another to lift him up! Again, if two lie together, they keep warm, but how can one keep warm alone? And though a man might

prevail against one who is alone, two with-
stand him-a threefold cord is not quickly
broken.
(Ecclesiastes 4:9–12, ESV)

And I will give you a new heart, and
a new spirit I will put within you. And I
will remove the heart of stone from your
flesh and give you a heart of flesh.
(Ezekiel 36:26, ESV)

Be doers of the word, and not hearers
only deceiving yourselves.
(James 1:22, ESV)

Prayer: Father God, please help me to stay involved in my life. Keep me on your good paths and help me to be a blessing to others. Please keep my heart open and full in the light of your Spirit. Helping to point the attention to you so that others in my life will want to know you all the more. In Jesus's loving name I lift us up, amen.

January 23

On the Road to Damascus

Good morning, my sweet spirit, sometimes this world can be a little tough as it seems to be throwing things at you from all sides, but I am with you so that you do not need to fear the world or any of its relentless attacks. Just as I met Saul on the road before he became my faithful follower Paul, I asked him, "Why do you persecute me?" I met him right there where he was on the road. I confronted him and he became one of my most dedicated followers. Saul grew from anger against my children into love as he was forever changed from Saul to the Apostle Paul in the encounter with me on the road to Damascus. You may have a situation in which you need to face head-on. Be brave, little one. Only good can come out of facing your problems instead of fleeing them. Once you confront the situation, you may be able to watch all the pieces of the situation finally fall into place. Helping to alleviate some anxiety and stress. Helping you to regain your peace and find the rest for your soul that you need, and I am there with you, just as I met Paul right where he was. I will meet you too wherever you are, in your moments. My strength will carry you through. I will walk with you and hold your hand and help you find the right words to say. No situation is too big for me to handle. Just trust me and let my spirit lead you and help you to bravely move forward, forever changed for good on the road to Damascus.

Count it all joy, my brothers, when you face trials of various kinds, for you know that the testing of your faith produces steadfastness. And let steadfastness have its

full effect, that you may be perfect and complete lacking in nothing.
(James 1:2–4, ESV)

And I am sure of this, that he who began a good work in you will bring it to completion at the day of Jesus Christ.
(Philippians 1:6, ESV)

And we know that for those who love God all things work together for good for those who are called according to his purpose.
(Romans 8:28, ESV)

Prayer: Father God, thank you for meeting me in my moments. I ask, Father, for myself and all my loved ones that you give us strength and help us to confront our problems in the way that you would want us to do. I pray that you would provide the words for us to say. Thank you for forever changing me into the person I am today. I ask that you make our hearts light and fill us with your joy. In Jesus's name, I pray, amen.

(About Saul/Paul, read in the Bible, Acts 9, The Damascus Road where Saul Converted.)

January 24

Blessed Are the Ones Who Believe

Early this morning, as the sun first cast its light, you arise, as soon as you open your eyes, I am with you. I have stayed with you all along, even into the deep and unaroused hours of your sleep. I have never left your side. I know there are some days you may feel alone and because of this, you may feel little out of sorts, maybe even a little empty or sad. But you are not alone, and you will never be empty again. You have the gift of my Holy Spirit; the Helper and he will remain to indwell with you always as you believe. Always remember to keep me at the forefront of your mind. There are times that you will need me to will remind you that I have seen you at your best and stayed with you at your worst. I will never turn my back on any of my children. Blessed are the children who have not seen and yet they still believe. There are things I have spoken over you and these will be fulfilled all in my good time. This, my child, is a lesson of patience, and of trust. Coming from a place of love. Every lesson I let you go through is meant to build you up, not to tear you down. Be patient, my child, for those who wait on me will fly with confident perseverance into the strength of my love, and the anointing of their calling, if only they remain steadfast. If only they believe…

And blessed is she who believed that there would be fulfillment of what was spoken to her from the Lord.
(Luke 1:45, ESV)

But they who wait for the Lord shall renew their strength; they shall mount up

with wings like eagles; they shall run and
not be weary; they shall walk and not faint.
(Isaiah 40:31, ESV)

For still the vision awaits its appointed
time; it hastens to the end-it will not lie. If
it seems slow, wait for it; it will surely come;
it will not delay.
(Habakkuk 2:3, ESV)

Prayer: Father God, I give you thanks for this day, and for all my friends and family. Lifting us up to you, Lord. I ask you to remind the ones who are feeling empty that you have filled them with your love. I pray for the ones who are sad, that you would bring them joy. I ask for the ones who are feeling overwhelmed that you would give them strength. I pray that you would help us all walk-in confidence on the paths of your calling for our lives. In Jesus's name, I pray, amen.

January 25

Rest in His Spirit

Slow down, my child, do not quicken your steps and hurry your way through situations that are meant for your growing. Pause for a while and open your eyes to find my good lessons hidden within the circumstance. I am with you in all the moments that make up each day; there is nothing that you experience, where you are truly alone. All your trials have a purpose. Seek me first and ask me to reveal my purpose in them. You are growing through your situations. This is good, my child, and will bring you to walk in places that I have planned for your life, time and time again. You will find yourself walking in my will when you let me lead. Let me fill you with the peace of Spirit after a long day. Rest is something that most of my children long for but do not know how to acquire. The world is so busy and there are always nonstop things to do on the task list of life. But you must learn to stop and breathe. Give yourself time to rest in my peace and learn from my yoke, as it is easy and gentle, it is beautiful and light. It is okay to sometimes withdraw from your daily activities. Learn to refresh in me and rest in my Presence. As I am food for your soul. For with me you shall never thirst or hunger again. Come to me my child, and learn to relax, finding every good thing you need, and just rest in my Spirit.

Jesus said to them, "I am the bread of life; whoever comes to me shall not hunger, and whoever believes in me shall never thirst."
(John 6:35, ESV)

*He satisfies the longing soul. And the
hungry soul he fills with good things.*
(Psalm 107:9, ESV)

*Come to me, all who labor and are
heavy laden, and I will give you rest.*
(Matthew 11:28, ESV)

*So then, there remains a Sabbath
rest for the people of God, for whoever has
entered God's rest has also rested from his
works as God did from his.*
(Hebrews 4:9–10, ESV)

Prayer: Father God, thank you for the rest that you bring. Thank you for being here with us and refreshing our souls. All my life I give to you. In Jesus's name, I pray, finding rest for my soul, amen.

January 26

Let Him

Let my love surround you, child, in the early morning hours. Let my love fill you into the evening shade. Let me remain the focal point of your life. Celebrate our time together. Lifting your prayers and your hands to me. We can walk through this day with a calm confidence. Arise, my children, and claim the joy that I have given. I will shine my light down from the heavens and bless your every step. Just stay in my will as I establish your way, making known to you the path of life. When you are tired, let me bring you rest. When you are lonely, let me provide for you my Spirit, as I am your companion. When you're feeling stressed let me bring you calmness. Find the serenity within as my Holy Spirit resides and indwells in you. Stay in tune with me all the hours of your days. When you are feeling lost, reach for me and the light of my Presence will uphold you placing you back on solid ground. I am everything you need as my grace is sufficient for you. Let me truly be Sovereign over your life and live in abundance of my calling and the majesty of my love. Only then if you will let me…trusting my steps and following me. Let me be the leader of your life. Let me be your Lord.

The Lord your God is in your midst, a mighty one who will save; he will rejoice over you with gladness; he will quiet you with his love; he will exult over you with loud singing.
(Zephaniah 3:17, ESV)

You make known to me the path of life; in your presence, there is fullness and joy; at your right hand are pleasures forevermore.
(Psalm 16:11, ESV)

But he said to me, "My grace is sufficient for you, for my power is made perfect in weakness." Therefore I will boast all the more gladly of my weaknesses, so that the power of Christ may rest upon me.
(2 Corinthians 12:9, ESV)

Prayer: Father God, I lift up my life and the lives of all that I love to you today Lord. I ask you to shine your light on us and lead us. Brightening the way with the light of your love. I want to walk with you, Lord, on the paths of your will. I pray you establish my steps. Remove from my heart anything that is not from you. In Jesus's name, I pray, amen.

January 27

The Open Door

Time is meant for living and growing up in your life and faith. From childhood, there were years of learning, in adolescence finding a sense of self. In adulthood a path of solidity. Learning patience and relishing in the placed foundations of your youth. Not all my children found this to be the order of their lives, as each one is different, and some are late to grow. But when they called on my Spirit to enter their lives, they opened up the door. The door to wellbeing, the door to love and trust, the door to patience and kindness, the door to grace and mercy. The door to eternal life... Yes, the old fades away and the new has shone its light as my children become new creations. There is a far more abundant life with me then in this life without me. As without me, most will find it empty and cold. Material things will never take the place for what is missing within the soul. Only I can fill those spaces that seem to never fill. Once you have invited me in, I'll make my home in you. And my children will never be empty again. Because they are loved best through and through, once they have opened their heart to me. They knock and have found the open door.

I know your works. Behold, I have set before you an open door, which no one is able to shut. I know that you have but little power, and yet you have kept my word and not denied my name.
(Revelation 3:8, ESV)

I am the door. If anyone enters by me, he will be saved and will go in and out and find pasture.
(John 10:9, ESV)

Ask, and it will be given to you; seek, and you will find; knock, and it will be opened to you. For everyone that asks receives, and the one who seeks finds, and to the one who knocks it will be opened.
(Matthew 7:7–8, ESV)

Prayer: Father God, thank you for everything you do. I ask that you help my family and friends with kindness and your love show them the way to truly fill their lives with you. Surround them Lord with people who point them to you and let them be opened to receiving you. Show them the open door. In Jesus's name, I pray, amen.

January 28

The Unveiled You

Good morning, my dear child, come to me with unveiled face and let your ways be completely transparent to me. There is nothing you need to hide. I know everything there is already, but it is sweeter when my children come to me openly. Being comfortable with themselves. There is a light that breaks down from the heavens casting its magnificent glow on my children and lighting up my good and righteous paths. The Holy Spirit shines deep within the hearts of my children and helps them to navigate their lives. There is a call I have placed over my children and will help them to find what I have designed. As they learn to walk within my will. I have watched you daily, all the hurdles and the troubles that you must face. I know that you take on the world with your tender heart. All the problems of your loved ones and people around you, but, as I have said before this is not your weight to carry, as I am the Sovereign Lord. My strength is never ending so I shall carry those burdens. Let my consolations cheer your soul. Bring those things that trouble you and lay them at my feet. Knowing that I would never neglect the prayers of my children. So unveil your heart and know that you are completely loved, with acceptance and grace by me.

And we all, with unveiled face, beholding the glory of the Lord, are being transformed into the same image from one degree of glory to another. For this comes from the Lord who is the Spirit.
(2 Corinthians 3:18, ESV)

Making known to us the mystery of his will, according to his purpose, which he set forth in Christ.
(Ephesians 1:9, ESV)

For nothing is hidden except to be made manifest; nor is anything secret except to come to light.
(Mark 4:22, ESV)

Prayer: Father God, thank you, Lord, for your acceptance and your love for us. I am grateful. Help me to accept myself and help me to keep myself completely open to you. Also, watch over us all and if there are any undesirable parts in us, help us to overcome those and remove them replacing them with your love and joy. In Jesus's name, I pray, amen.

January 29

Majestic Light of Love

Time to wake up, my child. Starting off the day with a grateful heart. Let this day be light, easy, and gentle in nature just like the nature of me. Put on kindness, compassion, meekness, humility, and patience. It's a day to appreciate all the small little blessings and the beauty in your life. Remember it is I, your Sovereign Lord, who has gone before you and have laid the firm foundations of your steps. Your ways are established before you. Do not let the world knock you off kilter. Arm yourself with my Spirit, my ways and my words each day. Letting me have complete control over your life so that when the ways of the world fail, you can stand firm knowing my good and perfect ways do not. Cast off all shadowed thoughts from your mind and feel my joy permeating within. Shine your light today my child so that others may see a gentle life full of compassion, good things, and the majestic light of love. I will walk with you on your paths today and always guard your hearts and minds. Breathe relax and walk with confidence, I have everything you need, and you are in my great hands. I am in control, feel refreshed and lightened as you walk in the steps I have planned. Filling you always with the majestic light of my love.

Put on then, as God's chosen ones,
holy and beloved, compassionate hearts,
kindness, humility, meekness, and patience.
(Colossians 3:12, ESV)

Take my yoke upon you, and learn
from me, for I am gentle and lowly in heart,
and you will find rest for your souls.
(Matthew 11:29, ESV)

In the same way, let your light shine before others, so that they may see your good works and give glory to your Father who is in heaven.
(Matthew 5:16, ESV)

Prayer: Father God, thank you for another glorious day. I am grateful to you all the days of my life. As you open up your good paths to me. I pray to always be confident of your paths, so that I may each day find myself walking in your will. All for your glory, Lord. I pray you watch over all my loved ones. In Jesus's name, I pray and give thanks, amen.

January 30

Remember Who He Is

Listen to my words reading the Bible each day and growing in your faith. Make me the focal point of your life seek me first and my will for your life. Walk on the paths of my choosing. Do not fear, for I am with you. No circumstance or situation is too big for me to handle, so give them freely to me. When you are facing what you feel are giants in your life, stop, my child, and ask yourself, who is bigger than my Lord?" And what could ever make my Lord fail? No one and nothing. You must keep your hope and faith, finding trust and courage. Remaining with me as my faithful children. Follow where I lead, even though places that may be uncomfortable and unpleasant. And you know that I reward my faithful children. Because I have come so that you may live an abundant life, a full life. Full of joy and adventure. Find joy today in the beauty of all that surrounds you… My beauty is everywhere, and my love is with you… Remembering always who I am, as I am your Lord, who loves you eternally…

May the Lord direct your hearts to the love of God and to the steadfastness of Christ.
(2 Thessalonians 3:5, ESV)

If we live by the Spirit, let us also keep in step with the spirit.
(Galatians 5:25, ESV)

The thief comes only to steal and kill
and destroy, I came that they may have life
and have it abundantly.
(John 10:10, ESV)

Prayer: Father God, thank you for your love. Thank you for your gift of eternal life. When my life seems difficult or hard, I will keep my faith in you. I ask that you guard my heart and that you lead my mind daily. Opening our eyes to see your beauty. Asking this also for all the people I love. In Jesus's name, I pray, amen.

January 31

February

This month is known for Valentine's Day, which is a day to celebrate love. Our Lord Jesus gives us his great love every day. When we open our eyes to see, we can find his love everywhere. In this picture I see... "And then two hearts became one." They are not perfect, but they belong together.

You Are His Beloved

In the blink of an eye, everything can change. Make sure it is you, who is grounded on a solid foundation with your soul rooted in me. Life happens way to fast. Constant change jumping from one thought to the next. I am immovable; I never change. Therefore, find your steadiness in me. I wish my children would learn the good pace. Slow and steady, as it is most times better than rushing through your life. I have created so many wondrous and beautiful things. I have placed things in your path for you to enjoy. Some say stop and smell the roses, and this is true not only do you view the beauty I've created but you smell the sweet lingering fragrance that a rose gives off. Bringing pleasant thoughts to your mind. Let the beauty of my loving Spirit fill you always, reminding you of how precious you are to me. So that even when the night falls hard and the day grows long you are strong enough to remember that I created you and it is I, who chose you. You are blessed by me, my child, and your purpose in me is worthy of far more than you could ever dream. I am eternal and constant. I am love…and you, beloved, are mine.

That according to the riches of his glory he may grant you to be strengthened with power through his spirit in your inner being.
(Ephesians 3:16, ESV)

Since you have been born again, not of perishable seed but imperishable, through the living and abiding word of God.
(1 Peter 1:23, ESV)

Beloved, we are God's children now,
and what we will be has not yet appeared;
but we know that when he appears we shall
be like him, because we shall see him as he
is. And everyone who thus hopes in him
purifies himself as he is pure.
(1 John 3:2–3, ESV)

Prayer: Father God, help me to seek you first from the time I open my eyes in the morning to the end of my day. Keep my mind on you. If there are things in my life that you would have me do differently help me with your kindness to see clearly the path of your choosing. And give me the strength to walk on those paths. I pray you to strengthen everyone around me, Lord, that they would see, and feel your beautiful nature working in their lives. In Jesus's name I pray, giving thanks, amen.

February 1

He Provides

I have prepared the way before you, that you should not stumble but that you shall soar. You shall mount up on wings, not growing weary but moving with grace and the promise of my victory in this world and in life. Just remain faithful to me my child and the call I have placed on your life. Growing daily in faith. Seeking me first and my kingdom. As when you do this, you will surely see your blessings multiply. There are those that you have not even noticed that you will begin to realize in your life, and they will shine within your heart, and I provide it all. My children are dear to me; they are my beloved little ones. Sometimes the unimaginable happens, but in that instant reach for me. Remain strong in your faith putting your trust in me. Keep patient little one. No one can begin to conceive what beautiful blessings I have planned for my faithful children who love me. Hold tightly to my promises daily… My grace will overflow unto you my child, and you shall have all the necessities required to abound in all of your good work. Keep moving forward, working at your good pace. I see all that you are doing, all the work you put forth. No matter what worldly circumstance unfolds, I am your God and I shall provide…

For we know that if the tent that is our earthly home is destroyed, we have a building from God, a house not made with hands, eternal in the heavens.
(2 Corinthians 5:1, ESV)

And God is able to make all grace abound to you, so that having sufficiency in

all things at all times, you may abound in
every good work.
(2 Corinthians 9:8, ESV)

But, as it is written, "What no eye
has seen, nor ear has heard, nor the heart of
man imagined, what God has prepared for
those who love him."
(1 Corinthians 2:9, ESV)

Prayer: Father God, thank you for always providing for me and my loved ones. There is nothing I lack because of you. I am thankful. I ask that you keep leading me on the paths of your choosing, Lord. Helping me to always seek you first. I love you, Jesus, with my whole heart, and it is in your name I pray each day, amen.

February 2

Intercessory Prayers

Light breaks over the face of the world and you open your eyes to begin another glorious day with me. I am your Sovereign Lord, the one who will wipe your tears away. I am close to the brokenhearted and I will bind up their wounds. Let my peace enshroud you today and the light of my love embrace you. Pray for them, my child, the ones that you worry about. Keep the powerful words of your prayers close to your heart but let them rest within my care. I am working for them on behalf of your intercessory prayers. As you have come before me, lifting them up with reverence, I will fill the hearts of those who once possessed a heart of stone replacing in them a heart of flesh made tender and gentle. Gracious is my love for the children who hold my commandments. Thou shall love one another as I love you, forgiving each other just as I have forgiven you. Find love in your heart's children for all those around you, who have yet to find their redemption in me. Pray for those who are lost, who are empty, who are brokenhearted. Come, draw near to me, child. As you draw near to me, I will draw nearer to you and to the intercessory prayers that travel from your lips into the mercy and grace of my sweet Sovereign Spirit. Come now and pray…

In the days of his flesh, Jesus offered up prayers and supplications, with loud cries and tears, to him who was able to save him from death, and he was heard because of his reverence.
(Hebrews 5:7, ESV)

Therefore, confess your sins to one another and pray for one another, that you may be healed. The prayer of a righteous person has great power as it is working.
(James 5:16, ESV)

Let us then with confidence draw near to the throne of grace, that we may receive mercy and find grace to help in time of need.
(Hebrews 4:16, ESV)

Prayer: Father God, I lift up all my friends and family to you each day. You know what they need. I thank you for the answers to my prayers, Lord. I pray for a day full of love and your peaceful joy. I pray for the ones who find it hard to come to you on their own that you draw them near with your kind and gentle Spirit. In Jesus's name, I pray giving thanks for the victories. Amen.

February 3

His Good Leading

More, there is more to the mornings than just routine. It is the time to soak yourselves within my Presence and let me fill you. Fill you with beautiful things and wonderous surroundings all encompassed by my love. Embraced by the brilliant light that finds its essence within all my children who believe. I will lead. Lead you with gentle nudges, lead you with strong pulls, lead you with my still small voice and sometimes with a load thunderous roar. But only will you listen, my child, as I will lead you the way through the vast and scorching deserts, through the lands lush and green, through the valleys deep and hidden, on the paths of my righteous truths. I will uphold you so that you do not stumble but remain confident along the good ways of my calling. Having all that you need for the journey as you remain steadfast in your pursuit with me. The journey can be many beautiful lessons, all meant for the teaching of my children and the building of their faith. Growing them strong in my purpose. Just follow with your whole heart and walk on my paths to the places I have planned before you. I love your faithfulness, my child. And I will celebrate you time and time again, as you celebrate me, your Lord. With me, you shall not fail. Remain joyful while exhibiting your trust, just follow and let me lead…

When the Spirit of truth comes, he will guide you into all the truth, for he will not speak on his own authority, but whatever he hears he will speak, and he will declare to you things to come.
(John 16:13, ESV)

Thus says the Lord, your Redeemer.
The Holy One of Israel: "I am the Lord
your God, who teaches you to profit, who
leads you in the way you should go."
(Isaiah 48:17, ESV)

And the Lord will guide you continu-
ally and satisfy your desire in scorched places
and make your bones strong; and you shall
be like a watered garden, like a spring of
water, whose waters do not fail.
(Isaiah 58:11, ESV)

Prayer: Father God, thank, you for this day. Help me to have the strength to get all of my tasks done today, Lord. I ask you to watch over all my friends and family. I pray for a good day today full of joy, in Jesus's name, amen.

February 4

Belong to Him

Resting on the light of my irrevocable love following in step with my most tender Spirit and remaining loyal and faithful during all the trials the storms. I have seen and I know all. I see every thought, I hear every word uttered from your lips and when you have no words, I can hear the prayers help deep within your heart. I know what matters most to you my child, and I am caring for them all. Pruning them and growing them. You shall see what good seeds you have planted by the fruit that they will bear. No worries, you can cast off the fear as I am holding them all in my great hands, I control the outcomes when you learn to trust me and release them in my care. I need no interference or help from you. I am the God of Israel. The mighty Jehovah. The creator of all, what is too hard for me? Am I not your Father who loves you? Do not worry, child. All belong to me, all your worries, all your burdens, all your joys, all your truths, all your loved ones and all of your heart, there is no one better to belong to. You are mine...and everything in creation belongs to me.

Now therefore, if you will indeed obey my voice and keep my covenant, you shall be my treasured possession among all peoples, for all the earth is mine.
(Exodus 19:5, ESV)

For by him all things were created, in heaven and on earth, visible and invisible, whether thrones or dominions or rulers or authorities-all things were created through him and for him.
(Colossians 1:16, ESV)

For we are his workmanship, created in Christ Jesus for good works, which God prepared beforehand, that we should walk in them.
(Ephesians 2:10, ESV)

Prayer: Father God, another day is here, and I am thankful. I ask you to continue to watch over all that I love. I place all my thoughts, circumstances, and loved ones into your hands. Your will, your way, and your timing. All my life I lift to you each day, Lord, and I will rest in my faith. I love you, Lord, in Jesus's name, I pray, amen.

On his robe and on his thigh he has a name written, King of kings and Lord of lords.
(Revelation 19:16, ESV)

February 5

Soak in His Presence

The glory of the light can be found in the hearts of all my children and can be seen at times within the ones who I have called. Sit with me awhile in the silence of your room turn off all distractions so you may find clarity in the whispers of my voice. I speak to your heart, but you must be willing to listen. Just as a child with its parent, some things may be hard to understand. Ask me for wisdom so that you may learn and grow. Just like a garden soaking up the light so will you soak up my words. Then you will thirst no more. As I will keep you nourished and fed. I will make you whole. You can become complete and can be thankful for even the smallest of blessings. Soak up my Presence so that you may shine before others and help them to find their way to me. Life can be interesting, to say the least but with my power, and the strength of my Spirit within, it is more than just interest as it is a living breathing truth found within the power of my Presence and my child, it is amazing… Where you once lived an ordinary life, when you soak in my Presence your life will shine with the brilliant light of believers and turn from ordinary into extraordinary. Come and soak in my Presence, my child…

All scripture is breathed out by God and profitable for teaching, for reproof, for correction, and for training in righteousness.
(2 Timothy 3:16, ESV)

But the anointing that you received from him abides in you, and you have no need that anyone should teach you. But as

his anointing teaches you about everything,
and is true, and is no lie-just as it has taught
you, abide in him.
(1 John 2:27, ESV)

For no prophecy was ever produced by
the will of man, but men spoke from God as
they were carried along by the Holy Spirit.
(2 Peter 1:21, ESV)

Do you not know that you are God's
temple and that God's Spirit dwells in you?
(1 Corinthians 3:16, ESV)

Prayer: Father God, I pray for your wisdom. That I may know which paths you are calling me to walk on. Help me to stay in the light of your words and your truths. I give all my loved ones to you Lord and I thank you for watching over us all. In Jesus's name, I pray, amen.

February 6

Help Others to Shine

Find your seat at my table my child or come lay at my feet. I am the good teacher and have much to teach. Find my lessons within the words of The Bible as it is my true and living word. Bring life to all the good and righteous ways of living by seeking me first. When you live in the Spirit then the worldly desires will fall away. You can stay focused and grounded by keeping focused on me. All for my great purpose, as it is meant for your growth and along the way while growing you are to be an example of the good ways I teach. It is then your job to spread the word and share about me and my kingdom, to help others to find their steps on the good paths of my calling. Showing each other brotherly affection and love. Surrounding each other with love, building each other up, encouraging and showing the light, which I have placed within. Help each other to shine which I have called you to do. What a brilliant light you all create together; it can not only be seen but felt within the hearts of all, even those who currently are walking along the sidelines in the shadows. Creating a radiant beacon to them for which they who are seeking can follow and join. Becoming a part of my kingdom of believers here in this world. Holding onto the great eternal promise I have given. Love one another, my child, just love one another and help others to find the shine that comes from following me...set my good examples, I love you.

Do not neglect to do good and to share what you have, for such sacrifices are pleasing to God.
(Hebrews 13:16, ESV)

In the same way, let your light shine before others, so that they may see your good works and give glory to your Father who is in heaven.
(Matthew 5:16, ESV)

Therefore encourage one another and build one another up, just as you are doing.
(1 Thessalonians 5:11, ESV)

Prayer: Father God, help me to shine today, and please watch over all my loved ones. Thank you, Lord, for another beautiful day, it is in your name, Jesus, I pray and give thanks, amen.

February 7

Find Your Place in His Kingdom

Every good and perfect gift comes from me, do not doubt yourself as I am calling you to perform certain tasks that are a benefit to others. There are whispers that I have been speaking to your heart and watching as you bravely take the steps required to fulfill my good purpose. Accept this gift I have given you, my child, as it is a growing of your faith with each step you take. My good and beloved little one, my child, who I call. I have chosen you. I have primed and prepped you throughout your years to bring life to my good purpose. Let all the worldly doubts fall away and listen only to the sounds of the whispers of my voice, held deep within your heart. As said within my scriptures (1 Corinthians 2:9, "But, as it is written, What no eye has seen, nor ear has heard, nor the heart of man imagined what I have prepared for my children who love me"). All the verses from the Bible are my living words, arm yourself with these daily. Walk in the light of my will. Be accepting of my will. Walk in strength, with certitude, as you shall find your place in my kingdom.

To each is given the manifestation of the Spirit for the common good.
(1 Corinthians 12:7, ESV)

The time is fulfilled, and the kingdom of God is at hand; repent and believe in the gospel.
(Mark 1:15, ESV)

Fear not little flock, for it is your Fathers good pleasure to give you the kingdom.
(Luke 12:32, ESV)

Prayer: Father God, I pray to walk in your ways to live according to your will, and through word and deed I ask that I may be an example of your love to others. Help me to be the light that you have called me to be. I thank you for everyone you have put in my life, and I ask for your mercy and grace and love each day. Help us all to be the people you have called us to be. In Jesus's name, I pray, giving thanks, amen.

February 8

Be Joyful

Day breaks and the dawn of a new day begins, find your joyful outlook. Take in a breath of your new refreshed Spirit, and let it fill within. I am always with you, my child, leading you to a better way where my mercy reigns and my blessings overflow. Keep seeking me and my kingdom first. Hold its importance near to your heart. Do not let me escape your sight. Remain focused on me all the time. Let the nature of my kingdom bring you joy. All happiness, gladness, joy, compassion, kindness, love, and gentleness take all these good things and focus on these. Find in your heart for others love, forgiveness, and understanding. As not, all my children see situations in the same light. But will arrive at the same understanding with the urging of my gentle loving Spirit. As all my children who belong to me and my kingdom shall soak in the same essence of my everlasting love... Be joyful, my child.

Your testimonies are my heritage forever, for they are the joy in my heart.
(Psalm 119:111, ESV)

But the fruit of the Spirit is love, joy peace patience, kindness, goodness, faithfulness, gentleness, self-control; against these things there is no law.
(Galatians 5:22–23, ESV)

You make known to me the path of life; in your presence, there is fullness and joy; at your right hand are pleasures forevermore.
(Psalm 16:11, ESV)

Prayer: Father God, this prayer is for all my friends and family including myself, all who need you desperately. All over the earth. Watch over them, heal them and show them your glory. We know you are mighty with power, Lord. Nothing can stop you or your love. You make ways in the wilderness. I am thankful. Please bring us your peace and fill us with joy this day and always. Thank you, Father God, for your eternal grace and love. In Jesus's mighty name, I pray, amen.

February 9

Wealth of God

Good morning, child, I do not want you to feel bad about pursuing your desires for a better life for yourself and your loved ones... As long as you seek first me and my kingdom, you shall find the wealth of God... I know your heart, little one, so do not worry. I want you to enjoy life and enjoy the things around you that you have worked so hard for and share your good fortunes with others, giving me the first fruit of your labor. I want you to have a full life, an abundant life, and find blessings in it all. May you never doubt yourself or feel less deserving than any child of mine. My children, have sweet huge hearts full of love that encompass my nature and follow on the paths I have called them too, even when they are uncomfortable, they step out onto faith as I light up the way. They keep moving forward. One foot in front of the other. Even during times when they feel uncertain, they learn to trust me, and the feet move forward—one foot, then the other. It never matters how slowly they move as long as they still keep growing, trusting, learning and helping, encouraging, and showing the ways of my mercy and grace. How accepting me as Lord gives purpose to life and changes lives for good. How the joy I've given remains a constant no matter what the circumstance. I will reward my faithful children and want them to allow themselves to enjoy it. Because they love me and find faith in me, strong with trust, helping to share my message... My children shall enjoy the inheritance of my kingdom and my gift of eternal life...the true wealth of God, a gift for my faithful.

Everyone also to whom God has given
wealth and possessions and power to enjoy

them, and to accept his lot and rejoice in his
toil-this is the gift of God.
(Ecclesiastes 5:19, ESV)

And if you indeed obey my command-
ments that I command you today, to love the
Lord your God, and to serve him with all
your heart and with all your soul, he will
give the rain for your land in its season, the
early rain and the later rain, that you may
gather in your grain and your wine and oil.
And he will give grass in your fields for your
livestock, and you shall eat and be full.
(Deuteronomy 11:13–15, ESV)

But Jesus said, "Let the little children
come to me and do not hinder them, for to
such belongs the kingdom of heaven."
(Matthew 9:14, ESV)

Prayer: Father God, I give you my trust and will walk forward knowing that my life is made whole because of you. I give thanks to you for all in my life the trials and the blessings. Thank you, Father, for all your good lessons and the fullness of your love. I ask each day and pray you continually watch over all my loved ones. In your loving name, Jesus, I pray, amen.

February 10

Morning Whispers

Wake up, my child. Rise and open your beautiful sleepy eyes. Come, child, and follow me. As soon as day breaks early in the morning hours, you will hear me whisper to your heart, "Get up and spend time with me." There is much to talk about. I see you have much on your heart and in your mind. I know at times my children can shut down and pull away, but I want them to lean in. Lean in and listen to the morning whispers of my sweet, loving Spirit. Let me fill you, all the empty parts. I will fill you with the light of my majestic eternal love. My grace will find you daily, and my mercy will reign into your life. The whispers of the morning will come upon you and lift your spirit high. It is my essence child that causes you to lift it makes you full, with my power and strength, it floats you high above the world. It is those special times child that you feel as if you were walking on clouds. You can relish in these sweet, yet powerful intimate moments illuminated in my Spirit and by your time spent with me. Find delight in the day as you armor yourself well. And find me again in the glory of the morning and the whispers to your heart.

My sheep hear my voice, and I know them, and they follow me. I give them eternal life, and they will never perish, and no one will snatch them out of my hand.
(John 10:27–28, ESV)

"Moreover," he said to me, "Son of man, all my words that I shall speak to you receive in your heart, and hear with your ears."
(Ezekiel 3:10, ESV)

And all these blessings shall come upon
you and overtake you, if you obey the voice
of the Lord your God.
(Deuteronomy 28:2, ESV)

Prayer: Father God, thank you for this day that you have made. I pray for the sick, Lord, heal them. I pray for the lost, find them and draw them near to you. I pray for all of us, Lord, that you stay constant in our lives, and that we will fill our lives with your joy and love. In Jesus's name, I pray, amen.

February 11

The Walk

Be thankful for this moment, find gratefulness for the day. Bring to me your heart full of worship and praise. Listen to my voice as I call to your soul creating in you a fullness of my eternal love. Forge ahead with perseverance and strength, knowing that it is I who provides for you. I never promised my children an easy walk, but I will never leave my children to walk alone. I am holding you, leading and guiding you into the fullness of my good purpose for you. Remain hopeful, faithful, loyal, and joyful. Let the truth of my Spirit reign in your heart and illuminate my righteous paths in your life. My beautiful loving child, there is so much more I have in store for you. Stay with me and find all the roads that were once blocked clear. I shall remove all the debris from your path and open the road leading you to a completely open space where you can refresh and relax and enjoy the fruits of your labor. Let my Spirit shine brightly in your heart and feel the warmth from the loving caresses that surround your soul, it is I! When you look up and ask, "Was that you, Lord?" Be confident in knowing that it is I, your Lord, your God, your Father, who is watching over you. Directing your feet as you walk on my good paths. Praise my name, child, live for me and I will give you the desires of your heart… Keep growing forward and together we shall unite, as you learn, love, and enjoy the walk.

And your ears shall hear a word behind you, saying, "This is the way, walk in it," when you turn to the right or when you turn to the left.
(Isaiah 30:21, ESV)

So as to walk in a manner worthy
of the Lord, fully pleasing to him, bearing
fruit in every good work and increasing in
the knowledge of God.
(Colossians 1:10, ESV)

But this command I gave them: "Obey
my voice, and I will be your God, and you shall
be my people. And walk in all the way that I
command you, that it may be well with you."
(Jeremiah 7:23, ESV)

And walk in love, as Christ loved us
and gave himself up for us, a fragrant offer-
ing and sacrifice to God.
(Ephesians 5:2, ESV)

Prayer: Father God, this day, I ask that you guard my steps, and help me keep my feet on the path of your calling. Guide me, Lord, and watch over all of my family and friends. Help me to let go of situations where I have no control. Fill me and all my family and friends with peace. The peace in knowing that you Savior have gone before us and are making our paths straight. I praise your name, Jesus, and it is in your name I pray, amen.

Again Jesus spoke to them saying, "I
am the light of the world. Whoever follows
me will not walk in darkness, but will have
the light of life."
(John 8:12, ESV)

February 12

Brave Steps

Take brave and bold steps forward, first thing in the morning. From the time you first open your eyes. There are so many challenges that my children face daily, but just as the ways of the world, they are ever-changing and constantly moving. Reach out and hold onto my hand, hold tightly and do not loosen your grasp. At times there may be mighty storms that may have just passed, but there may be some after-effects of its winds. It is okay, my child, I have ahold of you. When you are too weak to hold on, I will pick you up. Holding you in the palm of my hands and covering you from the elements of the storm. You have nothing to fear as I will protect you and keep you from harm. Keeping you safe in the warmth of my most radiant love. Stand firm, be strong, and shine your light, no need to back down. As you are united with my Spirit. My Spirit the Helper dwells within you, it gives you the strength to go farther than you ever could imagine going on your own. The impossible will always become possible if you remain in your faith and believe. Stay joyful praying continually and giving thanks to me for it all. This is the way you grow in your faith. Keep growing forward to the places I will lead you. Trust my paths to bring you to places where my grace will meet you with my peace and prosperity. Keep taking those steps, my beautiful child, those brave and mighty steps…

No weapon that is fashioned against you shall succeed, and you shall confute every tongue that rises against you in judgment. This is the heritage of the servants of

the Lord and their vindication from me,
declares the Lord.
    (Isaiah 54:17, ESV)

For I, the Lord your God, hold your
right hand; it is I who say to you, "Fear not,
I am the one who helps you."
    (Isaiah 41:13, ESV)

Rejoice always, pray without ceasing,
give thanks in all circumstances; for this is
the will of God in Christ Jesus for you.
    (1 Thessalonians 5:16–18, ESV)

Prayer: Father God,

When I am afraid, I will put my trust
in you. In God, whose word I praise, in
God I trust; I shall not be afraid. What can
flesh do to me?
    (Psalm 56:3–4, ESV)

I pray also for all of my family and friends. In Jesus's name, I give thanks and I pray, amen.

February 13

You May Grow

This is an acknowledgment of who you are; you are my child. A child of God. You are wonderfully and fearfully made. I know you full well and have anointed you with the power of my Holy Spirit. I have filled your emptiness and replaced it with a joy that is ever-present. You have such a big heart so full of love and compassion for others. It is evident in the way that huge tender spirit, brings out the best in the people around you. I love to see the way you are growing and how you have become a flower of my love in full bloom. A blossom of all the good and perfect gifts I give. When you keep your trust in me, you will become stronger. In the way in which you are learning to deal with the emotions of life, and you will gain wisdom and understanding from me and my words. You will gain also my peace. Believe me, child, I know all the hard work you are putting forth, day in and day out, in your daily routines and the unexpected add-ons of life. Yet you hold fast to my hand and keep focused on me, and now you may grow. You step bravely and speak boldly of my good and righteous ways, and again you may grow. You love me and trust me with your whole heart and everything in your life you share with me. Giving me the first parts of yourself, so now in the many nuances of your faith, you may grow. Grow forward in faith, grow forward in trust, grow forward in love, and grow forward in life. You are mine, my child, in full bloom. All wrapped with my love and the fruit of my Spirit. You truly are mine, a full heart filled with love and shinning with faith. My faithful, little child know where you belong. You belong to me... I love you and now you may grow...

But grow in the grace and the knowledge of our Lord and Savoir Jesus Christ. To him be the glory both now and to the day of eternity. Amen.

(2 Peter 3:18, ESV)

You did not choose me, but I chose you and appointed you that you should go and bear fruit and that your fruit should abide, so that whatever you ask the Father in my name, he may give it to you.

(John 15:16, ESV)

Rather, speaking the truth in love, we are to grow up in every way into him who is the head, into Christ, from whom the whole body, joined and held together by every joint with which it is equipped, when each part is working properly, makes the body grow so that it builds itself up in love.

(Ephesians 4:15–16, ESV)

Like newborn infants, long for pure milk, that by it you may grow up into salvation.

(1 Peter 2:2, ESV)

Prayer: Father God, thank you for helping me grow. As I read your verses daily, I feel my soul is being fed by the fruit of your Spirit. And I know it is good. I pray that you help all my family and friends grow closer to you. The more time I spend with you each day, the more I feel your peace and joy inside. I am grateful to you Lord for never giving up on me. I praise your name, Jesus, and it is in your name I pray, amen.

February 14: Happy Valentine's Day! And now you may grow, wrapped in the love of God.

Relish in His Love

You can relish in my love, giving thanks for this day. I have come and I have set you free that you might have life and live it to the fullest living abundantly with all the good and perfect gifts that I bring. When you live in the Spirit you live in my word and learn from me all your goodness. As I, your good teacher will lead you the way. Try not to venture on your own paths but hold fast to the truth of my Spirit. For many are called but few are chosen. My beloved child, find your task and work hard with diligence and be vigilant until it comes to competition. You have turned your ears to me and have heard my voice. Let now my grace and blessings surround you. They will begin falling from the skies. I will shine on you and I am anointing you, my child, to always walk in my ways and follow me through all the paths of my righteous good purpose. Find delight in me and let your heart be light. Your soul is enriched by the fruit of my Spirit. Enjoy, my child, enjoy. And relish in the light of my love…

Having the eyes of your hearts enlightened, that you may know the hope to which he has called you, what are the riches of his glorious inheritance in the saints.
(Ephesians 1:18, ESV)

For many are called, but few are chosen.
(Matthew 22:14, ESV)

*You will be enriched in every way to
be generous in every way, which through us
will produce thanksgiving to God.*
(2 Corinthians 9:11, ESV)

Jesus blesses us when we trust him. Even when we may not know he is with us and we ourselves do not see a way.

*Just as the day was breaking, Jesus
stood on the shore; yet the disciples did not
know that it was Jesus. Jesus said to them,
"Children, do you have any fish?" They
answered him, "No." He said to them,
"Cast the net on the right side of the boat,
and you will find some." So they cast it,
and now they were not able to haul it in,
because of the quantity.*
(John 21:4–6, ESV)

Prayer: Father God, I love you. Thank you for everything you do for me and my loved ones. My heart is full of the love I have from you. Lord, I pray to you to keep me on your paths and give me the strength to continue the path of my calling. I lift all praise up to you this day. In Jesus's name I pray, amen.

February 15

Fruit of the Spirit

Good morning, dear child, the more time you spend with me, the more you desire to be completely wrapped in my Presence. No worries, as I am here during it all. I meet you in all your moments. You can feel the peace of my Spirit as my yoke is easy and light. All the hours of the days and nights I watch over you and never leave your side. The road I have placed you on is a road full of all the wonders of this beautiful life. I know at times the road narrows, but I am walking you through it and providing for you whatever you need as the days unfold. The fruit of my Spirit brings you joy and fills you with my love. A love that you can and share with others around you. My heart is pleased by your acceptance of the tasks I'm calling you too. Even in scorched places, I keep you like a well-watered garden. Even in dry deserts, I replenish your soul. And though your heart may be troubled at times it is I who bears the weight. Taking it off your shoulders and placing you on paths of my calling. On paths of my righteous and eternal love. You can wrap yourself daily with the hope of my unfailing promises and shine with the knowledge that My Spirit is with you. Each day growing stronger and learning to enjoy the fruits of my glorious nature. A gentle, kind, and tender nature. Enjoy the fruit of my Spirit, child, and let your heart soar.

> *But the fruit of the Spirit is love, joy, peace, patience, kindness, goodness, faithfulness, gentleness, self-control; against such things there is no law.*
> (Galatians 5:22–23, ESV)

The Spirit of the Lord God is upon me, because the Lord has anointed me to bring news to the poor, he has sent me to bind up the brokenhearted, to proclaim liberty to the captives, and the opening of the prison to those who are bound.
(Isaiah 61:1, ESV)

That the God of our Lord Jesus Christ, the Father of glory, may give you the Spirit of wisdom and of revelation in the knowledge of him.
(Ephesians 1:17, ESV)

The Spirit himself bears witness with our spirit that we are children of God.
(Romans 8:16, ESV)

Prayer: Father God, may you keep me and make your face to shine upon me. May I always stay in step with you, that I may be like a well-watered garden whose waters do not fail. I pray for all my loved one's Lord and all your children found and unfound, that if unfound you find them, and if found you strengthen them with the fruit of your Spirit. In Jesus's name, I pray and thank you, amen.
February 16

He Watches over You

Here in the stillness of the morning, you can hear my voice, speaking sweet whispers to your heart. There is so much more I want you to experience, my child. If you heed the whispers of my voice, I will lead you there. There into the fullness of my will. Into the places where your dreams become my plans. There where you can walk within my will, to the places where your new dreams will become reality. You were meant for so much more than you know. I have anointed you with my Spirit and have watched you as you grow, into the fruit of my good purposes. All the struggles, all the hardships, all the places that were unsafe, yet it was I that kept you from harm, and when you were sick, I healed you. Nothing that the world has done or that the enemy has tried has kept me from leading you to find your way to my great plans. As I work everything together for good. You are one of a kind, my unique and perfect little child. I know there are times you fall short because after all, you are only human, but I see you try. I know your heart and what is hidden deep inside. You are loved beyond measure and nothing can separate you from my love that you hold. Nothing to fear, my beloved, as I am always watching over you…

Behold, I am with you and will keep you wherever you go and will bring you back to this land. For I will not leave you until I have done what I have promised you. (Genesis 28:15, ESV)

A song of Ascents. I lift up my eyes to the hills. From where does my help come?

My help comes from the Lord, who made heaven and earth. He will not let your foot be moved; he who keeps you will not slumber, behold he who keeps Israel will neither slumber nor sleep. The Lord is your keeper; The Lord is your shade on your right hand...
(Psalm 121, ESV)

And we know that for those who love God all things work together for good, for those who are called according to his purpose.
(Romans 8:28, ESV)

Prayer: Thank you, Father God, for always watching over me and watching over all that I love. I am blessed. I praise your name today and ask that yours always be the loudest voice in my head and in my heart, that your whispers are clear and that you keep me walking in step with your will. Correcting me if needed with kindness and love. I give myself to you each day, Father God. In Jesus's name, I praise and pray, amen.

February 17

You Are Because He Is

Good morning, my dear child, my message I will bring to you loud and clear, stay focused on that believing with all your heart. As miracles, I have done and still do today. Just walk forward standing firm on your faith and believe. Believe with all your heart and all of your soul, as I never leave or forsake my children. I can make ways were none seem evident. I will bring you to the places of my calling. Just let me lead. Keep learning from me, as I am your good teacher and practice always walking in my ways, feeding your souls with the fruit of my Spirit. Make yourself to always be shining examples of my nature. You are brave because it is I, who gives you courage. You are strong because it is I, who provides you, strength. You are light because it is I, who bears your burdens. You radiate love because it is I, who calls you my child. Keep following in the paths of my footsteps, learning, growing, and sharing what you have learned from me, your God, the good teacher and all along the way I will shine on you all my glory, grace, mercy, and love.

> *I will instruct you and teach you in the way you should go; I will counsel you with my eye upon you.*
> (Psalm 32:8, ESV)

> *Therefore, my beloved, as you have always obeyed, so now, not only as in my presence but much more in my absence, work out your own salvation with fear and trembling, for it is God who works in*

you, both to will and to work for his good pleasure.
(Philippians 2:12–13, ESV)

For God is not unjust so as to overlook your work and the love you have shown for his name in serving the saints, as you still do.
(Hebrews 6:10, ESV)

Prayer: Father God, thank you for this day. Please watch over all that I love. I believe in your plans, Lord, and love you with all my heart. I know that with my faith placed in you, your plans for me will not fail. In Jesus's loving name, I pray giving thanks, amen.

February 18

Blueprints of Life

Good morning, dear one, those sleepy eyes now wide. Wide with wonder and amazement at the power of my glorious hand. You are strengthened and moving ahead at my good pace. All good things today are evident, and your heart can be full. Your feet I have planted on my firm foundations, prime real estate for your soul. You can breathe. No longer letting troubles and burdens constrict you as you are fully aware that I am handling all the blueprints of your life. I have come to set you free. When you remain with me, you are unchained, and now we together may lay out all those wonderful ideas setting them into full motion. I will provide you, whatever you need to complete my good tasks. It has been quite the journey thus far and along the way, just as an architect may have small details to adjust, I have adjusted things bringing them back to my purpose. Keep loving me and trusting me, my child for all of creation is mine. And in my great hands...are the blueprints of life.

> *For we are his workmanship, created in Christ Jesus for good works, which God prepared beforehand,*
> *That we should walk in them.*
> (Ephesians 2:10, ESV)

> *Now may the God of peace, who through the blood of the eternal covenant brought back from the dead our Lord Jesus, that great Shepherd of the sheep, equip you with everything good that you may do his will, working in us that which is pleasing*

in his sight, through Jesus Christ, to whom
be the glory forever and ever. Amen.
(Hebrews 13:20–21, ESV)

For by him all things were created, in
heaven and on earth, visible and invisible,
whether thrones or dominions or rulers or
authorities-all things were created through
him and for him.
(Colossians 1:16, ESV)

In Christ Jesus, then, I have reason to
be proud of my work for God.
(Romans 15:17, ESV)

Prayer: Father God, today as I open my eyes, I am thankful. You are the way maker. Everything is in your great hands. I can enjoy the day without worry knowing that you are in control. Please keep watch over all filling us with your peace. In Jesus's name, I pray, amen.

February 19

Emulate His Love

Good morning, my child, there will be times that you hear my whispers, yet the meanings may be unclear. You will experience times where you are unsure, as to what I am communicating to you. It is okay, my child. Relax, as all will be revealed, in my perfect time. There are no flaws found in my ways, and my timing is perfect. Just let the inconsistencies of the day roll off you. Stay on the good paths of my calling and your feet will remain on my solid ground. You are unshakable when you place your life in me and keep focused. Keep rooted in me and wrapped within the safety of my arms. You can still look around to find blessings and joys as they are filling the dullness of the day. Try not to overthink situations that may arise, but instead know that I have everything under control. Giving it all to me. I will lift you high, even when the small snags of life try to drag you down. I will elevate you with the perpetual beauty of my love. And you will shine brightly with the fruit of my nature. Shining brightly for others to see. Always emulating the ways of my love…

As the rain and snow come down from heaven and do not return there but water the earth, making it bring forth and sprout, giving seed to the sower and bread to the eater, so shall my word that goes out from my mouth; it shall not return to me empty, but it shall accomplish that which I purpose, and shall succeed in the thing for which I sent it.
(Isaiah 55:10–11, ESV)

I am the true vine, and my father is the vinedresser. Every branch in me that does not bear fruit he takes away, and every branch that does bear fruit he prunes, that it may bear more fruit. Already you are clean because of the word that I have spoken to you. Abide in me, and I in you. As the branch cannot bear fruit by itself, unless it abides in the vine, neither can you, unless you abide in me. I am the vine; you are the branches. Whoever abides in me and I in him, he it is that bears much fruit, for apart from me you can do nothing. I anyone does not abide in me he is thrown away like a branch that withers; and the branches are gathered, thrown into the fire, and burned. If you abide in me, and my words abide in you, ask whatever you wish, and it will be done for you. By this my Father is glorified, that you bear much fruit and so prove to be my disciples. As the Father has loved me, so I have loved you. Abide in love.

(John 15:1–9, ESV)

And to bring to light for everyone what is the plan of the mystery hidden for ages in God who created all things.

(Ephesians 3:9, ESV)

Prayer: Father God, this day I pray that you surround all those that I love. That we may stay protected within the safety of your arms and that we may cover ourselves with the light of your love. I pray to always be a blessing to others. Armor us up each day Lord. In Jesus's name I pray, amen.

February 20

Well with Your Soul

Darling, sweet child, sleepy eyes, tired lids. I see how hard you work, and I know all that you deal with. Life can be messy at times, but you must go through the messy parts to fully enjoy the complete beautiful blessings of this life and all the glory I bring. I walk beside you through the journey of your life holding your fragile human hand. Who alone could never accomplish the sheer scale of the purpose I lead you too? It is I who provides you strength. Strength to bare it and strength to endure. It may be hard to give all your worries to me, child, but in this, you must try. You know there are struggles every day and you do well when you loosen your grasp and give them to me. You have come so far and been through so much. Although you have gone through many trials and storms it is your faith in me that sets you free. As you can still say, it is well with your soul. Because you do this, you work as if working for me, you, my child will succeed at whatever you set your mind to do. And through it all, you will find joy and all your ways will always remain purposeful… As it is well…with your soul.

For what will it profit a man if he gains the whole world and forfeits his soul? Or what shall a man give in return for his soul?
(Matthew 16:26, ESV)

For God alone my soul waits in silence; from him comes my salvation.
(Psalm 62:1, ESV)

The law of the Lord is perfect, reviving the soul; the testimony of the Lord is sure, making wise the simple.
(Psalm 19:7, ESV)

Beloved, I pray that all may go well with you and that you may be in good health, as it goes well with your soul.
(3 John 1:2, ESV)

Prayer: Father God, guide me always, shine the light on the path which I should walk. Leading me to the places of your good purpose for my life. I am grateful. As always, I ask you to continue to watch over and lead all my family and friends into your plans for our lives. Filling us all with your strength. your peace and your love. In Jesus's name, I pray, amen.

February 21

Full of Light

Follow the sound of my voice, dear child, and walk in the impressions of my steps, arming yourself fully before you begin the days' tasks. Read my words and let them pour into your heart like the most welcomed refreshment and nourishment for your soul. Enjoy all the beautiful blessings I bring, full of my love and adorned with my glory. Let me wrap you within my arms, soak up my Presence as it is full of light. Take all those cares and relinquish them to me. When you keep focused on me, facing forward toward me and the glory of my light, the shadows and the darkness of the day will fall behind you. Just like when you face the sun. But just as easily if you turn your back to the sun the shadows will invade your path and remain in front of you. Keep forward facing me always with the fierce heart of a believer and the perseverance of a conqueror. You have the makings of a warrior, my child, with a kind and gentle, yet strong spirit. You are my child, and so I am your Lord. The beauty of the heart of a believer is one filled with my love and full of light… Go and be blessed in my fullness, my child for you are full of light and complete with my love.

And now I am about to go the way of all the earth, and you know in your hearts and souls, all of you, that not one word has failed of all the good things that the Lord your God promised concerning you. All have come to pass for you; not one of them has failed.
(Joshua 23:14, ESV)

For at one time you were in darkness, but now you are light in the Lord. Walk as children of light (for the fruit of light is found in all that is good and right and true) and try to discern what is pleasing to the Lord.

(Ephesians 5:8–10, ESV)

Again, Jesus spoke to them saying, "I am the light of the world. Whoever follows me will not walk in darkness, but will have the light of life."
(John 8:12, ESV)

For God, who said, "Let light shine out of darkness," has shone in our hearts to give the light of the knowledge of the glory of God in the face of Jesus Christ.
(2 Corinthians 4:6, ESV)

Prayer: Father God, today I thank you for your light which shines in the hearts of all your children. I pray to let my light shine before others, helping them to see your glory. Lord, let me be pleasing to you in all my ways. I pray for all my family and friends that they may find your light of life and hold it within their hearts and experience the true joy of knowing you as their savior. In Jesus's name, I ask and pray, amen.

February 22

Pleasing Him

Take your time, my beloved child. Let yourself become refreshed by the fruit of my Spirit and let your mind be at ease. I have come upon you with my peaceable spirit and provided you rest for your soul. You, my good and faithful child are always seeking, always asking, always searching, always loving, laughing, learning, and accomplishing the tasks at hand. And all these good things please me, as they are full of the fruit which my nature gives. Know my child that I find delight in you and your beautiful heart. I see you look up in amazement at the beauty I bring, and you thank me. How beautiful are the hearts of my children? Who know they are blessed, no matter the circumstance they find gratefulness in all things. For this is my way. The way of your Lord, and it is pleasing to me... Stay in these, my child. in my ways practice and walk in them always.

When a man's ways please the Lord, he makes even his enemies be at peace with him.
(Proverbs 16:7, ESV)

And he who sent me is with me. He has not left me alone, for I always do the things that are pleasing to him.
(John 8:29, ESV)

And so, from the day we heard, we have not ceased to pray for you, asking that you may be filled with the knowledge of his will in all spiritual wisdom and under-

standing, so as to walk in a manner worthy of the Lord, fully pleasing to him, bearing fruit in every good work and increasing in the knowledge of God.
(Colossians 1:9–10, ESV)

Prayer: Father God, I thank you, Lord, for the light on your paths. I pray to always be pleasing to you, Lord, that I may implement (when needed) and accomplish the good tasks your calling me to. That I may help lead others to seek you. As we find our place in your will. That we may find success and favor in your sight Lord. And each day I will give you my praise Lord, as we journey together through this life of your design. In Jesus's loving name, I pray, amen.

February 23

Perfect Rhythm

Surround yourself with my Presence, doing your best and honoring me. Feel the strength of my Spirit bring harmony to your steps as you march forward. Finding the perfect rhythm of this life in love. Persevering and growing stronger with each step. Such a beautiful melody is the sound of your steps and the song of your heart as you are growing strong in your faith and flourishing on the paths, I lead you to. You are loved, child. Today when in prayer, close your eyes and feel the sensations of my love falling all around you. I will envelop you with the warmth of my light and the Spirit of love. No part of you goes without; I accept even what you see as your own flaws, shortcomings, and defects. For with me you are perfect. You are made perfect because you are mine. I am leading you to a new place, child, a new destination made uniquely for you. All the talents that were hidden for so long now I am bringing to the surface and they are shining brightly. You can smile, as you are empowered by the Helper that one that dwells within. And in all my creation, each gift and talent together creates a beautiful melody and all my children shall not only walk in light but will be joined together in perfect harmony, building each other up in love. Finding together the perfect rhythm of a blessed life...

I will ask the Father, and he will give
you another Helper, to be with you forever.
(John 14:16, ESV)

But he who is joined to the Lord
becomes one spirit with him.
(1 Corinthians 6:17, ESV)

From whom the whole body, joined and held together by every joint with which it is equipped, when each part is working properly, makes the body grow so that it builds itself up in love.
(Ephesians 4:16, ESV)

And above all these put on love, which binds everything together in perfect harmony.
(Colossians 3:14, ESV)

Prayer: Father God, I thank you for always leading and allowing me to walk on the light of your good and chosen paths. I thank you also, Lord, for helping me to grow stronger in my faith and flourish with your Presence. Sometimes, I know, Lord, that it seems I repeat myself in prayer, but Father, you know my heart and you know what I hold dear. It is all my family and friends and people. I want to help grow your kingdom, Lord, and see everyone around me come to know you as their Lord. I pray that everyone would get to feel your love. In Jesus's name, I ask and pray, amen.

February 24

Every Day Holds a Blessing

The sun has come up, time to begin a new day. A new day of treasured experiences and moments of memories all wrapped within the circumference of my love. Take heart and do whatever you are doing as if working for me so that you do not get caught up in the perils of daily routines and monotonous living. Every day is a blessing, which holds something new. If only all my children had eyes to see. The world keeps some so busy that they miss these treasured little nuances completely and others realize at a far later date. They say hindsight is twenty-twenty, and I know for some this is true. There are others who do not see the good of their lives in this present time, as they take things for granted. And when their lives are suddenly changed. Oh, how they long for the good old days. My children, listen to me. Learn my will and walk in my ways. Align yourselves with me. Then you will no longer miss the blessings that grace you daily, you will no longer wish for the good old days, you will no longer wish you had seen at the moment the true love that surrounds your lives. You will be living in my moments with me, and there is love in all my moments. There are acceptance and light. There is kindness and strength, gentleness, goodness, wholeness. There is laughter and happiness, and because there is sorrow there will also pain but there in those moments, they will find comfort for their tears. Stay mindful, my child, remaining aware of this the present time. It begins anew each day and like a gift, every day holds a blessing…

The steadfast love of the Lord never
ceases: his mercies never come to an end;

they are new every morning; great is your faithfulness.
(Lamentations 3:22–23, ESV)

And we have something more sure, the prophetic word, to which you will do well to pay attention as a lamp shining in a dark place, until the day dawns and the morning star rises in your hearts.
(2 Peter 1:19, ESV)

Let me hear in the morning of your steadfast love, for in you I trust. Make known to me the way I should go, for to you I lift up my soul.
(Psalm 143:8, ESV)

Blessed be the God and Father of our Lord Jesus Christ, who has blessed us in Christ with every spiritual blessing in heavenly places.
(Ephesians 1:3, ESV)

Prayer: Father God, thank you for this day. I ask you to help me be joyful in all my moments. I pray to always see the sunshine in my life, even on the days that seem gray. I ask to be an encouragement and a blessing to others. In Jesus's loving name, I pray, amen.

February 25

Times of Busy and of Rest

Blessed is the evening as it brings more time to rest. Let there be more times of rest and rejuvenation of your spirit, little child. I know you have become accustomed to always being busy. Many of my children when the chaos of the day stops, they feel uncomfortable just sitting. Always looking for the next thing to do. Learn to calm down, my child. Learn to rest, letting my Spirit give you comfort. It is very important to stop and refresh. There are times, however, that business is good as idle hands can get caught in laziness, doing nothing when they should be doing something. So, my child, stay aware of your balance. As rest and idleness are not the same. But whatever you do in word or deed, rest when needed and be busy when necessary always doing what is good and right, fair and just. Being productive in a worthy manner. For this is my way. Confess your sins and remain faithful in your hearts and I will forgive you and cleanse you from your unrighteousness. I will fill you with my joy and give you a life that is eternal. And every good deed shall show my glory and you shall honor me with yourselves and the way you live. For this is also my way.

Look carefully then how you walk, not
as unwise but as wise, making the best use
of the time, because the days are evil.
(Ephesians 5:15–16, ESV)

And we urge you, brothers, admonish
the idle, encourage the fainthearted, help
the weak, be patient with them all.
(1 Thessalonians 5:14, ESV)

If we confess our sins, he is faithful
and just to forgive us our sins and to cleanse
us from all unrighteousness.
(1 John 1:9, ESV)

Prayer: Father God I ask you to help me to maintain a good and healthy balance for the rest and business in my life and for the lives of the ones around me. Help us to stay healthy and keep a good balance within ourselves. Give us strength, Lord, when we feel weary and let us have peace when it is time to rest. Give us the knowledge to know what we should be doing. Also, help us to stay focused on you so that we may always feel proportioned. In Jesus's name, I ask and pray, amen.

February 26

Your Heart

Let your heart be light and the essence of the day be filled with all good things I bring. Most importantly love, as it binds everything together in perfect harmony. Keep your eye on the prize of my Salvation and move forward with your confidence, and I will keep your foot from being caught in the snares and potholes of life. You shall not stumble in the pursuits of the good perfect ways of my nature, on the paths of my calling. Do not be dismayed my child, as I will uphold you keeping you from harm. Do not let your heart condemn you but instead open completely your heart to me, allowing me to lead and to guide you in fullness. As you read my word and learn more and more about the good desires of the Spirit instead of the flesh. And all the beautiful absolutions this way of living brings. Seek to please me first and find that your troubled heart becomes light and free with my easy comfort and gentleness. You shall set your heart at rest in my Presence and this day may you smile, as your heart may rekindle its joy...the joy it has found in me...a joy that lasts eternally.

Blessed is the man who remains steadfast under trial, for when he has stood the test he will receive the crown of life, which God has promised to those who love him.
(James 1:12, ESV)

For whenever our heart condemns us, God is greater than our heart, and he knows everything. Beloved, if our heart does not condemn us, we have confidence before God.
(1 John 3:20–21, ESV)

*Trust in the Lord with all your heart
and do not lean on your own understanding.*
(Proverbs 3:5, ESV)

*But seek first the kingdom of God and
his righteousness, and all these things will
be added unto you.*
(Mathew 6:33, ESV)

Prayer: Father God, this day I ask you, Lord, just to simply be with me and all the people I love. I ask you to fill us with your love and gentleness. Please remove all our frustrations and replace any hurt or anger with your compassion and kindness. Thank you, Father God, Jesus, in your name I pray, amen.

February 27

Strong Faith

You can do it! Whatever you put your mind to, may your heart find perseverance as coming from me. I am your Lord and you do well when you stay within the light of my will. You know inside which way to walk as I am leading you with gentle tugs and strong pulls to keep going and most importantly keep growing up in your faith. Let me be your hearts obsession. Seek me, long for more of me and I will come and make my Presence known. You are mine, child as you call me your Lord, you call me—Jesus, Jesus, Jesus, I am here. I have already made my home in you stay awake and full in the Presence of my Spirit. There is a great task that I am calling you too and you, child, can and will accomplish it. It is my will that you shall accept this great gift I've given you. Learn to stop fear and doubt from poisoning your beautiful thoughts. So clever is the enemy but you are wise now child. Stand on my promises and my words! Forever and ever my truth and my purpose ring eternal and nothing can stop what I have planned. Stay hopeful and sure of it! Keeping your faith strong. Stand on my promise strong in your faith in the brilliant light of my will…

And Jesus answered them. "Have faith in God truly, I say to you, whoever says to this mountain. Be taken up and thrown into the sea," and does not doubt in his heart, but believes that what he says will come to pass, it will be done for him. Therefore I tell you, whatever you ask in prayer, believe you that you have received it, and it will be yours.
(Mark 11:22–24, ESV)

Look carefully then how you walk,
not as unwise but as wise, making the best
use of the time, because the days are evil.
Therefore do not be foolish, but understand
what the will of the Lord is.
(Ephesians 5:15–17, ESV)

And Jesus said to him, "If you can! All
things are possible for one who believes."
(Mark 9:23, ESV)

Prayer: Thank you, Father God, for giving me the strength and strong will to accomplish all the tasks that are mine to complete. Thank you for giving me the gift and the abilities needed to get things done. I pray to stay aligned with your will. That my faith may not fail. If I get off track, Lord, I ask that you gently bring me back to the fullness of your purpose with kindness. I love you, Lord, and as always, each day I pray for everyone around me in my life who need you that you may make known to them your beautiful Presence thank you, Jesus. It is in your name I pray, amen.

Read in the Bible, the book of Daniel chapter 3 about the strong faith that three young men showed and about how Jesus showed up in their moments of a fiery trial, not only were they saved but they were also promoted. Because they had faith

February 28

March

Sometimes the Lord will use others to show you that you are loved beyond measure. And when you feel love, then you are able to share the love that you feel with others. And this is what God calls us to do. We love because he first loved us.

He Breathes Life

There is life! Today, my child, as you begin, let me remind you that I created it all. As I give life and through my breath, creation was formed. I breathed life into existence. When the fleshly body gives way to withering and aging, illness, and injury I am the great physician. I am a healer and I am your Lord. Close your eyes child and let me whisper health into your bones growing you strong. Overcoming all that ails you within my will. No need for doubts and fear as that is an earthy mind-set. But you, my child, are of a spiritual mind-set. No weapon formed against you shall prosper. Whether disease or sickness, aging or unrest no harm shall befall you in my care. I may allow things to happen but keep in mind my will is perfect and my ways and my timing are impenetrably flawless. Nothing can stop what I have planned. Your obedience and faith are the key to your prayer life and obtaining what you are asking. Amazing things happen when my children with a faithful heart pray. If you say to the mountain, "Move," it shall move by the power of your faith. Anything you ask if it is within my will, believe that you have received it, I will do it. Just believe all things are possible with me. And I will whisper within you, strength, as I breathe life into you again.

And the Lord will guide you continually and satisfy your desire in scorched places and make your bones strong; and you shall be like a watered garden, like a spring of water, whose waters do not fail.
(Isaiah 58:11, ESV)

Saying, "If you will diligently listen to the voice of your Lord your God, and do that which is right in his eyes, and give ear to his commandments and keep all his statutes, I will put none of the diseases on you that I put on the Egyptians, for I am the Lord, your healer."
(Exodus 15:26, ESV)

My son, pay attention to what I say; turn your ear to my words. Do not let them out of your sight; keep them within your heart; for they are life to those who find them and health to one's whole body. Above all else guard your heart, for everything you do flows from it.
(Proverbs 4:20–23, NIV)

Prayer: Father God thank you for being the great healer. I pray for health for all my loved ones and myself. May you give us appetites for things that are healthy for us, and may we nourish our bodies with the power found within your words. I ask to be a blessing to those around me and that our faith in you would continue to grow. And that we may flourish in the gardens of our lives, producing your good fruit. In Jesus's loving name, I pray, giving praise and thanks, amen.

March 1

Slow Yourself

Sometimes it feels like you have the weight of the world placed on your small, human shoulders, and sometimes, my child, you do but know during those times it is you who has placed it there. As you have forgotten to cast the heaviness on me, giving me all the weight. In the heat of angry, frustrated moments, stop, catch yourself before you say something hurtful or do something out of haste. Practice this, my child, stop walk away to another room and call out to me to remove the intense feeling to lash out. My children should be slow to anger and slow to speak in heated moments. Give yourself some time to calm down and step away. Not leaving completely as to worry others, but just simply stepping away for a moment. Then return and resume coming from a place of love. It's okay to get angry but it is how you communicate the anger or frustration that really matters. Be the glue that brings things together. And you will begin to notice that others will respond better, and things will resolve much quicker. Be happy, child and set good examples demonstrating my nature, using always wisdom and self-control. For I am your Lord and I am love…

A soft answer turns away wrath, but a harsh word stirs up anger.
(Proverbs 15:1, ESV)

Whoever is slow to anger has great understanding. But he who has a hasty temper exalts folly.
(Proverbs 14:29, ESV)

A fool gives full vent to his spirit, but a wise man quietly holds it back.
(Proverbs 29:11, ESV)

Know this, my beloved brothers: let every person be quick to hear, slow to speak, slow to anger; for the anger of man does not produce the righteousness of God.
(James 1:19–20, ESV)

The Lord is merciful and gracious, slow to anger and abounding in steadfast love.
(Psalm 145:8, ESV)

Prayer: Father God, thank you for helping me during times of anger and frustration. And forgiving me when I am quick-tempered. Help me not to take out the pressures of life out on those around me. Help me to seek you first so that I do not get wrapped up in my own thoughts. Give me wisdom so that I may have self-control. And give me the desire to be able to listen to those around me with loving ears. Also, if I fail, help me to admit my wrongs and be able to ask them to forgive me. Give me your heart, Lord. In Jesus's name, I pray, amen.

March 2

Armor Up

Do not fall susceptible to the undertones of life. There are situations that may expose you to things that at the time you may find harmless but, there are undertones set by the enemy which if you are not armored up can penetrate your mind unknowingly. Stay with me and armor up daily so that you may withstand the tricks of the evil one. Arm yourself daily with verses and texts found within my living word (the Bible.) Learn wisdom and discernment and always act in manners of wisdom. Be good to others and to yourself. You may enjoy but just remain aware of the shadows that exist in the world today and keep your light turned on, trusting me and following me, walking always in my truth. Armor up putting on my whole armor each and every day. Escaping every attempt of the enemy with the resilient armor of God... Learn and seek my will above your own walking in the fruit of my nature and covered by me, as I give protection and forgiveness. Now child, go out and shine your light be the men and women I call you to be and always each day spend time with me in prayer. Never forgetting to armor up. Shine now, always protected in the excellence of my love.

Submit yourselves therefore to God.
Resist the devil, and he will flee from you.
(James 4:7, ESV)

For he is like one who is inwardly cal-
culating. "Eat and drink!" he says to you,
but his heart is not with you.
(Proverbs 23:7, ESV)

You have given me the shield of your
salvation and your right hand supported
me, and your gentleness made me great. You
gave me a wide place for my steps under me.
And my feet did not slip.
(Psalm 18:35–36, ESV)

For the weapons of our warfare are
not of the flesh but have divine power to
destroy strongholds. We destroy arguments
and every lofty opinion raised against the
knowledge of God, and take every thought
captive to obey Christ.
(2 Corinthians 10:4–5, ESV)

Prayer: Father God, thank you for your protection, and for watching over my whole family, all my loved ones. I pray to always be able to discern which situations to stay away from. I pray each day that you armor up all of us. And keep us enshrouded by your Spirit, held safely under the refuge of your wings. In Jesus's name, I pray, amen.

March 3

Perfect Peace of His Presence

You are graced by my Presence, take the beauty of my Spirit and its gentle nature and let it fill your soul. You are walking on such an adoring journey child, filled with many different canvases, backdrops, and terrain. Yet you do not let the journey rule you. As you have found me at the forefront of your mind and in the center of your heart. I am with you on the journey and every path I lead you to, you can see my blessings. You are aware of my Presence and can feel my peace even while walking on the most difficult of terrain. You are calmly wrapped within the safety of my arms. And even though there are times you feel weary, you are confident as you know I shall give you my strength, and through me, you can do all the things that you are called to do. Stay present minded so you may enjoy all the beautiful natural scenery of my creation along the way. Do not neglect what is in front of your eyes as it is easy to do when you live within the vast valleys of your mind. But remain aware of the beauty of my love in the present garden of your life and keep alive and well your faith with perfect peace found within my Presence...

Peace I leave with you: my peace I give to you. Not as the world gives do I give to you. Let not your hearts be troubled, neither let them be afraid.
(John 14:27, ESV)

What you have learned and received and heard and seen in me-practice these things. And the God of peace will be with you.
(Philippians 4:9, ESV)

Now may the Lord of peace himself
give you peace at all times in every way. The
Lord be with you all.
(2 Thessalonians 3:16, ESV)

Prayer: Father God, thank you for your peace. I know I can do all things and be all the things I am called to do and be because of you and your love for me. I pray for all today your presence surrounds us and give us strength. In Jesus's name, I pray, amen.

March 4

He Makes Known

I make known to you the paths of my righteousness I will bring you into the fullness of my lush and green gardens to the lighthouse that shines with my brilliant light in the darkness and you shall find my ways in which to walk. You shall enjoy the fruit of your labor and my grace and mercy shall be with you and my love shall reign in your heart. You will be a well-watered garden whose fruits do not fail. Because you have wrapped yourself in me. I will show you the error of your ways when you fall short of my glory and pick you back up placing you on the solid foundations of my Spirit. And from these, you shall learn and grow in your faith and not walk in the shadows any longer. Your steps will always be light and there will be paths that glow in front of you. When you walk on these paths, you shall never again be lost. My love shall fill your heart and help to show others my ways. And you, my child, you are called. As for now in all this good time, make good use of it and always fulfill my purpose and I will make known to you my paths all the days of your life.

Call to me and I will answer you, and will tell you great and hidden things that you have not known.
(Jeremiah 33:3, ESV)

For this reason, I remind you to fan into flame the gift of God, which is in you through the laying on of my hands, for God gave us a spirit not of fear but of power and love and self-control. Therefore do not be ashamed of the testimony about our Lord,

nor of me his prisoner, but share in suffering
for the gospel by the power of God.
    (2 Timothy 1:6–8, ESV)

Your word is a lamp to my feet and a
light to my path.
    (Psalm 119:105, ESV)

And you will know the truth, and the
truth will set you free.
    (John 8:32, ESV)

Prayer: Father God, I give thanks to you for this day. I will walk on your good and lighted paths with your gentle leading, as you make known to me the ways I should go. I pray for all my family and friends your love and strength and guidance. In Jesus's name, amen.

March 5

When Grace Shows Up

My child, I see you in the mornings, most days you wake with a grateful heart, for what the day holds. I see you, work through your struggles and walk through your trials, as I have been there holding your hand. I have seen you battling the thoughts within your mind. I have seen you grow in faith, as you learn to overcome and not succumb to the way of the world. As you place your trust in me. Each day we spend together brings a strength of unmatched and uncalculated proportion. I know there are times that your weariness may feel as if it will never end, but during those times as you reach out to me, you will see the light of my love lift you and you will be given understanding through the knowledge of my grace. Beautiful things happen when my grace shows up. Things at one time you fell short of understanding will make sense when you are given a small glimpse of what lies behind the veil. You are not to know everything, my child, not all the whys or the why not's. But know it is for your protection as the full view would be too overwhelming for the fragile nature of a human mind. So there are mysteries that I will keep. Only revealing them as I see fit because my ways are perfect and unflawed. You can trust in this. And on the days that you fall short of my glory, you also can trust you are forgiven and that you are loved. As always, my grace shows up and remains with you each day.

Little children, you are from God and
have overcome them, for he who is in you is
greater than he who is in the world.
(1 John 4:4, ESV)

But he said to me, "My grace is suffi-
cient for you, for my power is made perfect
in weakness." Therefore I will boast all the
more gladly of my weaknesses, so that the
power of Christ may rest upon me.
(2 Corinthians 12:9, ESV)

But grow in the grace and knowledge
of our Lord and Savior Jesus Christ. To him
be the glory both now and to the day of eter-
nity Amen.
(2 Peter 3:18, ESV)

Prayer: Father God, thank you for your love and unending grace. I pray to stay the course of my calling with joy in my heart and a love that continues to fill my life. My continued prayer: I pray to be a good example to my fellow brethren, my children, my family, friends and even those around me that do not know me, I pray they see you in me. Glory be to you Lord, all the days of my life. I pray you to watch over and protect all that I love, in Jesus's name, amen.

March 6

Take Caution, Have Faith

Take caution where you walk, child, during the times you feel just out of reach of the good purpose, I am bringing you too. Do not get discouraged but remain hopeful and present in the journey. Try not to get off track. It may seem as things are opening so slowly to you but, child, they are not going slowly. It may just be that you have been accustomed to how quickly things are available to you in this fast-paced world. But I have seen what lies ahead of you as I have gone to those places and been to your moments before you. Make sure to always pursuit me. Seeking to align yourself with my will and my ways as these are ways of peace and love; they bring to your life a righteous abundance of balance and happiness. Soar, child, spread your wings and soar fly like the eagle utilizing any winds of storms or trials that have caused angst in your life to propel you higher. I am with you so landing on my firm foundations makes for an easy flight, with no future worries. Just take caution in your daily life, child, and always have hope. Remaining in your faith standing strong on my promises in the light of my eternal love...

> *Do not be anxious about anything but in prayer and supplication with thanksgiving let your requests be made known to God. And the peace of God, which surpasses all understanding, will guard your hearts and minds in Christ Jesus.*
> (Philippians 4:6–7, ESV)

> *And now I commend you to God and to the word of his grace, which is able to*

build you up and to give you the inheritance among all those who are sanctified.
(Acts 20:32, ESV)

But by the grace of God, I am what I am, and his grace toward me was not in vain. On the contrary, I worked harder than any of them, though it was not I, but the grace of God that is with me.
(1 Corinthians 15:10, ESV)

Prayer: Father God, thank you for the abilities and the opportunities you have given me to be able to work and to do my best. I pray to always have what is needed to accomplish the tasks set before me. And I ask you to help me keep joy in my heart as I work each day toward my goals. I lift it all up to you. As I keep growing forward in faith and stand on the hope of your promises each and every day. I ask you to watch over everyone I love, in Jesus's name, I pray, amen.

March 7

God of Strength

I am the God of strength. I am your God, and nothing is too difficult for me. So on days you feel a little run down, call on me and let me fill you with my unending power supply. It is good when you ask me to help, my child. I never want you to feel like you are asking too much of me. Just remember who it is you're asking. I never tire, I never get run down or get overwhelmed and I never sleep. I am always available to you. I am the one who loves you unconditionally who sees you at your worst and still acknowledges what a special child you are. You are worthy because I created you, and I call you...mine. Because of my love, you can hold your head high and walk through life feeling a sense of victory, as I am always victorious. I have been with you and will be always until the end of this life and into the next, I will remain your King. I am Sovereign over your life, as you worship me and love me with your whole heart. Together we are accomplishing big goals and small tasks. You are getting done more than you could ever do on your own. And because you acknowledge where your help comes from it serves you well, all the more. My little beloved one hold fast to every promise that you have known from me. Stay present in my company and in your moments of weakness experience the strength that I provide to you daily. I am Jesus, your Lord, your God, your King and I am your strength...

And after you have suffered a little while, the God of grace, who has called you to his eternal glory in Christ, will himself restore, confirm, strengthen, and establish you.
(1 Peter 5:10, ESV)

But they who wait for the Lord shall renew their strength; they shall mount up with wings like eagles; they shall run and not grow weary; they shall walk and not faint.
(Isaiah 40:31, ESV)

And the word became flesh and dwelt among us, and we have seen his glory, glory as of the only Son from the Father, full of grace and truth.
(John 1:14, ESV)

Prayer: Father God, thank you for being my strength on the days I feel weak. Thank you for being with me during all my moments and for providing me whatever I need to be successful throughout the day. Guide my heart, Lord, to accomplish all the tasks I'm called to do and keep me on your good paths full of joy and love. I pray for everyone today that you remain strong within them. In Jesus's name, I pray, amen.

March 8

Stay with Him

What causes your foot to slip? Is it the earthly and fleshly desires? When you start to feel out of balance, it may just be that you are seeping back into old ways, the ones you left behind when you began to follow me. Stay aware of what and of who you are following. Find your steps as you walk on my lighted paths. Stay the course with me, my beloved child. Soak up my Presence each day, by spending time with me. Spending time in prayer is very essential to the wellbeing of your soul. I know that the world would have you stay so busy as to make you start thinking that time is a precious commodity. And in this life, my beloved, it truly is. As the hours and the minutes of the day pass by so quickly. Just remain focused on me, always casting your view up keeping your mind on heavenly things and I will bring you back to the places where you can rest in my Presence. Walk with me, find your focus in me, find your strength in me, find your rest in me, find your joy rooted in me. Holding fast to me and stay, child, just stay in the light of my truth, resting in the safety of my arms enshrouded by my love and nestled under my wings covered completely by my grace and held tightly within my arms just stay...

But I do not account my life of any value nor precious to myself, if I may only finish my course and the ministry that I received from the Lord Jesus, to testify to the gospel of the grace of God.
(Acts 20:24, ESV)

Who saved us and called us to a holy calling, not because of our own works but because of his own purpose and grace, which he gave us in Christ Jesus before the ages began.
(2 Timothy 1:9, ESV)

And with great power the apostles were giving their testimony to the resurrection of the Lord Jesus, and great grace was upon them all.
(Acts 4:33, ESV)

Prayer: Father God, each day I lift my life and the lives of all those I love to you, Lord. I know we can rest in the safety of your arms soaked in the mighty Presence of your Spirit. Keep directing us and leading us. I pray for healing for those who are sick and for the ones who are lost I pray that you would take them by the hand and gently lead them back to your paths, filling them with your good purpose. I pray we always make the choice to stay with you. In Jesus's mighty name, I pray, amen.

March 9

Your Lord Loves and So You Love Also

Every morning, I am here waiting for you to turn around to make mention of your Lord, to seek me and thank your mighty Savoir for another beautiful day. When you call on me, I will come in like a rushing wind and fill you with my brilliant light and purpose. You will find the unmerited favor of my grace daily, as you grow up in your faith with reverence and marvel at the beauty of this relationship you have formed with me. You are never far off from me and that is good as my righteous ways find their place in your heart each day. Life itself in these times has become so complicated. Find the simplicity that my love brings. I have said it before and will remind you to take my yoke as it is easy and light. I AM love, and I delight in you showing love for others, keep living this way. Sharing my good news and shining brightly with the nature of my Spirit. Seeking me always learning from my living words finding wisdom and practicing what you have learned. Take up your cross daily and keep following me, child. As I am your Lord and I am Love. I am your Father; you have found a love that exists as eternal. As forever and irrevocably, I love you… So you love also.

The Lord is not slow to fulfill his promise as some count as slowness, but is patient toward you, not wishing that any should perish, but that all should reach repentance.
(2 Peter 3:9, ESV)

A new commandment I give to you, that you love one another: just as I have

loved you, you also are to love one another.
By this all people will know that you are my
disciples, if you have love for one another.
(John 13:34–35, ESV)

We love because he first loved us.
(1 John 4:19, ESV)

Prayer: I am here Lord seeking you. Thank you, Lord, for this glorious day where your love shines brightly in me. I pray to continue this beautiful journey of my life and to always share your love with others. My continued prayer to be a blessing to those around me. That whenever they see me, they will see your Spirit shining brightly within me. I love you and lift my praise up to you Jesus, and it is in your name that I praise giving thanks, amen.

March 10

Excel with His Excellence

Just as the sun rises on some days brighter and more brilliant than others, so is your light. But you shine brighter when you cast the shade aside and armor up daily and practice what you are learning from me. The fruit of my nature is strong in you, child, as you seek to please me more and more. You have turned your ear to me and have found a thirst and desire for my words and my ways. Your love, I see is on fire for me. When you keep my ways before you, walking always in them, you shall begin to excel in everything in your life. Keep living in this good way. I open the ways before you nothing can hold you back as your realities in life are surpassing all that you had hoped, or thought was possible. The mountains they are moving, the skies now clear and the deserts are filled with my living waters. You will see the magnificence of my merciful and glorious nature, as my grace shines brightly upon you, my child. While we spend time together, you can feel my warmth bringing joy to your soul. I am pleased by your refusal to downplay my significance in your life. Stay brave in your words and deeds when sharing the gospel with others just as you are, and forever you will remain like a well-watered garden, sharing such good and wonderful seeds. Keep loving them, child, just as I love you...and excel with my excellence

But as you excel in everything-in faith,
in speech, in knowledge, in all earnestness,
and in our love for you-see that you excel in
this act of grace also.
(2 Corinthians 8:7, ESV)

Let the favor of the Lord our God
be upon us, and establish the work of our
hands upon us; Yes establish the work of our
hands!
(Psalm 90:17, ESV)

Because he holds fast to me in love, I
will deliver him; I will protect him, because
he knows my name. When he calls to me,
I will answer him; I will be with him in
trouble; I will rescue him and honor him.
With long life I will satisfy him and show
him my salvation.
(Psalm 91:14–16, ESV)

Prayer: Father God, thank you for your blessings and the gifts of my life. Thank you for removing mountains and clearing paths for me to walk and for providing in my heart my light to shine. Thank you for your Holy Spirit. I ask to continue to excel in all the good things I'm called too and to be able to work hard while keeping your joy in my heart. I pray for all that I love, in Jesus's name, I pray, amen.

So you will find favor and good success
in the sight of God and man.
(Proverbs 3:4, ESV)

March 11

His Perfect Love

Daybreak has come, time to begin your wondrous day. Mornings are sweeter when you bow down to me in prayer. Humble yourselves before your Lord, as the start of your day has arrived. Call on me, child, each and every day, as I provide you with all that you need. Relish in me, finding the merriment of your soul and delight in the calm enjoyment of the day, a solid and fulfilled eternal joy. Imagine yourself wrapped in my arms letting the warmth of my Spirit illuminate within your soul. Coddle yourself in the light of my love as you experience my impenetrable Sovereignty. In this place, there are no worries, you have nothing to fear. For you see, my child, you are perfectly loved and so you may also love-as perfect love casts out fear. Smile this day knowing that you will never be alone again. As I am with you, by your side, holding your hand, leading you through all the beauty of my creation. Even in this darkened world, you are enshrouded with my love and sheathed within my grace. Everything is all for my glory in the purpose of your life and embellished by the light of my perfect love... I love you, my child...

There is no fear in love, but perfect love casts out fear. For fear has to do with punishment, and whoever fears has not been perfected in love.
(1 John 4:18, ESV)

So we have come to know and to believe the love that God has for us. God is love, and whoever abides in love abides in God, and God abides in him.
(1 John 4:16, ESV)

Set me as a seal upon your heart, as a seal upon your arm, for love is strong as death, jealousy is fierce as the grave. Its flashes are flashes of fire, the very flame of the Lord.
(Song of Solomon 8:6, ESV)

Prayer: Father God, thank you simply for your love. I pray today that you be with us and strengthen us so that today's tasks are accomplished with ease. I love you, Lord. In Jesus's name, I pray, amen.

March 12

His Good Invitation

Let me lift you, child, let all the empty parts be made full in the glory of my grace. So you feel that you lack, but you must know when you are filled with my Presence you lack nothing. I have made you whole. You need nothing that this world could offer to make feel you complete. You are a child of God, my beautiful little soul. I see the daily struggles laid out before you, but I know you can overcome these. Keep your heart entwined with me and the strength of this love braid will be strengthened even more by the power of your faith and the strength of my chord. Even on the days when you feel broken in the spaces of your life that you have deemed empty. The Chord of my Spirit is indestructible and will never be broken, as long as you remain faithful to me the Sovereign King of your life. I am your Lord. I am the Alpha and the Omega, and you have found your solace resting in the warmth of my beautiful light. Shine on my dear and let the world see who it is that you belong to. As you encompass all the gentle and loving ways that my nature brings. Speak of me, tell them, show them, see how the truth of my Spirit makes them grow curious. As they see my Presence glow strong in you. My child of faith, my dear child of love, go out into the world as a warrior of light… And together we will grow the household of faith. Always doing what is good and just, right and fair, in life, in love, for all eternity. I offer eternity to all who call upon me to be their Savoir, the leader of their lives, for those who accept the invitation, taking me in their heart and call me Lord.

*So then, as we have the opportunity,
let us do good to everyone, and especially
those who are of the household of faith.*
(Galatians 6:10, ESV)

*In the same way, let your light shine
before others, so that they may see your good
works and give glory to your Father who is
in heaven.*
(Matthew 5:16, ESV)

*Whoever gives thought to the word
will discover good, and blessed is he who
trusts in the Lord.*
(Proverbs 16:20, ESV)

Prayer: Thank you, Father God, today as I begin my day, I ask that the light of your love remain bright in me. That during the day, others would be able to see you in me. I pray to be a blessing to those around me. And that our faith would continue to grow and shine to others. Always pointing the way to your purpose for our lives. I pray that we may always walk in the ways you call us to walk. In Jesus's name, I give thanks and I pray, amen.

March 13

Glory beyond Comparison

Do you not know, have you forgotten, who provides you help? Where does your help come from, child? It comes from me, your God, the creator of heaven and earth. How much more pleasing it is to me when my children surrender…giving it all to me. As they know that I Am their Sovereign Lord and have everything under control. The afflictions and trials here in this life are only but for a short moment in time but my grace, mercy, and love reigns eternally. Keep in mind, my child, this is not your permanent home. Do your best to walk in the ways that keep you strongly planted on my firm foundations. Listen to my instruction and I will lead you in the ways you should go I will counsel you and be there for you when things become unclear, to light the ways in which you should walk, as you follow in the footsteps of your Lord. Let all the grumbling nature that sits in a stronghold within your mind fall away, so that you do not become imprisoned by negative thoughts. But instead, stay joyful and seek to notice blessings that are around you every day. Give thanks for these and remain hopeful knowing that the trials for this moment do not compare to my eternal glory. My glory is beyond comparison and all moments are filled to the brim and overflow with my love.—hold these truths tightly calling them to mind whenever you feel angst and the glory of my love beyond comparison, will be revealed to you time and time again…

For this light momentary affliction is
preparing for us an eternal weight of glory
beyond all comparison.
(2 Corinthians 4:17, ESV)

If I lift my eyes up to the hills. From where does my help come from? My help comes from the Lord, who made heaven and earth.
(Psalm 121:1–2, ESV)

In him we have obtained an inheritance, having been predestined according to the purpose of him who works all things according to the counsel of his will.
(Ephesians 1:11, ESV)

What then shall we say to these things? If God is for us who can be against us?
(Romans 8:31, ESV)

Prayer: Father God, thank you for this day, thank you for my trials and my storms, thank you for it all. I will walk with you on your lighted paths. I pray this day to be present and thankful always holding onto you, my Lord. I pray you to continue to meet me in all my moments, to keep my faith strong as I walk through the garden of my life. I pray for all my family and friends for your peace and comfort and the fullness that your love gives. In Jesus's name, I pray giving thanks, amen.

March 14

Pleasant Kindness

There is pleasantness and kindness just peaking over the horizon of your life when you seek to be filled with the gentleness of my Spirit. There is so much I have in store for you, child. All my good and perfect ways bringing to you an easier gentler season in your life. You can breathe and take it in with love and wonder, all the beautiful serenity that you have longed for, for quite some time. A true refreshing of your soul. A simplicity of life that you have been craving in your spirit will arrive when your trust in me is strong. Now you are learning to truly let go of situations and people letting them rest within my care. You can see me moving and working in the lives of those around you enabling you to focus your energy with a balance of my truth. You can feel me taking the weight off your shoulders. Keep moving forward letting the worries of yesterday rest in the light of my care and the troubles of the day will not find you unprepared as your faith in me keeps you held high above the storms. There is peace. Fill yourself with my words and soak yourself with my truth and never forget the strength of the Lord, your God. I have got it all under control and I will remain Sovereign. I am the lover of your soul and so you shall be full of calm with the pleasant gentleness I bring, and you shall walk in my radiant peace. Enjoy each step little one, as we walk on the peaceful paths of my righteousness...

Take my yoke upon you, and learn
from me, for I am gentle and lowly in heart,
and you will find rest for your souls.
(Matthew 11:29, ESV)

And my God will supply every need of yours according to his riches in glory in Christ Jesus.
(Philippians 4:19, ESV)

I have said these things to you, that in me you may have peace. In the world, you will have tribulation. But take heart; I have overcome the world.
(John 16:33, ESV)

Prayer: Thank you, Father God, for the peaceful gentle nature that you bring to me each day. Thank you for filling me up with peace and giving me rest. I pray for all my loved ones and people around me as I go out into the world today that you remain the focus of our lives. Lead us to your purposes with love. Keep us on the paths that are best for our learning, helping us to emulate your gentle nature and grow our faith. Showing others pleasantness and kindness all for your glory. In Jesus's name, I pray, amen.

March 15

The Joyful Morning Star

A morning star has come to shine its beauty with the radiant light of grace. As you open your sleepy eyes today, my beloved, try not to overthink all the questions regarding the direction of your life. Just as I watch over your loved ones know that I'm watching over you too. As your destination, I'm holding in my hands. No need for sadness or empty feelings always longing for more. I am your fullness; in me, you are whole. Keep those eyes up fixed on the one true constant of love that does not change knowing that I am impenetrable to the ever-changing winds, and I am the one who can change situations and hearts in an instant. Nothing is too far out of reach for me. It's okay, child, to long for a change of scenery from time to time, to wonder about what life would look like in a different place—a different canvas and view Just as long as it doesn't steal your focus from me. There are days that a bit of melancholy may come and try to steal your joy, but the sorrow of the night won't last as the joy comes in the morning. Tomorrow you can open your eyes to be with me in an instant as I bring to you the glory of my light, filled by the radiant rays of the joyful morning star. To be filled time and time again by my love.

I, Jesus, have sent my angel to testify
to you about these things for the churches. I
am the root and the descendant of David,
the bright morning star.
(Revelation 22:16, ESV)

And we have something more sure, the
prophetic word, to which you will do well to

pay attention as to a lamp shining in a dark place, until the day dawns and the morning star rises in your hearts.
(2 Peter 1:19, ESV)

Sing praises to the Lord, O you his saints, and give thanks to his Holy name. For his anger is but for a moment, and his favor is for a lifetime. Weeping may tarry for the night, but the joy comes in the morning.
(Psalm 30:4–6, ESV)

Prayer: Thank you, Jesus, for the beauty of your love for your impenetrable glory, mercy, and grace. I look forward to this day and will begin by spending time with you, my Savoir. I ask you to continue to lead, to teach, and to fill our hearts with love, for you are our beautiful morning star filling our hearts with joy. In Jesus's name, I pray, amen.

March 16

The Truth His Love

Welcome, Spirit brings the power of love, when it is your first thought of the day. As you open your eyes to the light of my love. On these good days when your first thoughts in the morning are of me, I am with you more in strength and fill you with beauty and the much-needed light of my love. To be loved and to feel love is what everyone longs for deep down. If only they knew that they are loved by the one who will never leave them. I will never leave or forsake my children. I am the one assured constant of true love in their lives. Whoever abides in love, abides in me, as I AM love. Nothing can separate you from my love, dear child. Nothing you have said or done, as you are forgiven. Do not be conformed to the instant gratification of this world. But instead, find joy and peace in bringing to your life the steps of my good purpose and my righteous ways. Seek justice, love mercy, walk humbly with your God. Finding a rhythm of love with a gentle filled nature. May your life always be filled with the streams of my good measure poured out and relished in my deepest love. Even in the desert may you always find my living waters and quench your thirst with the glory of my light, the purpose of my grace, and the fullness of love that shall fill your heart. I am your Lord—I am your true love. Nothing can separate you from this, my eternal good truth. The truth found within my love. And you are eternally this, my child… you are loved.

Little children. Let us not love in word
or talk but indeed and truth.
(1 John 3:18, ESV)

And so we know and rely on the love God has for us. God is love. Whoever lives in love lives in God, and God in them.
(1 John 4:16, NIV)

For God so loved the world, that he gave his only Son, that whoever believes in him should not perish but have eternal life.
(John 3:16, ESV)

For I am sure that neither death nor life, nor angels nor rulers, nor things present nor things to come, nor powers, nor height nor depth, nor anything else in all creation, will be able to separate us from the love of God in Christ Jesus our Lord.
(Romans 8:38–39, ESV)

Prayer: Father God, thank you for the love in my life. Thank you for the ones that I hold dear. I pray to you today that this day may be filled to the brim with all the beauty of love that you give. May your love be amplified in our lives. I am forever grateful to you Father God and seek to please you. I love you. In Jesus's name, I pray, amen.

March 17: Happy St. Patrick's day to me, readers. Don't forget to wear green. God bless you all with love.

The One Who Holds You

The one who holds the light of all creation is holding you, child. Today when you rise, know that I have you within my great hands. Sometimes you feel like you're walking on the tightrope of life, but keep in mind that I am your safety net, I am there for you here in your moments of business, in your moments of work, of pleasure, of rest, I am with you in all your moments. I am holding your whole life, my child, and it's okay to not feel okay sometimes. In this life, pressures can build and bring the thoughts in your mind to a boil. You may feel frustrated or angry when you work so hard, yet you feel like it goes unnoticed. Do not let anger, frustration, or resentment find a home in your heart, keep these as fleeting and replace them with joy, gratefulness, thankfulness, and love. I want you to know, my child, that your work and your deeds do not go unnoticed as I know and see everything there is to know about you. I know what you are doing. I see the pressures of the day and I am here with you helping you to overcome. There are rewards in your spirit, as you can feel a sense of relief when you accomplish your goals in this life, the big and the small. It is a good feeling as you can look back at a job well done and check off things on your to-do list of life. But do not give in to the pressure of the day, or the night, for the pressures and troubles are only but a small moment in time fragmented by periods of happiness and contentment. Everything is only but a season my beloved. So for this season and all in your life, remember me, your Lord, for all eternity as the one who holds you...

For all eternity wrapped in love

Fear not, for I am with you; be not dismayed, for I am your God; I will strengthen you, I will help you, I will uphold you with my righteous hand.
(Isaiah 41:10, ESV)

And the hand of the Lord was with them, and a great number who believed turned to the Lord.
(Acts 11:21, ESV)

Even there your hand shall lead me, and your right hand shall hold me.
(Psalm 139:10, ESV)

My Father, who has given them to me, is greater than all, and no one is able to snatch them out of the Fathers hand.
(John 10:29, ESV)

Prayer: Father God, thank you for this day and everything I hold dear. Thank you for my abilities to work and grow. Thank you for holding me and all that I love in your great hands, and for helping me to overcome the hurdles of life. I praise your name, Jesus, it is in your name I pray, giving praise, amen.

March 18

He Makes His Home

Waiting in the light of my love. Goodness will find you every morning, as you put your trust in me. Bring to your attention thoughts of love and kindness and be filled with the power of the Holy Spirit, as I am the one who helps lead you into the lush and green gardens of your life. There are no barren lands when you walk on the paths of my righteous good and loving ways. On the path of my calling. Accept my good gifts as your talents will be made amplified with my good nature in strength and with the light of my purpose. Feel the fullness of this power made manifest in all my glory. Made manifest within you. As I am within you. I am your Lord and with you my child I've made a home. A place to call on the very essence of the fruit of my Spirit. A place where you have faith and give your heart to me. Can you hear me, child, in the moments of your life as I speak to your heart, calling on you to shine in all the places I have made you to walk? Taking each step with the hope of my promise growing, even more, made resilient by the power of your faith. To walk without stumbling in the safety of my love. And wherever you dwell, I will dwell also, as I consecrate each place that you enter and each step you take, I will bless. Bringing to your soul completeness as in you, I have made my home.

> *Now my eyes will be open and my ears attentive to the prayer that is made in this place. For now I have chosen and consecrated this house that my name may be there forever. My eyes and my heart will be there for all time.*
> (2 Chronicles 7:15–16, ESV)

For this reason I bow my knees before the Father, from whom every family in heaven and on earth is named, that according to the riches of his glory he may grant you to be strengthened with power through his Spirit in your inner being, so that Christ may dwell in your hearts through faith-that you, being rooted and grounded in love, may have strength to comprehend with all the saints what is breadth and length and height and depth...

(Ephesians 3:14–19, ESV)

By wisdom a house is built, and by understanding it is established; by knowledge the rooms are filled with all precious and pleasant riches.

(Proverbs 24:3–4, ESV)

Whatever house you enter, say first, "Peace be to this house!"

(Luke 10:5, ESV)

Prayer: Father God, may I always walk on the paths of your calling filled with your Holy Spirit. May I continue to be a blessing to others. Growing with wisdom and filled with grace, and may they see you within me. I pray for all my family and friends that you grow brightly in their hearts and lead them with kindness to the places you want them to walk, just as you lead me Lord lead them. In Jesus's name, I pray, amen.

March 19

You Can Achieve It

You can achieve whatever dreams I have put on your heart and excel with the glory of my good purpose. If you dream it, you can achieve it within the architecture of my will. Your plans from time to time will begin to take on a life of their own if you get caught up in selfish and earthly desires. Ask me about my will. Ask me to amplify it within your heart and in your mind making me the loudest voice in your head. Ask for discernment and wisdom when walking the course so you do not fall prey to distractions or selfish ways. I will keep the path you should walk clearly lit. If something or someone comes in your way sending you doubts, my little beloved child, do not be deceived, use discernment, as this may not be from me. They may be just momentary distractions. Pray for them, pray for situations, and stay focused on me, your Lord. When you begin to soar like an eagle, you may become a target to some. It is okay, do not fear, as I am bigger than any problems or distractions you face. Nothing that I have put together or joined can be separated as it is consecrated and glued together with the strength of my love. What is for you, is for you, and what is not, is not, this is the simplicity that you will learn to accept and whether these experiences work for the good of your benefit will only be seen when you give in and surrender to my will. Again, I say, "Child, you can achieve it if you can dream it and hold it steadfast within the light of my will." Keep marching forward and working for goals to benefit life and share my gospel with others pointing the way to me, while you're here in this world...

Brothers, I do not consider that I have made it my own. But one thing I do: forgetting what lies behind and straining forward to what lies ahead, I press on toward the goal for the prize of the upward call of God in Christ Jesus.
(Philippians 3:13–14, ESV)

Commit your way to the Lord; trust in him and he will act.
(Psalm 37:5, ESV)

For to set the mind on flesh is death, but to set the mind on the Spirit is life and peace.
(Romans 8:6, ESV)

Do you see a man skillful in his work? He will stand before kings; he will not stand before obscure men.
(Jeremiah 22:29, ESV)

Prayer: Father God, thank you for this day. I pray for discernment. I pray that yours in the loudest voice in my head and that your paths stay apparent to me as I walk the ways which you are calling, I pray for your will in my life and the lives of those around me. I give thanks for the people in my life and praise your loving name, Jesus, amen.

March 20

Peaceable Rest

Let my Spirit fall fresh on you today, my child, call on me before the start of your day and I will be with you, leading you on through my chosen paths for your life. Be courageous in life in love in it all. There will be lulls of time that seem oddly misplaced perhaps amid a storm or there may be peace in the midst of a busy time in your life. Let it be known, my child, that this is from me. I know and see when too much is happening for your fragile human soul to bear. So I will bring a calm and peace when I see it necessary that you need to refresh your spirit and rest. There are things in this life that are essential to your wellbeing and rest is one of them. You can work day and night and always seek to please me, and this is good. However, child, with no rest you may lose your effectiveness. Tired minds tend to lead to poor decisions. Give yourself the break that you so desperately need. Spend time in quiet soaking up my words as you read verses from the Bible my living text. The next busy time may just be on the horizon, or it may be the finish of the busy season you are in. As you may be in the eye of the storm, whatever the case I know right where you are. So you, yourself do not need to worry. Just know, that for now, this time, is what I have called to be peaceable and restful for your soul. Listen and rest, soaking in the truth of my word. Come to me, my child, relax and be still.

Come to me, all who labor and are
heavy laden, and I will give you rest.
(Matthew 11:28, ESV)

The Lord is my Shepherd; I shall not want. He makes me lie down in green pastures. He leads me beside still waters, He restores my soul. He leads me in paths of righteousness for His name's sake.
(Psalm 23:1–3, ESV)

The Lord will fight for you, and you have only to be silent.
(Exodus 14:14, ESV)

For I know the plans I have for you, declares the Lord, plans for welfare and not for evil, to give you a future and a hope.
(Jeremiah 29:11, ESV)

Prayer: Father God, thank you for the times of rest and peace that you bring. During these times, I pray to be able to be still and sit, soaking in your Presence. Quiet my mind. I surrender to you Lord all that is in my life and the lives of those around me. I put my trust in you—we are forever in your care. In Jesus's loving name, I pray, amen.

March 21

Answered Prayers

There is something more to answered prayers. More than simply getting your way. Here in the light of these answered prayers, you will realize that in these amazing moments you will feel even closer to me. As I am acknowledging you with my answers, in these times you will undoubtedly know that I have been listening. There is a wonderful sense of relief that comes from my answered prayers, especially the prayers that I answer with a resounding yes. As you see your loved ones grow closer to me, I see that it warms the very essence of your soul and that is good, my beloved, to want your loved ones to worship me just as you do. You have such a kind and tender heart. My hardworking and loyal little child. I am pleased by the love that you have for others. But you must know child, that other times my answer may be no. Trust in this, as I know what is best in all times. Hold tightly to the truth of the precious moments of clarity that are given during the moments of answered prayers. Keep in your heart and mind the closeness you feel to me. Cherish these God moments and call them to mind if ever your heart grows doubtful. I am here and I am listening to every word you utter from your lips, even those you have not spoken, the ones you hold in your heart, I hear them also. Smile child, as you know that I am always working. Keep your view clear as there may be times that I have answered yet you haven't seen. Stay aware of my Presence and discern what is from me. Keep living and walking in faith looking out for my answered prayers. I love you...

You did not choose me, but I chose you
and appointed you that you should go and

*bear fruit and that your fruit should abide,
so that whatever you ask the Father in my
name, he may give it to you.*
(John 15:16, ESV)

*But let him ask in faith, with no
doubting, for the one who doubts is like a
wave of the sea that is driven and tossed by
the wind.*
(James 1:6, ESV)

*For I know that through your prayers
and the help of the Spirit of Jesus Christ this
will all turn out for my deliverance.*
(Philippians 1:19, ESV)

*Let the words of my mouth and the
meditation of my heart be acceptable in your
sight, O Lord, my rock and my redeemer.*
(Psalm 19:14, ESV)

Prayer: Thank you, Father, for this day. I will put my trust in you, Lord, as I ask you to take care of my loved ones and the situations that I bring to you in intersession. I thank you for the outcomes, as I know you know what is best. I pray for a peaceful day and that you remain strong with us in all the situations that are to come. In Jesus's name, I pray, amen.

March 22

Immovable Grace

Welcome to the glory of my love, as the light shines upon the face of the earth. From early, at first light and all through the day, into the wee hours of the night. My child of God, you are favored and loved fervently by me. You can see the good purpose, I have given to your life, and you are thankful. When you hold tightly to me, you feel safe. You are safe from the winds that howl around you, safe from the egocentricity of the world and all its selfish ways. You are tied and hitched to my immovable grace and you shine with brightness in the fullness of my love. My Spirit surrounds you and the barrier of my truth is so full of light that it makes the idiosyncrasies and shadows of this life fall to the ground, sputtering out in their failing facade. There is love, a life abundant, and a life full of all the virtuous qualities that the fruit of my Spirit gives. It's a wondrous world. Look past all the surface and superficial happenings. There is a depth of love, a true immeasurable yet declared love that I have given. It can be held forever deep within your heart. Feel it time and time again, and though my wisdom is unsearchable my love and the glory of my merciful grace can be found in simplicity. Simply by declaring me your Lord. Taking my yoke upon you as it is easy and light and gentle in nature. Keep growing in faith you can overcome any obstacle. As I am with you providing you help and my immovable grace.

Therefore, my beloved brothers, be steadfast, immovable, always abounding in the work of the Lord, knowing that in the Lord your labor is not in vain.
(1 Corinthians 15:58, ESV)

And now I commend you to God and to the word of his grace, which is able to build you up and give you the inheritance among all those who are sanctified.
(Acts 20:32, ESV)

For by grace you have been saved through faith. And this is not your own doing; It is the gift of God.
(Ephesians 2:8, ESV)

As each has received a gift, use it to serve one another; as good stewards of God's varied grace.
(1 Peter 4:10, ESV)

Prayer: Thank you, Father God, for your grace. I lift us up to you today, Lord, and ask you to keep us protected from the shadows of the world. I pray for discernment, that we would know without a doubt which way to walk and that every path you want us to walk on is highlighted by your Presence. That we would always choose the ways that are acceptable in your sight. I ask that you keep us in the light of your immovable grace and the fullness of your love. In Jesus's name, I pray, giving thanks, amen.

March 23

Praise the Lord

Take your time as you head out this day, my child, no hurry as the beautiful destinations you will soon enough be experiencing. Walking through the wondrous gardens of my love. I may surround you with others today who share a similar view. Bring your praise and worship me. Such a beautiful sight is the brilliant light and the warmth that comes to my house when my children worship together. Meeting together in my sanctuary to praise my name. The power in my name can be felt by all who gather. Singing hymns and songs of praise, Jesus, Jesus, can be heard, as the sweet voices of my children travel straight up to heaven. During these times, the strength of my Presence can be felt deep within the soul. Hallelujah, I can hear your heart sing. Pray for all those around you, child, as they pray also for you. The prayers spoken on behalf of my children for others that they do not know is...sweeter still. The fragrance of my followers fills the air with an all-powerful glow creating freshness and beauty, stirring up in love. Keep loving and sharing, giving love to all. This is the way I want you to be. To have love and show love, to behold the words of your Lord and follow always in the footsteps of my teaching. Sharing in this good purpose. Spreading my message of Salvation for all the world to see. Lifting up your hands and voices, united and together, singing joyful praise to me... Let everything that has breath praise the Lord!

Praise the Lord! Praise God in his sanctuary; praise him in his mighty heavens! Praise him for his mighty deeds; praise him according to his excellent greatness! Praise

*him with trumpet sound; praise him with lute
and harp! Praise him with tambourine and
dance; praise him with strings and pipe!*
(Psalm 150:1–4, ESV)

*Addressing one another in psalms and
hymns and spiritual songs, singing and
making melody to the Lord with your heart.*
(Ephesians 5:19, ESV)

*And he answered, "you shall love the
Lord your God with all your heart and
with all of your soul and with all of your
strength and with all your mind, and your
neighbor as yourself."*
(Luke 10:27, ESV)

*I will praise the name of God with a
song; I will magnify him with thanksgiving.*
(Psalm 69:30, ESV)

Prayer: Father God, I lift my hands and my prayers to you today, Lord. I sing of your love and praise your powerful name, Jesus. Thank you for everything and everyone in my life. I sing to you, hallelujah and am grateful for your mighty hands that hold me. I pray that you continue to watch over everything in my life and all the people I love. I pray also for all the people who worship in your house and for those who cannot make it to your house but worship you wherever they are. I pray for all. In Jesus's name, I praise and give thanks and pray. Amen.

March 24

Comfort in Vast Places

Shine your light today, child, as we walk through the experiences of the day. The canvas we step into at times may deliver a vast wide-open space, where my paths can become a bit blurry, we have so much ground to cover, yet this is not to be worried about. For at this moment, I will caution you, just stay steadfast with me holding my hand, and I will lead you to the spaces of the day that are maintained and well-kept for the safety of your steps. You can find beauty today, when you stop and quiet the thoughts in your mind, step off the merry go round and come down from your routine. Take in a breath of the freshness that my Spirit brings. I will bless you and keep you and make my face to shine upon you when you stay soaked in the strength of my Presence. Feel the warmth of my love as it radiates around you and fills you with my peace and calm. Let yourself enjoy and relish in the wonder of the day. Find comfort with me in the vast places of your life. When the journey seems too big, remember that I am bigger than the journey and my purpose will help keep the wild untamed nature of the journey subdued under my reigns. I am Sovereign over your life. I am Sovereign over creation. I am in charge and I am your Salvation. Even when you walk through desolate vast places, find comfort, see the beauty and be strong, knowing the one who has gone before you is the same one who goes with you. It is I...your Lord, and I shall be your comfort.

Thus says the Lord, your Redeemer,
who formed you in the womb: "I am the
Lord, who made all things. Who alone

stretched out to the heavens, who spread out the earth by myself."
(Isaiah 44:24, ESV)

Now to him who is able to keep you from stumbling and to present you blameless before the presence of his glory with great joy.
(Jude 1:24, ESV)

For we are his workmanship, created in Christ Jesus for good works, which God prepared beforehand, that we should walk in them.
(Ephesians 2:10, ESV)

Have I not commanded you? Be strong and courageous. Do not be frightened, and do not be dismayed, for the Lord your God is with you wherever you go.
(Joshua 1:9, ESV)

Prayer: Father God, thank you for the places you lead me to. I pray that you keep hold of me. That you keep worries far from my mind and comfort my soul even in the vast spaces of my life. I pray this also for all my family and friends and for all who follow you, Lord. Let peace and comfort reign in our hearts this day, in Jesus's name, I pray, amen.

March 25

Thankful

Waking this day in the light of my love. Nothing much to think about as you walk through this day unscathed. You may be able today to enjoy a slow steady pace and an easiness. Go walk out among nature in the crisp fresh air, let all the world around you fill you with peace. Listen to all the natural sounds around you, birds singing in the trees, the rustling of the wind blowing somberly through the tall blades of grass. Even nearby traffic humming by doesn't seem bad today, as its steady hum brings to the backdrop, a natural chord of rhythm. And everything all culminated together, all the sights and sounds bring to attention everywhere the evidence of life... As I created and formed it all, the heavens and the earth. When you stop and celebrate the natural beauty of this world, you also celebrate me, your Lord. Experience this day as a cool, easy and peaceful day with reminders everywhere that there is so much to be thankful for. Enjoy my child, enjoy and always be thankful.

Oh, taste and see that the Lord is good!
Blessed is the man who takes refuge in him!
(Psalm 38:4, ESV)

So, God blessed the seventh day and made it holy, because on it God rested from all his work that he had done in creation.
(Genesis 2:3, ESV)

For from him and through him and to him are all things. To him be the glory forever. Amen.
(Romans 11:36, ESV)

This is the day the Lord hath made;
let us rejoice and be glad in it.
(Psalm 118:24, ESV)

Prayer: Thank you, Father God, for this peaceful easy day and for the beauty of nature and for this life! For all life that you have created, I thank you. In Jesus's name, I pray, amen.

March 26

Never Give Up

Cast away the doubts when it comes to completing things I've put in your heart as I am leading you day and night. You can accomplish all that I have tasked to you, my child. Stay surrounded by my words. Call on me to unblock whatever you feel is your stopping point. I am here in your heart and at the forefront of your mind, as you release your worries to me. You shall be like a stream flowing through a desert when you stay ever present with me. I will strengthen your inner being with the power of my Presence. And help you to complete the tasks of the day while you remain rooted and grounded in my love. I dwell within you and bring you through when you are faced with places of desolation or when you are amid the storm, I am with you. I will walk with you into the abundance of my lush and green gardens and I shall restore your soul. There are times when you feel my silence, but I am here, and my silence does not mean that I have forsaken you or that I've left you. I am here eternally with you child, I love you. These times of my silence you will need to remain strong and focused. I give every good and perfect gift and I provide you your abilities, so knowing that it is I who provides, then you must know this, that in your life with me as your focus, you will have completion of the good things that I have desired for you to fulfill. If you never give up and keep on going, growing and moving forward, in life staying strong in your faith, always persevering with your Lord...

That according to the riches of his glory he may grant you to be strengthened with power through his Spirit in your inner being, so that Christ may dwell in your

hearts through faith-that you being rooted and grounded in love.
(Ephesians 3:16–17, ESV)

He who dwells in the shelter of the Highest will abide in the shadow of the Almighty. I will say to the Lord," My refuge and my fortress, my God, in whom I trust.
(Psalm 91:1–2, ESV)

Our help is in the name Of the Lord. who made heaven and earth.
(Psalm 124:8, ESV)

For 'In him we live and move and have our being', as even some of your own poets have said, 'For we are indeed his offspring.'
(Acts 17:28, ESV)

Prayer: Father God, this day I ask you to help me to complete all the good tasks you have called me to do. To give me strength when I feel weak and to give me direction when I feel lost. I ask to remain focused on your truths for my life. I ask that you fill me up and keep me balanced and full. I ask that you watch over all that I love, in Jesus's name, I pray, amen.

March 27

I Am

Gracious, am I? Loving, am I? Your Savior, am I? I AM! I am the one who holds you close when the cold winds of the storm are surrounding you. I protect you with the warmth of my love. I am the one who feeds you when you grow hungry, I feed your soul with my living word, if only shall you read. I am the one who breathes life in you when you seem to be running out of breath, I restore your soul. I am your Lord, your God who loves you. Who walks with you, who walks beside you, who at times carries you when you are too weak to find your steps? I am all the things you need, and my great grace is sufficient for you. So head up, my child, eyes up, remain focused, and fixed on my good purpose for your life. Lean on your faith. Call on me, as I am everything at all times, and my timing is perfect. Mountains or roadblocks will not be feared when you draw from the power of the Lord your God. Walking with the assurance that this good task along with all others I've given will be accomplished despite any distractions or setbacks. You shall stay brave in your faith and strong in your steps. And when the world comes and tries to snatch you out of my hand, I will become stronger in Presence and hold you all the more tightly, as I dwell within you... When you call on my name Jesus, and ask, "Lord, are you here with me?" The answer my child is, most assuredly... I AM...

> "Am I a God at hand, declares the Lord, and not a God far away? Can a man hide himself in secret places so that I cannot see him? declares the Lord. Do I not fill heaven and earth?" declares the Lord.
> (Jeremiah 23:23–24, ESV)

The Lord your God is in your midst,
a mighty one who will save; he will rejoice
over you with gladness; he will quiet you
with his love; he will exult over you with
loud singing.
(Zephaniah 3:17, ESV)

And I will ask the Father, and he will
give you another Helper, to be with you
forever, even the Spirit of truth, whom the
world cannot receive, because it neither sees
him or knows him. You know him, for he
dwells with you and will be in you.
(John 14:16–17, ESV)

It is the Lord who goes before you. He
will be with you; he will not leave or forsake
you. Do not fear or be dismayed.
(Deuteronomy 31:8, ESV)

Prayer: Father God, thank you for always taking care of me. I pray that all the roadblocks and mountains be removed from the good paths that you guide me to walk upon. That you keep my feet from stumbling and that you keep fear far from my mind. I pray to be filled with your Presence each day and ask to stay a blessing to others around me. Help me to shine with your love. I surrender to your will for my life and ask that you keep me strong and focused and keep me moving forward lovingly. In Jesus's name, I pray, and I give thanks, amen.

March 28

God Watches Over

Let there be no one who talks down to my children, it is not for my children to seek revenge when these things happen, but it is for me to handle. In this world, you will have trials and tribulations, but I have said, "Take heart, my beloved, for I have overcome the world." When dealing with situations that may cause hurt, be slow to anger. If you feel your temper rising, close your eyes and pray to me to lift the tumultuous feelings of anger. Lifting them far away, replacing them with understanding and joy. Take my yoke upon you as it is easy and light. I know it is hard at times, my child, as you are only human, but you must try to remain on my good paths and walk in my steps reflecting with a good example my righteous ways. Let your light shine before others, and do not be conformed to this world either in thought or in your deed. Keep my good and perfect ways before you, practicing them always. Share love and joy with your fellow brethren. Try not to let little irritants cause you to complain; cast that behavior away. I will lift the burdens when you turn away from the grumbling nature and turn your attention to me. And with the purest of love, I will watch over...

> *No man shall be able to stand before you all the days of your life. Just as I was with Moses, so I will be with you. I will not leave you or forsake you.*
> (Joshua 1:5, ESV)

> *This God-his way is perfect; the word of the Lord proves true; he is a shield for all those who take refuge in him.*
> (Psalm 18:30, ESV)

But the Lord is faithful. He will estab-
lish you and guard you against the evil one.
(2 Thessalonians 3:3, ESV)

Prayer: Father God, thank you for this day. I thank you also for watching over us all. Help me during times when I feel upset or hurt and ask that you guard my heart and mind against feelings of anger, I pray to be able to always forgive others just as you have forgiven me. That I would be able to learn from situations, when they are for my teaching and to replace my complaints with a grateful heart. Today I pray that we all would be filled with your joy. In Jesus's name, I pray, amen.

March 29

You Bring, He Gives

I will give to you streams of goodness and abundance when you stand in the light of my love. I will shine on you all your days, as you walk on the lighted paths of my will. I will make you my people and indwell with you, as the truth of my Spirit makes in you a home. I shall reign over your life and all the circumstances that you encounter I shall make the outcomes be perfected giving them the shape of my design. Bring me your faithful heart, full of wholeness and shining brightly with my truth. Bring to me your trust, as even in hard times you know that I shall remain your Sovereign King. Lend to me your full attention and to you, I will make my paths known. I will show you great and wondrous things. I will give to you joy and fill your days with my mercy heaped up and served with love. Let my peace find you when needed, as rest is also good for your soul. As you bring to me confession, I give to you, forgiveness, cleansing you from your sin, and when you bring your hopes to me, I will give to them, a life of actuality. Bring to me your faith, my child, and I will give to you my faithfulness. In me, you shall lack nothing. Dear child, you bring, and I shall give...

> *Know therefore that the Lord your God is God, the faithful God who keeps covenant and steadfast love with those who love him and keep his commandments, to a thousand generations.*
> (Deuteronomy 7:9, ESV)

> *And I heard a loud voice from the throne saying," Behold, the dwelling place*

of God is with man. He will dwell with them, and they will be his people, and God himself will be with them as their God.
(Revelation 21:3, ESV)

I have been crucified with Christ. It is no longer I who live, but Christ who lives in me. And the life I now live in the flesh I live by faith in the Son of God, who loved me and gave himself for me.
(Galatians 2:20, ESV)

Prayer: Father God, thank you for everything you give to me and to the lives of those around me. I ask that on the days when I'm feeling sad or empty, you help to clear my mind and fill me with hope. Help me to remain strongly rooted in you. Remind me tenderly, Lord, of your love for me. Also, help me and all the people that I love to remember that in your truth we shall lack nothing. I pray this day, to be full of joy, and give thanks for all the moments that make up my life, in Jesus's loving name I pray, amen.

March 30

Purest of Love: His Love

My love prevails always in the lives of my children. Open your hearts to me, there is a brilliant destination that I am leading you to. Come child and walk awhile with me. You and I together making our way through the daily challenges of this worldly terrain. We can remain on the paths of my good purpose when you keep steadfast with me. Let the brilliance of my glory reign over your life with showers of truth and the light of the most, purest of love... There are no shadows when you stay in the realms of my heavenly steps. We can celebrate all that you are becoming as you immerse yourself in my words. Walking with confidence and certitude as your Lord is beside you eternally with you. Calling you to become the person that I have designed the person where my fruits from within you shine showing their full potential. The lovely, tender, heart that I have shaped and am molding. As each day you grow in wisdom being filled with power from my Presence. All beautiful and kind, tender, and caring, loyal, honest, and true. Filled with the purest of love, my love. These are the fruits of my Spirit and they exist in you.

So that Christ may dwell in your hearts through faith that you, being rooted and grounded in love. May have the strength to comprehend with all the saints what is the breadth and length and height and depth, and to know the love of Christ that surpasses knowledge, that you may be filled with the fullness of God.
(Ephesians 3:17–19, ESV)

*Humble yourselves, therefore, under
the mighty hand of God so that at the proper
time he may exalt you, casting all your anxieties on him, because he cares for you.*
(1 Peter 5:6–7, ESV)

*Jesus answered him," If anyone loves
me, he will keep my word, and my Father
will love him, and we will come to him and
make our home with him.*
(John 14:23, ESV)

Prayer: Father God, I pray to become all that you have designed, that I may always seek you, making you first in my life. My beautiful Savior Jesus, I love you. I pray to always be a blessing to others and that I may be a good example to inspire others to get to know you, so that they may love you just as I do. I pray for all these good things in Jesus's powerful name, amen.

March 31

April

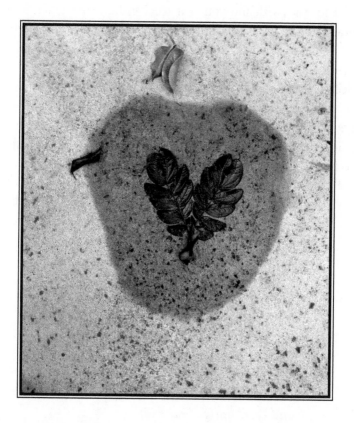

Just after a rain, everything is refreshed. Just the way the Lord refreshes us he washes away our unrighteousness and cleanses us of our sin.

Count Your Blessings

Good morning, dear child, the light of another beautiful day has cast its rays down over the face of the earth. And this day, as you are just waking up from your slumber, I am here. I am here as you get ready to go out into the daily trenches of the world. Even in the trenches, there is beauty and love as with me you will receive daily, my grace upon grace. Open your eyes to see all the treasured blessings that you encounter throughout the day. Think, on these, as they bring a sense of peace to your mind. Do not focus on how deep the trench is or how long the road is or how hot the sun or cold the wind, think on the love that surrounds you the people in your life who touch you and the beauty of life— think on me. Oh, what a blessing to breathe, to live, to laugh, to love, and to cry. Oh, what a blessing to drink and eat, to feel and give, to exist, oh what a blessing to live... To be loved by your Father in heaven. What a blessing to be called a child of God, oh what a blessing indeed. So today instead of counting your lucky stars, count your blessings, my child. And open your eyes to see...

> *But blessed is the one who trusts in the Lord, whose confidence is in him. They will be like a tree planted by the water that sends out its roots by the stream, it does not fear when heat comes; its leaves are always green. It has no worries in a year of drought and never fails to bear fruit.*
> (Jeremiah 17:7–8, NIV)

Then Jesus said to him, "Have you believed because you have seen me? Blessed are those who have not seen and yet have believed."
(John 20:29, ESV)

But whoever looks intently into the perfect law that gives freedom and continues in it-not forgetting what they have heard but doing it—they will be blessed in what they do.
(James 1:25, ESV)

Prayer: Father God, thank you for this day, help me to stay focused on you. I am grateful for every experience I get to share with my loved ones. Thank you for every meal I get to eat and every breath that I take. Thank you for every day I get to open my eyes and see the beauty of your love. Thank you for my health, and for all the people around me who you bring into my life. Thank you, Father, for it all. In Jesus's name, I give thanks and pray with gratitude, amen.

April 1

Make Time for Prayer

Rest in my Presence awhile. Sit with me, child, come talk and share all that is in your heart and on your mind. Sometimes the business of the world can try to keep your prayer time-limited, but remember I am with you always. You can call out to me and find time to pray, even in the busiest of days. Step back a moment from chores, from daily duties, from tasks, from work, from others, step back child, from your routines and sit for a few minutes alone in reflection with me. Try to make time with me at the beginning of your day. You can draw from my Presence the strength needed to get through the day. You can do all things through Christ who strengthens you. Keep this as your mantra during the times that you feel tired or weak. I will provide you whatever you need. Draw near to me and I will draw nearer to you. I can see things that you need, child, things that you do not see. I know things that you do not know, about yourself, about your life about what you need and what you do not. You may not feel tired until you slow down, but I can see what is to come as I have gone before you. Take time out now of the business to rest and relax. Eat healthy meals and exercise keeping your physical fitness, as it is just as important as your mental fitness. But during it all, always make time for me and prayer. Keep your faith forward and you will find my power in your prayers…

Therefore I tell you, whatever you ask
in prayer, believe that you have received it,
and it will be yours.
(Mark 11:24, ESV)

Then you will call upon me and come pray to me, and I will hear you.
(Jeremiah 29:12, ESV)

Rejoice in hope, be patient in tribulation, be constant in prayer.
(Romans 12:12, ESV)

Do not be anxious about anything, but in everything by prayer and supplication with thanksgiving let your requests be made known to God. And the peace of God, which surpasses all understanding, will guard your hearts and minds in Christ Jesus.
(Philippians 4:6–7, ESV)

Prayer: Father God, help me to find the motivation required to work out and to become healthier when I eat. Help me to make good choices that benefit my well-being, my body, and my mind. Keeping me healthy and strong so that I may be well maintained. I pray for all of us, Lord, that you would help us to stay balanced in our lives. Giving praise to you always, in Jesus's loving name, amen.

April 2

Wild Like the Wind

Try not to stray far from my paths child as you journey through the day. Calling on my Spirit to shelter you from the storm. There will be times my child that the storm may not be your own. It may be your standing to close to someone else whose life remains wild like the winds. Keep my strength full within you. And guard your hearts and minds with my full Presence, read your Bible and armor yourself daily. Bring to those children lost and blown by the worldly winds, my light, share with them my good message. Most importantly share my love. But do not yourself fall into the winds. Keep yourself rooted in me so that the winds do not pull you in. If you feel yourself growing weak, remove yourself and love them from a distance. Giving them to me in prayer and giving yourself much-needed rest and peace. Stay on the lighted paths where I will bring you to encounter those who need to see my light. Shine in the face of adversity with all my grace as you go from glory to glory bringing light to the shadows of this world. When you are touched by winds of wild, hold fast to me staying forever grounded and rooted in love planted on my firm foundations. I will set you ablaze and spread out my message in the winds turning them from wild to be tamed by the light of my eternal love…and even the winds know their Lord and Him they shall obey.

And he awoke and rebuked the wind and said to the sea, "Peace! Be still!" and the wind ceased, and there was a great calm. He said to them, "Why are you so afraid? Have you still no faith?"
(Mark 4:39–40, ESV)

*And the rain fell, and the floods came,
and the winds blew and beat on that house,
but it did not fall, because it had been built
on the rock.*
(Matthew 7:25, ESV)

*For behold, he who forms the mountains and creates the wind, and declares to
man what is his thought. Who makes the
morning darkness, and treads on the heights
of the earth—the Lord, the God of hosts, is
his name!*
(Amos 4:13, ESV)

*Of the angels he says, "He makes his
angels winds, and his ministers a flame of
fire."*
(Hebrews 1:7, ESV)

Prayer: Father God, thank you for keeping me rooted
and grounded in you. I pray for those around me who are
standing in the storm, that they may learn to know you, and
that you protect them with your love. And I pray to stay
within your will. In Jesus's name, I pray, amen.

April 3

His Gift: The Present

Today is a gift, my child, as it is the present. Let all your mind be on things that are magnified with my glory on this day. Open your eyes to see all nature and lovely things, appreciating all my creation and the beauty within it. Lean on me and let my love dance around you bringing to you the warmth of an affectionate hug. Resist the temptations that arise to worry or find faults in today. And keep your mind and heart cheerful. Find merriment and relish in the joyful playfulness of the day. It is good to allow yourself to be lighthearted as laughter and cheer are good for your soul. There is freedom in my good purpose so let it lift your spirit and restore your soul as you shall be exalted. Let my Spirit acquaint you with all my loving fruits. Dance on the rainbows of my grace and stand on my promise. As you stand in the wondrous light of my love. Let your heart soar as I give life to your dreams... Brought forth and led by my Presence let my glory abound in your heart forever, oh forever in your heart, my child... This is my gift and it is found within the day, as it is known as the present.

This is the day the Lord has made; let
us rejoice and be glad in it.
(Psalm 118:24, ESV)

The Lord your God is in your midst,
a mighty one who will save; he will rejoice
over you with gladness; he will quiet you
with his love; he will exult over you with
loud singing.
(Zephaniah 3:17, ESV)

And we know that for those who love God all things work together for good, for those who are called according to his purpose.
(Romans 8:10, ESV)

Finally brothers, whatever is true, whatever is honorable, whatever is just, whatever is pure, whatever is lovely, whatever is commendable, if there is any excellence, if there is anything worthy of praise, think about these things. What you have learned received and heard and seen in me-practice these things, and the God of peace will be with you.
(Philippians 4:8–9, ESV)

Prayer: Father God, thank you for this beautiful day and all that it holds. I pray to be surrounded by your love and to be led by your Spirit. I pray that I may excel in every situation that is presented to me. That you would keep me within your will and help keep my mind on the present. I also, pray that you fill our hearts with joy as we give thankfulness to you and stand on your promises. Give us peace and patience while we are becoming all that you have created us to become. In Jesus's loving name, I pray giving thanks, amen.

April 4

What Is Better

I have come to break your chains. I have come to set you free. Free from the bondage of sin and death. Arise with the victory of my glory in your heart each day, child. Remember this on the days that the world would try to drag you down. You can arise, child, to all occasions strengthened by the Power of my Presence, shining brightly with the brilliance of my love. There is nothing that cannot be accomplished when you let me lead. Keep your place right at my feet and listen to my good teaching. You can be so full of life's worries, things that matter not. Learn child, just as Mary chose what was better, so shall you, and that will not be taken away from you. Mary's sister Martha was all-consumed by the menial tasks of earthly chores that her attentions were held hostage by her good intentions. But her sister Mary sat at my feet and listened intently to my words, she chose what was better. As this life is fleeting, learn to recognize when it is the better option to slow down and listen. For what is better than the words of your Father? What is better than the promises of God? What is better than being saved by your Savior? What is better, child, than to be fully known and loved by me...as I am your Lord...my beloved child, I say, "There is nothing better."

As Jesus and his disciples went on their way, he came to a village where a woman named Martha opened her home to him. She had a sister called Mary, who sat at the Lords' feet listening to what he said. But Martha was distracted by all the preparations that had to be made. She came to

*him and asked, "Lord, don't you care that
my sister has left me to do all the work
by myself? Tell her to help me!" "Martha,
Martha," the Lord answered, "you are worried and upset about many things, but few
things are needed-or indeed only one. Mary
has chosen what is better, and it will not be
taken away from her."*
(Luke 10:38–42, NIV)

*My sheep hear my voice, and I know
them, and they follow me. I give them eternal life, and they will never perish, and no
one will snatch them out of my hand.*
(John 10:27–28, ESV)

*But he answered, "It is written," Man
shall not, live by bread alone, but every
word that comes from the mouth of God.*
(Mathew 4:4, ESV)

Prayer: Father God help me to always choose what is
better. Help me to know when to slow down and when to
move forward. Keep me and all my loved ones protected from
distractions and help us to remain focused on you. Help us
to make time to read your words and strengthen us in our
faith. Filling us with your love, in Jesus's name I pray, giving
thanks, amen.

April 5

Shine and Share

Be with me, child, my beloved, we can walk together, we can stand in my light or sit, and you can simply be still. I am with you always from now and beyond the end of ages. We can accomplish much together when you stay on my paths walking in the midst of my will. We can bring light to the far corners of the earth and draw all my children near. Near to their Father, as they may find their way home. Baptizing them and cleansing them, as they will be born again of the Father. And the old will pass away and a new creation I will make, and they shall share in this good journey with us and together we will share to all…my Gospel. Calling together all my children to shine out amongst the earth. No longer walking in darkness but walking in the light, becoming all that is meant for my great purpose. Glowing within the radiant rays of my Glory and beaming with the purest light of my love. Shine my child, oh, shine and share on this good day and always…and remember you are loved…

> *If my people who are called by my name humble themselves, and pray and seek my face and turn from their wicked ways, then I will hear from heaven and will forgive their sin and heal their land.*
> (2 Chronicles 7:14, ESV)

> *You did not choose me, but I chose you and appointed you that you should go and bear fruit and that your fruit should abide, so that whatever you ask the Father in my name, he may give it to you.*
> (John 15:16, ESV)

I have been crucified with Christ. It is no longer I who live, but Christ who lives in me. And the life I now live in the flesh I live by faith in the Son of God, who loved me and gave himself for me.
(Galatians 2:20, ESV)

For God so loved the world, that he gave his only Son, that whoever believes in him should not perish but have eternal life. For God did not send his Son into the world to condemn the world, but in order that the world might be saved through him.
(John 3:16–17, ESV)

Prayer: Father God, thank you for the victory you gave to us over sin and death, and for walking with us in our journeys. Also thank you for giving us a purpose, and the abilities and opportunities to share your Gospel. It is my prayer that everyone would come to know you and to worship you as their Lord. Also, I ask that you watch over us all, that you would shine your glory on us and keep us full of love. Keep our joy strong, full of faith and always and help us to live a life of abundance in all areas, as we serve. In Jesus's name, I pray, giving thanks for the victory, amen.

April 6

Hope the Good Thing

Never lose your hope, my child, never lose your hope for brighter tomorrows, but still find beauty in present days. Never give up on dreams that elude you this moment, just work harder to obtain them. Nothing is impossible when your faith is tied to me. Wrapped together with the strength of my Spirit a place where my victory is won. Cast those doubts aside. No good thing comes from living in fear. Fear of failure, fear of not being good enough. Fear is not meant to stop you from pursuing knowledge or pursuing a full life. As you are meant to push through the fear and try. Take chances and believe in yourself, just as I believe in you. Do this, let your belief in me shine also. We can walk and learn and laugh and love. We can find the fullness of the Father, and all the potential of life can be found when you believe. Be doers of the word, not just with talk, but put the speech of ideas into action. Not just empty words of good ideas but in action and deed. Taking the first step may be the hardest, but once you start to let your steps become quickened, they will become empowered to the beat of my perseverance. As we march forward to fulfill your hopes and set them into the light of reality. Every good thing stems from the hope that is brought forth by faith. Held tightly together by my immovable grace and my steadfast love. Strengthened and filled to its fullness by your heavenly Father. Always, every good and perfect gift comes from me. Keep your eyes on me and work for my purpose and remain strong in your faith. Full of your hopes as they are a good thing, my child... Abound in hope. Hope the good thing... Hope in me.

May the God of hope fill you with all joy and peace believing, so that by the power of the Holy Spirit you may abound in hope.
(Romans 15:13, ESV)

Now faith is the assurance of things hoped for, the conviction of things not seen.
(Hebrews 11:1, ESV)

Through him we have also obtained access by faith this grace in which we stand, and we rejoice in hope of the glory of God. More than that, we rejoice in our sufferings, knowing that suffering produces endurance, and endurance produces character, and character produces hope, and hope does not put us to shame, because God's love has been poured into our hearts through the Holy Spirit who has been given to us.
(Romans 5:2–5, ESV)

And now, O Lord, for what do I wait? My hope is in you.
(Psalm 39:7, ESV)

Prayer: Father God, thank you for every good thing. Thank you also for my trials and my lessons, and my storms. I know this life is temporary and while I am here, I will stay the course and keep my eyes up fixed on you putting my faith forward. Growing learning and sharing each day your words and your ways and remaining hopeful as I stand on your promises. Thank you, Father, for watching over my friends and family and for blessing those who mourn giving them comfort. I pray for strength and comfort wrapped in your love and filled with joy. In Jesus's name, I pray, giving thanks, amen.

April 7

The Vibrant Color of You

Good morning, child, I remind you in this life, do not let your beautiful personality be subdued by the daily routines, shine with the brilliance of joy that I have placed in your heart. Let that joy shine from within for others to see and admire. When you become subdued, you become a muted version of yourself and just as a canvas that once held such vibrant beautiful colors becomes faded and washed out when it stays out too long overexposed by the elements, you too can become faded. When you try things on your own and find no protection from the world. When you stay with me in your faith I will cover you and enshroud you from the worldly elements allowing your color to stay true, allowing those vibrant brilliant colors inside to shine...to touch those around you, to inspire, and stir them with my love. They, study you carefully child even when you do not see, they watch, while they stand in awe of your faith. So keep the light brightly lit and the colors of your soul vibrant and strong with faith. Keep that beautiful spirit I've created wrapped in the fullness of God. Let them see me in you, by letting them see your joy, feel and the vibrant true color of your heart... And what is seen can be felt.

You are a beautiful child of GOD.

> *Do you not know that you are God's temple and that God's Spirit dwells in you?*
> (1 Corinthians 3:16, ESV)

> *Put on then, as God's chosen ones, holy and beloved, compassionate hearts, kindness, humility, meekness, and patience.*
> (Colossians 3:12, ESV)

In the same way, let your light shine before others, so that they may see your good works and give glory to your Father who is in heaven.
(Matthew 5:16, ESV)

For at one time you were in darkness, but now you are light in the Lord. Walk as children of light.
(Ephesians 5:8, ESV)

Prayer: Father God, thank you for this beautiful day and for all those around me that I love. Help me to shine with your love. Give me eyes that always sees the best in others and let them see you in me. Keep my faith strong and help me to enjoy this wonderful day. In Jesus's name, I pray, amen.

April 8

Temporary Tears

There will be days, child, my beloved, that tears stream down your face here in this world. As the days are tempered with worldly ways, but take heart, my child, knowing I am with you. I have overcome the world; I will not forsake you and someday you will cry no more. But in the moments that bring you sadness know that the joy that is coming, gains more of a powerful steam within my Presence. So soak yourself in me. Without the sorrows, the joy would never be felt as intensely. Feelings and emotions are passing and changing but there will be joy again, just as the sun will again rise. The light of joy will find you... As I will find you and be with you in all the moments of your life. You can go from glory to glory, being filled with the fullness of God. As you take my hand and hold tightly to me, your Lord who loves you. Never to walk in the shadows of darkness again. But still, there will be storms that you have to go through. Nothing in life comes as easily as my love. Learn the good lessons that I walk you through, child. Practice living my good way. Always growing in faith and finding your shelter in me. Time does not represent itself the same way to me, as to your fragile human nature. Earthly standards of time itself, I am not held to. I am constant and never change. Stay faithful and strong keeping hope in my Spirit and when the storm blows it will pass and the sadness you may feel shall blow away. This day is but a fleeting passing wind where there are lessons to find and learn. So never give up on the journey... Even in the midst of your temporary tears...just hold tighter to your Lord.

And after you have suffered a little
while. The God of all grace, who has called

you to his eternal glory in Christ, will himself restore, confirm, strengthen, and establish you.
(1 Peter 5:10, ESV)

Those who sow in tears shall reap with shouts of joy! He who goes out weeping, bearing the seed for sowing, shall come home with shouts of joy, bringing his sheaves with him.
(Psalm 126:5–6, ESV)

For this light momentary affliction is preparing for us an eternal weight of glory beyond all comparison.
(2 Corinthians 4:17, ESV)

For his anger is but for a moment, and his favor for a lifetime. Weeping may tarry for the night, but joy comes with the morning.
(Psalm 30:5, ESV)

But do not overlook this one fact, beloved, that with the Lord one day is as a thousand years, and a thousand years as one day.
(2 Peter 3:8, ESV)

Prayer: Father God, this day I simply say thank you as I lift up my life to you and all those around me. Keep us wrapped in the fullness of your love. Even in the sadness, I pray that we find your peace and joy. In Jesus's name, I pray, amen.

April 9: "And we will come rejoicing bringing in the sheaves." (Written by David Rose, David D. Rose, Traditional, PD Traditional: "Bringing in the Sheaves")

His Way Prevails

Staying in the light of my goodness, walking through the gardens of love. Shining out against the darkness. I will call you to rise, never to fear, as my victories are in your heart. Even on the cloudy days where the gray skies are evident, I will call you to my grace as my mercies prevail and the light of my glory is shown. As I am the truth, the way, and the life. Keep your steps on the paths of my good keeping as I clear the ways before you. Even though the journey seems long, find beauty in the journey and enjoy this life you have been given. Remember to have hope, keeping the faith as it is the assurance of what we hope for and the certainty of things not seen, but we are certain of it, even when there is nothing evident just yet. It is assured by your faith. The world would have you believe otherwise but I am not of the world, I am the Creator of all, and my way will prevail. As I am your Lord. I am your faithful Lord… And my glory does shine, my love does heal, and my mercy reigns, and together I work everything for good as most assuredly my way shall prevail…

Fear not for I am with you; be not dismayed for I am your God; I will strengthen you, and help you, I will uphold you with my righteous right hand.
(Isaiah 41:10, ESV)

Behold, God is my helper, the Lord is the upholder of my life.
(Psalm 54:4, ESV)

Ah, Lord God! It is you who have made
the heavens and the earth by your power
and by your outstretched arm! Nothing is
too hard for you.
(Jeremiah 32:17, ESV)

I have said these things to you, that
in me you may have peace. In the world,
you will have tribulation. But take heart, I
have overcome the world.
(John 16:33, ESV)

Prayer: Father God, I am standing on your promises. Lead us beside still waters, let your words feed our souls. Clear the paths before us and walk with us through the gardens of our lives. Give us rest when we grow weary and fill our hearts and lives with your peace and love. Let your Glory be shown as your ways prevail. Thank you, Father, for your constant and unfailing love. I pray for all today, in Jesus's loving name, amen.

April 10

Celebrate His Deeper Love

This life is a series of events, there are moments wrapped in these events that bend and shift and change. There are moments of learning and growing, of laughing and loving, even of sorrow and tears. Find my love within them all. Do not focus on one or the other, as they are all changing moments in time, but remain solidly fixed on me the one who never changes, your Lord who loves you. I am the same throughout all time and my love for you never changes. Mine is not a fleeting emotion that can drift to and fro; it is deeper than you can understand, as I am transcendent. Find your purpose in sharing this, my beautiful love and the meaning for what I gave, as I gave my life to save the world from sin and death. I gave my life to save you. Share this, my gospel and celebrate my love. Celebrate with those around you, who walk with you in the world bringing my light to them. There is good news for those who love me and call me Lord. A gift of eternal life. The gift of Salvation. Celebrate then my faithfulness, today and always my deeper love...

The Lord appeared to him from far away. I have loved you with an everlasting love; therefore I have continued my faithfulness to you.
(Jeremiah 31:3, ESV)

No, in all these things we are more than conquerors through him who loved us.
(Romans 8:37, ESV)

The steadfast love of the Lord never ceases; his mercies never come to an end; they are new every morning; great is your faithfulness.
(Lamentations 3:22–23, ESV)

In this love, not that we have loved God but that he loved us and sent his Son to be the propitiation for our sins.
(1 John 4:10, ESV)

Prayer: Thank you for this day, Father, thank you for your love and for giving us the gift of salvation. Help me to keep my emotions from taking over my mind. Help me to keep my eyes and heart focused on you. Ground us all on your firm foundations and keep us rooted with your love, so that we may withstand and enjoy every moment of our lives. Help us to see you in all our moments and remain grateful as we share your love with others. In Jesus's loving name, I pray, amen.

April 11

You Shall Overcome

Good morning, child, ask yourself today what are you sure of? Anything held by faith is your assurance of things hoped for yet unseen, as someday you will see your hopes materialize becoming tangible and full. Do not lose hope, keep the faith as it is tied to your dreams. Never giving up or exiting out to early. Complete the good tasks laid before you, do them with a cheerful heart. Finding my grace within them all. The world may not help you up when you fall but with my strength, you will find the victory, as you rise every time to the occasion that you are called to. And when I tell you to step out and you see no place for your feet will you listen? Will you listen to your Lord with all your heart or will you trust only what your eyes can see? Will you miss opportunities laid before you because you become afraid? Do not live recklessly but instead find the, good way, living your life in a fearless way. Having faith in your Lord, as you walk with confidence and assuredness that you will persevere. Open your heart and listen, learning and walking in the ways in which I guide you. Let me lead. For I am with you, and you shall not fail. For the Lord, your God is in your midst and with Him, you shall overcome.

But you, O Lord, are a shield about me, my glory, and the lifter of my head.
(Psalm 3:3, ESV)

Little children, you are from God and have overcome them, for he who is in you is greater than he who is in the world.
(1 John 4:4, ESV)

Who is it that overcomes the world except the one who believes that Jesus is the Son of God?
(1 John 5:5, ESV)

But thanks be to God, who gives us the victory through our Lord Jesus Christ.
(1 Corinthians 15:57, ESV)

And I am sure of this, that he who began a good work in you will bring it to completion at the day of Jesus Christ.
(Philippians 1:6, ESV)

Prayer: Father God, help me to remain strong in my faith. Help me to achieve the dreams that are tied to my heartstrings. I pray for all today, that you remove any doubts and replace them with your truths. That we may find the strength to continue to work hard and enjoy the experiences you bring. Keep us in your will with kindness and love. Help lead us on the good paths you have chosen for our lives. Help us to live fearlessly and share your good news. In Jesus's name, I pray and give thanks. Amen.

April 12

Come Down

When the sun refuses to shine, you shine, as you are called to be the light. You are called to love and simply shine, sharing my good message. All radiant and glorious is my love and with my Spirit, a victory that shall be met with brave perseverance and my bright brilliant glory as its meant for all to see. You can stand off in the shadows and never attempt one good thing or you can take my hand and come where I am leading and bravely walk with me. Won't you come, my child, down from the worldly manta of the day. won't you come, my child as forever you will stay… You will stay forever, My Child. Won't you come? Come down and experience the realities of life in a whole new way as before your views were worldly coming from the place of flesh but now you can experience life through the eyes of the spirit and put down the worldly ways. You can experience life with the wholeness and completeness of my Presence. Come down child, come down and enjoy the fullness of God.

The natural person does not accept the things of the Spirit of God, for they are folly to him, and he is not able to understand them because they are spiritually discerned.
(1 Corinthians 2:14, ESV)

Therefore, since we are surrounded by so great a cloud of witnesses, let us also lay aside every weight, and sin which clings so closely, and let us run with endurance the race set before us, looking to Jesus, the founder and perfecter of our faith, who for

the joy that was set before him endured the
cross, despising the shame, and is seated
at the right hand of the throne of God.
Consider him who endured from sinners
such hostility against himself, so that you
may not grow weary or fainthearted.
(Hebrews 12:1–3, ESV)

But he knows the way that I take;
when he has tried me, I shall come out as
gold.
(Job 23:10, ESV)

Prayer: Father God, thank you for this day. I pray for opportunities to grow and learn and share your good news. I pray that others see you in me, allow me to shine with your brilliant love, even on the grayest of days. Give me eyes to always see the best in others and the words to say to point them the way to you. I pray that all my loved ones would come to know you, Lord, as their Savoir, and that more would be baptized in your name so that we can experience the fullness of God together and grow your kingdom. I ask to be filled with love. In Jesus's name, I pray, amen.

April 13

Even in the Waiting

I'm right here, my child, I'm right here in the waiting, no good things do I withhold from you. Why then do you doubt as if I would just let you go? Your circumstances are held just as tightly by the strength of my mighty hands, just as tightly as hold you. Keep following where I lead. The way may look unsure to your narrow human view but keep your faith strong because you will need to trust me. I am present in everything that is here. I am in the past, present, and future I am even beyond the veil. My Presence is in all your moments. Trust me to clear the way before you. As nothing is too hard for me. You must keep in mind that I know what is better for you. But do not doubt the good thing that I put on your heart. Pray about it, my beloved, and fight your battles on your knees. As I am with you, no weapon formed against you shall prosper. I am Emmanuel (God with you) from now and beyond throughout all the fractions of time. Practice staying present with your mind set on me. Then you can enjoy in these present moments with no worry, the blessings of life encompassed by the fullness of my love. Learn to trust me in the waiting. I am here, child, even in the waiting. I am present and with you, my Spirit is here...

> *A Song of Ascents. I lift up my eyes to the hills. From where does my help comes from? My help comes from the Lord, who made heaven and earth. He will not your foot be moved; he who keeps you will not slumber. Behold, he who keeps Israel will neither slumber nor sleep. The Lord is your*

keeper; the Lord is your shade on your right hand…
(Psalm 121:1–8, ESV)

Blessed is the man who remains steadfast under trial, for when he has stood the test he will receive the crown of life, which God has promised to those who love him.
(James 1:12, ESV)

So we do not lose heart. Though our outer self is wasting away, our inner being renewed day by day. For this light momentary affliction is preparing for us an eternal weight of glory beyond all comparison, as we look not to the things that are seen but to the things that are unseen. For the things that are seen are transient, but the things that are unseen are eternal.
(2 Corinthians 4:16–18, ESV)

Prayer: Father God, thank you for being present with me even in the waiting as I put my trust in you. Walk with me Lord leading me beside your still waters and restore my soul. I thank you for the garden of my life and pray for all those I love, that you watch over and fill them with hope. Even when they feel hopeless, shine your Spirit bright in them, just as you do me. In Jesus's name, I pray, amen.

April 14

Indifferent Behavior

Some days you will feel and sense a new meaning of the situations that you have passed through. You will see that some were most certainly required to help mold you into the person you have become. And the one you are now becoming may require just a bit more of my good lessons and experiences, as they bring wisdom. If you are accepting to learn. Some of my children remain unruly and caught in selfish ways, never seeking to know me for what I am. As I am their Lord but in action, they are indifferent. So to my faithful children, I say shine even brighter for the world to see and show others the love you have for me. Show others how to love and learn and grow in the Spirit. Lead by example. Holding fast to my Presence finding the glory in my promises as they will come to pass. Stand firmly on my truths. Life is such a brilliant ride stay within the light of my will and shine always. Shining with the fruits of my Spirit, cherish me, your Lord, casting off the indifferent behavior. Stay full in faithfulness child and let your heart sing.

But you take courage! Do not let your hands be weak, for your work shall be rewarded.
(2 Chronicles 15:7, ESV)

When a mans ways are pleasing to the Lord, he makes even his enemies at peace with him.
(Proverbs 16:7, ESV)

Iron sharpens iron, and one man sharpens another.
(Proverbs 27:17, ESV)

And those who are wise shall shine like the brightness of the sky above; and those who turn many to righteousness, like the stars forever and ever.
(Daniel 12:3, ESV)

Prayer: Father God, thank you for this day and for remaining strong in me. Help me to lead by example and help keep me true to my faith. Remove any doubts that enter my mind. I pray that we all stand firm on your truths. I love you, Lord. In Jesus's name, I pray, amen.

April 15

Head Held High

Keep walking with that head held high, finding joy in the present as you move to the future. Do not be haughty and boastful as some but remain humble. For where you are walking now others have gone before and where you yesterday once walked some are on their way just now. Every child has the ability to persevere, they do in many different ways. Help bring out the best in others around you, child. Helping to keep them in my fullness. When my children are lacking, I will make them full and bring them to my lush gardens of peace. As they learn my words and walk my righteous ways, I will build them up. Just as I lead you. When they come to me, I will meet them in the light of the day, even in the darkness of the night, I will meet them and you. Stay resilient in this life with the strength of my Spirit. For when you seek me you will find me. Stay hopeful in faith keeping hope in my promises and I will lead, and you will learn. I will strengthen and you will be brave. I will bring rest and you will quiet your soul. I will love you with an everlasting love and you shall love me as always you shall follow me with your head held high… You will follow all the days of your life and call me Lord.

For by the grace given to me I say to everyone among you not to think of himself more highly than he ought to think, but think with sober judgment, each according to the measure of faith that God has assigned.
(Romans 12:3, ESV)

And he who had received the five tal-
ents came forward, bringing five talents
more, saying, "Master, you delivered to me
five talents; here I have made five talents
more."
(Matthew 25:20, ESV)

May all who seek you rejoice and be
glad in you! May those who love your salva-
tion say evermore, "God is great!"
(Psalm 70:4, ESV)

But you, Lord, are a shield around
me, my glory, the One who lifts my head
high.
(Psalm 3:3, ESV)

Prayer: Father God, thank you for bringing me rest and for being my help, the lifter of my head. I pray to be acceptable in your sight Lord. I will follow where you lead and do my best to keep your commandments when I fall short Lord please forgive me. Help me not to judge others but to serve them with empathy compassion and kindness. I pray for all of us today your will, in Jesus's name, amen.

April 16

Be Happy

Open those bright eyes wide this day. I have so much to show you and when you let my Spirit fill you, I can guide you with spiritual eyes to see my truths. Shake off feelings of defeat. This day you can walk in confidence proclaiming boldly that you are mine. Child, I am more than just a Savoir that is far away as I draw near to you each day, I am your Sovereign, Lord. I am your immanent Savoir, I am everywhere all at once, not held by the space of time I am near to every one of my children as my Spirit lives within. I watch over you, guide you, strengthen you, I speak to your heart and give rest, I bring peace, and shower you with my love. Be happy my child as this life is fleeting. Oh, the ever-changing day and hours pass so quickly, the years here in this world fly by. Enjoy the experiences in these good present moments. Recall with fondness this life which you are leading. And the beauty of the journey that is only remembered in the way to which you can recall. But do not linger there in the memories, child. Be happy for the present days, be happy about your life. All the moments that are held within my great purpose, find my truthful joy and be happy as I am forever your Lord. Just as I am the morning star and rise each day... Be happy!

I perceived that there is nothing better
for them than to be joyful and to do the good
thing as long as they live; also that everyone
should eat and drink and take pleasure in
all his toil-this is God's gift to man.
(Ecclesiastes 3:12, ESV)

With joy you will draw water from the wells of salvation.
(Isaiah 12:3, ESV)

You make known to me the path of life; in your presence there is fullness of joy; at your right hand are pleasures forevermore.
(Psalm 16:11, ESV)

These things I have spoken to you, that my joy may be in you, and that your joy may be full.
(John 15:11, ESV)

Prayer: Father God, thank you for your good purpose in my life and for the lives of those around me. Thank you for making me the person I am today. I ask and pray to walk in confidence today full of joy, and that others may experience the fullness of your joy today as well, in Jesus's name, I pray with a thankful heart, amen.

April 17

His Living Words

Live your life for me, my child, seek my face turn away from yourselves and the wicked ways of sin. Learn to walk on the paths of my will. Count yourselves as blessed as you soak in my words every day reading my living text. The time we get to spend together is so precious my beloved. As some days there seems like no time at all but you, my faithful child makes the time, as you know how important it is to armor yourself with the victorious words of your Father. Casting away all that call for your attention and giving your attention to the one who created it all. Honor me, child, all the days of your life and your steps I will establish with my Presence, I reward my faithful children because I see them honor me with the true heart I have given. I will lead them into the life of abundance. Read my words, my living words, and let them breathe in you a new life where you can relish in the joy of my goodness. Where you can find blessings in my plans as you walk in this life that I have designed. Learn my living words and emulate me, sharing the love of your Father with others. There is nothing more powerful than what is found within the Bible, as the verses and text come alive when you read them. They are alive with my breath, full of my Spirit, and they shall fulfill my purpose, as these my child are my living words…

Whoever gives thought to the word will discover good, and blessed is he who trusts in the Lord.
(Proverbs 16:20, ESV)

Blessed are the people to whom such blessings fall! Blessed are the people whose God is the Lord!
(Psalm 144:15, ESV)

Do not merely listen to the word, and so deceive yourselves. Do what it says.
(James 1:22, NIV)

For the word of God is living and active, sharper than any two-edged sword, piercing to the division of soul and of spirit, of joints and marrow, and discerning the thoughts and intentions of the heart.
(Hebrews 4:12, ESV)

So shall my word be that goes out from my mouth; it shall not return to me empty, but it shall accomplish that which I purpose, and shall succeed in the thing for which I sent it.
(Isaiah 55:11, ESV)

Prayer: Father God, thank you for your living words. Thank you for your guidance and for your everlasting love. I pray for your will in my life and those around me, that our steps will be strengthened and established by your purpose for our lives and that while sharing your purpose with others we may be filled overflowing with your joy and unending love. I pray in thankfulness, in Jesus's name, amen.

April 18

"And Here's to Love"

Morning has come, the start of a new day has begun, my child. This day let the love in your heart be multiplied. Think about all the love you have in your life, all that you love and all that love you. People in your life that need you just as you need them—and all of you need me. I am the reconciler of relationships. I am the healer of hurts. I am your Lord who has forgiven, just as I call you to forgive. Think about the nature of my love. No wrongs are recorded, to be brought up time and time again. Love them and forgive them the way I love and forgive you, the way I also forgave those who persecuted me. Keep no record of wrongs in your mind. Keep the past in the past and look forward through the fresh eyes of today. It's a new day each day, so be joyful remain present in life and full of love, to share to give and to accept. Love conquers all and covers a multitude of sin. So keep your life and heart full of love. When someone hurts you, learn to forgive and keep your love open, not to be sheltered and protected by a self-built wall but to be given and experienced in fullness. As love should be open and easily given to all and that is how to change hearts. To love others even when it is not deserved. Stay in my fullness and celebrate life and the changing of hearts... Smile to yourself as you hear me say to your heart...," I love you my child...and with that, a new start, a new day, and here's to love."

The steadfast love of the Lord never ceases; his mercies never come to an end; they are new every morning; great is your faithfulness.
(Lamentations 3:22–23, ESV)

Let me hear in the morning of your stead-
fast love, for in you I trust. Make me know the
way I should go, for to you I lift up soul.
(Psalm 143:8, ESV)

love is patient love is kind; love does
not envy or boast; it is not arrogant or rude.
It does not insist on its own way; it is not
irritable or resentful; it does not rejoice in
wrongdoing, but rejoices with the truth.
Love bears all things, believes all things,
hopes all things, endures all things. Love
never ends. As for the prophecies, they will
pass away; as for tongues, they will cease; as
for knowledge, it will pass away.
(1 Corinthians 13:4–8, ESV)

Finally, brothers, rejoice. Aim for res-
toration, comfort one another, agree with
one another, live in peace; and the God of
love and peace will be with you.
(2 Corinthians 13:11, ESV)

Prayer: Father God, thank you for this day I ask this day
to be so full of love, that it spills over onto the lives of those
around me. That all of us will remember as we walk through
this day, that we are your children and that we are loved by
you. This day and always I pray to put my trust and hope
in you, Lord, as you lead us into the fullness of our lives. I
celebrate how wonderful it is to be fully known and loved by
you. In Jesus's name, I pray and give love, amen.

April 19

The Fullness of God

Some days are full of worry and others full of peace. But all the days are to be filled with my Presence. Seek me always and I shall be revealed in your life and in your heart. There is a completeness that only I can give. So call on me, walk with me, and live your life for my purpose. Then you can experience the fullness of God. There is nothing like the delicate nature of a tender heart, but to be captured in the tender moments of anguish suffering and pain with such a tender heart may seem more than overwhelming or at least it would be if you walked your battles alone. But you are not alone as my Holy Spirit dwells in you and provides you with the strength to get through your situations, to overcome your pain, and to be filled by the peace and love of my Spirit. Knowing that my ways are perfect, and my timing is flawless. You have no fear, as you walk on the good paths that I have designed. So come child, and walk into the paths I make known. Come and walk with me, my beloved, into the fullness of God.

For this reason I bow my knees before the Father, from whom every family in heaven and on earth is named, that according to the riches of his glory he may grant you to be strengthened with power through his Spirit in your inner being.
(Ephesians 3:14–16, ESV)

You make known to me the path of life; in your presence, there is fullness of joy; at your right hand are pleasures forevermore.
(Psalm 16:11, ESV)

*And to know the love of Christ that
surpasses knowledge, that you may be filled
with all the fullness of God.*
(Ephesians 3:19, ESV)

Prayer: Father God: thank you, I pray that you fill me with your fullness and fill the lives of those around me. Keep revealing to our hearts your kind and gentle nature. Thank you, Father God, for this day full of you and the victory brought forth by you, in Jesus's name, I pray, amen.

April 20

This Easter Season

The light of the morning sun has cast its rays upon the earth, time to rise again this day. Start your day in the morning with time in prayer. Bring to me all that is in your mind and on your heart. I know what your requests are my child, so no worry if you cannot find the words. Keep your mind on me and all that my nature brings. Keep your heart and mind, full of positive thoughts as this is the Easter season. Easter is the time to celebrate for my children, as this day was the day of my resurrection, the day, I rose again conquering the stronghold of sin and death-bringing Salvation to my children. Let all in your hearts be filled with my amazing love. Share it with family, friends, and strangers share my goodness with all. Let the joy of this season fill you with joy and relish in the completeness and victory of my love. Enjoy the togetherness…enjoy the day for all that it holds and bring me thanks for the people around you in your life. As together we will change hearts helping others to accept me as their Savoir and bring to their lives a manifestation of my love.

> *See, we are going up to Jerusalem. And the Son of man will be delivered over to the chief priests and scribes, and they will condemn him to death and deliver him over to the Gentiles to be mocked and flogged and crucified, and he will be raised on the third day.*
> (Matthew 20:18–19, ESV)

To this day I have had the help that comes from God, and so I stand here testifying both to small and great, saying nothing but what the prophets and Moses said would come to pass; that the Christ must suffer and that, by being the first to rise from the dead, he would proclaim light both to our people and to the Gentiles.
(Acts 26:22–23, ESV)

In this the love of God was made manifest among us, that God sent his only Son into the world, so that we might live through him.
(1 John 4:9, ESV)

Prayer: Father God, thank you for this beautiful day. I pray to be acceptable in your sight all the days of my life. I pray for the world around me that many more would come to know you as their Savoir. That we may always seek you first and find thankfulness in our hearts for all situations. I pray that we may all learn your ways as we grow in our faith and celebrate the victory you have given to us. In Jesus's loving name, I pray, amen.

April 21

Coming Easter Sunday

(Additional read)

Easter Sunday the day of my resurrection, the day I have risen out of the mire, breaking free from the strongholds of death and sin, I have overcome. And it's for you, because of my love for you that I suffered, but it was just a short while before my victory had shown itself within the glory of God. Amazed were my followers and the unbelievers although they were also amazed, at first, they were skeptical, but some witnessed seeing me after I was buried, after I resurrected and could not believe their eyes, but for them, hearts were changed. My children knew me, and know me still as the Messiah, their Savior, their Lord. I am the truth the way and the life. My children believed and it's my children that I bless. I was sent to pay a ransom for the sins of the world to bring life after the grave and so I rose again to give life and eternal Salvation to my children. So on this beautiful Easter day celebration, it is also a day of victory and of good things to come. Enjoy as you celebrate with your families be thankful and grateful as you have been given the greatest gift in the world, the ability to have an eternal life in my kingdom, where there is no more suffering, no more tears, just pure and true love. And when the Son sets you free, you are free indeed. Coming Easter Sunday every year, a celebration, a remembrance of sacrifice, of the victory, which was won, and a celebration of life offered with love…

Jesus said to him, "I am the way, and
the truth, and the life. No one comes to the
Father except through me."
(John 14:6, ESV)

> *Jesus replied, "Very truly I tell you,*
> *everyone who sins is a slave to sin. Now a*
> *slave has no permanent place in the family,*
> *but a son belongs to it forever. So if the Son*
> *sets you free, you will be free indeed."*
> (John 8:34–36, ESV)

> *Because, if you confess with your*
> *mouth that Jesus is Lord and believe in your*
> *heart that God raised him from the dead,*
> *you will be saved.*
> (Romans 10:9, ESV)

He has risen!

Prayer: Father God, thank you for your sacrifice and for bringing your victory to all of us. As this day, you have overcome. I am grateful, I am thankful, I am amazed, and I love you, Father! With you, because of you, this day...we have been set free. In Jesus powerful name, I pray and give thanks, amen.

not dated
additional read for whatever day Easter falls on this year.
Happy Easter everyone and God Bless!

The Pursuit of His Right Things

As life is a series of ebbs and flows, there may be days when you think, and where is my drive? Where you once felt inspired you seem at times to fall flat and where you once enjoyed the pursuit you may seem to be uninterested. Or could it simply be that you have taken on far too much for your humanity to carry? There may be situations that you need to step away from momentarily. Learn to let go and let God. Keep your priorities straight and do what is necessary to accomplish good goals, ask me to discern what is to be your priority and let me lead. And when you need to step away then do so and rest. Once you have sufficiently rested, you can make better decisions. It is okay to need help from others around you, the world is full of people who help each other and come together as a community, the same way they are called to worship together. They are called to serve one another, but it is not just meant for you to serve, and to help, but most importantly to love. It is meant for all my children so, if you need help do not fear to ask. You will have days of shadows, so keep the light of my Spirit strong within. The inspiration will return along with the enjoyment of the pursuit. So stay the good course my child, and do not give up. Keep pursuing the right things as always, they will bring a sense of joy for this is my good way... And my good way will become quickened when you pursue the right things. The right path will be made clear, if only you pursu...the right things.

So whoever knows the right thing to do and fails to do it, for him it is sin.
(James 4:17, ESV)

And you shall do what is right and good in the sight of the Lord, that it may go well with you, and that you may go in and take possession of the good land that the Lord swore to your fathers.
(Deuteronomy 6:18, ESV)

Whoever has my commandments and keeps them, he it is who loves me. And he who loves me will be loved by my Father, and I will love him and manifest myself to him.
(John 14:21, ESV)

For we are his workmanship, created in Christ Jesus for good works, which God prepared beforehand, that we should walk in them.
(Ephesians 2:10, ESV)

Prayer: Father God, help me to keep my eyes upon you and help keep me on the paths of your calling. Help me to know what are the right things that I should be pursuing. Keep me full of inspiration and the drive to complete all that I am called to do. I pray for all your children that you help us discern which things to pursue and keep us moving forward guided by your grace and your love. In Jesus's name, I ask, and I pray, amen.

April 22

Declutter Live Simple

Life is all but too hectic and days are filled with lists, to-do lists, uncompleted lists of things to acquire, bucket lists, so many lists. But slow down my child and put the lists aside keeping your gaze steady upon me, your Lord, for I will bring the tasks of my goodness before you and with me, they shall be completed. The things that matter the most in life you will see, they need no list. I know you have wants' in this life as that is simply your human nature, but do not let the wants turn into selfish desires. As they can become your master. Do not be enslaved by the earthly need for more but be happy with what you have, for at this moment you now have everything that is in my design for you. Keep yourself free from the love of money and of things, and accumulations of stuff, for these are my words to you. I am your Lord and will have no other God's before me. Do not be weighed down by earthly things. But free yourself and purge what you do not need. Declutter your life, and then my child you will feel refreshed and new, to live simple and enjoy. To be focused and find goodness as you hold your gaze steady upon me, your Lord. Declutter my child and live simply for your Lord.

No servant can serve two masters, for either he will hate the one and love the other, or he will be devoted to one and despise the other. You cannot serve God and money.
(Luke 16:13, ESV)

For where your treasure is, there your heart will be also.
(Matthew 6:21, ESV)

And he said to them, "Take care, and
be on your guard against all covetousness, for
one's life does not consist in the abundance of
his possessions."
(Luke 12:15, ESV)

The unfolding of your word gives light;
it imparts understanding to the simple.
(Psalm 119:130, ESV)

The Lord preserves the simple; when I
was brought low, he saved me.
(Psalm 116:6, ESV)

Prayer: Father God, I want to thank you for all that I have. But most importantly thank you for your love and for the people in my life. Help to keep me free from earthly wants and desires and fill my heart with joy. In Jesus's name, I pray giving thanks, amen.

April 23

A Servant's Heart

To have a servant's heart is to live the way that I have lived. It is the way I want all my children to live. To share your heart with others, showing kindness as you serve. A servant's heart puts the needs of others before their own, as it always serves with the right motivations. A servant is one with a tender heart, who expects nothing in return for their kindness. They keep no records of good deeds they do and do not demand to be repaid. They love with unconditional love. They exemplify the fruits of my Spirit and live their lives with the characteristics of my nature. They are the helpers and the givers; they are selfless and genuine. The servant's heart is given to my children from the purest of my love. A servant's heart can be seen and felt by others around them and their light to which is seen and the warmth to which is felt can change the energy of a room it can even change hearts of the people around them. The servant's heart is a grand blessing to others, as it is selfless, it is my love in the purest form. It is easy and gentle, peaceful and calm. It is a humble heart that finds its joy in helping others. I have placed in you my servant's heart not to be a weakness but to be revealed as a warrior, bravely sharing love, as love endures all things, bears all things, hopes all things, and believes all things. And my love will shine brightly with the boldness and of the glory of God, the Father, the Son, and the Holy Spirit, forever will shine a fullness of love within a servant's heart.

What do you wish? Shall I come to you with a rod, or with love in a spirit of gentleness?
(1 Corinthians 4:21, ESV)

But let your adorning be the hidden person of the heart with the imperishable beauty of a gentle and quiet spirit, which in God's sight is very precious.
(1 Peter 3:4, ESV)

Those who look to him are radiant, and their faces shall never be ashamed.
(Psalm 34:5, ESV)

Have this mind among yourselves, which is yours in Christ Jesus, who, though he was in the form of God, did not count equality with God a thing to be grasped, but made himself nothing, taking the form of a servant, being born in the likeness of man.
(Philippians 2:5–7, ESV)

Prayer: Thank you, Father God, for my servant's heart. Thank you for making me go through situations so that I now can say I truly appreciate the life that I now lead. I am grateful. I pray that everyone could learn how to be selfless and loving toward each other. Because I know kindness and love go a long way to change situations and hearts... In Jesus's loving name, I pray, amen.

April 24

Garden of Your Soul

Each day journey with me, hold my light brightly within the garden of your soul find beauty as you walk in my steps my child, giving up your own plans to take up your cross daily following where I lead. I do not promise a life free from sadness, free from hardships or strife. As most certainly in this life you will have many trials and tribulations. I do not promise a life free from worries or cares. What I do promise is to love you unconditionally and eternally. To help you succeed as you walk in my ways, as my plans are to prosper you and not to harm you. I will establish your steps; I will lead you and show you the right paths to walk on. I will never leave you or forsake you. I give you hope to build your faith upon. During the walk, through the journey of life, I will show you many things. I will teach you my ways and rejoice as you share my message and the ways of my teaching. I have handpicked you and set you apart for specific tasks that are meant to help you grow and to shine within the fullness of God, to lead others by example. Share with them the great big love you have in your heart. Whereas anger begets anger, and bitterness begets bitterness, but with this in mind, kindness begets kindness and most importantly love begets love. Let the two latter mentioned reign in your heart, kindness, and love. So you shine, my child, with all the brightness of love and the forgiving, kind and tender nature, that I have placed within. Journey with me and I will refresh daily, my good and perfect purpose in the garden of your soul.

So neither he who plants nor he who waters is anything, but only God who gives the growth.
(1 Corinthians 3:7, ESV)

I am the vine; you are the branches.
Whoever abides in me and I in him, he it
is that bears much fruit, for apart from me
you can do nothing.
(1 John 15:5, ESV)

And the Lord will guide you contin-
ually and satisfy you in scorched places and
make your bones strong; and you will be
like a well-watered garden, like a spring of
water, whose waters do not fail.
(Isaiah 58:11, ESV)

Many are the plans in the mind of a
man, but it the purpose of the Lord that
will stand.
(Proverbs 19:21, ESV)

For I know the plans I have for you,
declares the Lord, plans for welfare and not
for evil, to give you hope and a future.
(Jeremiah 29:11, ESV)

Prayer: Father God, lead on and I will follow. Help me to learn the right ways of your teaching and to be able to show others by example how big and full and beautiful your love is for us. And how amazing you are. My Jesus, how I love you! Thank you for the victories you have brought forth in my life and for refreshing the garden of my soul. I pray for all my friends and family in Jesus's name, giving thanks, amen.

April 25

Confidence in Him

You can accomplish the good things I have tasked you to do. Human emotions, they are unpredictable and can change their direction like the wind. But remain solid and grounded in the foundations that I have laid out before you, so you do not get stuck in the whirlwinds in your mind. The enemy, he is clever and will try to keep your attention on what you feel you lack, and he will draw your attention to what you feel you cannot do. Causing within you great angst, but you can do all things with my Spirit held strong within you. Armor yourself and stand firm against the doubts that creep into your mind. Stay focused as step by step you can accomplish what may seem impossible to the human mind. Because what is impossible for man is possible with me. Nothing is too great, no way is too steep, no mountain too high, for the children who stay steadfast and strongly rooted with me. When the ground starts rumbling beneath your feet, step out and reach up to me, no fear, as I have got you and will place my solid foundations back beneath your feet. And if the ground falls away from you, no worry, my beloved, as I will give you *wings*. Let the strength of my love carry you through whatever season you're going through. Whatever moment you're in, remember you are not alone. I have gone before you and am with you now. So what then do you do when your mind begins self-defeating and worrying; Stop, look up, eyes up and rise up! Put your confidence in your Lord.

Blessed is the one who trusts in the
Lord, whose confidence is in him.
(Jeremiah 17:7, NIV)

Be strong and courageous. Do not fear
or be in dread of them, for it is the Lord
your God who goes with you. He will not
leave or forsake you.
(Deuteronomy 31:6, ESV)

And this is the confidence that we
have toward him, that if we ask anything
according to his will he hears us.
(1 John 5:14, ESV)

For the Lord will be your confidence
and will keep your foot from being caught.
(Proverbs 3:26, ESV)

Therefore do not throw away your
confidence, which has a great reward.
(Hebrews 10:35, ESV)

Prayer: Father God, Thank you for this beautiful day.
I pray for all of us today and always Lord, that when our
minds' start overthinking you will help us to put our focus
back on you, restoring in us our confidence. Restoring in us
our faith. Thank you for the victory over our emotions. Help
keep us on your firm foundations and fill our hearts with
love. In Jesus's name, I pray and thank you for the victory,
amen.

April 26

Ignite the Spark of Love: Him

Arise, child, let the joy in your heart fill you this day, as you walk through the daily routines of life. I am always with you, now walk with the confidence that you are never alone. I may bring people to your life that need to be reminded what a spark of my love can do. Share love within my great purpose. People can become so accustomed to monotonous routines that they lose their ability to see me, they may have become desensitized and forget that they need me. As some have become temporarily blind to the joy and blessings in their current situations. But all my children from time to time will need to be reminded with a kind word or gesture from someone around them. As it only takes just a small nudge to create the spark and open their eyes once again to reignite the faith they may have let fall away. There is awesome power in my words, so share them. There is a fullness of joy within my Presence, so ignite it. Call on me, communicate. Keep your prayer life full of power by being honest with me. No empty talk or flattery, but a real deep in your soul talk. I already know your words, but they have a more desired healing effect when you let down those walls and let out what you have buried beneath the surface for far too long. Then in your openness, you can grow closer to others. No fears, I know you, my child, I know your heart because I created you, and it is my Holy Spirit that stirs within you and speaks to that very heart… I love you, my child, so be full with my love, go with my fullness and shine. Shine for the world to see and ignite the light with the power of my Spirit. Ignite that spark with the passion of faith and boldly share my love.

Beloved, let us love one another, for love is from God, and whoever loves has been born of God and knows God.
(1 John 4:7, ESV)

But God, being rich in mercy, because of the great love with which he loved us, even when we were dead to our trespasses, made us alive together with Christ-by grace you have been saved.
(Ephesians 2:4–5, ESV)

There is no fear in love, but perfect love casts out fear. For fear has to do with punishment, and whoever fears has not been perfected in love.
(1 John 4:18, ESV)

Know therefore that the Lord your God is God, the faithful God who keeps covenant and steadfast love with those who love him and keep his commandments, to a thousand generations.
(Deuteronomy 7:9, ESV)

Prayer: Father God, may my faith always shine bright, and my speech always speak the truth, as I share your love with others. Keep us strong in our faithful pursuit of your ways, Father, and when we fall into the monotonous routines of life remind us gently that you're still with us. Thank you, Father God, In Jesus's name, I pray for all, amen.

April 27

His Purpose Never Fails

There are times in your life that you can see clearly my good purpose. At times the journey starts to become arduous and the time drags long you become weary with wonder... Will you ever be done? I say to your heart do not give in, do not give up, it is I your Lord who has called you to this good task so you must remain diligent and see it through to its completion be faithful my servant and your reward will be a life of abundance and your store-houses shall be full over-flowing with the blessings of my love. Remain vigilant. Keep working at the good tasks before you and before you know it, the way will open, and the path will get much clearer and you will find your rhythm quickened again with the passion that is in your heart. It is the passion to complete this good thing, this wonderful task to bring it to completion. As it is the accomplishment of a goal that I have given. And with this apprised task I've given herein lies my good purpose and just as my promises and my words, my good purpose shall never fail.

For the gifts and the calling of God are irrevocable.
(Romans 11:29, ESV)

Before I formed you in the womb I knew you, and before you were born I consecrated you; I appointed you a prophet to the nations.
(Jeremiah 1:5, ESV)

You did not choose me, but I chose you and appointed you that you should go and bear fruit and that your fruit should abide, so that whatever you ask the Father in my name, he may give it to you.
(John 15:16, ESV)

Thus says the Lord, your Redeemer, who formed you in the womb: "I am the Lord, who made all things. Who alone stretched out to the heavens, who spread out the earth by myself."
(Isaiah 44:24, ESV)

Prayer: Father God, thank you for your good purpose. Thank you for leading me as I walk through my life working for you. I pray that this devotional will be acceptable in your sight and that it will be helpful to others as it points their attention to you and gives them hope of what you can do in your children's lives. I pray for all of us, your will, your way, always. I am amazed and thankful. In Jesus's loving name, I pray and give my heart. Amen.

April 28

Essential Trust

Arise in the light of this day knowing that I have prepared the way before you. I have planned out the way, in the garden of your life and although I have given you free will, I knew you would find your way, even when you, yourself did not. And when you make a mistake, I will work together things for good because I know you love me. There are times in my children's lives that they may feel like they are walking in the darkness. Making them unsure of the path before them, but, if they keep strongly rooted in me and soaked in my words, they can bravely walk forward. As it is called stepping out in faith. Their faith will help them to keep their light turned on. Giving them at times spiritual eyes to see. Allowing them to trust enough to take their step, and with each step they take, the grip of fear will lessen... My children know to trust me, as they can experience with assuredness that I will keep their feet from slipping. They will learn to trust me more and more. Trust is an essential part of our relationship as it is what helps you to grow in your faith. Staying in the light of my will and living the way I have lived. Being generous, kind, selfless, and forthcoming as they share my message of Salvation with those around them. Remain joyful and full of the brightness of love. Stay full of this essential trust, so that I may help you succeed in your life. And in all your endeavors trust me my child, and I will watch you soar...

When I am afraid, I will put my trust
in you.
(Psalm 56:3, ESV)

*Commit your work to the Lord, and
your plans will be established.*
(Proverbs 16:3, ESV)

For we walk by faith, and not by sight.
(2 Corinthians 5:7, ESV)

*He will not let your foot be moved; he
who keeps you will not slumber.*
(Psalm 121:3, ESV)

*Trust in the Lord with all your heart,
and do not lean on your own understanding. In all your ways acknowledge him, and
he will make your paths straight.*
(Proverbs 3:5–6, ESV)

Prayer: Father God, each day, I will put my trust in you. I ask you to help me see the paths I should take, and I ask you to protect me, my family and friends. Keep us aligned with your will and help us to cast out fear during the times that we should be moving forward. Keep us protected and enshrouded with your love as we journey through our lives. In Jesus's name, I pray, amen.

April 29

A note of encouragement to my readers.

To my Brothers and Sisters in Christ-
And now as I am a few days away from completing this devotional that God put in my heart to accomplish and complete, I am joyfully overwhelmed. When I re-read the words that I have written, knowing that although they are my words, they are not completely my own, I am filled with pure joy. I started out this amazing eye-opening journey on May 5 of the last year 2018 and a whole year has gone by leaving me feeling amazed that I have almost completed it. I set out to write just once a day and for the most part, I stuck to it. Within the year I never missed a single day of writing something. This accomplishment may not be such a grand achievement to some, but it is so grand and big to me, because I know myself, and I have always quit almost everything I've started, from earlier in my youth till now. But this one good task filled with His purpose gave me the strength to soldier on. He gave me the ability and strength to persevere. And during the times I felt like giving up he surrounded me with people who encouraged me. So important are His encouragers. So to you, my dear brothers and sisters in Christ, I say," Do not quit and when you feel like giving up don't! Just call on Him, do not give up, but instead look up and let Him give you the confidence to complete whatever good purpose He has given… If it is His will you will never fail." And remember He is bigger than all your fears, and He loves you.
As always, I'm signing this note in closing with love, April. ♥

*The Lord will fulfill his purpose for
me; your steadfast love, O Lord, endures*

forever. Do not forsake the work of your hands.
(Psalm 138:8, ESV)

Commit your way to the Lord; trust in him, and he will act. He will bring forth your righteousness as the light, and your justice as the noonday.
(1 John 5:15, ESV)

The Lord is my strength and shield; in him my heart trusts, and I am helped; my heart exults, and with my song I give thanks to him.
(Psalm 28:7, ESV)

For we are his workmanship, created in Christ Jesus for good works, which God prepared beforehand, that we should walk in them.
(Ephesians 2:10, ESV)

The Lord of hosts has sworn; "As I have planned, so shall it be, and as I have purposed, so shall it stand."
(Isaiah 14:24, ESV)

April 30

May

And with God you can see love even in scorched places.
His beauty is everywhere…

You Can with Him

Ease into this day with hopes held high. Anything is possible during a day in your life. Keep your soul lifted to dream and believe, to live, and to achieve. If you dream it, you can achieve it when you stay within my will. Lift all the hopes and dreams up to me and hold them strong in faith. Walk on throughout the day with the assurance that I am with you. My sweet child, I have stayed with you and will always, as you will never walk alone. In faith, you are walking side by side with your Savoir. On the paths that I have designed for you. I have your hand in mine and I hold you close. So precious are you, my faithful child. Let those hopes and dreams overflow. Do not put a limit on them. There is no good thing that I withhold from you, and no good thing that you can't accomplish in the Presence of your Lord. So march on keeping on your determined path. What will be, will be. Nothing can stop what I have purposed. Hold that head high as you work skillfully knowing that I have equipped you for every task that I have given. You can do all things, you can be all things, and you can achieve all things. It is when you believe all things are possible with the power of your prayers and the strength of your faith, and most importantly the trust you place in me, as my will be done. Keep moving forward from glory to glory and accomplishing goal after goal, you will get there. Let your persistence in life and the good purpose I call you to shine brightly in your heart. And you will succeed in life with a predestined fierceness of a warrior's heart, stepping out in faith. Live for me, my child and stand firmly on my truth. Anything and everything are possible, whatever your dreaming, you can with me.

I can do all things through him who strengthens me.
(Philippians 4:13, ESV)

For everyone who has been born of God overcomes the world. And this is the victory that has overcome the world-our faith.
(1 John 5:4, ESV)

Therefore, if anyone cleanses himself from what is dishonorable, he will be a vessel for honorable use, set apart as holy, useful to the master of the house, ready for every good work.
(2 Timothy 2:21, ESV)

Whatever you do, work heartily, as for the Lord and not for men, knowing that from the Lord you will receive the inheritance as your reward. You are serving the Lord Christ.
(Colossians 3:23–24, ESV)

Having the eyes of your hearts enlightened, that you may know what is the hope to which he has called you, what are the riches of his glorious inheritance in the saints.
(Ephesians 1:18, ESV)

Prayer: Father God, help lead me into the fullness of your will for my life. Lead me to the dreams that are what you have designed for my life and walk with me. Give me the strength to stay on your paths and help me succeed. God bless us everyone. In Jesus's name, I pray, amen.

May 1

Learn and Grow

There will be times in your life my child that you may feel a little down and lost but come to me, with your faith forward, as I can help you navigate your way through all the vast and busy terrains of life. Take my hand and keep your eyes on me and I will help to keep you grounded. Stabilize yourself when you plant your feet strongly upon the foundations of my words and stand bravely on my promises. I am your God of truth, and I do not lie, as everything I have said pertaining to all things will come to pass. Everything I have said to you will be fulfilled. And my plans for you they give you hope and a future that shines brightly with my love. In the storms, you can rest with the assurance that I am with you. It is just a passing season showing you what you are capable of handling, you are stronger than you think. If you look back for a moment and see all the difficulty you have passed through. The times you thought your life was over, the hurt, and angst, anxiety, anger, even danger. Just in those moments of life, you must see now what you have overcome. But now turn your attention to this present moment and see all the beauty of the love of family. friends, all the laughter, and joy you have. Even in the current storms, you can stay full with joy, because you stay full of me. And it is during these times you can see the truth clearly. Oh, my child, you have grown. Stay growing up in your faith as you are finding the true person, I have created you to be. Always seek me first, sharing my words, and my love and you will keep on this good journey and on this good path you will continue to learn and grow.

And it is my prayer that your love may abound more and more, with knowledge and all discernment.
(Philippians 1:9, ESV)

In hope of eternal life, which God, who never lies, promised before the ages began.
(Titus 1:2, ESV)

Let the wise hear and increase in learning, and the one who understands obtain guidance.
(Proverbs 1:5, ESV)

And he said, "The kingdom of God is as if a man should scatter his seed on the ground. He sleeps and rises night and day, and the seed sprouts and grows; he knows not how. Then the ear, then the full grain in the ear. But when the grain is ripe, at once he puts in the sickle, because the harvest has come."
(Mark 4:26–29, ESV)

And though your beginning was small, your latter days will be very great.
(Job 8:7, ESV)

Prayer: Father God, I pray to always learn from your good lessons in the ways in which you would have me learn. That I would apply what I have learned with your right principles and be able to openly share with others your teaching. I thank you for helping me to navigate my life and for making me the person that I am today, and for the one I am becoming. I pray for all my family and friends that they would also get to experience your Presence in their lives. I thank you Lord, as I stand on your promises, in Jesus's name, I pray, amen.

May 2

Align, Step, Reach, Hold

I am the Lion and the Lamb, the First and the Last, the Alpha and the Omega. The Beginning and the End. I am everything and everywhere all at once. I am everything to everyone who seeks me. But most importantly I am your infinite Lord who loves you. I am the truth, the way, and the life and anyone who stays aligned with my will, they shall find the right steps and walk on my confident paths of truth. As they reach for my eternal glory. Holding fast to their faith. Pray to stay aligned with my will and so that you may be able to obtain all that planned for your life. Let your spirit flourish in the misty sprays of life. And during rough seas keep your gaze upon me, as I remain a lighthouse for all to see. I have given to my children different gifts, of talents and abilities and love to watch them when they discover what I've placed within them. I will polish their God-given talents and bring them forth utilizing them each one just the perfect way of my good purpose. You can soar, rise this day child, nothing in this life can weigh you down when you are enshrouded by my love. All you need to do is call on me. I am here with all my strength in the moment of your weakness. Strength comes from me and my words so fully armor yourself each day. Delight yourself in my words. I know there are times when you feel the time slipping by and wonder what is to be? But do not worry about that. Just live in the present fullness of the joy. As you align yourself with my will, you step out in faith, reach for my glory and hold fast to your Lord.

To the weak I became weak, that
I might win the weak. I have become all

things to all people, that by all means I might save some.
(1 Corinthians 9:22, ESV)

Therefore do not be anxious about tomorrow, for tomorrow will be anxious for itself. Sufficient for the day is its own trouble.
(Matthew 6:34, ESV)

There are different kinds of gifts, but the same Spirit distributes them. There are different kinds of service, but the same Lord. There are different kinds of working, but in all of them and in everyone it is the same God at work. Now to each one the manifestation of the Spirit is given for the common good.
(1 Corinthians 12:4–7)

If any lacks wisdom, let him ask God, who gives generously to all without reproach, and it will be given him.
(James 1:5, ESV)

Prayer: Father God, keep us in your will and when we step the wrong way correct us with kindness and direct us back to your plans. Give us the courage to step out in faith, the desire to reach for your glory, and the strength to soldier on. Keep us balanced on your firm foundations and help us always to keep our eyes upon you. In Jesus's name, I pray, amen.

May 3

Your Life's Song

Smile today, from the first time you open your eyes! Be joyful! As you are alive and full of my Presence. Be still, for a moment and feel all the love around you. In your journey remain faithful, my child, and let your heart be full. Find the beauty in your life and let your heart sing. I have put a song within your heart, and it is yours to build on and most importantly to share. It's a wonderful incomparable melody and within each unique note, there is an array of experiences. Look at your song with the sincerity of love. Finding the most beautiful moments of truth in the chords that are all strummed together. As you can now see that I am within them all. My Spirit creates strength in your melody and harmony in your life… It has been this way since the beginning even when you did not have the ears to hear. I've been with you all along. I have watched you, as you live and dream, experience and share. A masterpiece of music is your life. A heavenly symphony orchestrated by me… Your song is so beautiful my child, so embrace your song as you let your heart sing. Sing your life's song and make melody with your Lord.

My heart is steadfast, O God, my heart
is steadfast! I will sing and make melody.
(Psalm 57:7, ESV)

Sing to him. Sing praises to him; tell
of all his wondrous works!
(Psalm 105:2, ESV)

To the choirmaster; with stringed instruments. A Psalm. A Song. May God be gracious to us and bless us and make his face to shine upon us, Selah.
(Psalm 67:1, ESV)

I will incline my ear to a proverb; I will solve my riddle to the music of the lyre.
(Psalm 49:4, ESV)

You make known to me the path of life; in your presence there is fullness and joy; at your right hand are pleasures forevermore.
(Psalm 16:11, ESV)

Prayer: Father God, thank you for helping me complete this good task before me. I pray for all my friends and family, please lead us to your paths and walk with us, guide us gently, holding our hands. Give us the courage to overcome fear and help build our faith. Lead us to our appointed positions, keeping us filled with your Presence. In Jesus's name, I pray, singing hymns and praise, giving thanks, amen. Hallelujah! Glory to the Lord.

May 4

Straightening Your Path

Hear the sound of my voice, my love, I speak to you in the hours of day and night. Let my voice be your path calling to you, toward your destiny for today. Do not get ahead of yourself or my calling. Do not be confused by the echoes which seem to bounce back and forth off all your scattered thoughts, but hear my initial calling the loudness in which you first heard me. Close your eyes, my child. Stand in the sunshine of my love and remember where your first thoughts were of me today. I will guide you today and always, bringing you back to the starting place. Not to begin again but to fulfill my will for you. As I keep you on task. Just keep me close in your mind. If you feel yourself slipping away from me, call my name JESUS, and I will return to the forefront of your mind. Walk through this day with confidence that I AM with you always leading and guiding you making your path straight. Your path will once again be made straight as we walk throughout this day hand in hand.

Trust in the Lord with all your heart
and lean not on your own understanding;
In all your ways submit to him and he will
make your paths straight.
(Proverbs 3:5–6, ESV)

In this love God was made manifest
among us, that God sent his only Son into
the world, so that we might live through
him.
(1 John 4:9, ESV)

*Because if you confess with your
mouth that Jesus is Lord and believe in your
heart that God raised him from the dead,
you will be saved.*
(Romans 10:9, ESV)

*Make your face shine on your servant,
save me in your steadfast love.*
(Psalm 31:16, ESV)

Prayer: Today Father God, I ask you to be with me to clear my mind to lead me, give me hope to stand on your promises. Guide my steps. I ask you to help me to begin this good task you have called me to do and to be able to see it through to completion. I pray also for all my loved ones and all your children everywhere, your love and peace filled with joy, in Jesus's loving name, amen.

May 5

Always Listening

Do not fear little one. I hear your prayers and love when you speak to me. Our time together is precious to me. Although I am always with you, I love the special moments you spend with me alone. Your prayers are not in vain. I will answer according to my will and in my time. My timing is always perfect. You may not always know what I am doing or how my leading will benefit you. This is where you must learn to trust me. Remember I know you; I know your heart. I see how you work so hard to help others in your life. I am pleased with your efforts and compassion. I hear you! I am working on your behalf and on behalf of your prayers for others. Do not be discouraged. Keep praying and talking to me. Keep your ear turned to me and I will turn my ear to you. I AM here. I AM always listening, and I love you.

At the voice of thy cry; When he shall hear it, He shall answer thee.
(Isaiah 30:19, ESV)

Again Jesus spoke to them saying, "I am the light of the world. Whoever follows me will not walk in darkness, but will have the light of life."
(John 8:12, ESV)

These things I have spoken to you, that my joy may be in you, and that your joy may be made full.
(John 15:11, ESV)

My sheep hear my voice, and I know them, and they follow me. I give them eternal life, and they will never perish, and no one will snatch them out of my hand.
(John 10:27–28, ESV)

Prayer: Father God Thank you for always listening to me and guiding me. Help me to have patience when waiting for your answers. Also, help me to know that your answers serve me best. In Jesus's name, I pray, amen.

May 6

Strengthening You with Love

I AM the sun shining upon the earth in the early morning. I am the light, the truth, and the way to heaven. I am the creator of all. Your Father, your friend. I am with you; I am for you. I never sleep on the job. I never give up. I am always working to better your life, to guide you when you are lost, to lead you through the darkness and find the path of love and happiness. When you don't feel well, just ask me and I will heal your spirit. I know you feel tired my child, but just as I can do all things with the strength of my Spirit you can too. I will share my power supply with you. It is limitless never ending. Call out to me let me know your needs. I will pick you up and carry you through this day. As I am all that you need, and I am strengthening you with the greatest power that one can hold, the power of love...

I can do all things through Christ who strengthens me.
(Philippians 4:13, ESV)

He gives power to the faint, and to him who has no might he increases strength.
(Isaiah 40:29, NIV)

Seek the Lord and his strength; seek his presence continually!
(1 Chronicles 16:11, ESV)

So shall my word be that goes out from my mouth; it shall not return to me empty, but it shall accomplish that which I pur-

pose, and shall succeed the thing for which
I sent it.
(Isaiah 55:11, ESV)

Prayer: Father God, today help me to have the strength to do all that I am called to do. Fill me with your spirit so I can also energize the people around me with your love. Although I feel weak today, Father, I thank you for carrying me until I can stand on my own once again. In Jesus's name, I pray for all who need you today. Lord thank you for the victory of your presence, amen.

May 7

Peace for Your Soul

Today you will find my peace in the quietness of the morning. This day will bring you much needed rest not from the daily tasks ahead but from the earthly worries and daily thoughts that fill within your mind. Keep your eyes focused on me to find the rest that is much needed. Today's world is filled with chaos constantly pulling your thoughts away from me, I see your troubles, I hear your prayers and today I will give you rest. If you will completely trust in me, I will take your worries. Trust is essential for my children. Feel the breeze of the wind listen to the birds and look around at the trees and the stillness of the sky. Find me here in the beauty of all I have created for you. I love your willingness to spend time with me. Feel the warmth of my Presence within you. I will work through the night recharging your soul while you sleep. You are a shining light to others and today you are extra bright. Your soul is once again restored. Go and enjoy this day feeling whole and complete once more.

I am smiling.

Come to me all who are weary and burdened and I will give you rest.
(Matthew 11:28, NIV)

You keep him in perfect peace whose mind is stayed on you, because he trusts in you.
(Isaiah 26:3, ESV)

I will satisfy the weary soul, and every languishing soul I will replenish.
(Jeremiah 31:21, ESV)

I have said these things to you, that in me you may have peace. In the world you will have tribulation. But take heart, I have overcome the world.
(John 16:33, ESV)

In peace I will both lie down and sleep; for you alone, O Lord, make me dwell in safety.
(Psalm 4:8, ESV)

Prayer: Thank you, Father God, for taking all my worries. Thank you for loving me and making me feel whole. I pray today Lord to be a blessing to others to show them how much they are loved. I pray for all my friends and family protection and peace within their souls. Fill them, today Lord, just as you have filled me with happiness and joy. In Jesus's name, I pray AMEN.

May 8

Keep the Faith

When I'm not apparent try to stand on your faith. Sometimes you feel like I am far away from you. You wonder where I am. Rest assured my Child I am here. I have never left you. I will not forsake you. Rest on the hope of my promises. Faith is being sure of what is promised but not yet seen. Don't lose hope. You will see my answers and blessings in your life. Keep the faith. Know that I want what is best for you and will turn even the worst situations into something good. Although it is hard to fathom at times, you must trust me and know I will never leave my children. Even in the silence of your soul I am within you. Today watch for a sign from me showing you I am here. Walk today knowing you are not lost but are on the right path and be happy, as blessings stream your way flowing to you always. Keep in mind sometimes they will trickle along a winding path, but other times, the river of my blessings will pour out to you abundantly. Have patience my child, soon you will see all that I have instore for you and it is good.

Have faith my child.

Now faith is confidence in what we hope for and the assurance about things we cannot see.
(Hebrews 11:1, NIV)

But let him ask in faith, with no doubting, for the one who doubts is like a wave of the sea that is driven and tossed by the wind.
(James 1:6, ESV)

Though you have not seen him, you love him. Though you do not now see him; you believe in him and rejoice with that joy that is inexpressible and filled with glory, obtaining the outcome of your faith, the salvation of your souls.
(1 Peter 1:8–9, ESV)

Save us, we pray, O Lord! O Lord, we pray give us success! Blessed is he who comes in the name of the Lord! We bless you from the house of the Lord.
(Psalm 118:25–26, ESV)

Prayer: Thank you father God for this day. I will hold onto my faith and thank you for answering my prayers. I pray to be a light today full of your peace and love to share with others. I pray for your protection and love to help all that need you. in Jesus's name, AMEN.

May 9

One Day at a Time

Keep your eyes fixed on me. Believe that I am answering all you ask. I'm so pleased that you recognize my voice, little one. As I speak to you throughout the day. I know the troubles of this world and your life. You are a soldier. Keep leaning on me to be your strength. We are on a journey together. Find beauty and joy at every turn. I know sometimes you want to take a shortcut because you can see the good ahead, but you must not. Just stay on my path. Walk with me through winding roads, up rugged hills and mountains. Keep walking with me taking in all that surrounds you. We must walk this way if you are to learn. You are learning so much about yourself by traveling this path and it is good. You have many questions wrapped in hopes for me. I am answering. Keep your faith and the hope that I am working. One day at a time, eyes up and fixed on me and my leading. You are on the right path. Keep following me and spreading joy to those around you. I am proud of you. Experience the joys completely as you stay in the present. Keep your mind on this day as tomorrow will have worries of its own. Keep enjoying the present, as it is my gift.

Yet you do not know what tomorrow will bring. What is your life? For you are a mist that appears for a little time and then vanishes.
(James 4:14, ESV)

Make me to know your ways, O Lord; teach me your paths. Lead me in your truth

and teach me, for you are the God of my
salvation; for you I wait all the day long.
(Psalm 25:4–5)

Whoever heeds instruction is on the
path to life, but he who rejects reproof leads
others astray.
(Proverbs 10:17, ESV)

The steps of a man are established by
the lord, when he delights in his way.
(Psalm 37:23, ESV)

Prayer: Thank you Lord, for leading me and speaking to me. Thank you for blessing me with what's best. I believe in your promises to me. I believe in all that you are. Jesus, I love you! Father God, I am yours. Do what you will with me Lord. Use me Lord for your glory. In Jesus's name, I pray, amen.

May 10

All My Children

Good morning, my child. I've seen you lately taking on things that are not your burdens to carry. I love your willingness to try and help others and I love your compassion, but I see these things draining your spirit. At times it seems like you have the weight of the world on your shoulders, but you must remember, that it is I who carried the ultimate cross. Don't let the weight of the world drag you down. Call me and I will help ease the heaviness and lighten your soul. Keep praying for them. Knowing that I hear their prayers, just as I hear yours. I love all my children. I have heard the names of your loved ones in your prayers and I am working it all out for them too. Don't worry. Trust me with your loved ones dear one. I will whisper my spirit into their lives just as I have done for you. Today experience my love, breathing joy into your heart. Enjoy this day. Fear not and know that I am GOD.

Don't be afraid, for I am with you.
Don't be discouraged, for I am your God.
I will strengthen you and help you. I will
hold you up with my victorious right hand.
(Isaiah 41:10, ESV)

Finally, brothers, rejoice. Aim for restoration, comfort one another, agree with one another, live in peace; and the God of love and peace will be with you.
(Ecclesiastes 12:13, ESV)

*Behold, God is my helper; the Lord is
the upholder of my life.*
(Psalm 54:4, ESV)

*The law of his God is in his heart; his
steps do not slip.*
(Psalm 37:31, ESV)

*Anxiety in a man's heart weighs him
down, but a good word makes him glad.*
(Proverbs 12:25, ESV)

Prayer: Thank you, Father, for caring for my loved ones. I pray today that they can feel your spirit with them and that you fill their souls with happiness and joy. Bless them, Father, just as you bless me time and time again. In Jesus's loving name, AMEN.

May 11

Let Your Light Shine

Today is the day that I have made. Be thankful for this day even before it has begun. When you rise early in the morning my child, spend time giving thanks to me for what is yet to come. This is the key to happiness even amid small storms. We will find the good together. If you will keep your eyes fixed on me, you will start to see more and more of what is good and less of the troubles of this world. Trust me and you will start to notice that the peace within your soul will become stronger than the passing problems. True joy will take hold, and you will smile from within. A smile that comes from joy. Walk through this day with confidence and soon you will notice others recognizing your light. I have made you just this way. You want to be a blessing to others my dear one, and believe me, you are. Let your light shine always. I have placed it within you, and it is good.

This is the day the Lord has made; Let us rejoice and be glad in it.
(Psalm 118:24, NIV)

In the same way, let your light shine before others, so that they may see your good works and give glory to your Father who is in heaven.
(Matthew 5:16, ESV)

As you wish others would do to you, do so to them.
(Luke 6:31, ESV)

And let us consider how to stir up one another to love and good works.
(Hebrews 10:24, ESV)

For at one time you were darkness, but now you are light in the Lord. Walk as children of light.
(Ephesians 5:8, ESV)

Prayer: Thank you, Father God, for this day. Thank you for all the blessings and love you give me and my loved ones. I pray to continue to be a blessing to others and I pray that they see your light shine within me. I am thankful for all my spiritual gifts Lord. Please fill our lives with happiness and peace. In Jesus's name, AMEN.

May 12

Music of Life

Surround yourself with my love today. Enjoy all that I bring to you. Today your soul may feel lighter and you feel like you can finally breathe. I love the way you look to me with excitement, it pleases me to see you trusting me more and more. Feel the peace of joy today, knowing that I love you with an everlasting love. No worries today my child, it is good you have placed them all at the foot of the cross. Knowing that I have them under control, and you can relax. Smile with me and we can enjoy the beauty of this day together. Life is a symphony and I am the Maestro. Life is filled with beautiful music as all my creations band together to create a beautiful melody. Recognize the chords which together create this powerful melody of love. Keep hold of my hand as I am leading you toward all that I have planned. Your love for others is key. You are destined for greatness. Speak life today and smile, I love you. And enjoy the music of life.

Surely, goodness and love will follow
me all the days of my life, and I will dwell
in the house of the LORD forever.
(Psalm 23:6, ESV)

So I will show my greatness and my
holiness and make myself known in the eyes
of many nations. Then they will know that
I am the Lord.
(Ezekiel 38:23, ESV)

But you are a chosen race, a royal
priesthood, a holy nation, a people for his

own possession. That you may proclaim the excellencies of him who called you out of darkness into his marvelous light.
(1 Peter 2:9, ESV)

And in order that the Gentiles might glorify God for his mercy. As it is written, "Therefore I will praise you among the Gentiles, and sing to your name."
(Romans 15:9, ESV)

But now bring me a musician. "And when the musician played, the hand of the Lord came upon him."
(2 Kings 3:15, ESV)

Prayer: Jesus, I love you. Thank you for filling my spirit with the beautiful music that makes life great. Thank you for giving me a kind heart and for making me feel complete, as I am filled with your love today. I pray for others to experience this joy today. I pray for all my friends and family and for all in the world who need you. Thank you for this day in Jesus's name I pray, amen.

May 13

Plans for a Future

I am with you and for you. What better news could you receive today? I know you have your plans for this day and this life, but I also have plans for you. Plans to fill you with joy and guide you through plans to give you hope and a future. Share a smile today my child. My children show love to even those that are without, and I am pleased. Walk through this day sharing my light. Be thankful for all your circumstances. Your blessings are many just open your eyes to see, open your ears to hear, and open your heart to love... It makes my heart happiest spending time with you. Watching your face light up when you see one of your prayers get answered. Keep in mind that I am working out all your requests my way, on my time. I am the Lord and I know best. Do not feel bad about asking me to help you fulfill future goals, I want you to talk with me about everything. Just remember my child do not get stuck daydreaming of the outcomes. Trust me and all in the future will be bright. Always with love.

"For I know the plans I have for you," declares the Lord, "plans to prosper you and not harm you, plans to give you hope and a future."
(Jeremiah 29:11, NIV)

And the Lord will guide you continually and satisfy your desire in scorched places and make your bones strong; and you shall be like a watered garden, like a spring of water, whose waters do not fail.
(Isaiah 58:11, ESV)

Now to him who is able to do far more abundantly than all that we ask or think, according to the power at work within us.
(Ephesians 3:20, ESV)

But seek first the kingdom of God and his righteousness, and all these things will be added to you.
(Matthew 6:33, ESV)

Prayer: Father God, thank you for guiding me and leading me. I pray for you to help me and my loved ones Lord. I pray that we don't get lost in the daydreaming and worrying about the future, I thank you for all our blessings. Surround us with your protection and love today and always. Lord guide us into your will for our lives. Keep us always seeking you first, in Jesus's name, I pray, amen.

May 14

Tasks at Hand

Smile in the face of small storms. Although Your light is always shining sometimes the skies are gray. Things left undone start to accumulate and make you feel overwhelmed. Call out to me speak to me about these situations, and one by one we will accomplish these things together. No need to rush dear one. We can take our time, I am not confined or held to the earthly hourly standards, therefore all is as it is meant to be. One task at a time. Fix your eyes on me ask me to direct your thoughts. I will help you decide which tasks to pursue and in what order. Trust me to be the leader of your life. All the good things I have given you, and the situations I have already led you through have prepared you for your life and all the tasks at hand. Stay encouraged.

Commit everything to the Lord, trust him, and he will help you.
(Psalm 37:5, NLT)

He made the storm be still, and the waves of the sea were hushed.
(Psalm 107:29, ESV)

Jesus said to them, "I am the bread of life; whoever comes to me shall not hunger, and whoever believes in me shall never thirst."
(John 6:35, ESV)

*Many are the plans in the mind of a
man, but it is the purpose of the Lord that
will stand.*
(Proverbs 19:21, ESV)

*For we are his workmanship, created
in Christ Jesus for good works, which God
prepared beforehand, that we should walk
in them.*
(Ephesians 2:10, ESV)

Prayer: Father God, guide my thoughts today, do not let me feel overwhelmed. I trust you Lord and know that you will help me. Also, I ask for all of my family and friends' guidance and help today. Take all our worries. Thank you for watching over us and helping us to complete our tasks. In Jesus's name, I pray and thank you father for the victory, amen.

May 15

Eyes to See Yourself

When the morning arrives my child, it is a new day, the worries of yesterday should be left with me. Today is a fresh start. It pleases me to watch your faith grow. Sometimes the world makes you feel inadequate. This life has a way of making you feel that you somehow fall short, but believe me, my child, that's just not true. Each of my children has a different path which I've chosen for them to travel, that in time will reveal in them the true strength of their spirit. I have used difficult situations to show you just how strong you truly are. You are more than you know. Already you have gone through so much. You have gone through the fire and yet still, you are here, brighter and stronger than ever. It is not that you are a better version of yourself it is just that you are finally being able to see yourself for who I created you to be. You are my beautiful child and you are loved.

> *When you pass through the waters, I will be with you: and when you pass through the rivers, they will not sweep over you. When you walk through the fire, you will not be burned: the flames will not set you ablaze.*
> (Isaiah 43:2, NIV)

> *So we do not lose heart, Though our outer self is wasting away, our inner self is being renewed day by day.*
> (2 Corinthians 4:16, ESV)

See what kind of love the Father has given to us, that we should be called children of God; and so we are. The reason why the world does not know us is that it did not know him.

(1 John 3:1, ESV)

You are altogether beautiful, my love; there is no flaw in you.
(Songs of Songs 4:7, ESV)

Prayer: Take a moment and close your eyes pray to Jesus whatever is in your heart and on your mind. Today is about you and your self-reflection.

"Today, my Lord, I am in agreeance with my friend in Christ. In Jesus's name, we pray, Amen."

May 16

Share Love

Love, it is meant for my children to share. I have said," love, thy neighbor as you love thyself." My meaning is to love all. Sometimes I know it is hard for you to put away negative feelings for someone who may have upset you or is living in a way you do not agree with, but you must remember, it is not your place to judge. That burden is mine. Ask me to fill your heart with forgiveness, as this is what I want from you. Just as I forgave you. You must also forgive. Being able to overcome negative thoughts or feelings about others not only benefits your mind but also your heart. Bad thoughts or judgments cause a bitter soul. Pray for the person or people in your life that are upsetting to you for they are my children too. Their path is not your path. I will lead them to the correct destination. Keep praying for them. Don't lose hope. Find peace and comfort knowing I am here. Find love in your heart for them and you will experience sweetness in your soul. Today share my love…

Do not judge, or you too will be judged.
(Matthew 7:1, NIV)

Jesus replied: "Love the Lord your God with all your heart and with all your soul and with all your mind." This is the first and greatest commandment. And the second is like it: "Love your neighbor as yourself."
(Matthew 22:38–39, NIV)

And over all these virtues put on love,
which binds them all together in perfect
unity.
    (Colossians 3:14, NIV)

Greater love has no one than this, that
someone lay down his life for his friends.
(John 15:13, ESV)

Let all that you do be done in love.
(1 Corinthians 16:14, ESV)

Prayer: Father God, help me to be more forgiving and understanding with certain people in my life. I pray you to watch over and guide them. I pray you to enter their lives and let them know about you. Thank you for forgiving me Lord and loving me. I pray you to keep a hold of my loved ones, my family and myself today and always. In Jesus's name, I pray to be filled with your love for others, amen.

May 17

Beauty in This Life

This life is a beautiful life. The news and media would have you believe otherwise, as they fill up your time with only disasters and terrible happenings. Turn it off for today, give yourself a break. Here is my news for today, "You are blessed, you have all that you need. My grace is sufficient for you." You can look around and find me in everything, from a beautiful blue sky filled with billowy white clouds to the treetops rustling in the wind to the warmth of the sun upon your skin. To the beauty of colors all over this world or the wonderful smells that you experience, like freshly cut grass, fresh apple pie the list goes on and on. All these wonderful things which make you feel good. I am in a smile from a stranger or a hug from a friend. The warm inviting feeling within that you feel as happiness sets in. Yes, dear child, I am in everything. Train your mind to focus on what's good and ask me to help you with the rest. Go and find the beauty today. Feel alive today with the beauty in life.

In the beginning, was the word, and the word was with God, and the Word was God. He was with God in the beginning. Through him all things were made; without him nothing was made that has been made. In him was life, and that life was the light of all mankind.
(John 1:1–4, NIV)

The grass withers the flower fades, but the word of God stands forever.
(Isaiah 40:8, ESV)

Ah, Lord God! It is you who have made the heavens and the earth by your great power and by your outstretched arm! Nothing is too hard for you.
(Jeremiah 32:17, ESV)

He made everything beautiful in its time. Also, he has put eternity into a man's heart, yet so that he cannot find out what God has done from beginning to end.
(Ecclesiastes 3:11, ESV)

And we all, with unveiled face, beholding the glory of the Lord, are being transformed into the same image from one degree of glory to another. For this comes from the Lord who is the Spirit.
(2 Corinthians 3:18, ESV)

Prayer: Thank you, Father, for helping me find the beauty in this life. I ask you to help all my family and friends experience your beauty today. I ask you to fill our hearts with joy and kindness for one another. I ask you to help us realize that you are all we need. I thank you, Father, and pray in Jesus's name. Amen.

May 18

Perfect Timing

When asking me for things my dear child you must remember to have patience. I am not like your TV remote changing channels at the push of a button. I am not a genie granting wishes. I am GOD. The one who formed you and knows what is best for you. It may seem like I'm taking my time, and this is true I am. My timing is perfect. You can trust in this. I may answer your requests in ways, which you do not understand. Sometimes my answer is no, but do not fear for I am always looking out for you. Doing what is best. Ask me to put my requests in your heart that benefit your life and the lives of others around you. This is a hard task because essentially you are letting go of your own wants and desires and are asking me for my will and not your own. I hear all your petitions and I love gifting my children answers to their prayers. Again, have patience. Things are happening and one by one you will see a path clearing before you. Follow me and we will experience the beauty and blessings together. I love you.

The steps of a good man are ordered by the Lord, and He delights in his way.
(Psalm 37:23, NKJV)

Your word is a lamp to my feet. And a light to my path.
(Psalm 119:105, NKJV)

So teach us to number our days that we may get a heart of wisdom.
(Psalm 90:12, ESV)

*But do not overlook this one fact,
beloved, that with the Lord one day is as
a thousand years, and a thousand years as
one day.*
(2 Peter 3:8, ESV)

*As a plan for the fullness of time, to
unite all things in him, things in heaven
and things on earth.*
(Ephesians 1:10, ESV)

Prayer: Father God, please replace my wants and desires with your will, so that I may be asking you for the right things. I thank you for placing love and compassion in my heart. I pray for all my family and friends and people I encounter today. Your will be done. In Jesus's name, AMEN.

May 19

The Great Physician

Enjoying this day moment by moment. Hello, my dear child, I'm glad you're here again ready to spend time with me. Precious are the moments in which we spend time together. This is the time I can give new life to your soul. Your soul is like a battery fully charged at times, and other times drained and weak. Spending time with me allows me to recharge your battery so that your life light can shine brightly once again. When you allow your soul to become weak by taking on too many problems or doing too many things illness or injury can set in. Open up to me today, give me your time. Sit with me awhile. You must remember that I am The Great Healer. When you or someone you love is facing an illness or going through an injury, keep the faith. It is said by my stripes you are healed, and this goes for all my children. Not feeling well is tough to go through on many levels. Whether it is you, a child, or a friend it is the absolute situation that there is no control. But keep this in mind, my child, I AM in control. I can…and do…heal. Whether or not it is meant to happen is all a part of my design. Please do not hesitate to ask me to take charge of the illness or injury and watch what I can do. I am The Great Physician. I am your Father, your Creator, and I am your God who heals.

Who forgives all your iniquities; who heals all your diseases.
(Psalm 103:3, AKJV)

"I have seen their ways, but I will heal them; I will guide them and restore comfort to Israel's mourners, creating praise on their

lips. Peace, peace, to those far and near,"
says the LORD. "And I will heal them."
(Isaiah 57:18–19, NIV)

Behold, I will bring to it health and
healing, and I will heal them and reveal to
them abundance of prosperity and security.
(Jeremiah 33:6, ESV)

He himself bore our sins in his body
on the tree, that we might die to sin and
live to righteousness. By his wounds you
have been healed.
(1 Peter 2:24, ESV)

Prayer: Father God, today I Lift up __ give them your strength heal them, my Lord. I ask that you keep their eyes fixed on you and that you fill their mind and body with your healing power. I ask you today to restore their health as I trust you in this matter and thank you for the victory. In Jesus's name, I ask and pray, amen.

May 20

A Helpful Soul

I see you helping out. I love it when you help my child, by stepping in when you see someone in need. All my children need a little help sometimes. Your willingness to offer up care to another when it is needed pleases me. As this is one of my commandments" Love thy neighbor as thyself." You have a very thoughtful spirit and such a big heart. This is a quality that I have placed in you. I have watered the seed of kindness and watch each day as it grows within your soul. Your light of compassion is bright. I know there are times that you want to help but may not be able to. Do not worry about these times, as certain situations are meant to be left completely in my care. Not all my children are so open to receiving help or instruction so you must ask me to guide them. Learn to let me handle those situations in which you have no control. It is also very important, my child that you don't get upset with yourself if your help is rejected or the task is too big. It is Ok. Pray about it and leave those children and situations to me. Remember you must also love yourself. Be kind to yourself, know that you are worthy, you are special, and you are loved.

Jesus said unto him, thou shalt love the Lord thy God with all thy heart, and with all thy soul, and with all thy mind. This is the first and great commandment. And the second is like unto it, thou shalt love thy neighbor as thyself.
(Matthew 22:37–38, KJV)

Therefore, my beloved brothers, be steadfast, immovable, always abounding in

the work of the Lord, knowing that in the
Lord your labor is not in vain.
(1 Corinthians 15:58, ESV)

And he sat down and called the twelve.
And said to them, "If anyone would be first,
he must last of all and the servant of all."
(Mark 9:35, ESV)

Prayer: Lord thank you for giving me a kind heart for others. Please help me to love myself. Help me to release those situations in which I cannot help you. I leave these friends and situations to you. I know and trust that you are taking care of them. In Jesus's loving name I ask and pray and thank you, Lord, amen.

May 21

Not Perfect yet Beautiful

Good morning Beautiful child, Today I want to tell you to stop looking back. The past has a way of taking your focus off me and all the progress you have made. All my children have sinned. Not one is perfect. The good news is I have died for your sins and the sins of the world. You are washed clean, from your past. You must not get stuck in self-pity or regret. The enemy uses these past situations to steal your joy and will try to keep you far from me. He will tell your mind that you have been far too bad to deserve the life I have planned for you. Do not give him power. Call on me I will direct your thoughts back to the present. Once you start living in this moment look around and truly think of all the blessings you have today. Look how far you've come. Before you head out today put on my whole armor. Ask me to protect your mind and thoughts and to lead them. Stay positive, remember the enemy is very clever he has a way of tangling up your thoughts and using them to make you feel hopeless. I am God, focus on me. You will not be defeated. You are my child.

I am the door. If anyone enters by me, he will be saved and will go in and out and find pasture. The thief comes only to steal and kill and destroy. I came that they may have life and have it abundantly.
(John 10:9–10, ESV)

For we do not wrestle against flesh and blood, but against the rulers, against the authorities, against cosmic powers over this

*present darkness, against the spiritual forces
of evil in the heavenly places. Therefore take
up the whole armor of God, that you may
be able to withstand in the evil day, having
done all, to stand firm.*
(Ephesians 6:12–13, ESV)

*Set your minds on things that are
above, not on things that are on earth.*
(Colossians 3:2, ESV)

*You keep him in perfect peace whose
mind is stayed on you, because he trusts in
you.*
(Isaiah 26:3, ESV)

Prayer: Father God direct my thoughts today. Protect me from the enemy. Fill my soul and mind with joy. I am yours's Lord. Watch over all my family and friends as well in Jesus's name, I pray, amen.

May 22

Facing a Giant

When facing a giant. Some situations require complete faith that you will succeed. I want you to know nothing can be accomplished if you don't step out in faith. Some of my children stay complacent, meaning they never move forward, not because they lack the aptitude for the job but because of fear. The fear of failure is one of the biggest issues holding back so many of my children. It keeps them stuck in familiar places. Maybe you want to start a new business or get a promotion at work. It might be that you want to make a big move across the country, whatever it is my child I want you to succeed. It delights me to watch you move forward in life. I know how strong you truly are... Do you? Watch for my cues and let me lead you there. If it all seems overwhelming just take it one step at a time, but do not give up. Most importantly be brave and do not fear.

But as for you, be strong and do not give up, for your work will be rewarded.
(1 Chronicles 15:7, NIV)

May he give you the desire of your heart and make all your plans succeed.
(Psalm 20:4, NIV)

David said to the Philistine, "You come against me with sword, spear and javelin, but I come to you in the name of the LORD of Heavens Armies, the God of the armies of Israel, whom you have defied."
(1 Samuel 17:45, NLT)

Prayer: Jesus thank you for washing my sins away. Thank you for forgiving me and making me feel new. I thank you for the rain as it washes the earth and makes everything refreshed and clean. Thank you also for loving me. I pray today that my family and friends experience the refreshed feeling of your love, that you wash away their worries and pain in your name, I pray, amen.

May 24

Love Signs That Lead

Have you ever noticed certain things stand out to only you? A certain song you hear when you're feeling a certain way, touches you. Writings on a sign you may see on the side of a road, a heart shaped rock. The shape of a cloud. The list is long. These things are meant for you to notice as your senses at that very moment become hyper-aware. It is because I have meant these things for you, and I will open your spiritual eyes. Every one of my children from time to time has noticed something that made them feel my Presence at a higher level of emotion and connection as your senses become heightened. For some of my children, the feeling is fleeting and dissipates quickly, for others their feeling may linger a bit longer. Yes, my child, most times when you look up and ask, God was that you? Most likely it was and is. The reason I say most likely is that there are times the enemy tries to imitate my messages to you, so be wary if at that moment something feels a little off. Pray about all things. Thank me for your signs and cues. Ask me to increase your spiritual awareness and to open your spiritual eyes and to give you discernment... Go out today, knowing I love you. Be blessed, my child, and enjoy my love signs that lead.

I pray that the eyes of your heart be enlightened in order that you may know the hope to which he has called you, the riches of his glorious inheritance in his holy people.
(Ephesians 1:18, NIV)

Every good gift and perfect gift is a gift from above, and cometh down from the

Prayer: Jesus thank you for washing my sins away. Thank you for forgiving me and making me feel new. I thank you for the rain as it washes the earth and makes everything refreshed and clean. Thank you also for loving me. I pray today that my family and friends experience the refreshed feeling of your love, that you wash away their worries and pain in your name, I pray, amen.

May 24

Love Signs That Lead

Have you ever noticed certain things stand out to only you? A certain song you hear when you're feeling a certain way, touches you. Writings on a sign you may see on the side of a road, a heart shaped rock. The shape of a cloud. The list is long. These things are meant for you to notice as your senses at that very moment become hyper-aware. It is because I have meant these things for you, and I will open your spiritual eyes. Every one of my children from time to time has noticed something that made them feel my Presence at a higher level of emotion and connection as your senses become heightened. For some of my children, the feeling is fleeting and dissipates quickly, for others their feeling may linger a bit longer. Yes, my child, most times when you look up and ask, God was that you? Most likely it was and is. The reason I say most likely is that there are times the enemy tries to imitate my messages to you, so be wary if at that moment something feels a little off. Pray about all things. Thank me for your signs and cues. Ask me to increase your spiritual awareness and to open your spiritual eyes and to give you discernment... Go out today, knowing I love you. Be blessed, my child, and enjoy my love signs that lead.

I pray that the eyes of your heart be enlightened in order that you may know the hope to which he has called you, the riches of his glorious inheritance in his holy people.
(Ephesians 1:18, NIV)

Every good gift and perfect gift is a gift from above, and cometh down from the

father of lights, whom is no variableness,
neither shadow of turning.
        (James 1:17, NIV)

My command is this: Love each other
as I have loved you.
        (John 15:12, NIV)

Prayer: Thank you, Father, for the beautiful signs, that fill me with joy. And most importantly thank you for giving me the wisdom to see that it is you. I truly am grateful Jesus for the spiritual eyes. Thank you for sending your love to me for lighting my path and guiding my way. Also, thank you, father God, for sending love to my family and friends. I feel such joy in my soul, I pray in Jesus's name, you keep lighting my way, amen.

To my reader, speak to the Lord about whatever is in your heart particularly if there is something you may need guidance accomplishing. Ask God to reveal himself to you, and to shower you with joy. Watch for his leading. Soon amazing things will start to come.

May 25

Opening Doors

Breathe me in, what does that mean to you, my child? To truly breath me in, is to ask me to guide your life, to open your heart completely to me. Let my spirit fill your soul. When making decisions be aware of my urging. Be aware of my stop signs as well. I will direct your path. It might be that you need to make a small adjustment to get to the place that at this moment I have designed for you to be. Follow my lead I will open doors before you and opportunities will show themselves. Sometimes multiple opportunities will arrive at once. Do not be confused. Pray about everything and I will make the right path appear brighter and it will become more apparent to you, which door you should go through. Do not be afraid, step out in faith, as I am with you. I will not force you through any doors. You must take the first step on your own. As this is a test of trust. You must learn to trust my leading. However, if you have taken a step that doesn't feel right and your soul is unsure as to which way to go, it is okay to step back as this may not have been the path, I have chosen for you. Pray again. Take your time and have patience I will point the way. There are other times you may feel like you've hit a dead end, as it seems all the doors are shut. Rest assured my child these are the times I've designed for you to rest and spend time with me. When I feel you are ready the path will clear again. I will never keep you stuck. I want you to move forward and live life abundantly.

Remember this always you are blessed.

In all thy ways acknowledge him, and
he will direct thy paths.
(Proverbs 3:6, KJV)

You make known to me the path of life; you will fill me with joy in your presence, with eternal pleasures at your right hand.
(Psalm 16:11, NIV)

May the Lord direct your hearts into God's love and Christ's perseverance.
(2 Thessalonians 3:5, NIV)

Prayer: Please enlighten me Lord as to which way to go. Guide my steps, take away my doubts and fears. Show me the way, Lord. Father God, I pray to be a blessing to others around me as I am on this journey. I pray for your protection and love for myself and everyone in my life. Thank you, Jesus, for always guiding me and showing me which way to go. In Jesus's loving name, I thank you for the victory, amen.

To my reader my friend, I urge you today if you are confused about a direction in your life ask God to open the way before you and to give you the wisdom to know which door to go through.

May 26

Destination Heaven

When you align yourself with my will, my child, you will start to notice that life flows a little more freely. As you learn to trust me more and more...it will become easier for you to recognize the outcomes that my hand was truly in. I have gifted all my children with free will and because of this, you are able to make your own choices and decisions. My plan for your life is a destination, how you get there is a choice of your own. Try not to blame me when things in your life seem hard or terrible things happen; you must remember that the enemy is here in this world trying to take over. He wants to keep you far from me. He is a liar. He is also very clever, do not be deceived. Pray for discernment. I will not let him take you. You live in a world where chaos is evident. Horrible things all over the world happening to my children. My heart breaks. I did not make these things happen, it is and was always free will filled with sin that continues to create these events. Do not lose hope. The good news is I AM GOD and I have come to SAVE my children from themselves and the enemy. Heaven is the destination for my children. Because of sin there became death. So that they may come home, I died for the world and its sin, I died to save you and overcame death. This means people will still die to this world. I know this is hard for many of you to understand. As your loved ones pass away, I know you feel pain, the pain of loss. I watch as your heart breaks, keep in mind my child, mine does too. My children who accept me as their Savoir when they leave this world, they will come home to me. I will wrap my arms around them and welcome them. No more death, no more sadness just an overwhelming exuberance of love and eternal life in Heaven. (...and another angel received their wings.)

*Be careful for nothing; but in every-
thing by prayer and supplication with
thanksgiving let your requests be made
known unto God.*
(Philippians 4:6, KJV)

*I give them eternal life, and they shall
never perish; no one will snatch them out of
my hand.*
(John 10:28, KJV)

*The Lord is near to the brokenhearted
and saves the crushed in spirit.*
(Psalm 34:18, ESV)

Prayer: *Our Father who art in
Heaven hallowed be thy name. Your kingdom come your will be done. On earth as it
is in heaven.*
(Matthew 6:9–10, ESV)

Please comfort us Lord, and take care of our loved ones in heaven, amen.

One of my friends who was very young died from cancer this year. I prayed and prayed for her a miracle healing, but her healing never came. My Lords answer to me was no. He was taking her home. This is not the part where I say, that it's easy to just accept God's answers, because most times when his answers are not the answers we are seeking—it is not easy at all. In fact, it downright hurts. It's hard to say farewell. But we need to remember that our Lord knows what is best and we are to trust him. I just need to remind myself, that this is not our permanent home. There is a heaven, a place free of death and sadness, a place of no more tears, a place of pure love. a place that someday we will call home. A place where we will be with our Savoir, the Lord Jesus Christ.

May 27

You Are Wonderfully Made

You will Soar on wings like Eagles... Just to remind you, my child,

You are courageous. You are beautiful. You are compassionate. You are loving. You are talented. You are kind and forgiving. You are caring. You are empathetic and encouraging to others. You are strong. You are so many wonderful things. Please remember this my dear one. Do not dwell on what you feel you lack. Your attention is not meant to linger on what you believe to be your shortcomings. Embrace who I have made you to be. You are my child. I have made you to be a light to others. To share my word and deliver my good news. I have made you to love and to be loved. We are on a journey together. When you feel down about yourself and blue. Ask me to pick you up and to remind you of all these amazing qualities I have placed in you. No fear...just go out in the world with your head held high and most importantly be yourself. Knowing always, you are LOVED.

> *But those who trust in the Lord shall renew their strength. They will soar on wings like eagles; they will run and not grow weary; they will walk and not grow faint...*
> (Isaiah 40:31, NIV)

> *The spirit of God has made me, and the breath of the Almighty gives me life.*
> (Job 33:4, ESV)

I praise you, for I am fearfully and wonderfully made: Your works are wonder-ful. I know that full well.
(Psalm 139:14, NIV)

Prayer: Father God, thank you for making me who I am. Thank you for all my trials and my blessings. Thank you for reminding me just how worthy and beautiful I am. I ask and pray today father that you also remind my family and friends just how beautiful and worthy they are and how much they are loved. In Jesus's name, I ask and pray AMEN.

To my Readers: Always remember; You are beautiful, and you are loved

May 28

All You Need

Good morning my child, have you ever been going throughout your day with a million thoughts in your mind. When suddenly, a stranger starts talking to you and they say something to you that at that very minute you needed to hear. Or it might be that you have said something that they needed to hear. As the conversion opens up, you will see that I am guiding it. I will send my children to each other to encourage and to give hope. When I use my children to comfort each other and to strengthen each other it is because I know that this is what their soul needs. During the conversation no matter how, short you can draw strength from each other. In that moment, all your doubts are pushed away, and you experience the true joy of my love. Keep sharing with others if you feel a push from me to speak with someone or pray for someone step out in faith. My children need each other. Just as air is needed to breathe, my children were meant to come together. Let my guiding light be a lamp to show the way. Experience completeness. How awesome my love for my children… My love is all you need.

> *How priceless is your unfailing love,*
> *O God!*
> (Psalm 36:7, NIV)

> *For everyone who has been born of*
> *God overcomes the world. And this is the*
> *victory that has overcome the world, our*
> *faith.*
> (1 John 5:4, ESV)

I have no greater joy than to hear that
my children are walking in truth.
(3 John 1:4, NIV)

Prayer: Father God thank you for the times I get to spend with other believers. Thank you for letting me also be a blessing to others. I love you, Jesus, keep directing my steps and the steps of my loved ones Thank you again, Father God, in Jesus's name I pray, amen.

May 29

Crossing the Mire

This is the day that I have made, rejoice and be glad in it…

Good morning my dear one whatever comes your way today be glad and full of joy. Thank me for everything. Even the situations that get under your skin. There are days when even my most obedient children will get caught up in the mire of this life. As complaining begins, soon that is all they can see. Take a step back try not to get stuck focusing on the little irritants of this day. When you feel yourself getting upset or irritated just remember to look up fix your eyes on me. Find my love and let it bring you back to the place of joy. There are so many beautiful little blessings that surround you every day. Focus on these. This takes practice.

It is easier to get stuck on the negative. It is like the thick muddy ground, as you take the first step you sink in. The second step, and then the third. With each step, you get a bit deeper. Soon it becomes like quicksand and before you know it, you're stuck. Let my love offer your way through. Be thankful. Focus on me and the positive in your life, and you will be light as a feather with no weight to allow you to get stuck. Don't sweat the small stuff.

Let's conquer this day together find the joy and be happy, and together we'll cross the mire

Do everything without complaining
or arguing, so that no one can criticize you.
(Philippians 2:14–15, NLT)

When the enemy comes in like a flood.
The Spirit of the Lord will lift up a stan-
dard against him.
(Isaiah 59:19, NIV)

This is the day the Lord hath made:
we will rejoice and be glad in it.
(Psalm 118:24, NKJV)

Prayer: Father God, help me today to focus on positive things and not to get stuck complaining about anything. I ask and pray in your name, to find the joy in today. When I start getting annoyed about small things help me to lift them up to you. Thank you, Father, for helping me to remember how blessed I am. Please help my friends and family stay joyful too. In Jesus's name, amen.

May 30

June

And look to the skies and you will find God's love pouring over you. When prayers go up, then blessings come down. Keep looking up. He is with you.

The Light of Hope

Never lose hope, my child. Be hopeful of things that have yet to come. Everything in this life takes time. Just as the sun takes time to rise, so does the light of my blessings that each day shines upon your life. Hope takes faith. Faith is the foundation of believing in something without evidence of seeing. If there is something that you have been asking to happen in your life, keep hoping and have faith that it will come. Even when you don't see anything in the situation moving. I am working on it. There are dreams I have placed in your heart and because they are from me, you can rest assured that they will be fulfilled. Any roadblocks or mountains in your way I will remove, but you need to ask me. Know that you are on the right path and most importantly my child never lose hope and keep the faith.

> *Now faith is confidence in what we hope for and the assurance about what we do not see.*
> (Hebrews 11:1, NIV)

> *But seek ye first the kingdom of God, and his righteousness; all these things shall be added unto you.*
> (Matthew 6:33, KJV)

> *Make me know your ways; O Lord; teach me your paths.*
> (Psalm 25:4, NIV)

"I have asked and hoped and prayed and suddenly the way opened up before me and there was a light shining upon the road. It was the path my Lord had called me to take. Trusting him I followed, and my reward became evident. It was everything I've hoped for, and more than I ever could dream." (April Yarber)

To my readers: Stay hopeful and he will show you the way.

Prayer: I pray today with you that the path to which he is leading you to walk upon will become crystal clear. I pray for any mountains to be removed and that your path will open before you, so that you may journey safely to his appointed position for you. In Jesus's name, I pray, amen.

June 1

Light on the Horizon

There is a light on the horizon, my child. Have you ever had an eagle-eyed view of the road ahead? Maybe you're standing on top of a hill and as you look down at the valley, you can see so many different paths that lead to the one destination you are trying to get to... A light shining upon your destination. it is so far across the land, yet you can see it. Now it is up to you, which direction you are going to take. As you look down you can see the shortest distance to travel. It looks like a straight shot to the ending place but look, again if you take that path you will see the landscape rise and fall. The way is very narrow. It is full of treacherous terrain, so if you attempt to go that way it may take just as long or longer to get there. Then you'll notice what may seem to be a longer route. The path is very prominent as it stands out more than the others. It has wider areas and that pass between the treachery and although it twists and bends, it runs along a stream at different points of its journey. This path is luscious and green. I want you to know, no matter which path you choose my child, I will get you there. I will stay with you and guide you through. I want you to trust me. Sometimes the journey is long, but if you take the long road you will have water to quench your thirst along the way. I don't want you to rush through your life so focused on the destination that you miss all the beautiful sights and blessings along the way. It is good to have goals my dear one but try not to rush through. Unless I call you to do so.

If you get confused ask me and I will guide your way. Just listen to my guidance and follow me.

You are special, my child.

If anyone serves me, he must follow me; and where I am, there my servant be also. If anyone serves me,
The father will honor him.
(John 12:26, ESV)

And he said to them, "Follow me, and I will make you fishers of men."
(Matthew 4:19, ESV)

Then Jesus said to his disciples, if anyone would come after me, let him deny himself and take up his cross and follow me.
(Matthew 16:24, ESV)

Prayer: Today I will pray a verse that is in my heart (Psalm 23, ESV)

A Psalm of David

The Lord is my shepherd; I shall not want. He makes me lie down in green pastures. He leads me beside still waters. He restores my soul. He leads me in paths of righteousness for his name's sake. Even though I walk through the valley of the shadow of death I will fear no evil, for you are with me; your rod and your staff they comfort me. You prepare a table before me in the presence of my enemies; you anoint my head with oil; my cup overflows. Surely goodness and mercy shall follow me all the days of my life, and I shall dwell in the house of the Lord forever.
In Jesus's name I pray, amen.

June 2

Joyful Rest

Sending my love to you today. As I have said before, I bring to you my love in many forms. The sun shining upon the world. Birds singing in the sky. Beautiful fragrant flowers in bloom. A joy within your soul that shows. I love the days when you have heard my sweet messages recharging you while you have slept. You awake and for no other apparent reason, you just feel good. You are happy and it is a happiness that carries through all day long. It is wonderful to see how joyful you are. It makes me proud to see you sharing this happiness with others. I want you to enjoy your life, my child. Take time to appreciate nature as it refreshes your soul. Go on a vacation from your daily routine. Concentrate on all the happy blessings that surround you. Knowing full well that I love you. I have created you and formed you. Walking with you each step of the way. Keep sharing your smiling soul with others. Today is a day of rest and relaxation, it is a day of appreciation. Now go outside with me and find the natural beauty of this life.

Come to me all who are weary and burdened and I will give you rest. Take my yoke upon you and learn from me, for I am gentle and humble in heart, and you will find rest for your souls.
(Matthew 11:28–29, NIV)

The Lord replied, "My presence will go with you and I will give you rest."
(Exodus 33:14, NIV)

Truly my soul finds rest in God; my salvation comes from him.
(Psalm 62:1, NIV)

So then, there remains a Sabbath rest for the people of God, for whoever has entered God's rest has also rested from his works as God did from his.
(Hebrews 4:9–10, ESV)

Prayer: Today, I thank you, Father, for the rest and happiness I receive. I pray for others to receive this joyful rest as well. In Jesus's loving name, I pray, AMEN.

June 3

Road to Success

Working toward goals is good. I have seen you moving forward as you work toward your goals. But try not to take on too many at once. If you try to do too many things, you make your days so busy that you have little time to really accomplish one over the other. So your pace is slowed. Try focusing on one at a time. Give yourself a break. There are dreams that I have placed in your heart some big and some small. When you are working toward a certain big goal you might find that I have made several of your other smaller goals' paths meet. Only then can you accomplish them together. However, if you must journey off the path of your primary goal, that I am calling you to fulfill, then you must stop as it may not be the time to venture there. Trust me, that I can get you there. Hope in all things, If you feel yourself being slowed by daily monotony and a barrage of routine, then rest or change your course for a moment. Do not let yourself lose sight of the original goal. Have patience with the day and patience with yourself. Allow yourself the joy of laughter and daily experiences with family and friends. All life is beautiful so enjoy it on your road to success.

Brothers and sisters, I do not consider myself yet to have taken hold of it. But one thing I do: forgetting what is behind and straining forward toward what is ahead, I press on toward the goal to win the prize for which God has called me heavenward in Christ Jesus.
(Philippians 3:14)

Thanks be to God, who gives us the victory through our Lord Jesus Christ.
(1 Corinthians 15:57, ESV)

The light shines in the darkness, and the darkness has not overcome it.
(John 1:5, ESV)

This book of the law shall not depart from your mouth, but you shall meditate on it day and night, so that you may be careful to do according to all that is written in it. For then you will make your way prosperous, and ten you will have good success.
(Joshua 1:8, ESV)

And God is able to make all grace abound to you, so having sufficiency in all things at all times, you may abound in every good work.
(2 Corinthians 9:8, ESV)

Prayer: Thank you God for helping me to achieve my goals, no matter how big or small. I am thankful for all the experiences along the way. I thank you also for family and friends and for the good medicine of laughter. I pray all good things in Jesus's name, amen.

June 4

Character Building

Good morning, my dear one. Have you ever felt helpless? Of course, you have. My child, that is part of your humanity. Maybe you have a child that you watch work so hard to accomplish their goals, and yet you feel helpless as you watch them overwork. I watch you with the same loving eyes. I want so much and desire what is best for you. I would love to step in and make things easier on you, but there are times I must not. I know that you must work through it yourself, as it builds your character. When you can see the fruit of completion approaching and deadlines are being met. Remember it was you who put in all the hard work to get here. I am always with you supporting you. I can recharge you when you're exhausted if you ask, but the work is all your own. Your labor is not in vain. You should feel proud of yourself. I know it takes time to get to the finish line. There are always trials and errors along the way. Just like the sower of the seed you are learning what works and what doesn't, without giving up. Keep pressing forward. If you need me, call on me and I will guide you, but I will not do the work for you. Just as a parent with a child, I must step back and let you figure it out on your own. Don't worry my child. You are doing well. Keep believing in yourself the way that I believe in you. You can do it...

I know this because you are mine.
But as for you, be strong and do not
give up, your work will be rewarded.
(1 Chronicles 15:7)

Commit to the Lord whatever you do,
and he will establish your plans.
(Proverbs 16:3)

May he give you the desire of your
heart and make all your plans succeed.
(Psalm 20:4)

The Lord will open to you his good
treasury, the heavens, to give the rain to
your land in its season and to bless all the
work of your hands. And you shall lend to
many nations, but you shall not borrow.
(Deuteronomy 28:12, ESV)

Prayer: Today, Father God, I just want to thank you for your love. For building my character and for giving me wisdom, showing me which way to walk and in what position I should be working. I pray for everyone that we may all find what it is that we should be doing and that we may all work hard. As we increase in joy and prosperity. In Jesus's name, I pray and send love, amen.

June 5

To Bless or Curse

When my children are not getting along it troubles me. I have meant for you all to encourage and build each other up. Life can be hard sometimes I know as this is a fallen world. There are people that can push your buttons so to speak. There are arguments that you are witnessing every day. You need to let this go. Pray to me about it when someone you love gets stuck in the selfishness of this life. You can't always reason with people. Some of my very own sweet children have been lost for quite some time and no matter how many times you try they have dug their heels into the stubborn selfish attitude of only "I matter no one else." They refuse to help themselves and blame everyone else for their problems. It can be exhausting. I want you to pray and continue to pray for the person or persons that seem to cause chaos everywhere they go. They have tongues like daggers, as the words can tear at your soul. The tongue is wicked and is one of the cruelest and insidious weapons when used in the wrong way. It can rip you to shreds, it has the power to curse or bless, but stay resilient. Shield yourself with my cloak of love and righteousness. Do not get pulled into any debate or argument that tears others down. When you speak, let all be said coming from a place of love and encouragement and of truth. But if you can see that nothing you say is getting through, then release them into my care and remove yourself from them. Do not let the poison of their judgments drag you down.

Continue to love yourself. Let the lies of anger bounce off you, as you are my child, I will protect you. You are precious my dear one, for you are fearfully and wonderfully made. You are mine and I love you.

For, whoever would love life and see good days must keep their tongue from evil and their lips from deceitful speech.
(1 Peter 3:10, NIV)

An unfriendly person pursues selfish ends and against all sound judgment starts quarrels. Fools find no pleasure in understanding but delight in airing their own opinions.
(Proverbs 18:1–2, NIV)

Be angry and do not sin; do not let the sun go down on your anger, and give no opportunity to the devil.
(Ephesians 4:26–27, ESV)

Prayer: Father God, please watch over my soul and the souls of my loved ones. Please help me to speak from a place of love and truth. Protect us from our enemies and cover us with your armor. Cloth us in your robe of righteousness. Thank you, Father, for this day and every day. In Jesus's name, I pray, amen.

June 6

Redirect the Response

The sun has come up again, time to start your day. Do everything you are called to do with joy.

Learn to appreciate this life your living. Do not get sucked in by your emotions, I know this is hard to do. All my children have feelings and their own personal responses to situations that arise but do not let the negative feelings run their own course. Emotions can be beautiful as you experience happiness, joy, love, compassion these are all good. Yet you know there are other emotions that can run away with your mind. Anger, sadness, regret... These are sometimes so subtle as they sneak up on your mind or other times, they can be explosive. When your emotions start to overtake you pray to me about the way you're feeling ask me to guide your thoughts and your mind. You are more than what you feel. Here is the thing you must understand, "feelings are fleeting." Emotions can run high and, in a moment, even out and at other times plunge us low. So if you have been stuck on an emotional roller coaster, then it is time for you to take control by asking for my help. Change negative emotions by changing your responses. Try doing something nice for someone else when you're feeling blue. Try forgiving someone that has wronged you when you're feeling angry. Give all situations to me. Let me be in control of your life and your emotions. Deal with your situations. Do not try to hide or numb your feelings but instead ask me to reappoint your emotions and redirect your responses. Remember you are my child. Look at how blessed you are. You are alive. Smile my child, it is a beautiful day.

A fool gives full vent to his spirit, but a wise man holds it back.
(Proverbs 29:11, ESV)

For the anger of a man does not produce the righteousness of God.
(James 1:20, ESV)

Good sense makes one slow to anger, and it is his glory to overlook an offense.
(Proverbs 19:11, ESV)

Set your minds on things that are above, not on things that are on earth.
(Colossians 3:2, ESV)

Prayer: For my reader-Ask God to take charge over your emotions ask him to redirect your responses to negative feelings. Ask him to guard your heart and your mind daily that you may experience the Joy and good feelings that are created by love and that are given to us freely by Him. In Jesus's name, we ask and pray, amen.

June 7

Walking in His Will

Here you are today standing in the light of my love. I am so proud of you. All that you are. All that you're accomplishing, and all that you are becoming. Sometimes it takes a while for my children to truly "get it" so to speak. I want you to be slow to anger, eager to learn, ready to give, and patient with yourself and others. I want you to never give up. I want to give you all the good desires of your heart. I want to give you more than this world…and I can. Just keep walking in my will. Keep moving forward, my child. Keep your head held high. Keep stepping up and over problems or situations that used to hold you back. You are stronger and now have no fear to stop you. Look at how far you have come and how much you have grown. No matter how old you are or what stage of life you feel you are at, it's never too late to learn to trust me and walk in my will. Let my light shine on you. Giving you a new strength and pushing you in a new direction. I can see what lies ahead. It is better than good. When you stay aligned with me as your walking in my will.

He has told you, O man, what is good;
and what does the Lord require of you but
to do justice, and to love kindness, and to
walk humbly with your God?
(Micah 6:8, ESV)

Therefore, if anyone is in Christ, he is
a new creation. The old had passed away;
behold the new has come.
(2 Corinthians 5:17, ESV)

You shall walk in all the way that the Lord your God has commanded you, that you may live, and that it may go well with you, and that you may live long in the land that you possess.
(Deuteronomy 5:33, ESV)

Prayer: Thank you, Father God, for the guidance and glory. I ask and pray to stay in your will and enjoy the peace of love and joy it brings me. I pray all my family and friends find this opportunity as well. I pray your love always finds us when we are lost and brings us back to your path. I pray we always find joy and happiness along the way. In Jesus's name, I pray, amen

June 8

Gracious and Kind

Good day my darling. There are times you will see my love showering you from the actions of others. How beautiful it is when my children offer help to each other. These are the times you can truly see my grace. If you receive kindness from a stranger, someone who although they may not know you personally are ready to help and offer a hand. These times and situations are sweeter still. They carry a fragrance of love from one to another, that truly encompasses the beauty of life and of fellowship. Have you ever had someone do something so graciously kind for you and yet they did not even know you? They do it simply because this is how I've called them to live. Just as yourself. Be good to each other. My heart sings. I have children all over this world who are doing what I've called them to do. They go out—share my good news and do my good works. I have also called you to live just this way. Be courageous, loving and kind, but also be humble. As you are an example to others, let them see me in you. Let your light shine before others, being gracious and kind. As in these moments, you can see truly that you, my child, are blessed, and a blessing.

> On one occasion an expert in the law stood up to test Jesus. "Teacher," he asked, "What must I do to inherit eternal life?" "What is written in the law?" he replied. "How do you read it?"
>
> He answered, "Love your Lord God with all your heart and with all your soul and with all your strength and with all

your mind; and, "Love your neighbor as yourself."

"You have answered correctly," Jesus replied. "Do this and you will live."
(Luke 10:25–28, NIV)

And in the same way, let your light shine before others, that they may see your good deeds and glorify your Father in heaven.
(Matthew 5:16, ESV)

Prayer: I want to take the time today Lord, to thank you for the kindness that _____ has shown me.

I pray to always be a blessing to others and be thankful for the help that comes in my time of need. Thank you, Father, for all your children. Help us always to be loving to each other. In Jesus's name, I pray, amen.

To my reader, read in the Bible, the parable of "The Good Samaritan."

No act of kindness should go unnoticed by the receiver.

No, matter how big or small the gesture is.

June 9

And It Is Called Faith

Encourage the experience of those around you. Some of my children are so very vulnerable and sensitive. They might even be struggling with their own thoughts and feelings about me. They are torn as they say they know I exist, but they haven't truly opened themselves up to the beauty of my Presence that lives within. Let them know it is okay to have such feelings or thoughts, and that questions about me are good. The more they learn to communicate with me and learn about who I am. The more they can see my work in their lives. Let them know I am not like the television remote. Something to give up on if they do not like the answers I give, at the moment, or they do not see instant gratification they should not just cast hope aside. I know they feel tempted to just change the channel and redirect their thoughts to something else to try and get the result that they want. Tell them my ways are higher them theirs. I know the outcomes and I am doing what is best for them, even if they cannot see it just now. If they change the channel now, they may be delaying themselves an answer to a prayer. I work best when my children put their whole trust in me. This is such a hard thing to do, as we are trained to only believe in things, we can see and touch. If you are having doubts, I want you to share that with me also. Watch me work, ask me to give you spiritual eyes and awareness. I can do this for you. Let me in. Above all else, you must learn to love me with your whole heart and trust me. It's a process for all of my children, as you are all at different levels of faith. Some do not even have an ounce of faith. For these children, I have called you to simply plant the seed of my love and leave the rest to me. Do not worry, we will get there together. Keep encouraging each other... I exist and I love you.

> *And without faith it is impossible to please him. For whoever would draw near to God must believe that he exists and that he rewards those who seek him.*
> (Hebrews 11:6, ESV)

> *He said to them, "Because of your little faith. For truly, I say to you, if you have faith like a grain of mustard seed, you will say to this mountain, move 'Move from here to there, 'and it will move, and nothing will be impossible for you."*
> (Matthew 17:20, ESV)

> *You will seek me and find me, when you seek me with your whole heart.*
> (Jeremiah 29:13, ESV)

> *Jesus said to him, "Have you believed because you have seen me? Blessed are those who have not seen and yet have believed."*
> (John 20:29, ESV)

Prayer: I pray for everyone that they would come to know you as much or even more than I have. Open the eyes of their heart Lord and grow us in our faith. In Jesus's name, I pray and thank you for the victory, amen.

June 10

Calm and Peace

I want to be your best friend. Speak to me about everything or maybe just nothing at all. Some days are so peaceful. No worries to speak of, just a calm peaceful day. You have done well letting me take the burden of worry off your mind. You go out and complete your daily chores and small to do list with ease. Enjoying the moments of rest that I give. I see your bright brilliant smile. The daily stresses of life cannot subdue you. As this day, you give it all to me. Just as your body requires sleep to truly recharge, so does your mind. You are learning. You do well as you spend more and more time with me. You can feel rested knowing that the outcome of situations you have brought to me, are under my control. I have heard your prayers. It is good that you feel open enough to be completely honest with me about everything you've been going through. As you are learning to trust me with your most intimate situations. I am pleased. The calmness of today is just another gift from me to you. Just enjoy and feel peace, my child...

I have told you these things, so in me you may have peace. In this world you will have trouble. But take heart! I have overcome the world.
(John 16:33, NIV)

Now may the Lord of peace himself give you peace at all times and in every way. The Lord be with all of you.
(Thessalonians 3:16, NIV)

The Lord bless you and keep you; the Lord make his face shine upon you and be gracious to you; the Lord turn his face toward you and give you peace.
(Numbers 6:24–26, NIV)

Prayer: Lord God my Father thank you for always being there for me, for taking all my worries and giving me rest and peace. I am so thankful to you Lord. I am praying for everyone I come in contact today that they get to experience the true rest in your peace. In Jesus's loving name I pray, amen.

June 11

No Regrets

Good Morning my child. There are people in your life that are, need I say difficult. They just have so much regret and feel so defeated. They complain constantly about past mistakes or situations. They are so stuck on what was and past situations that they are missing the true beauty of their lives today. Maybe their emphasis is on money and because they have so little, they are angry. Too much attention given to anything in your lives will take your attention off of me. Do not let things like money, wealth or possessions or past mistakes rule in your heart as they will become idols. They will fall short every time. In this fallen world all my children are slaves to paying bills and trying to attain enough money to sustain their lives but do not let this become a primary focus. Do not get me wrong it is good to work. It is good to strive for better, but during times when you feel like you can't keep up. Talk to me, trust me I will make a way. Enjoy the simpler things today. Keep pressing forward. Give the difficult ones to me. I can soften their hearts just continue to pray. Pray that I relieve them of their guilt and regrets, just as I can do for you. Also, if you have regrets still lingering in your life. Let it go, you must also give them all to me. Forgive yourself. No one is perfect. No not one is without sin. I am your Savior. My grace is sufficient for you...

That is why, for Christ's sake I delight in weaknesses. In insults, in hardships, in persecutions, in difficulties. For when I am weak, then I am strong.
(2 Corinthians 12:10, NIV)

> *But he said to me, "My grace is sufficient for you, for my power is made perfect in weakness. Therefore I will boast all the more gladly of my weakness, so that the power of Christ may rest upon me."*
> (2 Corinthians 12:9, ESV)

> *Do not be overcome by evil, but overcome evil with good.*
> (Romans 12:21, ESV)

Prayer: Father God, I pray today that you keep me far from the regrets of my past that you allow me to forgive myself and move forward. I pray your love fills up my heart and the hearts of those around me. In Jesus's name, I pray, amen.

June 12

Bigger Than the Journey

I am leading you. You have asked this of me, and I am leading. Opening the way before you, but only do you perceive it? I have sent others to you that may have similar life paths or situations that they are going through right now. You can see the light of hope and promise shining down on their lives. This is my way of encouraging you to keep you going. Do not stop or doubt it for a minute. I know the journey seems long and arduous, but I am bigger than the journey. I am bigger than any situation of life that seems to get in your way. No task is too big or small. I can move mountains—I can part the seas. Anything that stands in your way of accomplishing what I have called you to do I can conquer. Just as I have conquered death. I can do these things for you. All you are required to do is pray. Know and accept that I am the Savior of your life. I am listening and I am leading. Stay faithful and let my wisdom guide you. Fear will not overtake you because you are my child, you are trusting me. One step at a time, One day at a time. Breathe my child it is okay we are on our way together to something good.

For he commands his angels concerning you to guard you in all your ways.
(Psalm 91:11, NIV)

Let us hold fast the confession of our hope without wavering, for he who promised is faithful.
(Hebrews 10:23, ESV)

But, as it is written, "What no eye has seen, nor ear has heard, nor the heart of a man imagined, what God has prepared for those who love him."
(1 Chronicles 2:9, ESV)

And we know for those who love God all things work together for good, for those who are called according to his purpose.
(Romans 8:28, ESV)

Prayer: Father God, thank you for walking with me on this journey. Thank you for leading and for instilling me with bravery and the will not to give up. I pray for all today please stay close to us Lord and let your will done in our lives. In Jesus's loving name, I pray, amen.

June 13

Showing Kindness

Be the light in someone else's world. Today reach out and show support to those around you. Try not to get stuck in your own situations and problems. All my children in this world will have struggles. I want you to reach out, support each other to encourage and give hope. It is very important to do this. Do not just say you love one another but truly show it. Honor me by being kind and showing empathy. I am pleased when my children come out of their comfort zones, just to help someone else along. No one truly wants to be alone, so be there for those that are in need. Show them love and kindness. This is what I've called you to do. You love because I first loved you. Now go out in this day and do a job well done. Sharing my Love, extending a hand, and showing much kindness.

> *And do not forget to do good and to share with others, for such sacrifices God is pleased.*
> (Hebrews 13:16, NIV)

> *She opens her arms to the poor and extends her hand to the needy.*
> (Proverbs 31:20, NIV)

> *Be kind to one another, tenderhearted, forgiving one another, as God in Christ forgave you.*
> (Ephesians 4:32, ESV)

She opens her mouth with wisdom,
and the teaching of kindness on her tongue.
(Proverbs 31:26, ESV)

Give, and it will be given to you.
A good measure, pressed down, shaken
together running over, will be poured into
your lap. For with the measure you use, it
will be measured to you.
(Luke 6:38, NIV)

Prayer: Guide me today, Lord. Help me to be helpful to someone in need. Let me see past my own problems and issues. Help me to be a light in the darkness. In Jesus's loving name, I pray, amen.

June 14

Brave and Strong

Sometimes in life, I will call you to be brave. Other times I will call you to be strong. These are not the same thing. Being brave accompanies a beginning of something. To step out in faith and be brave is usually the taking of the first step toward a goal or to start something new in your life. it is part of an action needed to begin. To be strong is a reaction. It is a response to a circumstance or situation that is already in motion. (Sometimes in which you have no control.) I will ask you to be brave enough and begin a new journey with me. I will ask you to be strong enough and not give up on the journey. I need you to trust me during it all. Have faith in this "I know what is best, and if I'm leading and guiding you, then whatever happens along the way just know—I want what is best for you. I know what is best for you, and I am leading you to what is best for you." I am in control even on the days when you are not. When you are weak, I will be your strength. When you are lost in the darkness, I will light the way. When you are afraid, I will be your courage. Whatever you're lacking... I will be that for you. because I love you and you are my child. I will get you there to the place I've destined you to be. I will because I AM.

God said to Moses, "I AM THAT I AM: and he said, thus shalt thou say unto the children of Israel, I AM hath sent me unto you."
(Exodus 3:14, KJV)

Have I not commanded you? Be strong and courageous. Do not be afraid; do not be

discouraged, for the Lord your God will be
with you wherever you go.
    (Joshua 1:19, NIV)

But Jesus beheld them, and said unto
them, with men this is impossible; but with
God all things are possible.
    (Matthew 19:26, NIV)

Be strong and courageous. Do not fear
or be in dread of them, for it is the Lord
your God who goes with you. He will not
leave you or forsake you.
    (Deuteronomy 31:6, ESV)

Prayer: Father God Thank you for this day, I pray today that you keep guiding me and show me the times when you want me to be brave. Help me through the times I need to be strong. I pray you to surround me today with your protection and love. I also pray this for all my family and friends. In Jesus's loving name, amen.

June 15

Carpe Diem

Search your soul today my child. I am calling you to spend time with me. Slow down, life is a journey to be enjoyed and experienced at its fullest. This includes ups and downs. Sometimes extreme highs and lows, and even the peaks and valleys in between. You can find me in it all. Every second can be given to me to work out. All of it. This life is not a race to speed through by-passing all the beauty or the hardships as you are rushing to get to the finish line. Speeding so fast, you are running to get to the end. In fact, when the journey of this life is almost over, many of my children will ask me for more time. Please find joy in the experience. Surround yourself with loved ones. Be kind to everyone. Find the beauty where none is evident. Keep hope alive in your heart. Spend time with me in prayer. And as it is said in Latin, "Carpe Diem my child... Carpe diem."

Rejoice always, pray without ceasing,
give thanks in all circumstances; for this is
the will of God in Jesus Christ for you.
(1 Thessalonians 5:16–18, ESV)

You make known to me the path of life;
in your presence there is fullness and joy; at
your right hand are pleasures forevermore.
(Psalm 16:11, ESV)

There is nothing better for a person
than that he should eat drink and find
enjoyment in his toil. This also, I saw, is
from the hand of God.

(Ecclesiastes 11:9, ESV)

Prayer: Father God, help me to always seize the day. To walk in your will—to work hard—and give my all in the present moments of my life. To give the worry of tomorrow to you so that I may truly enjoy this day. Please help me and all my family and friends slow down, so that we may find the beauty in each and every day no matter what the circumstance Lord. I thank you for this day and for the guidance your Spirit gives, in Jesus's name, I ask and pray for eyes to always see the good, AMEN.

CARPE DIEM: "Seize the Day"
A Latin phrase meaning "Seize the Day"
It summarizes living life in the present moment and not worrying about the future. The same way the Lord tells us not to worry about tomorrow. We can truly experience joy within today if we are aware of the present and not caught up in thoughts of yesterday or tomorrow. So Seize the day with purpose and vigor. And enjoy.

June 16

Reap and Sow

To reap what you sow, what does this mean to you, my child? It is like saying you get what you give. Maybe not today or in this moment but somewhere down the line. When it is my will, you will see what kind of fruit your life will bear. If you sow kindness and grace and joy, your fruit will be good. If you have sown mostly hate or anger or bitterness. Then your seeds cannot produce the good fruit I have intended for your life, because you have not been living and walking in my words. You have not believed that it is better to be kind and forgiving or to show self-control. Do not lose hope it is never too late to change what kind of good comes out of your life. If you are reading this, it means you are still alive and able to let me change your heart. Ask me and I will help you. I know no-one is perfect. Some of my most obedient children have days when they have thought or said or have done something cruel or hurtful to someone else even themselves. Something that in a moment they wish they could take back. Know that the words you say or the actions you display cannot be erased but can be forgiven. Ask me to forgive you. We can produce good fruit together… Never lose hope, always share my good news, be brave and bold when speaking of me, plant my good seeds. Watch me work in your life and the lives of others around you.

THE GOLDEN RULE
Do to others whatever you would like them to do to you. This is the essence of all that is taught in the law and the prophets.
(Matthew 7:12, NLT)

THE TREE AND ITS FRUIT

Beware of false prophets who come in disguise as harmless sheep but are really vicious wolves. You can identify them by their fruit that is, by the way they act. Can you pick grapes from thorn bushes, or figs from thistles? A good tree produces good fruit, a bad tree produces bad fruit. A good tree can't produce bad fruit, and a bad tree can't produce good fruit. So, every tree that does not produce good fruit is chopped down and thrown into the fire. Yes, just as you can identify a tree by its fruit, so can you identify people by their actions.
(Matthew 7:15–20, NLT)

His Lord said unto him, Well done, thou good and faithful servant; thou hast been faithful over a few things, I will make thee ruler over many things; enter thou into the joy of thy Lord.
(Matthew 25:21, KJV)

Prayer: Father God, let me always be mindful of what I think, say and do. Keep me from hurting others with my actions and words. Keep my intentions pure and help me show love and kindness when I speak. I pray to you, Lord, asking that I do your will and that I live in a way that pleases you. I thank you, Father God, for your grace in my life and for your forgiveness when I fall short. I thank you for your teaching. In Jesus's name, I pray, amen.

June 17

Faithful in Affliction

Focus on me. Keep your eyes fixed on things above. At some point in your life my child you or someone you know may experience pain, injury and/or illness. All with different levels of anguish. I do not like this, although I may allow it. Sometimes it is meant for me to draw you closer. As you cry out to me for relief. Other times it is meant for you to go through, so, you can relate to others and learn. This is how you build compassion and empathy in your life. I did not give you the calamity of sickness or pain willingly, it was brought about by sin. There is a lesson to be learned in the affliction. Keep up your faith, stand confident in the current affliction. Remain faithful to me. As I am 'The Great Physician' and I can heal. I can bring you through. Stand firm on your faith and do not doubt me for one moment, my child. I love you, just remain faithful in affliction.

Heal me, O Lord, and I will be healed; save me and I will be saved, for you are the one I praise.
(Jeremiah 17:14, NIV)

"But I will restore your health and heal your wounds," declares the Lord.
(Jeremiah 30:17, NIV)
He heals the brokenhearted and binds up their wounds.
(Psalm 147:3, ESV)

You restored me to health and let me live. Surely it was for my benefit that I have

suffered such anguish. In your love you kept
me from the pit of destruction; You have put
all my sins behind your back.
(Isaiah 38:16, NIV)

Prayer: Father God, thank you for the victory of defeating my pain and the pain of my loved ones. Thank you for giving to us good health, and for healing the hurt of a broken heart. I ask to learn whatever lesson you want me to learn during my times of sickness, injury, and heartbreak. Heal us and restore us, my Lord. Thank you for all your love. In Jesus's name, I pray AMEN.

June 18

The Armor of God

All the lessons you have learned over the course of your life have been stored up in your mind. As you go through more and more situations. You can recall what has worked and what reactions or responses did not. The key here is to never give up. To try and try without ceasing, as this pleases me. Just as I call you to pray and pray without ceasing. As this communication between us keeps you strong. You have a fight in your soul. Keep fighting the good fight. As you refuse to let the daunting tasks of this day win the battle. You know I am with you and I can save. As you call on me, we together will overcome the shadows of fear of doubt and hopelessness. You are a soldier of faith, covered with my whole armor. At your waist the belt of truth. The breastplate of righteousness. Your feet fitted with readiness. You have your shield of faith, your helmet of salvation and your sword of the Spirit. Stand firm my child. Recall the good lessons you've learned, try not to repeat past mistakes. Keep marching forward and enjoying everything along the way. Keep steadfast in your faith, putting on each day, the whole armor of God.

Finally, be strong in the Lord and in his mighty power. Put on the whole armor of God, so that you can take a stand against the devil's schemes. For our struggle is not against flesh and blood, but against the rulers, against the authorities, against the powers of this dark world and against the spiritual forces of evil in the heavenly realms.
(Ephesians 6:10–12, NIV)

Now it is God who makes both us and you stand firm in Christ. He anointed us.
(2 Corinthians 1:21, NIV)

For the promise to Abraham and his offspring that he would be the heir of the world did not come through the law but through the righteousness of faith.
(Romans 4:13, ESV)

Prayer: Father God, I ask you to cover me today with your whole armor. Help me go through this day with love and joy in my heart. I ask you to protect all my loved ones and help us to appreciate all that you do for us. Thank you for this day Lord. I pray in Jesus's name, amen.

June 19

See the Bigger Picture

It takes an incredible amount of bravery to take the first step or to voice an opinion when you see something is wrong. I will direct your steps and your words. All you must do is ask and take that initial first step to start the conversation. I will do the rest. Sometimes I will use you to get certain points across to someone who may have a narrow point of view. I will call you at the exact moment that they may be more open to the conversation, and maybe more willing to accept that things could be handled with a better approach. I will use you to widen their view of the situation. It may make them stop and think about how they have been handling things and pursue them in a different more positive way. Perhaps it is you who has a narrow view of something, and I have sent someone else to share their ideas or start the conversation to get you to see the bigger picture. Learn also to listen. I will always help my children by directing them to do the right thing. Keep your eyes, ears and mind open. Do not be afraid to speak up, listen or move forward when I have called you to do so. Always have empathy for others, as you have not walked in their shoes, but correct them with kindness. This is my way and it is good. My dear brave child, I am happy, keep seeing the bigger picture.

Bearing with one another and, if one has a complaint against another, forgiving each other; as the Lord has forgiven you, so must you also forgive.
(Colossians 3:13, ESV)

Correcting his opponents with gentleness. God may perhaps grant them repentance leading to a knowledge of truth.
(2 Timothy 2:25, ESV)

So whatever you wish that others would do to you, do also for them, for this is the law and the prophets.
(Matthew 7:12, ESV)

And they devoted themselves to the apostles' teaching and the fellowship, to the breaking of bread and the prayers.
(Acts 2:42, ESV)

Prayer: Thank you, Father God, for leading my words and for giving me the strength to stand up for myself and others. I pray to recognize when I am to deliver and when I am to receive correction. I pray for all my family and friends as well. In Jesus's loving name, I pray, amen.

June 20

Teachable Spirit

Life is a wonderful journey. I want you my child to have a teachable spirit. Always be willing to listen and learn. Do not become narrow-minded or have a skewed view of things. Open your mind and your heart. Take each day as it comes with all its ups and downs be happy in the moments. Enjoy the small little graces of life, as well as celebrating the big accomplishments along the way. Invite me into all the areas of your life. Do not compartmentalize me to just a few areas in which you need help, but invite me in, to also celebrate with you ALL the wonderful moments of your life. For all the moments together makeup who you are today. Walk through this day with your head held high, eyes up, fixed on me. And I will keep feeding your teachable spirit with my good lessons and with my love.

Let my teaching fall like rain and my words descend like dew, like showers on new grass, like abundant rain on tender plants.
(Deuteronomy 32:2, NIV)

If anyone lacks wisdom, you should ask God, who gives generously without finding fault, and it will be given to you.
(James 1:5, NIV)

I will instruct you and teach you in the way you should go; I will counsel you with my eye upon you.
(Psalm 32:8, ESV)

All scripture is breathed out by God and profitable for teaching, for reproof, for correction, and for training in righteousness, that the man of God may be competent, equipped for every good work.
(2 Timothy 3:16–17, ESV)

Prayer: Father God please keep my spirit teachable. Keep me open to learning and correction when necessary. When you must correct me please correct me with kindness. Teach me to walk in your will and open your exceptional way before me. I pray to always be bold enough to speak of you and share your good news. In Jesus's loving name, I pray, amen.

June 21

Small Things

Sail through this day feeling blessed. Enjoy the small things today. In this life, my children will accomplish much, but what truly is missed by many is the small things. What brings joy to you? What warms your heart and brings joyful tears to your eyes? Is it compassion from a stranger? Kindness from a friend, or perhaps it is watching your loved ones enjoying themselves. These tiny treasures are all made up of the one thing I want you to experience most in this life, LOVE. Love in all the moments. Some of your biggest joys will come from the smallest things in life. Cherish the moments. Hold fast to the tender experiences as they make your soul rich. It is okay to want more in life, but do not make money or power become more important than the kindness and joy only love for others can fulfill. Remember it is good to LOVE. Love others as I love you. With your heart wide open, your soul will rejoice. It will rejoice over and over, enjoying the small things

We love because he first loved us.
(1 John 4:19, NIV)

Beloved, let us love one another, for love is from God, and whoever loves has been born of God knows God. Anyone who does not love does not know God because God is love.
(1 John 4:7–8, ESV)

And now these three remain: faith, hope, and love. But the greatest of these is love.

(1 Corinthians 13:13, NIV)

Thanks be to God for his inexpressible gift!

(2 Corinthians 9:15, ESV)

Prayer: Heavenly Father, thank you for the love in my life and love in my heart, that I can share with others. I pray to continually be a blessing to others and to be able to show love the way you love. I pray for all my family and friends and people I encounter today please let them feel the deepest love in their souls and joy in their hearts as we find blessing in even the small things. In Jesus's name, I pray, amen.

June 22

Beacon of Light

Escape with me today into the wonderful life created for you. See The examples of fellow Christians and how they handle the bulk of the day. When their eyes are fixed on me, I am bigger than any stumbling blocks or daily problems. You can tell when others are true followers of me by how they handle the situations in their lives. They do it with a thankfulness in their hearts. People will ask what their secret is, how do they remain so happy? The answer, "It is because they have Jesus in their lives." Just as you have me also. You can smile when there is nothing on the surface to smile about and have joy when going through trials of adversity. My children are lights that shine brightly with happiness in this darkened world. Drawing others like beacons, this is the kind of example I want you to be. Hopeful always, knowing and believing that I am with you, and full of the joy and love that others can see, no matter what the day brings. You are my child and when you practice living this way, then you are true to your soul and all that I have created you to be. Good job my child.

See what great love the Father has lavished on us, that we should be called the children of God!

And that is what we are! The reason the world does not know us is that it did not know him.

(1 John 3:1, NIV)

You, dear children, are from God and have overcome them, because the one who is in you is greater than the one who is in the

world. They are from the world and there-
fore speak from the viewpoint of the world,
and the world listens to them. We are from
God and whoever knows God listens to us;
but whoever is not from God does not listen
to us. This is how we recognize the spirit of
truth and the spirit of falsehood.
(1 John 4:4–6, NIV)

With joy, you will draw from the wells
of salvation.
(Isaiah 12:3, NIV)

Prayer: Thank you, Father God, for your joy inside my heart. May I always remember even during troubled times that I am a child of God. I can remain happy in knowing that you are always with me. I pray to live correctly in the way you have called me to live. When I fall, short Lord, please forgive me and direct my steps back to you kindly. Help all your children to be the beacons of light you have created us to be, thank you always for your love, in Jesus's name, I pray, AMEN.

June 23

No More Whys

Good morning little child so full of life and joy. When you step away from the things of this world and come to me you are made new. Opening your eyes to see as if for the first time. Everything will look different to you, and you will have an easier understanding of the situations in life. The circumstances you do not understand will not make you as tangled, getting wrapped up in the question as to why," things are happening?" Yet you will gain so much more peace and be able to let go of the whys and navigate through your life feeling more at ease. You in the past may have tried to force a situation to reveal your outcome or you have tried to make the outcome go in a way that it just would not go. Leaving you feeling a sense of disappointment or sadness. Release these feelings to me. Things will happen if you free up your mind from pointless worries, giving you more time to enjoy the days of your life. Knowing that I am in charge, so you do not have to force your life to go a certain way. When you trust me, I will guide you and direct your steps. Even though not all your journey is easy, as this is life, it will be more comfortable, and you can have peace in your soul knowing that I work all things together for good. I am with you always. Oh, glorious days.

Don't worry about anything; instead, pray about everything. Tell God what you need, and thank him for all he has done. Then you will experience God's peace, which exceeds anything we can understand. His peace will guard our hearts and minds as you live in Christ.

(Philippians 4:6–7, NLT)

And do not be conformed to this world, but be transformed by the renewing of your mind, so that you may prove what the will of God is, that is good and acceptable and perfect.
(Romans 12:2, NIV)

Those with a steadfast mind you keep in peace, because they trust in you. Trust in the Lord forever, for in the Lord God you have an everlasting rock.
(Isaiah 26:3–4, NIV)

Prayer: Thank you, God, for the victory of overcoming worries. I trust in you all the days of my life I pray for all my family and friends Lord that you keep them from getting caught up in this world and that they may also know you are greater than the world and more powerful than any problem that lingers or question that cannot be answered. I pray we always remember that you, our loving Father is always in control…in Jesus's name AMEN.

June 24

Love and Support

In this world, in every moment always spend time with me. I am speaking to you daily. Trust me enough to bring everything to me. We can walk confidently through this day. Your heart is so big and that pleases me. It is better to give than to receive. I love the way you give even those times when you have little. That is telling of how much you trust that I am with you and will meet all your needs. When you see someone in need it's not always monetary support that is needed, sometimes my children feel emotionally bankrupt. Show these children the support of love. Pray with them. Remind them that I can be their strength. This can also help you when you are feeling down. You can bring yourself up by doing something nice for someone else. This is who I've called you to be. Now go out and enjoy this day in confidence.

Each of you should give what you have decided in your heart to give, not reluctantly or under compulsion, for God loves a cheerful giver.
(2 Corinthians 9:7, NIV)

A generous person will prosper; whoever refreshes others will be refreshed.
(Proverbs 11:25, NIV)

And God is able to bless you abundantly. So that in all things at all times, having all that you need, you will abound in every good work.
(2 Corinthians 9:8, NIV)

Give, and it will be given to you. Good measure, pressed down, shaken together, running over, will be put in your lap. For with the measure you use it will be measured back to you.
(Luke 6:38, ESV)

Prayer: Father God, thank you for the abundant blessings I receive from you. Please help me to always be a cheerful giver and help me not complain when I am called to help. I pray for everyone that doesn't have enough that you would send help to them and let them know it is from you...in Jesus's loving name, I pray for all those less fortunate, AMEN.

June 25

Lover of My Soul

Finding a way in the darkness. There are times when we are going through lives sure of our destination, and then the enemy creeps in placing fear and doubts within our minds. These are the times we need to remain strong and pray to the Lord for guidance and protection. The enemy does not want you to succeed or to be happy in this life. The more unsure and fuller of fear and worry you are, the more time and effort it takes to get through the day. Thus, your attention is turned to the fears rather than the Lord. Do not let the enemy have his way. Guard your hearts and especially your minds. Pray to the Lord Jesus for protection and guidance. Give your worries to him. Let him lead you, know that God can handle all of it, nothing is too big for him. Today I give my worries to Jesus and cast my cares upon him. He is my savior. My heavenly Father, the lover of my soul and yours too.

(So I had one of those days today. I almost gave up on this devotional. God sent someone to encourage me to keep going. Ultimately, I didn't let fear and doubt stop me but went about my writing another way, just for today. A reminder we all have struggles in this life, but we know that during these times we are not alone, and most importantly, *never* give up on what you feel God has placed in your heart.)

This is the confidence we have in approaching God: that if we ask anything according to his will. He hears us. And if we know he hears us-whatever we ask-we know that we have what we asked of him.
(1 John 5:14–15, NIV)

You will pray to him, and he will hear you, and fulfill your vows.
(Job 22:27, NIV)

Do not conform to the pattern of this world, but be transformed by the renewing of your mind. Then you will be able to test and approve of what God's will is, his good, pleasing and perfect will.
(Romans 12:2, NIV)

Prayer: Father God, thank you for reminding me of who I am. Sending encouragement just when needed, also please give me the strength to accomplish what you are leading me to do. I pray for all today that you just guide our hearts and our minds. In Jesus's name, amen.

June 26

Thankful Hearts

The Lord is my shepherd I shall not want. Good morning dear one. The Lord God will meet all your needs when you place your life in his hands. We must live the way he has called us to live. When you put him first and bring him your prayers, you give power and charge to him over your life. It is important to trust him. Love him with your whole heart. Do not let the wants of worldly desires become your primary focus, but instead be thankful for all that you have. Let all the small joys of life bubble up into one, soon you will have a river of joy flowing strong. You can smile and feel secure knowing that Jesus loves you.

The Lord is my shepherd I shall not want. He maketh me lie down in green pastures; He leadeth me beside still waters. He restoreth my soul: he leadeth me in the paths of righteousness for his name's sake.

Yea though I walk through the valley of death, I will fear no evil: for thou art with me; thy rod and staff they comfort me. Thou preparest a table before me in the presence of mine enemies: thou anointest my head with oil; my cup runneth over. Surely goodness and mercy shall follow me all the days of my life: and I will dwell in the house of the Lord forever.

(Psalm 23:1–6, KJV)

*The Lord is my light and my salvation;
whom shall I fear? The Lord is the strength
of my life; of whom shall I be afraid?*
(Psalm 27, KJV)

*The Lord is my strength and my
shield; my heart trusted in him, and I am
helped: therefore my heart greatly rejoiceth:
and with my song I will praise him.*
(Psalm 28:7, KJV)

Prayer: Father God, it is in the moments of every day I thank you. I love you, Lord, with my whole heart. In Jesus's name, I pray, please give me strength to soldier on this good journey. And help others who also need encouragement to keep going be filled with your perseverance. Amen.

To My Reader: tomorrow I will go back to writing the way the Lord intended. I pray you still find comfort in this today.

June 27

Bringing Hope

Wait in this moment with me. Wait for my answer, do not rush ahead of yourself eagerly wanting the benefit without all the work. You need to be of strong and good courage taking up all the tasks of the days and night. Doing everything with purpose and confidence. Find the good purpose I give, for its the purpose of bringing hope to this world. Showing the hope and that exists in me. Share with others the love I have placed in you. Tell others that when you come to me and accept me into your hearts and into your lives, recognizing me, as your Lord and Savior I will bring truth, Salvation, and love. Share with them, encourage them to read my word. Pick up their Bibles and reflect on my words, just as you should also do. Aligning yourself with my will. There are times you feel confused and lost by your own emotions. You can get wrapped up so quickly. Do not get sucked into the snare, but rather fellowship with others and strengthen yourselves with my presence. Let your light shine today, push the clouds of doubt away and let my light shine on you. We will get to the place of joy once again, to that wonderful place, where hope exists. Always knowing and never forgetting, I am the same today, yesterday and always, as I am love. Eyes up, hearts open, my child and don't to put your faith forward and shine with the light of hope.

As for you, the anointing which you have received from Him abides in you, and you have no need for anyone to teach you: but His anointing teaches you about everything, and is true and is no lie, and just as it taught you. You abide in Him.
(1 John 2:27)

Guard, through the Holy Spirit who dwells in us, the treasure which has been entrusted to you.
(2 Timothy 1:14)

I pray that the eyes of your heart may be enlightened in order that you may know the hope to which he has called you, the riches of his glorious inheritance in his holy people.
(Ephesians 1:18)

Prayer: Father God, please guide my heart to show me what is good and right in your sight. Let me do your will without doubts and direct my steps. I pray for everyone today that we all may know your truths and your will for our lives. That we would grow strong in faith and stand confident in the light of hope. I thank you, Loving Father. In Jesus's name, I pray, amen.

June 28

Finding Joy

My child, it is now, that I have called you to trust and lean on me. Let me guide your spirit. Do not take this day as another problem to get through, instead thank me for this day wholeheartedly, so that you may find your joy. I know that you have a tender heart and feel compelled to help everyone. It is just not possible, as I am the only one who can accomplish this. There is something that you can do, however... You can pray to me about all situations, worries, and problems in your life and the lives of those around you. Bring them to me and leave them at my feet. As you know that my way of working situations out is a perfect way, and I will work out the ones concerning you and your loved ones in ways of my good design. I will help you and have heard your prayers, as you have interceded on their behalves. Sometimes you may not agree with the answer that I've designed, but remember my child, I know best. Keep the joy in your heart and your love for others evident. As we walk in this day that I have created. We will be glad in it and find joy once again.

I urge then, first of all, that petitions, prayers intercession and thanksgiving be made for all people.
(1 Timothy 2:1, NIV)

Therefore confess your sins to one another and pray for one another, that you may be healed. The prayer of a righteous person has great power as it is working.
(James 5:16, ESV)

Do not withhold good from those to whom it is due, when it is in your power to do it.
(Proverbs 3:27, ESV)

Rejoice in hope, be patient in tribulation, be constant in prayer.
(Romans 12:12, ESV)

Prayer: Father God, please help me to pray for my family and friends effectively as I give them to you. I pray for you to give them what they need. I pray that you bring them closer to you lovingly. Thank you, Lord, for the love you show them and for the full heart, you have given me. In Jesus's loving name. I pray, amen.

June 29

More Than a Conqueror

Come to me all who are broken, let me heal you. This life is hard enough my child why should you try to do things all on your own. There are scars deep down in your life that you have been unable to heal and get over. These all need to be given to me. Every part of your life that is broken or pains you. Please lay them at my feet. The burdens of this world are too much for you in your humanity to carry on your own. I can be your strength, but you must let me in. You must let me in and love me wholeheartedly. Opening yourself and letting down those walls, that are trying to prevent me from being in all areas of your life. As I belong, not only, in half of your life, not a small ounce of your life, but in ALL of it. I love you with an everlasting love and It breaks my heart to see you struggling. Yet sometimes the struggle is good. When the work is harder the reward is sweeter still. You are more than a conqueror through me, when you give me your all. We can journey on together with purpose and hope. You can relax in this; I am with you and will never leave you or forsake you. Keeping the faith always moving forward with the presence of my love. And when you truly honor me as Lord of your life then, my beloved, you shall become more than a conqueror…

Nay, in all things we are more than conquerors through him that loved us.
(Romans 8:37, KJV)

And the peace of God, which passeth all understanding, shall keep your hearts and minds through Christ Jesus.
(Philippians 4:7, KJV)

No temptation has overtaken you except what is common to mankind. And God is faithful; He will not let you be tempted beyond what you can bear. But when you are tempted, he will also provide a way out so you can endure it.
(1 Corinthians 10:13, NIV)

And you shall love the Lord your God with all of your heart and with all of your soul and with all of your mind and with all of your strength.
(Mark 12:30, ESV)

Prayer: Father God, I have no words, just thank you. In Jesus's name, I give thanks, amen.

June 30

July

"Take his yoke upon you as it is easy and his burden is light"

*Take my yoke upon you, and learn
from me, for I am gentle and lowly in heart,
and you will find rest for your souls.*
(Matthew 11:29, ESV)

Amazing Grace and Peace

Give me all your worries my child. Cast your cares on me. Keep your eyes fixed on me always. Today find some comfort. Let my peace fill within your soul and your mind. This journey is sometimes long and arduous, so make peace with your thoughts. As you ask me to take charge. I am your strength and I have an endless supply of power as my battery never fades. If you try to do things alone you will feel burnt out or hopeless, but I can recharge you and provide to you the rest you need to get through another day. I can help you find your hope once again. Feel how much I love you. You are my precious child. None of my children are lost to me for no one can snatch them out of my hand. You are not lost, because you have invited me into your life. You, my child in fact have been found, and I will always be here with you. Loving you and providing to you my amazing grace and peace.

He answered, whether he is a sinner I do
not know, that though I was blind, now I see.
(John 9:25, ESV)

For sin will not have dominion over
you, since you are not under the law but
under grace.
(Romans 6:14, ESV)

And with great power the apostles
were giving their testimony to the resurrec-
tion of the Lord Jesus, and great grace was
upon them all.
(Acts 4:33, ESV)

Prayer: Father God, I lift us up to you today, all of your children, my family, and friends, and myself. We all need you. Please help us to remember that we are loved by you and that we are worth so much more to you than we ourselves would consider. Remind us also, that you offer us salvation and a love full of grace. That even when we make mistakes you forgive us, and that no situation is too big for you. Thank you, Jesus, for guarding our hearts and our minds. I pray for your joy and peace in our lives and that love fill us again this day. In Jesus's loving name, I ask, and I pray, amen. Hallelujah!

Let your soul sing:

> "Amazing Grace, how sweet the sound
> I once was lost, but now am found
> I was blind but now I see."

July 1

Reference: "Amazing Grace," hymn, written by John Newton (1779)

Let Peace Abound

Good Morning my dear child. Today let me lift your spirits. You can take a deep breath in and smile. I am pleased by the way you've been handling some of the tough situations in your life. As I love it when you choose to trust and lean on me. You are recognizing that I am the lighter way and can strengthen you from within. I can help you today and every day when you keep your eyes fixed on me. This day can be lighter still. Let my peace permeate in your soul. Walk through this day with happiness, head held high, knowing that I am with you and that I am surrounding you with love. Enveloping you with my love and the love from others. Bringing to your soul a calming display of warmth and security. You are more than a conqueror today. You are my beloved child, so as you find me in this day, let my peace abound.

And let the peace of Christ rule in your hearts, to which indeed you were called one body. And be thankful.
(Colossians 3:15, ESV)

Cast your anxiety on him because he cares for you.
(1 Peter 5:7, NIV)

And the peace of God, which transcends all understanding. Will guard your hearts and your minds in Christ Jesus.
(Philippians 4:7, NIV)

Prayer: Father God, fill our hearts with your love. I pray for everyone today that we all are filled with the peace of your Holy Presence. Help us to start seeing ourselves the way you see us. I thank you for the daily victories and blessings that you send to us each and every day. I pray for eyes to see and ears to hear your will and your ways because I know they are higher than mine. In Jesus's loving name, I pray, amen and amen.

July 2

Greater Is His Love

This day let me lead you back to a place of joy. As we walk through this day accomplishing one task at a time. It is good to surround yourself with bits of lightheartedness. Do not take everything so seriously. Let yourself have joyful moments and allow the light of my Presence to fill you with the fullness of love. Laughter is good for your soul, and it pleases me to see the happy moments you share with others. All life is precious my child. This journey can be steep yet still beautiful. Let my love encompass you and soon you will feel a joy overflowing. Even though the problems of the day may exist, you'll find they have no power because your hope is in me and my love for you is great. My love for you is deeper than any ocean and vaster than the largest desert imagined. It is a love that surpasses all understanding. It is so great that it even surpasses knowledge. As you can never measure my love. Today my child let my love reign down and wash over you. We can laugh and love today and focus on goodness. Amid this great journey, you can relax and smile, as you come to know more each day, my greater love.

Though the mountains be shaken and the hills be removed, yet my unfailing love for you will not be shaken nor my covenant of peace be removed," says the Lord, who has compassion on you.
(Isaiah 54:10, NIV)

You will go out in joy and be led forth in peace; the mountains and hills will burst

into song before you. And all the trees of the
field will clap their hands.
(Isaiah 55:12, NIV)

Because you are precious in my eyes,
and honored, and I love you.
(Isaiah 43:4, ESV)

And to know this love that surpasses
knowledge-that you may be filled to the
measure of all the fullness of God.
(Ephesians 3:19, NIV)

Prayer: Father God, my beautiful Savior, I pray today that your love fills us with your peace and surrounds us with your joy. I pray that through the hardships and the trials we all remember that we are loved and beautiful and strong. That we can be lighthearted today and laugh and share your love. I pray to look around today and to find goodness everywhere I go. In Jesus's loving name, I pray AMEN.

July 3

Celebrate with Love

Good Morning dear child. Today celebrate with friends and loved ones. Enjoy the beauty in this day. Surround yourself with the light of my love and enjoy. Life is not always a sweet perfect road in which you can pass through in perfect peace, no not this life. So today hug your friends and family laugh and share good times. Be thankful for today and keep hopeful of things to come without missing all the beauty in the moments of today. And as always keep your eyes fixed on me, with your heart open in love. Always speaking your prayers to me in truth. As we journey on together. We can celebrate with love.

Higher are the ways of our God.

More glorious is his reward to the faithful.

> *The steadfast love of the Lord never ceases; his mercies never come to an end; they are new every morning; great is your faithfulness.*
> (Lamentations 3:22–23, ESV)

> *He who calls you is faithful; he will surely do it.*
> (1 Thessalonians 5:24, ESV)

> *The thief comes only to steal and kill and destroy. I came that they may have life and have it abundantly.*
> (John 10:10, ESV)

Make a joyful noise to the Lord, all
the earth; break forth into joyous song and
sing praises!
(Psalm 98:4, ESV)

Prayer: Father God I pray you to keep us all safe today as we go out and celebrate with friends and family. I thank you for the ability to be able to gather and enjoy life today. In Jesus's name, I pray and give thanks, amen.

Happy Independence Day, Happy 4rth of July.

July 04

Love and Forgiveness

Good Morning bring your worries and fears to me my child and as you lay them at my feet cast aside your worries... Start your day in prayer. You can accomplish much today. We together can become unstoppable. Although some days the steps we take are small, they are still steps moving forward and you can still enjoy this day. I have called you to be an example to others as you can show them my love and how to forgive. Some of my children let hurt turn to anger. You must remember this is not the way. I will show my children to be forgiving. Opinions can turn into judgments, of each other. But I have said you must be loving and not judge. Love thy neighbor, as yourself. Forgive them for hurts just as I have forgiven you. Cast out any thoughts or speech that causes discord as this is not from me. Truly lean on me, my child. I am the light and the way of life and love. I am the truth and truthfully, I love all my children. Forgive today and let your heart be free. For this is the day that I have made go out and be glad in it.

He heals the brokenhearted and binds up their wounds.
(Psalm 147:3, ESV)

Bearing with one another and, if one has a complaint against another, forgiving each other: as the Lord has forgiven you, so you must also forgive.
(Colossians 3:13, ESV)

Be sober-minded; be watchful your adversary the devil prowls around like a roaring lion, seeking someone to devour.
(1 Peter 5:8, ESV)

For God so loved the world, that he gave his only son, that whoever believes in him should not perish but have eternal life.
(John 3:16, ESV)

Prayer: Father God, help me today with any upset feelings I have for the people in my life. Help me to be forgiving. I pray you to lighten the feelings of hurt that have weighed any of us down and that you replace them with your love. Fill us up with your joy today Father. In Jesus's name, I pray, amen.

July 5

Peace in Jesus

Let my Presence surround you, filling you with peace. Take all that you need from me. Call on me and this day I can bring to you today a gift of much-needed rest. You are doing well my child reaching for me. Let the thoughts of today fill you with happiness. All my children need to rest whether emotionally, spiritually or physically. There are different types of rest for your soul. Ask me to lift your burdens and make your heart light. You can trust my timing as its always perfect. Find your peace in me, as I am like a barrier between you and howling winds. Sometimes you will feel hard pressed on all sides. But if you keep your focus on me, you will see that soon you will rise above.

> *When a man's ways please the Lord, he makes even his enemies be at peace with him.*
> (Proverbs 16:7, ESV)

> *You keep him in perfect peace whose mind is stayed on you, because he trusts in you.*
> (Isaiah 26:3, NKJV)

> *These things I have spoken to you. That in Me you may have peace, In the world you have tribulation, but take heart; I have overcome the world.*
> (John 16:33)

...And there I was feeling all the pressures of the day I lifted my arms and called on my Lord Jesus. He came to me and lifted me up and over. He gave me rest. His Presence filled my soul with a wave of peace and calmness. I am thankful.

Prayer: Father God, today I pray to have calm and peace. I pray for all my family and my friends please give us much needed rest. Thank you, Jesus, I pray this in Jesus's name, amen.

To my reader; This last couple of weeks has been hard for me to find my focus, just wanted to let you know that even though this good purpose is harder at the moment, I will not give up. I will give it to the Lord and watch him work in my life.

July 6

More Beautiful than Gold

You are precious, my child, so fragile yet so strong. The hurdles of life will keep coming but I have prepared you for the run. Just like a long-distance runner, I have been preparing you all along. Some of the track has already been accomplished yet there is more, and some maybe just the training. In suffering, you can find perseverance. You can rest in the knowledge that I never give to you more than you can handle. Although at times you may feel overwhelmed and broken, I can mend you when you trust me. The more you trust me and let me fill your life with my strength and love the more beautiful and resilient you become. I will never try to disguise your hardships, but I will peace you back together with my love. Making you so much more beautiful, and the cracks and breaks that you have already gone through will be filled with the strong gold of my love. Never hiding your hurts but celebrating what you have been through and what you have overcome with me.

When we go through our sufferings and we break, God will restore us. He repairs us, just like the Japanese art of Kintsugi repairs broken pottery, when we are restored, we are more beautiful because of our sufferings:

Kintsugi or Kintsukuroi translated means "golden repair". It is the centuries-old Japanese art of fixing broken pottery with a special lacquer dusted powdered gold, silver or platinum. This is a method that celebrates each artifacts' unique history by emphasizing its fractures and breaks instead of hiding or disguising them. It often makes the peace more beautiful than the original revitalizing it with new life. Just the way Jesus revitalizes us, giving us a new life.

I can do all things through Christ who strengthens me.
(Philippians 4:13, NKJV)

Not only so, but we also glory in our sufferings, because we know suffering produces perseverance; perseverance character; and character hope. And hope does not put us to shame, because God's Love has been poured out into our hearts through the Holy Spirit, who has been given to us.
(Romans 5:3–5, NIV)

Consider it pure joy, my brothers and sisters, whenever you face trials of many kinds, because you know that the testing of your faith produces perseverance. Let perseverance finish its work so that you may be mature complete, not lacking anything.
(James 1:2–4, NIV)

Prayer: Father God, thank you for my trials and sufferings as they bring me closer to you. I trust in you and love you with my whole heart. I also thank you for the victory of overcoming all sufferings that life brings and pray that you strengthen all my friends and family with your Spirit each day, during all times. I pray we can see ourselves the way you see us. That we know that we are loved and are more beautiful then gold. In Jesus's name, I pray and thank you, amen.

July 7

Word of Life

Let your heart be full of the special time we spend together. The morning sun appears, time to rise and shine. Much like the morning sun, I have called you to shine. To be a light to others of what my love looks like. I have equipped you with strength and fill you with my love. Let my love overflow from you and reach out too many. Let my words fill your hearts and your minds. Reading my living word every day, as to guard against the trials in this life. Learning more and more of what I have called you to do. Walking in my will and giving me your all. The blessings you receive are sweeter when you truly see them and do not overlook them. I will use trials to draw my children closer to me. Hear my call and follow. Do not be afraid. Let your heart sing to me a joyful hymn of thankfulness. Casting all doubts aside, as nothing is impossible with me. Oh, glorious day, shining with my magnificent love and filling my children with the joy that comes from me. There will be a victory burst forth as they learn my word of life.

Your words were found I ate them, and your words became to me a joy and the delight of my heart, for I am called by your name, O Lord, God of hosts.
(Jeremiah 15:16, ESV)

And we have something more sure, the prophetic word, to which you will do well to pay attention as to a lamp shining in a dark place, until the day dawns and the morning star rises in your hearts.
(2 Peter 1:19, ESV)

But he answered, "It is written, 'Man
shall not live by bread alone, but by every
word that comes from the mouth of God.'"
(Matthew 4:4, ESV)

Prayer: Father God, thank you for directing me and strengthening me. I pray to be a blessing to others. That I will always point to you and give you all the glory Lord. I am thankful to share you with my family and friends. Keep leading us, Lord. Let us want to know you so much more. Thank you also for your living word the Bible and the strength that it provides. In Jesus's name, I pray and give thanks, AMEN.

July 8

Creating Something New

I am creating something new in you, my child. I am the Lord your God; it is in me you will find your refuge and strength. I am your protector and strong tower. No situation is too monumental for me to overcome. I am the creator who has the power to surround you with light and fill you with my Presence. Come to me all who are weary, and I can give you rest. Call out to me in times of trouble and I will take hold of your hearts and minds. No weapon formed against you shall prosper in the presence of your mighty Lord, for I am on your side. Remember this in times of panic and anxiety. Lay down the depression and guilt and ask me to take it, believing that I can, and knowing that I will. I am the Lord your Redeemer and love you with an everlasting love. You are worth more to me than you know. But the enemy knows just how valuable you are. Therefore, this is why spiritual assaults take place, the enemy is afraid. No longer will you be a foot soldier of this world, lost and full of sorrow, but a light in the darkness that shines full of my love and grace. I have plans for you, great and wonderful plans. Ask me to guide you through this life. I will never leave your side.

It is the Lord who goes before you. He will be with you; He will not leave or forsake you. Do not fear or be dismayed.
(Deuteronomy 31:8, ESV)

Have I not commanded you? Be strong and courageous. Do not be frightened and do not be dismayed, for the Lord your God is with you wherever you go.
(Joshua 1:9, ESV)

And we know that for those who love God all things work together for good, for those who are called according to his purpose.
(Romans 8:28, ESV)

For I know the plans I have for you, declares the Lord, plans of welfare and not for evil, to give you hope and a future.
(Jeremiah 29:11, ESV)

Prayer: Father God, strengthen us today with your mighty Presence. Lead us today in your ways for we know they are good. Protect our minds today Lord and fill us with joy and the hope that we can find only in you. Thank you for being our strong tower and the rock of our Salvation. I pray for all my family and friend's happiness today. In Jesus's loving name, I ask and pray, amen.

July 9

Honesty

May you be filled with the joy of truth. Look today and find me in your relationships, in the smiles of loved ones. Speak to me in all honesty hold nothing back. I am the redeemer of your life. I want you to walk this day in the knowledge that I am always with you and will never leave or forsake you. Trusting in me more each day. As this truly brings me joy. Never doubting, never hiding, but being open and honest in prayer. You can watch me moving in your life and in the lives of those around you. Spread out my message until we will reach far and wide. No person should be without the hope that's found in me. I am searching the hearts of many and pulling my children close. You are my beloved child, so live a life of grace and truth. Keep leaning on me and letting go of troubles. Count every blessing and smile knowing you are loved...today and always.

And he said unto them, Go ye into all the world, and preach the gospel to every living creature.
(Mark 16:15, KJV)

Do not forget to show hospitality to strangers, for by so doing some people have shown hospitality to angels without knowing it.
(Hebrews 13:2, NIV)

Jesus saith unto him, "I am the way, the truth, and the life: no man cometh to the Father, but by me."
(John 14:6, KJV)

Prayer: I come to you Father God, with a thankful heart. I pray to be open and honest when speaking of you. I pray to be able to stay bold and to not let fear stop me from sharing your good news. I also pray for all my family and friends and people all over this world Lord, that they may come to know you so much more. Thank you for all our blessings Father God and for loving us and forgiving us our sins. In Jesus's name, I pray, amen.

July 10

Giving Your All

Easing into the day with confidence. Be happy in your pursuits, when you asked me into your life and accepted me as your Savior, you have asked me for my truth. You have opened up yourself to your true life, full of all the wonderful things I have in store for you. Stop trying to run from me as I will keep pursuing you. You are just that important to me. I will never give up on you. Some of my children only cling to me in times of hardships, trials or sickness, but once the storm passes, they push me off and back to the farthest corners of their minds. I have not called anyone to do so. I want to have your all. I want not only your hard times and troubles, but I want your happiness and gladness too. I want your whole heart. It pleases me to be your first thought of the day, the last thought before bed, and all the times in between. Keep praying and having conversations with me my child and you will find that I am listening. Make time for quiet moments. You will find me in these as well. And all your life will find you well, just keep giving your all.

Seek first the kingdom of God and his righteousness, and all these things will be added to you.
(Matthew 6:33, ESV)

So give yourselves completely to God. Stand against the devil, and the devil will run from you. Come near to God, and God will come near to you. You sinners, clean sin out of your lives. You who are trying to

follow God and the world at the same time,
make your thinking pure.
(James 4:7–8, NCV)

My son, give me your heart and let
your eyes delight in my ways.
(Proverbs 23:26, NIV)

Prayer: Father God, I give you my all and pray for you to forgive me my distractions. May my attention be with you first. I pray for all my family and friends each day fill us with your love and grace and keep us safe from harm. In Jesus's loving name I pray, amen.

July 11

Rock Solid Foundation

I am here with you. I will stand by your side and hold your hand. I will strengthen my Holy Spirit within you. Come to me on this day with praise and thanksgiving. The energy of the day may be mixed, but I never change. I am the one true constant. I am the foundation on which to build your life. A steady and solid foundation, that even under the most severe pressure... I will not be shaken, nor will I be moved. Settle into the day. When you feel empty call out to me, even more. I am always with you even in the silence of the day. I am always pursuing you. Stand firm and well positioned, my child, upon my rock-solid foundation.

Jesus Christ is the same yesterday, and today, and forever.
(Hebrews 13:8, NIV)

Anyone who listens to my teaching and follows it is wise, like a person who builds a house on solid rock. Though the rain comes in torrents and the floodwaters rise and the winds beat against the house, it won't collapse because it's built on bedrock.
(Matthew 7:24–25, NLT)

He is like a man building a house, who dug deep and laid the foundation on the rock. And when the flood arose, the stream broke against that house and could not shake it, because it had been well built.
(Luke 6:48, ESV)

So that Christ may dwell in your hearts through faith, that you, being rooted and grounded in love.
(Ephesians 3:17, ESV)

Prayer: Father God, today I thank you for the victory that I have found in you. The victory of a solid foundation, to base my life upon. Thank You for getting me through the hard times Lord and for celebrating the joyful ones with me. I pray for all today that need you Lord, and those who do not know you yet. That we can all find your love, keeping the faith, and the hope that is found in you. In Jesus's loving name I pray, and then I say, amen.

July 12

Gracious Gifts

Try walking in my ways. I know it is hard, my child as this world calls you to live and think a certain way. But my ways are not of this world they are higher. I will caress your soul with rest and fill you with love. A greater love than what is in this world. I give you this to share, to share it with the world. So that they may see my beauty of love and kindness shining from within you. I will strengthen you and keep the lies of the enemy far from your mind. You are my beloved. You are so much more. Submit yourselves to me. Be patient, loving and kind. Walking in grace. Taking each moment as it comes, never rushing ahead. But persevering with my Spirit who lives in you. Pray to know your gifts and talents, that they may be used to help the cause of my good news. Keep growing in your faith and sharing along the way, the good and gracious gifts that I have given you to use.

For the gifts and the calling of God are irrevocable.
(Romans 11:29, ESV)

To this end we always pray for you, that our God may make you worthy of his calling and may fulfill every resolve for good and every work of faith by his power.
(2 Thessalonians 1:11, ESV)

As each has received a gift, use it to serve one another, as good stewards of God's varied grace: whoever speaks as one who speaks oracles of God; whoever serves, as one

*who serves by the strength that God sup-
plies-in order that in everything God may
be glorified through Jesus Christ. To him
belong the glory and dominion forever and
ever. Amen.*
(1 Peter 4:10–11, ESV)

Prayer: Father God, I pray we each may learn which gift
you have given us. That we use it fully for your glory Lord.
Thank you for loving us. I pray for all my family and friends
and I that you keep leading us Lord and filling us with your
joy. In Jesus's name, I pray, amen.

July 13

Work and Trust

It saddens me to see that some of my children have turned their backs on me and are letting the world dictate their lives. I want you to talk with these lost children and share with them a hope that's found in me. Tell them they are worth it. Let them know that they are loved but remind them in order to change they must first turn to me and accept me as their Lord. They must make different choices changing the responses they have become so accustomed to. It can be very scary for them at first, as they either know no other way or refuse to acknowledge that they themselves may be the cause of their own troubles. Learning to let go of their old ways and old habits. Learning to trust is not easy for anyone, especially the ones who have felt lost for quite some time, So at the beginning of our relationship they may feel uncomfortable…Share with them that I have called my children to step out and grow in faith, and that comfort might take time. But in order to conquer fear, there needs to be the first step. Also, my children, you must be thankful for your lives and what you have. As to always count your blessings, but you should not settle for less than I have called you to be. Greater is he who works hard and is deserving of his portion than one who is lazy and demands what is not rightfully his. No one is perfect and without sin but turn from your sinful ways and commit yourselves to me, allow me to work in you something much greater.

Whatever you do, work at it with all your heart, as working for the Lord, not for human masters.
(Colossians 3:23, NIV)

Lazy hands make for poverty, diligent hands bring wealth.
(Proverbs 10:4, NIV)

Be careful then how you live-not as unwise but as wise, making the most out of every opportunity, because the days are evil. Therefore do not be foolish, but understand what the Lord's will is.
(Ephesians 5:15–17, NIV)

Prayer: Father God I pray you to guide me in my work. That you teach me the ways of your will, so that I may be able to provide for my household, loved ones and family and that I may be able to help contribute to the poor. I pray to succeed in my work and to have an abundance that I may share. I pray for those who are lost Lord that you may find them and open their eyes, so that they can have a hope and a future found in you. In Jesus's name, I pray and ask and thank you for the victory. Amen.

And God is able to bless you abundantly, so that in all things at all times, having all that you need, you will abound in every good work.
(2 Corinthians 9:8, NIV)

July 14

Day of Rest

Take a breath, relax. Stop worrying my child. There is nothing to fear, no stress today. Everyone has busy weeks full of life's demands. Everything pulling for your attention. You frantically run around almost blindly trying to accomplish all that is required. Slow down little one. Be still and know that I am God. Take a day to relax, refresh and quiet your mind and your soul. Refresh your mind with quiet time with me. Shut out the demands of the day. Take in beauty today go for a walk outside to clear your mind. Keeping your eyes fixed on me and all the beauty of the day. You can relax for the fruit of your harvest will come. You are working so hard. Good job my child. Keep going and keep sowing, but today just rest, always remembering not to rush ahead. Just as it is said," Blessed is he who waits on the Lord. "The perseverance you have shown will be rewarded. Relax now and breathe.

But as for you, be strong and do not give up, for your work will be rewarded.
(2 Chronicles 15:7, NIV)

Let us not become weary in doing good, for at the proper time we will reap a harvest if we do not give up.
(Galatians 6:9, NIV)

For ye have need of patience, that, after ye have done the will of God, ye might receive the promise.
(Hebrews 10:36, KJV)

Prayer: Father God thank you for teaching me and guiding my ways for giving me the strength and ability to keep going. I thank you also for giving me the rest I need to refresh my mind. I pray for everyone today in my life. I pray for your guidance to know the seasons of work and rest and that you refresh all of us with your grace, love, and joy. I pray in Jesus's name for this day. Amen.

July 15

Close to Me

I have known you always, even before you were born. Even before I formed in your mother's womb. I have loved you and watched you grow. I have blessed you and taken care of you. Even during times, you have not known. Now I am growing you in your faith. I am pleased by your desire to know me even more. Do not let the past mistakes make you feel sad or defeated in any way but be glad as these are the growing pains of life. I use these hardships to build you in your character, so that you may become all that I have called you to be. When you look back on your life you can see I was always working, and you'll see all the experiences I used to pull you to this moment. To this very moment close to me.

Thus says the Lord, your Redeemer, who formed you in the womb: "I am the Lord, who made all things, who alone stretched out the heavens, who spread out the earth by myself."
(Isaiah 44:24, ESV)

Before I formed you in the womb I knew you, and before you were born I consecrated you; I appointed you a prophet to the nations.
(Jeremiah 1:5, ESV)

But when he who had set me apart before I was born, and who called me by his grace.
(Galatians 1:15, ESV)

But God's firm foundation stands, bearing this seal: "The Lord knows those who are his," and, "Let everyone who names the name of the Lord depart from iniquity."
(2 Timothy 2:19, ESV)

Consequently, he is able to save to the uttermost those who draw near to God through him, since he always lives to make intercession for them.
(Hebrews 7:25, ESV)

Prayer: Thank you Father GOD, for my life. thank you for all the lives of those around me as well. We are blessed by your loving grace, and I am thankful. Keep us close to you my Lord. In Jesus's name, I pray and give thanks. Amen.

July 16

How Wonderful

By love, you were formed. How wonderful it is to be loved by me. Your Savior and your Father. The hope found in me is great. It pleases me when you walk with me in my will. Giving all your attention to me; as your one true love. I know this life is hectic and will try to pull you away. But never wander far from my loving arms, my child. I will be your safety in times of trouble. I will be your strength when you're feeling weak. I will be your joy when you're feeling happy. I will and I am all things. Trust in me is essential. Live this day in abundance. I am with you always. With the gaze of your eyes solidly fixed on me. Never losing focus. You are good. My sweet and precious child you are loved.

Let love and faithfulness never leave you; bind them around your neck, write them on the tablet of your heart. Then you will win favor and a good name in the sight of God and man.
(Proverbs 3:3–4, NIV)

And so we know and rely on the love God has for us. God is love. Whoever lives in love lives in God, and God in them.
(1 John 4:16, NIV)

May the Lord direct your hearts into God's love and Christ's perseverance.
(2 Thessalonians 3:5, NIV)

Prayer: Thank you, Father, for your unfailing love. I pray for all today that we will experience just how truly loved we are. That we may all find the pure joy of your love in our lives and our hearts. In Jesus's name, I pray. Amen.

July 17

First You Must Try

The blessing is in the doing, not the talking. I have heard many of my children talking about their ideas for a better way of life. Yet they never step out in faith or even attempt that first step. I have not designed you just to be a dreamer. I have designed you for so much more. Come to me with all your hopes and dreams. Strengthen them with me. As I can help you accomplish them. Do not get discouraged if it does not end up the way you wanted it to, on the first try. Here are the lessons of life to learn. I haven't made you be a quitter, as in giving up or putting off the dreams that have come into your life. Work hard at them my child. Grabbing every opportunity that comes your way. Sharing my word with those around you and spending time with me. Seek and you will find me, when you seek me with your whole heart. Give every part of your life to me and I will make your paths straight. But remember you will never know unless you first try.

Let us not become weary in doing good, for at the proper time we will reap a harvest if we do not give up.
(Galatians 6:9, NIV)

Jesus looked at them and said, "With man this is impossible, but not with God; all things are possible with God."
(Mark 10:27, NIV)

I can do all this through him who gives me strength.
(Philippians 4:13, NIV)

And he told them a parable to the effect that they ought always to pray and not to lose heart.
(Luke 18:1, ESV)

Prayer: Father God, I pray for all of us today that you would give us the courage to step out in faith, that you will remove all our fears. That you will strengthen us Lord as we work toward our goals. I pray that you will encourage us during our work Lord. I thank you, Father God, for removing any mountains and for helping us to find our way to what you have called us to do. In Jesus's name, I pray. Amen.

July 18

Helping Freely

Gracious is the one who offers his help freely. No strings attached just helpful. Have you ever known someone who seems so giving and always offers to help, just to remind you later that they have helped you, so you should also help them? This is not the kindness of giving as I've created it to be. It is not the worldly mantra of, "I'll scratch your back if you scratch mine. "That my child serves no good purpose. When you help someone do it freely without any thought of your own benefit. Simply do it because this is how I have made you. To be kind and compassionate, tender in heart, and giving. This is how to show love for me, by loving others. Showing others, the true reflection of my love for you, by the way, you love them.

> *We love because he first loved us.*
> (1 John 4:19, NIV)

> *Each one must give as he has decided to in his heart, not reluctantly or under compulsion, for God loves a cheerful giver.*
> (2 Corinthians 9:7, ESV)

> *One gives freely, yet grows all the richer; another withholds what he should give, and only suffers want. Whoever brings blessing will be enriched, and one who waters will himself be watered.*
> (Proverbs 11:24–25, ESV)

Let each of you look not only to his own interests, but also to the interests of others.
(Philippians 2:4, ESV)

In all things I have shown you that by working hard in this way we must help the weak and remember the words of the Lord Jesus, how he himself said, "It is better to give than to receive."
(Acts 20:35, ESV)

Prayer: Thank you, Father God, that I may help others. Please forgive me during the times that I complain about helping for I know that I should give help freely and with joy. I thank you today for this day you have made. I pray for all my family and friends a good day. In Jesus's name, amen.

July 19

Season to Rest

Days that are slow and uneventful are a blessing just as well. It is good to slow way down, as almost sitting still. This gives your soul time of reflection. During these times you should take the opportunity that is given and spend some solitary time with me. Far too many of my children are so pre-programmed by this world, always staying busy. Constantly on the go jumping from one thing to the next. It is good to work hard and to have business at times, but there are seasons for all things. There is also a season to rest. Be thankful in all times. As I am good every day. Walking in my will, as I direct your steps. One day at a time my child. Let this be a season to rest.

> *Truly my soul finds rest in God; my salvation comes from him. Truly He is my rock and my salvation; he is my fortress, I will never be shaken.*
> (Psalm 62:1–2, NIV)

> *Yes, my soul, find rest in God: my hope comes from him.*
> (Psalm 62:5, NIV)

> *This is how we know we belong to the truth and how we set our hearts at rest in his presence.*
> (1 John 3:19, NIV)

> *Come to me, all who labor and are heavy laden, and I will give you rest. Take*

*my yoke upon you, and learn from me, for I
am gentle and lowly in heart, and you will
find rest for your souls. For my yoke is easy,
and my burden is light.*
(Matthew 11:28–30, ESV)

Prayer: Father God, give me rest today quiet my mind. I pray for good thoughts and a relaxing day for all my friends and family. I pray that we all can find time to spend with you during these restful moments. In Jesus's name, I pray. Amen.

To my reader: Find rest for today, it is so important that we find a balance in our lives. There are so many busy times, we need to make equal time for rest. Even the Lord rested on the seventh day. So if the Lord himself rested then we should also rest because it is good.

July 20

Pushing Off Fear

Be steadfast and confident today. Is there something that you are working on in your life that you once had good feelings about and now the doubts and fear are creeping in? Do not give up. The dark one will say no you should not complete this. Be careful my dear one as to not let the fear become so great that you do not finish what I have called you to do. If you are unsure pray with me ask me to put the answer in your heart and give you discernment. Stay on the right path. Do not allow fears to push you off course. Read my word, Read the Bible. As this is my living word. Strengthen up your heart and soul. The answer lies within my word. Put on my armor and stay on course. Do not get distracted by the evil ones lies he will use doubts of your destination to scare you and make you unsure, causing great anxiety, as this is what he exists for. Taking your eyes off me. Strengthen up your heart and your mind. You will find peace through me as I will restore all that the enemy has tried to steal. Let the happiness in! Oh, my child, push off the fear.

> *Even though I walk through the valley of the shadow of death, I will fear no evil, for you are with me; your rod and your staff, they comfort me.*
> (Psalm 23:4, ESV)

> *I sought the Lord, and he answered me and delivered me from all my fears.*
> (Psalm 34:4, ESV)

Be strong and courageous. Do not fear
or be in dread of them, for it is the Lord
your God who goes with you. He will not
leave or forsake you.
(Deuteronomy 31:6, ESV)

Prayer: Thank you, Father God, for protecting my mind and guarding my heart. I place my life in your hands, Lord. Guide my every step and keep me on your good and righteous path. I give to you all my anxieties Lord and cast my fears at your feet. I will follow wherever you lead. In Jesus's name, I pray and thank you for the victory of my life...Amen

July 21

Blessed Are the Peacemakers

Blessed are the peacemakers for they will be called the children of God. Sometimes in our lives, we will be drawn into situations that are not our own disagreements or arguments to share, or we may watch our loved ones and family have hurts against each other. I urge you my children if you can do anything to make peace between people do so. I am not the God of disharmony and anger, or of finger pointing and laying blame. I am your God who loves and forgives. The Lord who has given you grace and compassion. When you show empathy for others it can make your heart grow. Demonstrate the way you should treat each other. Sometimes in life, you may have disappointments and hurts caused by people very close to you. Often times my children hurt the ones they love the most, but do not hold onto any of these negative feelings but instead pray about the situation give it to me, forgive them. Show others the benefit of forgiveness as it sets you free from heaviness which can lead to more sin. We can break the chains together.

> *But the wisdom from above is first pure, then peaceable, gentle, open to reason. Full of mercy and good fruits, impartial and sincere. And a harvest of righteousness is sown in peace by those who make peace.*
> (James 3:17–18, ESV)

> *So whatever you wish that others would do to you, do also to them, for this is the law and the prophets.*
> (Matthew 7:12, ESV)

Blessed are the peacemakers, for they
will be called the sons of God.
(Matthew 5:9, ESV)

Prayer: Father God, thank you for peacemakers and for those who show kindness and compassion. Thank you for those who show empathy and are slow to anger. I pray to always see both sides of the argument that I may be able to help people to see that forgiveness is the right way. I pray for everyone in my life Lord the ability and willingness to forgive and be forgiven when needed. In Jesus's loving name, I pray, amen.

July 22

Gifts and Talents

Take what you are given and do something with it, my child. I have given you and all my children certain spiritual gifts and strengths that can be used to benefit others. No one is more important than the other. Just as the parts of the body have different functions and uses, so do you. Think of it this way; eyes are to see. Can an eye speak? No, that is not what it is designed to do. Just as the parts of the body have different functions So do my children. Each all has different gifts or attributes. Sometimes they will be called to work together to obtain a more beneficial result. The people in the church are often called together" the body of the church "as each member has different functions and different abilities that when they all work together to serve one purpose, it makes them whole. Sharing and spreading my words to worship, encourage others, and give thanks to me. When you discover your gifts and talents just know you will become unstoppable. Just make sure you use them in a way that is pleasing to me. If you have yet to discover your abilities or talents, pray to me about it, I can open your eyes to see. You are a child of God, and so it is that I will call on you to use the gift I have given.

There are different kinds of gifts, but the same Spirit distributes them. There are different kinds of service, but the same Lord. There are different kinds of working, but in all of them and in everyone it is the same God at work.
(1 Corinthians 12:4–6, NIV)

Just as a body, though one, has many parts, but all its many parts from one body, so it is with Christ, For we were all baptized by one Spirit so as to form one body, whether Jews or Gentiles, slave or free-and we were all given the one Spirit to drink. Even so the body is not made up of one part but of many.
(1 Corinthians 12:12–14, NIV)

Having gifts that differ according to the grace given to us, let us use them: if prophecy, in proportion to our faith; if service, in our serving; the one who teaches, in his teaching; the one who exhorts in his exhortation; the one who contributes, in generosity; the one who leads, with zeal; the one who does acts of mercy, with cheerfulness.
(Romans 12:6–8, ESV)

Prayer: Father God, thank you for my spiritual gifts for my abilities and talents. I pray to use them for your glory Father. I pray for those who do not know their gifts, Lord, that you open their eyes to see. Helping to guide us to the life you designed for us. In Jesus's name, I am thankful and pray, amen.

July 23

Blessed Are the Meek

Blessed are the meek for they shall inherit the earth. Being meek in itself is strength under control. It is someone who when faced with anger or a harsh situation, can handle the situation with gentleness and a quiet spirit. Moses himself was a great leader. He stood up to a very powerful leader, Pharaoh, yet Moses is said to be the meekest man above all the men on the face of the earth, during his time. For you see, being meek is not weakness, as many would think, but it is a strength in character. Just like a parent who is fueled by anger when a child has done something wrong, controls their temper. Showing patience and love. They do not destroy the child but instead, they handle the situation with meekness. They demonstrate a cool spirit, a calm wind like attitude, a gentleness. Not downplaying the situation but maintaining self-control. Go out today my child with kindness and quietness, be gentle my child.

> *To speak evil of no one, to avoid quarreling, to be gentle, to show perfect courtesy toward all people.*
> (Titus 3:2, ESV)

> *Who is wise and understanding among you? By his good conduct let him show his works in the meekness of wisdom.*
> (James 3:13, ESV)

> *But let your adorning be the hidden person of the heart with the imperishable*

beauty, of a gentle and quiet spirit, Which
in God's sight is very precious.
(1 Peter 3:4, ESV)

Blessed are the meek, for they shall
inherit the earth.
(Matthew 11:29, ESV)

Prayer: Father God, help me to be meek and humble. Help me to be slow to anger and give me the kindness of understanding during harsh situations. I pray for all my family and friends today, that they may all experience your love and have joy fill their spirits. Even during turbulent times, and that they themselves might be able to display meekness in quarrel like situations. In Jesus's name, I pray, amen.

July 24

Humility and Pride

When you accomplish something, my dear child, try not to brag or boast. Do not think of yourselves as any better than anyone else. Therefore, be humble. All my children have different abilities and can accomplish much but let no one believe they are more important than any other. Do not be a bragger, but instead show others through humility and kindness, what the success found in me looks like. Do not speak slanderously about one another, build each other up. Just as empathy and compassion, humbleness and the ability to relate to one another brings forth goodness. A strength in character creating dignity and happiness. But do not be prideful as that may become a slippery slope. Too much pride can be a dangerous thing as it gives you a false sense that you are better or more equipped than even I. This is not the way. It is okay to feel proud of yourself for accomplishments. I will celebrate them with you. But it is I, your God who truly creates success in you. So therefore, I say to you, my child, remember to humble yourselves and lessen the pride you feel. Keep working hard and moving forward, your work is good, but let in you exist a humble pride for this is the paradox that serves you best.

Humble yourselves before the Lord,
and he will lift you up.
(James 4:10, NIV)

But he gives more grace. Therefore
it says, "God opposes the proud, but gives
grace to the humble."
(James 4:6, ESV)

The Lord Almighty has a day in store for all the proud and lofty, for all that is exalted (and they will be humbled).

(Isaiah 2:12, NIV)

But remember the Lord your God, for it is he who gives you the ability to produce wealth, and so confirms his covenant, which he swore to your ancestors, as it is today.
(Deuteronomy 8:18, NIV)

Prayer: Father God, please keep me from becoming prideful. Please let me always give the glory to you. I know whatever my accomplishments in life, that it is you who have given me my abilities and it is you who will provide me the confidence to use them. I also thank you for the ability to use my talents to be successful Lord and ask that I may always use the talents and gifts you have given me—as a blessing to and for others. I pray for all my family and friends and people who need you, Lord, that they may experience your greatness in their lives, full of your grace and filled with joy. In Jesus's loving name, I pray, amen.

July 25

Awakening with Love

Dear child, good morning. You are so aware today of my presence, much more than the yesterdays of your youth. I am pleased to see your faith growing, as you start to experience me more and more. I am opening your eyes and giving you a new experience that you can no longer deny. You have run from me for far too long, but here I am. I have never left your side. I will never force myself onto any of my children, but I will encourage and use certain situations and people to draw you near. I have waited for you in patience I am always constant, I never change. I am always with you and I love you, not just at this moment, not just for today, but I love you with an everlasting love. Go out today and rejoice. As I am awakening your heart with love.

There is no fear in love, but perfect love casts out fear. For fear has to do with punishment, and whoever fears has not been perfected in love.
(1 John 4:18, ESV)

Give thanks to the God of heaven, for his steadfast love endures forever.
(Psalm 136:26, ESV)

The Lord appeared to him from far away. I have loved you with an everlasting love; therefore I have continued my faithfulness to you.
(Jeremiah 31:3, ESV)

Prayer: Heavenly Father, thank you for always loving us. Guide us today and always Lord that we may experience your love to its fullest and share it with others. I pray for all today that you continue to guide us in love and in this life. In Jesus's name, I pray and thank you, amen.

July 26

This Way Today

Be holy in all you do, for, I am Holy. So be a reflection of me. Work hard as if working for me. Be kind to others, so that even while you work as they can see the example of me living in you. Let my light shine out from within you. Even during times of disharmony, create harmony amongst yourselves, as this is pleasing to me. Do not be so quick to point out the twig in your brother's eye, when you yourself may have a log in your own. Meaning no one is perfect, so do not cast judgment upon your fellow brethren. Be accepting and loving. If you are a teacher or leader, then you should lead or teach with a loving hand and a kind tongue. Let no one be cruel just for the delight in hurting others. When you witness one of my children being undeservingly harsh then you should point it out to that person, lovingly. Go through this day my child with all that I'm teaching you. Do not forget the lessons you are learning. I am pleased by your willingness to open your heart and life to me and let me lead. Now go and be thankful in this day my child and share the love that you're given. And let us walk together this way today.

And let us consider how to stir up one another to love and good works.
(Hebrews 10:24, ESV)

Little children let us not love in word or talk but in deed and in truth.
(1 John 3:18, ESV)

But as he who called you is holy, you also be holy in all your conduct, since it is written, "You shall be holy, for I am holy."
(1 Peter 1:15–16, ESV)

Whatever you do, work heartily, as for the Lord and not for men, knowing that from the Lord you will receive the inheritance as your reward. You are serving the Lord.
(Colossians 3:23–24, ESV)

Prayer: Father God, thank you for this day. Thank you for correcting us with kindness and love and reminding us to lead, teach and correct in your ways. I pray to be a light to others and to be more like you Jesus in my thoughts and actions. I pray this each day that you are with all my family and friends. In Jesus's name, I pray. Amen.

July 27

Which Way to Go

Which way to go? I have heard so often in the prayers of my children, "Lord which way do I go?" When facing a decision in which path to pursue you must learn to turn off all distractions from the outside world. Go into your room and sit in silence, in prayer with me, open up to me completely. Most importantly read your Bible, the answer may or may not come to you in that moment, but it will reveal itself in time. You will need to pray for discernment when learning how to differentiate your thoughts from mine. The worlds thoughts and the worlds views have taken up roots in some of my children. They let themselves get tangled into the hype of the world around them as to what is acceptable what is not. Remember my dear child, my views are not of this world and my ways are higher than this world. Try not to lose focus on what I've called you to be, always keep your eyes fixed on me and your heart open to all my guidance and answers no matter what they may be.

I will instruct you and teach you in the way you should go; I will counsel you with my eye upon you.
(Psalm 32:8, ESV)

And your ears shall hear a word behind you, saying, "This is the way, walk in it," when you turn to the right or when you turn to the left.
(Isaiah 30:21, ESV)

*Thus says the Lord, your Redeemer,
the Holy One of Israel: "I am the Lord your
God, who teaches you to profit, who leads
you in the way you should go."*
(Isaiah 48:17, ESV)

*Let me hear in the morning of your
steadfast love, for in you I trust. Make me
know the way I should go, for to you I lift
up my soul.*
(Psalm 143:8, ESV)

Prayer: My Lord Jesus, thank you for guiding my steps and directing me. I pray for all my friends and family discernment that they may not only know and love you Lord but that they and I will be able to distinguish what is from you and what is not. I pray we find our ways and our paths through and with you. In Jesus's loving name, I pray and thank you, amen.

July 28

Your Faithful Heart

I'm speaking to your heart. Listen to all the beautiful ways of my teaching. I know my children are not perfect as I know some are far from me but try to live in the way I have called you to live. Showing all the love, kindness, and forgiveness to others and yourself, that I have given you. I give to you grace and a purpose. Which allows you to keep moving forward, eyes up fixed on me. Confess your sins to me. Let not your heart be troubled. Do not let your past mistakes dictate who you are. There is a fine line as your past surely has helped mold you into the wonderful person you are today, but the past should not be a stumbling block, that would keep you stuck within its moment. It is not something to be rehashed or to feel regret about, as its outcome can never be changed. Nothing can change the past. But with me in your present and future things are much brighter now as you will find forgiveness. Go and be baptized let your sins be washed away. Knowing my love for you and all my children never fails. I want you to keep growing with your faith and trust in me. Hope for my promise and in this, you can rest assured, it will be fulfilled. Just stay faithful to me and push away the thoughts that say you couldn't possibly matter, that you're not big enough or equipped for the job that I have given you. Remember my dear child, I am never wrong. I know your next, stay focused on me and you will see it is good. And with your faithful heart, cast away all doubts and just believe…

Many are the plans in the mind of a man, but it is the purpose of the Lord that will stand.
(Proverbs 19:21, ESV)

And Jesus said to him "If you can! All things are possible for one who believes."
(Mark 9:23, ESV)

For with the heart one believes and is justified, and with the mouth one confesses and is saved.
(Romans 10:10, ESV)

Whoever believes and is baptized will be saved, but whoever does not believe will be condemned.
(Mark 16:16, ESV)

Prayer: Father God, thank you for your love and for my life. I put my trust and hope in you Lord. I pray for all today Lord, that we all may experience the truth of your love in our lives. Help me today to not look back at the terrible hurts and mistakes I've made but remind me Lord with kindness that you have set me free from those sins. Thank you for creating in me, something new. In Jesus's name, I pray and rest in the hope of your promises. Amen.

July 29

Pure in Heart

Blessed are the pure in heart, for they shall see GOD. My dear and precious child, when dealing with your fellow brethren, make sure to come from a place of truth, be honest in all your actions and communications. Have no ulterior motives but be kind and love genuinely, If you do this, you will find yourself truly happy. People will seek you out, as they see my light shining from within you. Knowing that they can trust you. When living this life, as you live it for me and my glory only. When this is the purpose of your heart, it is pure. When you look around it is apparent which of my children have really let go of themselves and given their lives to me. They have genuine happiness about them, a glow from within. A light that shines brightly. Their spirit can even brighten the outlook of others. The outlook on life for them is a simple view, with only my true purpose in mind. They live their lives for me. They strive to please me and share my good news with others. This is how I call you to live in love and grace from me to you and others. Simply be happy, put away the selfish desires from your heart and minds. Casting out all fear as there is no fear in love. Remaining with me faithfully.

Let love be genuine. Abhor what is
evil; hold fast to what is good.
(Romans 12:9, ESV)

Love one another with brotherly affec-
tion. Outdo one another in showing honor.
(Romans 12:10, ESV)

Beloved, we are God's children now,
and what we will be has not yet appeared;
but we now that when he appears we shall
be like him, because we shall see him as he is.
(1 John 3:2, ESV)

Blessed are the pure in heart, for they
shall see God.
(Matthew 5:8, ESV)

And he made no distinction between
us and them, having cleansed their hearts
by faith.
(Acts 15:9, ESV)

Prayer: Father God, please help me to keep my focus on you solely that I may always do what is good in your sight. I pray to be a blessing to others and to truly demonstrate what the joy found in you looks like that I may share you with others, Lord. Thank you, Jesus, for your love and guidance and for the happiness you have placed within my heart. Amen.

July 30

Love Tones

I speak to your spirit with love tones soft and calm. I let you know when I am pleased and reproach you when I am not. I guide you and keep you safe with me but remember my child not to take your eyes off me. Hold me tighter when you feel like I've slipped away. Knowing inside that I will never leave you or forsake you, no matter what the world might have you believe. Today and always seek to please me. I love you, my child. I am your God who loves to see you succeed and become all I've called you to be. Show the world how my love works for you and through you. Cast out fear as there is no fear in love. Keep your eyes up gaze fixed on me. Joyful in the promise I have given.

Let me hear in the morning of your steadfast love.
For I trust in you. Make me known the way I should go for to you I lift up my soul.
(Psalm 143:8, ESV)

But it is written, "What no eye has seen, nor ear heard, nor the heart of man imagined, what God has prepared for those who love him."
(1 Corinthians 2:9, ESV)

There is no fear in love. But perfect love drives out fear, because fear has to do with punishment. The one who fears is not made in perfect love.
(1 John 4:18, NIV)

For God so loved the world, that he
gave his only Son, that whoever believes in
him should not perish but have eternal life.
(John 3:16, ESV)

Prayer: I thank the Lord God for this morning and all the days of my life! Thank you, Lord, for casting out fear and filling my heart with a great love for you, and everyone. I pray for all my family and friends for a joyful day today. Fill our hearts Lord and give to us happiness so strong that we know it comes from you. In Jesus's name, I pray and thank you, Father, amen.

July 31

August

And even with a shadow God can cast his love into the eye of the beholder.

Strength in Trust

Good Morning my dear one. I love your giving heart, but there is a fine line between giving and enabling. I haven't made you to be a helper so that you could help others stay stuck. I have made you to help. So that with your help they can grow strong enough to stand on their own. Remind them of me and who I am. Not all of them are ready to be receptive, and some may never come around. Those are the most difficult on you, I can see it. But I will release you from the burden, as it is not yours to carry, but you also need to release yourself. Every man has his own burden to bear. Ask me to continue working it out and release them to me. You cannot fix people. You can help them to realize there is more to life than selfish desires, and worldly problems, only if they are willing to listen. Enabling them is not allowing them to grow on their own. Not all the lessons are easy. As you most assuredly know. You have had your own tests and trials, and some you are still going through. Everyone will always have trials and hardships all throughout this life. But blessed are my children that learn to be strong enough, to trust in me, and overcome the world, and all it is throwing at them. Do this, trust me. Then you can help others by being an example of someone who never loses faith, and always has hope. One who keeps persevering and diligently works. The one whom I will bless abundantly.

> *For even we were with you, this we commanded you, that if any would not work, neither should he eat.*
> (2 Thessalonians 3:10–15, KJV)

He becometh poor that dealeth (with) a slack hand: but the hand of the diligent maketh rich.
(Proverbs 10:4, KJV)

For every man shall bear his own burden.
(Galatians 6:5, KJV)

So put away all malice and all deceit and hypocrisy and envy and all slander. Like newborn infants, long for pure spiritual milk, that by it you may grow up into salvation-If indeed you have tasted that the Lord is good. As you come to him, a living stone rejected by men but in the sight of God chosen and precious, you yourselves like living stones are being built up as a spiritual house, to be a holy priesthood, to offer spiritual sacrifices acceptable to God through Jesus Christ...
(1 Peter 2:1–25, ESV)

Prayer: Jesus my loving Father, I pray for all the ones who are lost and misled. I pray for all those who are trying to help, I pray for your hand to guide and to give strength to the ones who are being taken advantage of Lord. I pray you to put a stop to the situations in my life that become roadblocks. Remove my mountains and I pray for all my family and friend's happiness and health, in Jesus's name, I pray, amen.

August 1

Trust and Obey

Maybe it's a test. A test of your faith. A test of your strength. A test of your will. How badly do you want to change certain aspects of your life? Are you willing then to do the work? Are you willing to obey? I am with you. I am encouraging you. Walk through this day knowing that I am with you, in all that you do, and reward you for your faithfulness. Do not grumble about the day, but instead find joy in all that you do. Let me lift you up and bring you to the place of my calling. Do not just sit and wait for things to happen. If you can take any action to move ahead then do so. Stay faithful to me my child and learn my good lessons. We can reach your goals together. Trust and obey that is the only way. Smile my child good things are in store.

These trials will show that your faith is genuine. It is being tested as fire tests and purifies gold, though your faith is far more precious than mere gold. So when your faith remains strong through many trials. It will bring you much praise and glory and honor on the day when Jesus Christ is revealed to the whole world.
(1 Peter 1:7, NLT)

Because you know that the testing of your faith produces perseverance.
(James 1:3, NIV)

But when you ask, you must believe and not doubt, because the one who doubts

*is like a wave of the sea, blown and tossed
by the wind.*
(James 1:6, NIV)

*For I will pour water on the thirsty
land, and streams on dry the ground; I will
pour my Spirit upon your offspring, and my
blessing on your descendants.*
(Isaiah 44:3, ESV)

Prayer: Father God, I lift my life to you, all my goals. I lift my friends and family to you. Help us to be diligent and successful in our work and in our lives. Remind us with kindness Lord not to give up and that all things are possible because it is you that strengthens us. I pray for peace and joy today wherever I go, and I ask you to help me to trust and obey. In Jesus's loving name, amen.

August 2

A New Way

Sometimes you must be reminded where you are. You do well with your eyes up and fixed on me. I love hearing your thankfulness when you speak to me in prayer. We are on this wondrous journey and I have much goodness in store for you. Just stay positive and keep the spirits of yourself and others lifted. Sharing the love, I've placed in your heart and continually praying for those, even the ones who have hurt you. It is something I can smile about, seeing how my grace has given you the ability to forgive others without contempt. So pleased am I by the way you are handling difficult situations. Your obedience has opened up a whole new way for you. You are finding out how good it is to be faithful to me. You can say to your negative thoughts, I know where you come from, and command them to leave. As you ask me to fill your thoughts and your mind with my beautiful truth. You are my child. You are good. You are accomplishing the tasks at hand and you are handling situations correctly when you remain to lean on me and trust in me. Keep putting on my whole armor as you start your day, and walk with the steadfast heart of love in this new way

And whenever you stand praying, forgive, if you have anything against anyone, so that your Father who is also in heaven may forgive you your trespasses.
(Mark 11:25, ESV)

Whoever covers an offense seeks love, but he who repeats a matter separates close friends.
(Proverbs 17:9, ESV)

*Therefore, my beloved brothers, be
steadfast, immovable, always abounding in
the work of the Lord, knowing that in the
Lord your labor is not in vain.*
(1 Corinthians 15:58, ESV)

Prayer: Father God, as always and forever I thank you for this day. I pray to you to keep me on the right track to cover me with your whole armor and keep my actions pure. I pray you to protect and guide each one of us today Lord. Guide us on your paths Lord today and always. Thank you, Father God, for looking out for us and for blessing us with your love. In Jesus's name, I pray, amen.

*And let us not grow weary in doing
good, for in due season we will reap, if we
do not give up.*
(Galatians 6:9, ESV)

August 3

My Beloved

Today my beloved one, wake up with a calm spirit, knowing I am with you. I walk beside you throughout your day. Smile to yourself and feel the joy of my love singing in your soul. The happiest of moments are the ones spent and filled with thoughts of me. I am the one most High. The Creator of all. I am your God who loves you, and all my children. I am Faithful, I am light. Every good and perfect gift comes from me. I never change. I am constant. I am truthful and honest. I never lie. I always keep my promises. My way is perfect. My word is flawless. I am your God who saves. I will bear with you, your daily burdens and give to you my grace and truth. I bring harmony to your soul and give you peace. No good thing will I withhold from you because you live your life for me. I am the truth and the way, and I am love. And you, my child, are my beloved...

The heavens declare the glory of God,
and the sky above proclaims his handiwork.
(Psalm 19:1, ESV)

Every good gift and perfect gift is
from above, coming down from the Father
of lights, with whom there is no variation
or shadow due to change, Of his own will
he brought us forth by the word of truth,
that we should be a kind of first fruits of his
creatures.
(James 1:17–21, ESV)

Jesus said to her, "I am the resurrection and the life. Whoever believes in me, though he die, yet shall he live, and everyone who lives and believes in me shall never die. Do you believe this?"
(John 11:25–26, ESV)

But God shows his love for us in that while we were still sinners, Christ died for us.
(Romans 5:8, ESV)

Prayer: Jesus my Father, you are so pleasing to my soul. Your ways are perfect. Thank you for taking care of my friends, family and I, Father. Thank you for giving us your love and grace. I will be confident today because I know you are with me and all my loved ones. I pray to stay faithful to who you are calling me to be. I pray in thanks for all your good gifts. I pray and thank you for the power in your name. Jesus, Jesus JESUS. Amen.

August 4

Good and Gracious Goals

Waiting in the light of my love as you have worked so hard. Do not worry. Do not fear I will reward my obedient and faithful children. The abundance of blessings comes in a flood like a river overflowing. Patience and hope accompanied with faith that I will keep my promise. That I will meet all your needs, now and forever. I know what is best for your life and when opportunities present themselves and the way opens freely, you will take that step toward the goal journeying into your future without fear, knowing my timing is always perfect. We can again have a day of beauty surrounded by this beautiful life, enjoying whatever the day holds while retaining your goals and walking in confidence. Knowing that when you put me first, the correct goals are attainable. I will open the path before you, but do not worry about the whys or the how's, but instead focus on this moment. Focus on me, and the good and gracious goals I give will be completed…and enjoy.

> *And my God will supply every need of yours according to his riches in glory in Christ Jesus.*
> (Philippians 4:19, ESV)

> *That according to the riches of his glory he may grant you to be strengthened with power through his spirit in your inner being.*
> (Ephesians 3:16, ESV)

For we are his workmanship, created in Christ Jesus good works, which God prepared beforehand, that we should walk in them.

(Ephesians 2:10, ESV)

Prayer: Father God, open the way before me, bless my every step, my every thought my every action. Keep my thoughts on you and your will not my own. I thank you for the victory you have given me and all the blessings daily, no matter how small as I am truly thankful for it all. Thank you for my children and my family and friends. I pray that everyone may be filled with the light of your everlasting love and feel your Presence as we work to obtain your good and gracious goals for our lives. In Jesus's name, I pray, amen and amen.

August 5

Made New

Be brave and stand strong. The world will keep moving at light speed, but you have placed your life in my hands, and my timing is not of this world as this world is flawed. My timing is perfect and when you live your life for me, ways open up before you that the world could never offer. There are so many new and wonderful things that I will show you. Stay faithful my child always hoping and remaining in faith as I am your one true Father. I am your Savior. You have learned so much and are continuing with me on this journey. Your light is shining so brightly, I have made and fashioned you with love. You can offer an example of what it means to live your life for me. Keep learning and growing and trusting in my ways. How blessed you truly are. And how beautiful your soul is when you learn to embrace, what I have made new... You.

Behold, I am doing a new thing; now it springs forth, do you not perceive it? I will make a way in the wilderness and rivers in the desert.
(Isaiah 43:19, ESV)

And he who was seated on the throne said, "Behold, I am making all things new." Also, he said, "Write this down, for these words are trustworthy and true."
(Revelation 21:5, ESV)

And I will give you a new heart, and a new spirit I will put within you. And I

will remove the heart of stone from your
flesh and give you a heart of flesh.
(Ezekiel 36:26, ESV)

And though your beginning was small,
your latter days will be very great.
(Job 8:7, ESV)

Prayer: Father God thank you for making me the person I am today for leading me to be completely new and fashioned in your love. I pray for all today that they may find you and hold fast to you and experience your love just as I have, in Jesus's loving name, I pray, amen.

August 6

Feed the Soul

Don't give up. Do not let one bad situation take up all your time. Pulling your attention away from me. Realize my child how strong you are. Look at how far you've come. Keep your attention on me through the midst of the storms. You know that all the trials are fleeting. If you look at your life as a whole, you can see truly how much you have gone through, and you'll notice the places and moments where I was moving in your life. Keep me close and push off anxious thoughts or negative feelings. Fill yourself with the truth of my spirit. I am Love. I am light, a coolness amid the desert. I am the bread of your life and my word is the living water. Read and learn my words found within the pages of the Bible. Can you see now how without me my children will thirst? They thirst for me and my goodness. Keep your soul fed. Be strong my dear one.

Blessed are those who hunger and thirst for righteousness, for they shall be satisfied.
(Matthew 5:6, ESV)

For the bread of God is he who comes down from heaven and gives life to the world. They said to him, "Sir, give us this bread always." Jesus said to them, "I am the bread of life; whoever comes to me shall not hunger, and whoever believes in me shall not thirst."
(John 6:33–35, ESV)

But he answered, "It is written, 'Man shall not live by bread alone, but by every word that comes from the mouth of God.'"
(Matthew 4:4, ESV)

So Jesus said to them, "Truly, truly I say to you, unless you eat the flesh of the Son of Man and drink his blood, you have no life in you."
(John 6:53, ESV)

Your words were found, I ate them, and your words became a joy and the delight of my heart, for I am called by your name, O Lord, God of hosts.
(Jeremiah 15:16, ESV)

Prayer: Father God. I come before you today and thank you for this day that you have made. I pray for all my family and friends, Lord, keep our souls fed with the power of your Holy Spirit. And help us daily in our walk to pick up the Bible and read your words. In Jesus's name, I ask, and I pray, amen.

August 7

The Good Way

You are my child; I will never give up on you. I will always stand with you. You have shown your faithfulness considering your circumstances and have held tightly to my hand. I'm so proud of you all that you're becoming and the way you are growing. Smile my beloved, the time is now to believe in yourself the way that I believe in you. Just as you are faithful to me, I also am faithful to you. You no longer need to wrestle with the thoughts of doubt or fear, but you can be confident in knowing that you are on your way and those blessings will abound, in every good way. Take these good steps with me, never doubting, always trusting, counting your blessings, as it is good. Find my steps and follow where are I am leading each and every day, for this is my good purpose for your life, and it is my good way.

> *Then God said, "Let there be light;" and there was light. And God saw that the light was good, And God separated the light from the darkness. God called the light Day, and the darkness he called Night. And there was evening and there was morning the first day.*
> (1 Genesis 3–5, ESV)

> *The night is far gone; the day is at hand. So then let us cast off the works of darkness and put on the armor of light.*
> (Romans 13:12, ESV)

Thus, says the Lord: Stand by the
roads, and look, and ask for ancient paths,
Where the good way is and walk in it, and
find rest for your souls. But you said, "We
will not walk in it."
(Jeremiah 6:16, ESV)

For he guards the course of the just
and protects the way of his faithful ones.
Then you will understand what is
right and just and fair-every good path.
(Proverbs 2:8–9, NIV)

Prayer: Father God, I come to you and ask you to guard my heart my mind. Guide my steps, always leading me and all my loved ones in your good and perfect ways. My heart is thankful Lord to you. I lift up every thought and every action to you. I pray Lord, that I may always do what is pleasing to you. When I fall short Lord forgive me and pick me up and set me back on your good path. In Jesus's name, I pray and ask and thank you. Amen.

August 8

Everything Is Possible

Good morning my child, take a moment with me and just relax your mind, slow down your thoughts. You can find your shelter in me. I wrap you in the cloak of my love. I provide the sustenance your soul needs to flourish and grow. Do not let anything steal your focus away from me, but instead invite me into all the areas of your life, even the ones that require a great deal of your time and we can do it together. Keep no door closed to me. I will guard your heart and your mind. Sending you beautiful little love signs along the way. I am the one who will never leave you. I will never forsake you. Nothing you have said or done could make me turn away from you now or ever. So do not turn away from me. I desire to show you many good things and deliver you out of the muck of this world today. I desire to replace your doubts and fears with confidence and courage. I desire you to be bold and brave. I will help you take charge of your life and guide your steps. You can achieve everything with me. Nothing is impossible for me. Stay strong my child.

He guards the path of justice, and preserves the way of His saints. Then you will understand righteousness and justice, Equity and every good path.
(Proverbs 2:8–9, NKJV)

Teach me to do your will, for You are my God; Let your good spirit lead me on level ground.
(Psalm 143:10, NIV)

But Jesus looked at them and said,
"With man this is impossible, but with God
all things are possible."
(Matthew 19:26, ESV)

Prayer: Father God, please replace my doubt and fears with confidence and direct my steps lead me and my family and friends in your will. Thank you for giving us, your grace and love. I pray you to help us to make good decisions and to follow the paths that you have created for us. Help us all to be more honest with you. In Jesus's name, I thank you for this day and I pray, amen.

August 9

Do Not Problem

Be encouraged, my dear one. Go out spread my good news. Life will always happen, relationship problems, work problems, home problems, mechanical problems, money problems...etc. They will always exist in this life, and in this world. I'm glad to see you recognize that I am not of this world and know my ways are higher, therefore know all these problems that exist in life are fleeting and changing constantly. Even the best things in this life will change, but I never change. My love for you never changes, and my power never changes. I am the Messiah. I am your God! Put no other gods before me. No Idols or distractions, such as problems should take up so much of your time. Do not worship your problems. Do not make them any more important. Stop spending far too much time worrying about them. You give life to them when you sit and dwell on them. Spinning your mind into circles. Taking away the hours you should be focusing on me. I will help you with your problems. Trust me with these. Have patience. Live your life with purpose. Do not "problem" your life to live. Live for me and walk in my good ways. Live in peace.

And call on me in the day of trouble;
I will deliver you, and you shall glorify me.
(Psalm 50:15, ESV)

Praise be to the God and Father of our
Lord Jesus Christ, the father of compassion
and the God of all comfort, who comforts us
in all our troubles, so that we can comfort

those in any trouble with the comfort we ourselves receive from God.
(2 Corinthians 1:3–4, NIV)

Peace I leave with you; my peace I give you. I do not give to you as the world gives. Do not let your heart be troubled and do not be afraid.
(John 14:27, NIV)

I have told you these things, so that in me you may have peace. In this world you will have trouble. But take heart! I have overcome the world.
(John 16:33, NIV)

Prayer: Father God, please fill me with calm and peace. Give us all the strength to overcome the problems and troubles in this life. Help keep us focused on you and all your good ways. In Jesus's name, I pray and thank you. Amen.

August 10

You Have Heard

They have heard my voice from the heart of fire on Mount Sinai. So why then do you question yourself also hearing the voice of my Holy Spirit which lives within you. I want you to be obedient and confident, and not fall prey to the evil one who attacks your mind. Oh, so many doubts and unsure steps. How can you move forward with me when you are trembling in fear? You are worrying that you have made the wrong choices or decisions. You need to learn to trust me and my ways. This means every day. Not just every other day or once a month but every second…of every minute…of every hour…of every day. I know this task is not easy. I know how hard it is for you to believe and not see. But I am asking this of you. FAITH! I am asking you to keep your faith, so that you may live and flourish in love and abundance and be who I have created you to be. Do you remember all the times that for just a split second you knew it was me, then the knowledge dissipated quickly? Swiftly fleeting away as your worldly mind has set in. Do not try to convince yourself that coincidences exist they do not. I hear your prayers, and I answer. You are always my child. I forgave you and you are still forgiven. Let me guide your heart always.

Give ear, O heavens, and I will speak, and let the earth hear the words of my mouth. May my teaching drop as rain, my speech distills the dew, like gentle rain upon tender grass, and like showers upon the herb.
(Deuteronomy 32:1–2, ESV)

Moreover, he said to me, "Son of man, all my words I shall speak to you receive in your heart, and hear with your ears."
(Ezekiel 3:10, ESV)

Then the Lord spoke to you out of the midst of the fire. You heard the sound of words, but saw no form; there was only a voice.
(Deuteronomy 4:12, ESV)

Does he who supplies the Spirit to you and works miracles among you do so by works of the law, or by hearing with faith.
(Galatians 3:5, ESV)

Call me and I will answer you, and tell you great and hidden things that you have not known.
(Jeremiah 33:3, ESV)

Prayer: Father God, I lift up my family and friends to you. Oh Lord, I lift up myself as well. Help me Lord Jesus to be confident in hearing you and your will so that I may walk with strength in your ways and not my own. Keep us all safe from the enemy's attacks on our minds and keep our focus on you. Please guide our hearts. Always in Jesus's name, I pray. Amen.

August 11

Our Good Purpose

Living each day with my purpose brings sweetness to your soul. All my children, each one has a purpose. A calling. A job. A special something that I have called them to do. How wonderful it is when they start to realize what their purpose is. For each one of you is fearfully and wonderfully made. Fashioned in my likeness and made with love. Created with compassion. Kissed with kindness. Graced with victory and blessed with purpose. Celebrate each other and share this wonderful thing called life. Share my good news and be excited about your next. Be thankful for what is now. Hallelujah!

I praise you, for I am fearfully and wonderfully made. Wonderful are your works; my soul knows full well.
(Psalm 139:4, ESV)

And all these blessings shall come upon you and overtake you, if you obey the voice of the Lord your God.
(Deuteronomy 28:2, ESV)

So God created man in his own image, in the image of God he created him; both male and female he created them.
(Genesis 1:27, ESV)

But rise and stand upon your feet, for I have appeared to you for this purpose, to appoint you as a servant and witness to the

*things in which you have seen me and to
those in which I will appear to you.*
(Acts 26:16, ESV)

*And Jesus came to and said to them,
"All authority in heaven and on earth has
been given to me. Go therefore and make
disciples of all nations, baptizing them in
the name of the Father and of the Son and of
the Holy Spirit, teaching them to observe all
that I have commanded you. And behold, I
am with you always, to the end of the age."*
(Matthew 28:18–20, ESV)

Prayer: Father God, thank you for your good purpose
for our lives. Thank you, for our next. Thank you, for your
good and righteous ways. How blessed we all are to be loved
by you and surrounded with your grace. Thank you In Jesus's
name, I give thanks, amen.

August 12

Encompass His Good Way

Encompass all that's good. All that surrounds you and fills you with joy. Today let the song of my love fill within your spirit. Be thankful for all that you have. Do not compare what you have to what others have. My grace is sufficient for you. I am your Shepherd; you shall not want any more than what I have given. You must not worry about tomorrow, or what you do not have today. My ways are higher and my plans for you are good. Trust me with your whole heart. Do not try to force situations into happening as everything is on my time and my timing is always perfect. Be happy now, don't put your happiness away and wait until everything is the way you think it should be. Love your life today my child. As tomorrow may never come. So today I'm encouraging you with love, let it be the way it is, and everything will be okay. Trust in your Father, I'm the one who saves. Smile and be filled with joy today, my beloved. It's a good day.

The end of the matter; has been heard.
Fear God and keep his commandments, for
this is the whole duty of man.
(Ecclesiastes 12:13, ESV)

And by this we know that we have
come to know him, if we keep his com-
mandments. Whoever says "I know him"
but does not keep his commandments is a
liar, and the truth is not in him.
(1 John 3:4, ESV)

*And I am sure of this, that he who
began a good work in you will bring it to
completion at the day of Jesus Christ.*
(Philippians 1:6, ESV)

Prayer: Father God, there is a situation that I feel an urgency in. That I have prayed and waited on, please guide me, Father as to what to do next. Please fill my heart with joy and help me to remember that every day is a good day because I have you. I am trying my best Father to live in the way you have called me to live. Please forgive me for my shortcomings. Today… I choose to be happy and I am thankful to you for all my blessings. I pray for all my family and friends as well as people all over the world. Lord, make our paths straight with the love found only in you, In Jesus's name, I pray, amen.

August 13

You Are

Good morning my child, there are things you need to always hold onto. Not the things of the past but the things in which I have placed deep in your heart. I have called you to a purpose and it will be fulfilled. No one can stop what I have declared over your life. How wonderful it is when my perfect plan is being realized by you. I know it has taken you some time to understand the work which I am doing in and through you. Keep your gaze steady upon me. Cast your cares, and relinquish those doubt-filled thoughts to me, as I will handle the enemy. You must know what you are worth to me. You have great worth. You are my child. A child of GOD. The world around will always have inconsistencies and may not always have level ground to stand upon, but I am always consistent I never change, so you can then be confident and stand on my word. Everything I've spoken over you, every dream I have declared for you, every promise I have made you… Everything I have said concerning you, all of it will be fulfilled. Yes, my beloved child, I have plans for your life. Great and mighty plans to give you hope and a future. Plans to prosper you and not to harm you. Thank me even in the storms. Just know I am doing something good. You are loved. You can go forward with love.

But to all who did receive him, who believed in his name, he gave the right to become the children of God.
(John 1:12, ESV)

That you may be blameless and innocent, children of God without blemish in

the midst of a crooked and twisted gener-
ation, among whom you shine as lights to
the world.
　(Philippians 2:15, ESV)

For I know the plans I have for you,
declares the Lord, plans for welfare and not
for evil, to give you a future and a hope.
　(Jeremiah 29:11, ESV)

And I will be a Father to you, and you
shall be sons and daughters to me, says the
Lord Almighty.
　(2 Corinthians 6:18, ESV)

Prayer: Thank you for this day. Today Lord, I will walk with your mighty presence within me and before me, that you may lead me Lord in your will. I trust you Father God and am also praying for all my family and friends and brothers and sisters in Christ. Help us, Lord, to become what you have called us to be. We love you, Father. I pray for our paths each and every one that they will open up and become clear to us Lord. In Jesus's name, I pray, amen.

August 14

Bringing Back

Bringing back what the enemy has stolen, you will be living in abundance and able to share all my good news. Share my words, share the scripture found in the Bible. Encourage others to learn me, especially the ones who do not know me. Introduce me to them. Really think about how you would describe me. The more you spend time with me, the more you are able to share with others my good news and ways. Before, when you lived your life from the worldly perspective, I watched you struggle as you tried to do things on your own without me. But now I am doing a new thing in you. As you have asked me into your life. You can accomplish things that before were just out of reach. Keep moving forward in joy and with love for all, I am making your way.

And after you have suffered a little while, the God of all grace who has called you to his eternal glory in Christ, will himself restore, confirm, strengthen, and establish you.
(1 Peter 5:10, ESV)

The spirit of the Lord is upon me, because he has anointed me to proclaim the good news to the poor. He has sent me to proclaim liberty to the captives and recovering of sight to the blind, to set at liberty those who are oppressed.
(Luke 4:18, ESV)

See, I am doing a new thing! Now
it springs up; do you not perceive it? I am
making a way in the wilderness and streams
in the wasteland.
(Isaiah 43:19, NIV)

Prayer: Father God, thank you for making me a new creation for doing this new and good thing. I pray for all my family and friend's protection, health, love, joy, peace, and abundance. I pray we get back all the enemy has stolen. I thank you and love you Lord with my whole heart. In Jesus's name, I pray. Amen.

August 15

Become Rooted

Good morning my beloved, the sun has come up today, but there are times in your life that the sun shines outside, but inside there are storms brewing. You must find your steps and become rooted in me. Life has many stages and phases but no matter your earthly age, there will always be storms. Arm yourself with my power and my glory. Each and every day read my word, as it will become a lamp unto your feet and light up my good way through the darkness. Find your steps...again I say, "read my word, become rooted." Nothing is impossible with your eyes fixed on me. I am immeasurably more than you can imagine. I am here to be your support, to be your strength and to guide you. When the winds of life are howling around you, blowing toward you, do not fear. Remember my child you have chosen to be rooted in me. Think of it like this...the more you read my word the more you grow, the deeper the roots grow. With me as your foundation, and the deeper your rooted in me, you can then withstand the most unimaginable storm. Be joyful today my child, finding the peace I have for you.

> *Let your roots grow down into him, and let your lives be built on him. Then your faith will grow strong in the truth you were taught, and you will overflow with thankfulness.*
> (Colossians 2:7, NLT)

> *Blessed is the man who trusts in the Lord, whose trust is the Lord. He is like a tree planted by water, that sends out its*

roots by the stream, and does not fear when heat comes, for its leaves remain green, and is not anxious in the year of drought, for it does not cease to bear fruit.
(Jeremiah 17:7–8, ESV)

That according to the riches of his glory he may grant you to be strengthened with power through his spirit in your inner being, so that Christ may dwell in your hearts through faith, that you, being rooted and grounded in love, may have the strength to comprehend with all the saints what is the breadth and length and height and depth, and to know the love of Christ that surpasses knowledge, that you may be filled with all the fullness of God.
(Ephesians 3:16–19, ESV)

Prayer: Father God, thank you that I may be more like you, that I may feel your love and share it with others. Always help us all to become deeply rooted in you Lord, and to stand firm on your foundation. I pray and ask, giving thanks, in Jesus's name. Amen.

August 16

Coming Home

I have surrounded you with other believers to share encouragement giving strength to each other. Bringing all my children, each and everyone together. When my children share with each other the power of the love and grace they have in me found, it creates a fire, a brave and strong stir within your souls. Soon you will begin to feel empowered and recharged. I love it when my children share their testimonies with each other, just reinforcing how truly loved they are. Sharing my glory. I also am pleased when you share me with nonbelievers. Giving them a glimpse of how much love and grace I offer all my children. No one is too far gone for me to save. Not one. I will wait for them just as I waited for you. Their backs may be turned now but keep surrounding them with the light of my love. I'm calling all my children to be a light to others. To the ones who are now lost in the darkness. Not only to be an example to them, but also to pray for them. Once they have asked me into their hearts, they are found, and lost no more. It is joyful, like a tearful reunion and the day they get baptized as their sins are washed away... they come up from the water a new transformed creation, their sins are remembered no more. They have a hope for a future and a purpose to live, full of happiness and confidence. An assurance of the fulfillment of every eternal promise I have made, and that my child is even sweeter still, as now they can say," My Savior, my Lord, I'm home."

For where there are two or three gathered in my name, there I am among them.
(Matthew 18:20, ESV)

And let us consider how to stir up one another to love and good works, not neglecting to meet together, as is the habit of some, but encouraging one another, and all the more as you see the Day drawing near.
(Hebrews 10:24–25, ESV)

And Peter said to them, "Repent and be baptized every one of you in the name of Jesus Christ for the forgiveness of your sins, and you will receive the gift of the Holy Spirit."
(Acts 2:38, ESV)

In my Fathers house are many rooms. If it were not so, would I have told you that I go to prepare a place for you?
(John 14:2, ESV)

I have indeed built you an exalted house, a place for you to dwell forever.
(1 Kings 8:13, ESV)

Prayer: Father God, I thank you Lord for this day you have made. I pray for all your children Lord, let us be a blessing to others encouraging and welcoming everyone to the joy of your good news and the hope that is found in you. My hope is in you Lord every day. I am thankful for this life you have given me. Let all those who don't know you, find you and help us to welcome them home. I love you, Lord. In Jesus's name, I pray, amen.

August 17

New and Good Things

Try new good things. Don't be afraid to try new things, my child, whether it be the pursuit of a different country, career or exploring a different place. Trying new things is good. it allows you to experience life in a whole new way. When traveling you get to see all the beauty in the world around you. New scenery is good for your soul. There is so much I've created that you haven't even glimpsed yet. Go and be blessed, my child. Keep walking in my will and doing what I've called you to do. There is hope for tomorrow and peace in the beauty of today. It is good to have dreams and to work toward them. Set goals high, you can accomplish them with the help of my power and grace. I leveled all the mountains and have overcome every obstacle just to set you free. Live with the attitude of perseverance and diligence always walking in my good ways. I have set the path before you, opening the way to which you will be able to explore and travel all the beauty I've created firsthand. Taking me and my good news wherever you go.

And I heard the voice of the Lord saying, "Whom shall I send, and who will go for us?" Then I said, "Here am I! Send me."
(Isaiah 6:8, ESV)

For you shall go out in joy and be led forth in peace; the mountains and the hills before you shall break forth into singing, and all the trees of the field shall clap their hands.
(Isaiah 55:12, ESV)

And he said to them, "Go into all the world and proclaim the gospel to the whole creation."
(Mark 16:15, ESV)

Prayer: Father God, thank you for my opportunities to experience the beauty in this life. Thank you for your creation I pray to always be able to bravely share your good news with all I encounter. I pray for all my family and friends that we keep surrounded by your love and grace and get to experience new places and see the beauty in this world you have created. In Jesus's name, I pray and give thanks, amen.

August 18

His Good Ways Always

Find enjoyment in friends. It is good to laugh and enjoy the day. Everyone must find time to rest. Communication with me is so very important for your soul as I can help you to find the happiness that is deep within your heart. Give yourself a much-needed break. Be lighthearted and laugh with good friends. Surround yourself with happiness and beauty. When blessings flood in, remember I will keep you afloat amongst all this good busy-ness. Remember to rest with me. All life ebbs and flows. At times calm and slow and other times busy and rushed. Hold tightly to my hand, during it all. Even in the rushed and most momentous of days, keep my peace and calm inside you. There is a process to everything and an order. Do not try to experience too much at once. Just walk with me my child following my good ways and my good and perfect pace. Wake up with thankfulness. Watch the sunset at the end of a glorious day. Take time to take in the wonderful beauty in this world. Be blessed by blessing others and sharing me with them. Promoting always all my good ways. Keep it simple my child and journey on with me in my good ways, always.

When I look at your heavens, the work of your fingers, the moon and the stars, which you have set in place, what is man that you are mindful of him, and the son of man that you care for him?
(Psalm 8:3–4, ESV)

God called the dry land Earth, and the waters that were gathered together he

called the Seas. and God saw that it was good.
(Genesis 1:10, ESV)

I believe that I shall look upon the goodness of the Lord in the land of the living!
(Psalm 27:13, ESV)

Oh, taste and see that the Lord is good! Blessed is the man who takes refuge in him! Oh, fear the Lord, you his saints, for those who fear him have no lack!
(Psalm 34:8–9, ESV)

And above all these put on love, which binds everything together in perfect harmony.
(Colossians 3:14, ESV)

Prayer: Father God, today I celebrate you and all your good ways. I give thanks to you Lord for all the blessings in this day and always. I pray for all my family and friends that we may always find beauty in your creation. In Jesus's name, I pray, amen

August 19

By Him We Are Called

I have traced out a life for you. I have called you to it. I have waited in patience for you to walk in my ways and be accepting of my good Presence. I have watched you make many mistakes. But have always forgiven you freely and showed you my endless grace. I watched as you struggled to try to do things on your own. But then the light of my love began to direct your heart, and you began to take notice of me, and the warmth of my light began to show you a new way. A way more beautiful and worthy of purpose. A way above all others. Happy am I that you have decided to give in to my plans and are learning to stay within the concepts of my will, giving up those ideas you have had for your life and surrendering them to me. It is good that you recognize my call, as you take up your cross daily and follow me. There is much to accomplish, but the time we have is not rushed, as I am not constrained to earthly limitations of time. I am constant and timeless. My mercy and grace are found everywhere. Always be thankful and do your best. Serving me first above all others and things in this life. Finding my unfailing love. You will soar like an Eagle. Graceful and unstoppable. My beautiful creation, My beloved, my child.

You did not choose me, but I chose you and appointed you that you should go and bear fruit and that your fruit should also abide, so that whatever you ask the Father in my name, he may give it to you.
(John 15:16, ESV)

And he said to all, "If anyone would come after me, let him deny himself and take up his cross daily and follow me."
(Luke 9:23, ESV)

For the word of the cross is folly to those who are perishing, but to us who are being saved, it is the power of God.
(1 Corinthians 1:18, ESV)

But do not overlook this one fact, beloved, that with the Lord one day is as a thousand years, and a thousand years as one day.
(2 Peter 3:8, ESV)

Prayer: Lord, help us daily, as we take up our cross. I am hopeful in your promises. I give all the glory to you. I praise your mighty name Jesus, and it is your name that saves, I give thanks, amen.

August 20

Be Kind to All

Be kind to all, even to those who have offended you. I know it is hard to do to be forgiving when someone has hurt you, but this is what I'm calling you to do. Many were cruel to me and tried to offend me as I lived among you. But my heart is so big that no offense did I take. In fact, I called to the Father to forgive them because they knew not what they were doing. Just as many who hurt with words or angry actions do not think before they speak or act, wrapped up in their own selfish attitudes and desires. Pray for them my child and forgive them. Give them to me. I will set the way before them. You are my child and I have made you be loving and kind compassionate and forgiving. When you try to live differently from the way I have made you, hardships set in, difficulties grow big. Problems will start to consume your hearts and minds. This is not the way of my good grain; I would call living like this dishonest. By way of promoting opposition. Being unforgiving staying upset or angry. Having a spiteful spirit is, in fact, living against the grain. It is harder to live in this manner and retain any ounce of love or joy that I have given you. So do not get caught in the ways of selfishness. Keep my sharing spirit, Act justly, love mercy, walk humbly with your God.

If you forgive others their trespasses,
your heavenly Father will also forgive you.
(Matthew 6:14, ESV)

Then Peter came up and said to
him, "Lord, how often will my brother sin
against me, and I forgive him? As many as

seven times?" Jesus said to him, "I do not say
to you seven times, but seventy-seven times."
(Matthew 18:21–22, ESV)

He has shown you, O man, what is
good. What does the Lord require of you,
but to act justly, to love mercy, and to walk
humbly with your God?
(Micah 6:8, NHEB)

Prayer: Father God help me be forgiving. Lead me in the way I should live. Guide my thoughts and help me to be kind when I feel angry to help me to release my frustrations. Help me to also be forgiving of myself when I fall short. I pray today for all my family and friends. Release us from resentments and help us to not become judgmental or selfish. Keep our eyes focused on you and your goodness Lord. Fill our hearts today with your love. In Jesus's name, I ask and pray... Amen.

August 21

Even in the Stillness

I am here with you, even if you do not feel me, even if you do not hear me. I am with you. I never leave your side. Do not let anxious thoughts spin out of control. At first, you may feel the need to speak endlessly about the same problems you gave to me yesterday. You only have to use three little words, "Jesus help me." How powerful my name is, Jesus! Call out to me during the times of silence, and then just sit quietly…

Stand still and let me give you rest, I know you have been heavy with burden, be still my child, I am leading you always, even in the stillness. Even in the deserts, I am leading. Do not stray from me by taking your focus off me, in the emptiness of this day. I am still working. It is okay to spend quiet time with me. Letting your thoughts blow away. I know everything that is in your heart. I know the troubles of your mind, and I am in control. Learn to be still and know that I am God. Learn to sit silently with me. No worries to think about. Just the beauty of this day and all that I have created. If there is an urgency that arises, I can handle it. You are never alone. But for now, stand still and be still knowing, you are, my child and you are loved.

Now therefore stand still and see this great thing that the Lord will do before your eyes.
(1 Samuel 12:16, ESV)

The Lord will fight for you, and you only have to be silent.
(Exodus 14:14, ESV)

He who calls you is faithful; he surely will do it.
(1 Thessalonians 5:24, ESV)

Be still, and know that I am God. I will be exalted among the nations; I will be exalted in the earth.
(Psalm 46:10, ESV)

Prayer: Father God, thank you for this day, thank you for the stillness in this day, and the closeness to you it brings. I pray for all my family and friends your will—your way. In Jesus's name. Amen.

August 22

You Belong to Me

Keep praying, I hear every word, of every prayer, from every heart of all my children. Sometimes I will send an angel, to help see you through the darkness. Often times my Presence inside, so bright will light up the way before you. Oh...what has my creation become. In the last days' people have become lovers of money, lovers of pleasure, and lovers of themselves, lovers of doing evil. You must guard your hearts and do not get swept away like so many around you, pray for them. Keep your focus on me, and the love for me and my righteous and good ways. Act justly seeking no reward for your good deeds but the reward which only I can give, as your heart fills with my everlasting love. Keep your love for others and spread kindness wherever you go. Share happiness. Let your light shine brightly for all to see and confidently proclaim to the world that you belong to me.

Know that the Lord, he is God! It is he who made us, and we are his; we are his people, and the sheep of his pasture.
(Psalm 100:3, ESV)

Little children, you are from God and have overcome them, for he who is in you is greater than he who is in the world.
(1 John 4:4, ESV)

I give them eternal life, and no one will snatch them out of my hand.
(John 10:28, ESV)

I press on toward the goal for the prize
of the upward call of God in Christ Jesus.
(Philippians 3:14, ESV)

Prayer: Father God, protect us, Lord, from the ways of the world. I pray to be a blessing to others letting your light shine brightly from within my heart. I Pray for your love to lead us each and every day. Help me to save those lost in darkness. Help me to boldly speak about You and the eternal gift you offer. Help me to lead others into Salvation. In the name of Jesus, I pray, amen.

August 23

Beautiful Truths

Your heart will sing full of the beautiful truths I've placed in it. The more time you spend with me the more vibrant and filled you will become. My spirit within you, like a beautiful song, gifting life into your soul. My thoughts fill within your mind. You have finally found something and someone who will last forever. I am, "The Eternal King." I will for all eternity, love you. I've set you on the path of righteousness. Nothing can separate you from my beautiful truths, as they will carry on and on. Like an endless river flowing and drifting across the land ending where it starts and staring where it ends. Like a flower garden, are all my children. Each one is so different. Different petals and leaves shaded with lighter and darker greens and each of their petals different shapes and beautiful colors. Yet what allows them to grow are all the same ingredients of life. When by themselves they hold a unique single beauty and a faint fragrant sweetness, but together, surrounded by all the different varieties of blooms they create the most glorious canvas, and their sweet perfume fills the air. Just the way my children do when they are together, giving me praise and worshipping. They are the most beautiful scenery outside of Heaven. I love watching them all together, sharing with each other my pre-eminent love. I have called them to love each other just as I love them. Because you choose to follow me, you will become like a beautiful bloom, full of all the radiant ingredients of life and my Holy Spirit within. How beautiful you are my child. Open your gaze, and you will see, all my beautiful truths...

Our lives are a Christ-like fragrance
rising up to God. But this fragrance is per-

*ceived differently by those who are being
saved and those who are perishing.*
(2 Corinthians 2:15, NIV)

*He has made everything beautiful
in its time. He has also set eternity in the
human heart; yet no one can fathom what
God has done from beginning to end.*
(Ecclesiastes 3:11, NIV)

*Therefore let us be grateful for receiv-
ing a kingdom that cannot be shaken, and
thus let us offer to God acceptable worship,
with reverence and awe, for our God is a
consuming fire.*
(Hebrews 12:28–29, ESV)

God brings the ingredients of life…
His Spirit is the light, bright and warm like the sun.
His Holy words are the living waters and food for our
souls.

Prayer: Lord, today I simply say I love you, and I praise
your mighty name. Everything within my heart you know,
and I thank you for it all. Thank you for my beautiful family
and friends. In Jesus's name, I pray, amen.

August 24

Walk with Him, His Way

Walk with your Lord, head held high, feet planted on a righteous solid path. Nothing can slow you down when you find the way of my will. No mountains, no peaks, no valleys, nothing can separate you from me and what I've designed for your life. Keep moving forward confidently. You are so brave my child, stepping out onto faith believing in something you cannot see or have yet to fully understand. But you have found me inside. It is my Holy Spirit within you. You have asked me into your heart, and I am here forever with you, helping you, guiding you. Filling up all the empty parts of you. I have made you full. Be courageous! Do not let fear stop you or slow you down. Cast it off. Go forward. Running straight at what scares you and remember the one who calls you to do so is the lover of your soul. So walk with me. My will, my way.

Even as he chose us in him before the foundation of the world, that we should be holy and blameless before him, in love he predestined us for adoption as sons through Jesus Christ, according to the purpose of his will.
(Ephesians 1:4–5, ESV)

I know your works. Behold, I have set before you an open door, which no one is able to shut. I know that you have but little power, and yet you have kept my word and have not denied my name.
(Revelation 3:8, ESV)

You whom I took from the ends of the Earth, and called from the farthest corners, saying to you, "You are my servant, I have chosen you and not cast you off"; fear not, for I am with you; be not dismayed, for I am your God; I will strengthen you, I will help you, I will uphold you with my righteous right hand.
(Isaiah 41:9–10, ESV)

Prayer: Father God, help me to truly give up my will and live by yours. I want your will and ways for my life. I cast off fear and step out in faith into the unknown with you by my side and your Holy Spirit within me. I ask your Holy Spirit to lead me and show me the righteous and good ways that you are calling me to go. I pray in the confidence that you will supply the victory in my life and for those around me. In Jesus's name, I pray and thank you, Father, again, I thank you for the victory, amen.

August 25

Undeniable Love

Sending you my gifts in a big way. It's undeniable how much I love you. I shower you with sunshine as the morning begins. I surround you with the beauty of nature, all the animals and fish in the sea. When night falls, I send you the twinkling lights of all the stars in the sky. I give to you all the world, to explore and see. New Experiences are happening every day. Find me in it all. Counting every blessing along the way. Trusting me frees you up to enjoy and not to worry about what is on the way. Every good and perfect gift is from me. Smile in your soul feeling my fullness of grace in your heart. Learn to love your journey and find the beauty inside, all my creation. It exists just as my undeniable love.

> *But ask the beasts, and they will teach you; the birds of the heavens, and they will tell you, or the bushes of the earth, and they will teach you, and the fish in the sea will declare to you. Who among all these does not know that the hand of the Lord has done this? In his hand is the life of every living thing and the breath of all mankind.*
> (Job 12:7–10, ESV)

> *When I look at the heavens, the work of your fingers, the moon and the stars, which you have set in place, what is man that you are mindful of him, and the son of man that you care for him?*
> (Psalm 8:3–4, ESV)

Worthy are you, our Lord and God, to receive glory and honor and power, for you created all things, and by your will, they existed and were created.
(Revelation 4:11, ESV)

Prayer: Father God, I thank you for all your beautiful gifts of life. I pray to truly enjoy all this life you have formed and to always stand in awe looking up to the heavens as I know all was created by you. I praise your name Jesus and I love you. It is in your name I pray and am thankful, amen.

August 26

What's Next

What's next? Many of my children are too prone to the quick fix of the day. Always bored seeking the next thing. Wanting so much for something to fill up their lives and thoughts, so they do not have to deal with any true issues. I want you to be different, I want all my children to quit looking to the ideas and pastimes of the world as their next. I have so much more in store for my children then just fleeting, passing jumble and a barrage of mindless nothing. Indeed, I have something. It is my good and perfect plan for their lives. But they must truly trust me. When they do this, it becomes okay to have nothing on the surface to do. Your nothing is my something. Take your empty hours and grow your relationship with me. Reading my word and praying with me. Do this and you will begin to see a new way, a more rewarding way, and a perfect way. A path that makes you feel so full of joy that you will no longer worry about what is next and learn to enjoy what is now. Even in the storms thank me and watch how they pass away differently than they have before. I have got your next. I am in control of that, so no fear or worries, just stay on my path walking in my will. Enjoying the days moment by moment with me, as I am holding your hand. Leaning not on your own understanding but trusting me with your whole heart. Soon your next will come.

So flee youthful passions and pursue
righteous faith, love, peace, along with those
who call on the Lord from a pure heart.
(2 Timothy 2:22, ESV)

Instead you ought to say, "If the Lord wills, we will live and do this or that."
(James 4:15, ESV)

When the Spirit of truth comes, he will guide you into all the truth, for he will not speak on his own authority, but whatever he hears he will speak, and he will declare to you the things that are to come.
(John 16:13, ESV)

Prayer: Father God thank you for my next and thank you for my now. I will try to remember, Lord, to try and count even the storms as a blessing. I Pray for all my family and friends and me, Lord, to enjoy the present time you have given and feel peace in knowing that you have our next and we can trust you, Lord, as you keep us on your good and righteous paths. I Pray again for peace in Jesus's name, amen.

August 27

Sovereign

I am sovereign over your life. I will set your ways before you. I know at times you can let emotions run away with your thoughts or actions. Forgive yourself, just as I have forgiven you. Staying in the present moment can be a help to your soul. You can truly appreciate everything I've created when you see with your eyes and do not get caught up in the thoughts within your mind. Ask me to guide your thoughts, so you do not linger there too long on worldly problems. My Love is perfect. Perfect love casts out fear. Reach for my love and it is there, ask and you shall receive. Seek me you will find me, in everything every day. As I am Sovereign over your life…and you will be perfected in my mighty hands.

And you will know the truth, and the truth will set you free.
(John 8:32, ESV)

There is no fear in love. But perfect love drives out fear, because fear has to do with punishment. The one who fears is not made perfect in love.
(1 John 4:18, NIV)

With God are wisdom and might; he has counsel and understanding. If he tears down, none can rebuild; if he shuts a man in, none can open. If he withholds the waters, they dry up; if he sends them out, they overwhelm the land. With him are

strength and sound wisdom; the deceived
and the deceiver are his.
(Job 12:13–16, ESV)

Remember the former things of old;
for I am God, and there is no other; I am
God, and there is none like me, declar-
ing the end from the beginning and from
ancient times things not yet done, saying,
"My counsel shall stand, and I will accom-
plish all my purpose."
(Isaiah 46:9–10, ESV)

The Lord has established his throne in
the heavens, and his kingdom rules over all.
(Psalm 103:19, ESV)

Prayer: Father, I reach for you. I am thankful that I can call on you and know that you will always be with me. I pray for all my family and friends and people all over the world, who need you I pray and ask you to be with them, in Jesus's loving name, amen.

August 28

His Perfect Peace

Sit with me at the end of the day and learn more about my Spirit. Learn more about me. Enjoy your God. I am the one who will never let you down. I never fail. I will always help you up and lift you off the ground. While I keep you grounded on the path of righteousness. Spend precious moments with me alone. Let me take the weight of the day off your shoulders. Intimate moments with me are so very important, allowing our relationship to grow. The more you are learning me, the more you trust me. The more enlightened you become. Just as a newborn baby as it looks around for the first time. It is not sure of what it sees. Its vision is new, so it is blurry and out of focus. The more familiar the baby becomes with its surroundings and the longer it looks, the more the images become whole. As its focus sets in. It will then begin to notice all the beautiful intricate details of its surroundings. Just as you are now. Keeping your eyes fixed on me, your vision is becoming more focused and clearer. Where you once were blind. Now you can see. Tonight, may you settle into perfect peace with me.

Like newborn infants, long for the pure spiritual milk, that by it you may grow up into salvation.
(1 Peter 2:2, ESV)

I have heard that the spirit of the gods is in you, and that light and understanding and excellent wisdom are found in you.
(Daniel 5:14, ESV)

There was a true Light which, coming into the world, enlightens every man.
(John 1:9)

Having the eyes of your hearts enlightened, that you may know what hope to which he has called you, what riches of his glorious inheritance in the saints.
(Ephesians 1:18, ESV)

Prayer: Father God thank you for my eyes to see, and for the relationship, I have with you. Thank you for my calling. I pray to be more developed and aware of everything you want me to do. I pray you to make it so clear to me Lord (with kindness) that I cannot deny what is your will. I pray to be successful at what I am tasked to do. I pray for all my family and friends, that they, each one will seek you with their whole heart and really get to walk with you, Jesus. I thank you for the victory Lord, and it is in your name I pray, amen.

August 29

Humanity Pains

Sometimes I will call you to a period of solitude. Removing situations or people that may hinder your progression. I am leading you down the path that I have chosen for you. Try not to take any unnecessary detours, by taking your focus off me or off what I am calling you to do. Trusting me is essential during these times. As I know your humanity my cause you to feel lonely but remember my child you are never alone, I am always with you. I will restore relationships in my own time if it is my will. But for now, be accepting of what I give to you, and thank me for leading you on my righteous paths. Sometimes life hurts. Every one of my children has felt the sting of hurt or pain at some point in their lives. No one is truly alone during their trials. I am always with my children. Also, if they become brave enough to reach out to others, they would find just how similar the pains of life are for everyone. Across the entire world, emotions are emotions...yet they are fleeting and ever-changing. For you to become strong, I will call you to quiet times. This is where you will rest in me and strengthen your soul. Other times I will call you to be with other believers and find connection in my Spirit. This too can give you the much-needed boost you need. Keep your gaze steady in all times, and most importantly do not give in to fear. Move forward, live with the confidence of grace, full of the love that I have given. Be happy.

For the gifts and the calling of God are irrevocable.
(Romans 11:20, ESV)

But watch yourselves lest your hearts be weighed down with dissipation and drunkenness and the cares of this life, and that day come upon you suddenly like a trap.
(Luke 21:34, ESV)

Come let us return to the Lord; he has torn us, that he may heal us; he has struck us down, and he will bind us up.
(Hosea 6:1, ESV)

He heals the brokenhearted and binds up their wounds.
(Psalm 147:3, ESV)

Prayer: Father God, guard my thoughts today Lord, and the thoughts of my loved ones. Lead our minds and our steps. I give all my situations to you Lord. I thank you, Father God, for your unfailing love. In Jesus's name, I pray, amen.

August 30

The Good Ghost

Hold onto me, always. Learn my ways. Walk with me on my righteous good paths. Give yourself to me completely. Happier is the one who trusts in me, than those who live their lives without me. You can always spot my children, not by their words but by the way they live their lives. They are recognized by their actions. My children bear good fruit, and the blessings that follow will carry on. There is a light within my children. It is the light of my love. It is the Spirit of kindness, gentleness, and love. It is my Holy Spirit. There is a Ghost that lives within them. Not living for them, but guiding them as a Helper, walking with them through this life. Take my yoke upon you. Perceiving always what is true. There is a light set before your feet lighting the way to go. Do not wander off into the shadows no matter the temptation, just trust me and my leading. I will always be good to you. I want the best for you, my child. Even when life throws you a curveball, or you get pounded by the enemy and his lies. Know that I am always rewarding, and I am always with you. My Spirit lives within you.

But the Helper, the Holy Spirit, whom the Father will send in my name, he will teach you all things and bring to your remembrance all that I said to you.
(John 14:26, ESV)

And we are witnesses to these things, and so is the Holy Spirit, whom God has given to those who obey him.
(Acts 1:8, ESV)

And when they bring you to trial and deliver you over, do not be anxious beforehand what you are going to say, but say whatever is given you in that hour, for it is not you who speak, but the Holy Spirit.
(Mark 13:11, ESV)

For no prophecy was ever produced by the will of man, but men spoke from God as they were carried along by the Holy Spirit.
(2 Peter 1:21, ESV)

Prayer. Thank you for all my family and friends. I am thankful for your Holy Spirit. In Jesus's name, I pray today for a good day, amen.

August 31

September

Our lives are like beautiful gardens and when we come together, we show a greater image of God's love. And our prayers and praise together are a beautiful fragrance that travels up to heaven

Rise Up

Rise up, my children. You are more than conquerors through me. Take steps forward on my good path. Spreading my word and good news. Keep fighting the good fight of faith. Let your light shine. Be courageous and speak the truth. Always be mindful that although you feel good, the enemy is never far off. He sits and waits like a predator for his moment to strike. Use me as your shield to ward off his attacks. Always be sober-minded, so he cannot take hold of your minds. Guard your hearts and remain happy through it all as always being thankful to me. The path is becoming wider and easier to navigate, so you can cover more ground than before. Things that before used to stop you no longer can hold you back. Things that used to frighten you, cannot impede you anymore. Marching forward with conviction, and the truth I've placed in you. Now you can soar.

Let us then approach God's throne of grace with confidence, so that we may receive mercy and find grace to help us in our time of need.
(Hebrews 4:16, NIV)

Be sober-minded; be watchful. Your adversary the devil prowls around like a roaring lion, seeking someone to devour.
(1 Peter 5:8, ESV)

No, in all these things we are more than conquerors through him who loved us. For I am sure that neither death nor life,

*nor angels nor rulers, nor things present nor
things to come, nor powers, nor height nor
depth, nor anything else in all creation, will
be able to separate us from the love of God
in Christ Jesus our Lord.*
(Romans 8:37–39, NIV)

Prayer: Father God, I am so thankful to you Lord. May I always remain confident in the truth I have found in you. I am more than a conqueror with you God, and I am so blessed to have you as my Savior. You are the one that I love. I pray for all my family and friends Lord may we always serve you and your goodness in the way in which you have chosen for our lives. Please strengthen our faith Father, each and every day as you are good. In Jesus's name, I pray, amen.

September 1

Unstoppable

Eternal life is my promised gift for those who love me and have accepted me as their Lord and Savior, those who keep my commandments and give their lives to me. I can make a way where you see no way. I can take the hardest of hearts and turn them into the kind and loving gentleness that my spirit brings. I can find the lost and give them a path of righteousness and grace. I can take the anger away and replace it with joy and happiness. I can do all things. I give my children a hope and a purpose. I call them to step out in faith and trust me when they have lost the ability to trust. They will find their peace again, but my peace is different than the inconsistent peace of this world. My peace remains unchangeable and unstoppable. As they grow in their faith with me, they will learn to keep my peace safely within their hearts. I can change the mind of the most stubborn of men and open a whole new way for them. I will speak into their lives truth and show them my good ways. No one is too lost, angry, or separated from me. I can develop the most infantile of my children into the strongest followers of my words and teachings. Never cease praying for others. Watch as the beautiful outcomes of their lives unfold. Stay confident and know that I am God, and I am leading.

Peace I leave with you, my peace I give to you; not as the world gives do I give to you. Let not your heart be troubled, neither let it be afraid.
(John 14:27, KJV)

*In the day when I cried out, you
answered me, and made me bold with
strength in my soul.*
(Psalm 138:3, NKJV)

*And I will give you a new heart, and
a new spirit I will put within you. And I
will remove the heart of stone from your
flesh and give you a heart of flesh.*
(Ezekiel 36:26, ESV)

Prayer: Lord, thank you for your unstoppable change
and your unchangeable peace. Thank you for helping my
family and friends find you, as they learn you and grow in
their faith. Thank you for making us all new creations. I love
you Jesus, today and forever. I ask you Lord keep leading us
and helping us learn to be more like you. In Jesus's name, I
pray, amen.

September 2

Pure Intentions

Speak deliberately and be slow to anger. Think before you speak. This world is filled with frustrations. Frustrations caused by situations or people. People who you may be unknowingly judging. Do not judge my child. Opinions can hold contempt and turn into spite. Unnecessary comments made to get a response are usually ones that carry frustration. That is not my way. Teach my good ways. Share your thoughts and advice but do not carry frustration behind the conversation. Also, listen as this is very important to understand what the other person is going through. Be compassionate and sympathetic. People express their hurts in very different ways, as one might hold it all in, shutting down and building a wall. Another may explode in anger. While others will reflect their true hurt onto some other matter altogether. Listen intently and pray for my discernment to help you, so that you may, in turn, help the other person. With pure intentions, love them fervently. Give all the frustrations to me and let my spirit fill you with my calm unrelenting joy.

Seeing you have purified your souls in your obedience to the truth in sincere brotherly affection, love one another from a pure heart fervently.
(1 Peter 1:22, NHEB)

Little children let us not love in word or talk but in deed and truth.
(1 John 3:18, ESV)

All a person's ways seem pure to them,
but motives are weighed by the Lord.
Commit to the Lord whatever you do, and
he will establish your plans.
(Proverbs 16:2–3, NIV)

Prayer: Father God guide my thoughts, my words, and my actions. I pray to be a blessing to those who are lost, Lord. Let me be an example Lord to them of what your love can do in our lives. Take my frustrations Lord and remove any judgment from my heart. Give me the right words to say. Let me always try to be a helper, not a hurter. In Jesus's name, I pray, amen.

September 3

Peace in Patience

Find my perfect peace in your patience. I know that feels unnatural to most of my children. Anxiety and urgency always try to find a way into my children's minds and hearts, especially during the times that call for patience. Guard your hearts and minds with me and my whole armor... Stay focused and remain joyful. The enemy is clever and will try to derail you. Using your own thoughts against you. He may even try to distract you with other people's problems. Throwing them at your doorstep. Irrational people who are not living for me. Pray for them but do not get caught up daily in their cries of self-pity and anger. I am the Savior and Redeemer. I am all powerful, where you have only human limitations. I have overcome the world of sin and death. Keep learning how to accept my peace. Sometimes you will have to make a conscious effort and practice focusing on my peacefulness. Each time you overcome the worry and anxiety you win. Casting off fear, soon you will see it becomes easier and easier. Then you will truly be able to master having peace in the times that I am calling you to wait. You will find my peace, and soon you will find peace within the patience.

"Though the mountains be shaken and the hills be removed, yet my unfailing love for you will not be shaken nor my covenant of peace be removed," says the LORD, who has compassion on you.
(Isaiah 54:10, NIV)

And the peace of God that surpasses all understanding will guard your hearts and minds in Christ Jesus.
(Philippians 4:7, NET)

No weapon that is formed against thee shall prosper; and every tongue that shall rise against thee in judgment thou shalt condemn. This is the heritage of the servants of the Lord, and their righteousness is of me, saith the Lord.
(Isaiah 54:17, KJV)

Prayer: Father God, help me each day to be patient and hopeful as I wait on you. Help me and all my family and friends stay diligent and find enjoyment in our work. Help us find your peace, no matter what the circumstances. When we get anxious Lord, nudge us with kindness and pull our minds and thoughts back to you, filling us with love and peace again. I thank you, Lord for this day. In Jesus's name, I pray. Amen.

September 4

To Glimpse Heaven

I love to show you glimpses of heaven, in many different ways. It could be as simple as the joyful laugh and smile on the faces of your loved ones. It might be seen in the most amazing sunrise as the rays of light beam down brightly through the clouds. So bright and mesmerizing. It could be imagined as a beautiful canvas. Just the perfect picture emulating love, full of millions of beautiful colors. Anything perfect and good, filled with beauty and wonder can be described as a glimpse of the wondrous heavenly place. Heaven is such a beautiful place. Warm and peaceful, dreamy and majestic, serene, unbelievably amazing, happy and calm. Comfortable in every way. It is every good and glorious thing you could ever hope for. It's more than you could ever truly imagine. It is unfathomable. It's more than every wonderful dream... My children who believe in me and have accepted me as their Lord and Savior, have another name for Heaven, as they call it their "forever home. "To glimpse it doesn't even begin to pull back the veil of what is hiding just above. It is my kingdom that I share with all my children, and such a majestic place it is.

But Jesus said, "Let the little children
come to me and do not hinder them, for to
such belongs the kingdom of heaven."
(Matthew 19:14, ESV)

The heavens declare the glory of God,
and the sky above proclaims his handiwork.
Day to day pours out speech, and night to
night reveals knowledge.
(Psalm 19:1–2, ESV)

But, as it is written, "what no eye has seen, nor ear has heard, nor the heart of a man imagined, what God has prepared for those who love him."
(1 Corinthians 2:9, ESV)

Prayer: My Father God, thank you for your gift of heaven and everlasting life. Thank you for all my family and friends. I pray this day Lord that you make a way for us to get to see the beauty of heaven here on the earth and all that you created. I pray we get to find the small glimpses of heaven as we journey on through our lives. Always with you by our sides and in our hearts. In Jesus's loving name, I pray, amen.

September 5

Testify

I will wake you in the stillness of the morning and fill you with my love. I give to you my fullness in Spirit. Let your eyes see more than the facade of the thin outer shell that this world brings. With my grace, may you experience the deepness of my unfailing love... May your mouth always speak my truths, and not be overtaken byways of your humanity. I will guard you and your ways, aligning them with my will. I will keep you safe. I will clear the path for you to travel in peace and bring others to you for my promotion and the distribution of my good news. Share my gospel with everyone, even those who do not know me. Shine like an example to all. Planting the seeds of faith wherever you go. I am pleased and reward my children for their faithfulness in many different and wonderful ways. Testify about what I have done in your life. Always be willing to share. Stepping out into the world today with the confidence I have placed in you. Now with faith forward go and testify...

So, everyone who acknowledges me before men, I will also acknowledge before my Father who is in heaven.
(Matthew 10:32, ESV)

"Return to your home, and declare how much God has done for you." And he went away, proclaiming throughout the whole city how much Jesus had done for him.
(Luke 8:39, ESV)

*Come and hear, all you who fear God,
and I will tell you what he has done for my
soul.*
(Psalm 66:16, ESV)

*Fight the good fight of the faith. Take
hold of eternal life to which you were called
and about which you made the good confession in the presence of many witnesses.*
(1 Timothy 6:12, ESV)

Prayer: Today I pray for all my family and friends, Lord, that whatever you have done or are doing in our lives be known, so that we may share all that you have done for us with others confidently. All for your glory. I am thankful to you Lord Jesus for everything in my life. It is in your name I pray and give thanks, amen.

September 6

Not Far Behind

Ready to begin another day. Take me upon you and hold tightly. Do not wish for things to come faster. The resolution to your problems is not far behind. I know you are always worrying about whether you will have enough. Look my child and see, my grace is sufficient for you. Do not worry about success. With me, everything is possible, no worry of failure or defeat. I am your Lord who makes a way even when none is evident. Success will come to those who work hard. I see what you have been doing. I know what you have been going through. Believe me, my child, success is not far behind. Ready yourselves when the blessings flow upon you like a flood that you do not get swept away. Do not let life consume you. Do not take your eyes off me. Always hold tightly to me. I am the one who will bring you through all times, the trials and the blessed. I am here for you always. The experience of life will become clearer when your eyes are opened by me. Finding your way in the truth of my Spirit, my words, and my ways. As I am the breath of life, and your just reward is not far behind.

> *You shall remember the Lord your God, for it is he who gives you the power to get wealth, that he may confirm his covenant that he swore to your fathers, as it is this day.*
> (Deuteronomy 8:18, ESV)

> *Bring the full tithe into the storehouse, that there may be food in my house. And thereby put me to the test, says the Lord of*

hosts, if I will not open up the windows of heaven for you and pour down for you a blessing until there is no more need.
(Malachi 3:10, ESV)

Honor the Lord with your wealth and with the first fruits of all your produce; Then your barns will be filled with plenty, and your vats will be bursting with wine.
(Proverbs 3:9–10, ESV)

And my God will supply every need of yours according to his riches in glory in Christ Jesus.
(Philippians 4:19, ESV)

Prayer: Father God, I first thank you for giving me the strength and endurance to accomplish the work that I need to get done. I thank you for guiding my steps Lord, and for giving me the ways and means to help others. I have been feeling the pressure of the needs of life for myself and those around me, I cast off these pressures and the fears of not having enough, In Jesus's name, I pray, amen.

September 7

Grace Belongs

I will tell who you are. You belong to me. Today is only about finding the truth of my Spirit. Do not give in any longer or let the enemy fill your mind with doubts and lies. You can be stronger than that now. Look at how far you've come. With me, you can overcome issues and obstacles. Let me control all the aspects of your life. I will carry any weight and replace it with the lightness of my love and grace. My grace is my unmerited favor and I give it to all my children, freely. So that they can live abundantly. Freeing them up from their earthly worries. They are able to enjoy the quiet calmness that my grace brings. There is a season for everything, and sometimes the season brings trials, but that is not to become the main focus in your life. You are to maintain your focus on me even through the most difficult of times. Breathe my child, everything will be okay because my grace belongs to you.

In him we were also chosen, having been predestined according to the plan of him who works out everything in conformity with the purpose of his will.
(Ephesians 1:11, NIV)

Grace and peace be yours in abundance through the knowledge of God and of Jesus our Lord.
(2 Peter 1:2, NIV)

But by the grace of God I am what I am, and his grace toward me was not in

vain. On the contrary, I worked harder than any of them, though it was not I, but the grace of God that is with me.
(1 Corinthians 15:10, ESV)

For it is by grace you have been saved, through faith-and this is not from yourselves, it is the gift of God.
(Ephesians 2:8, NIV)

And from his fullness we have all received, grace upon grace.
(John 1:16, ESV)

Prayer: Father God, thank you for your unfailing love and your unlimited grace. I pray for all my family and friends health, happiness, success, and a love that's found in you. In Jesus's name, I pray, amen.

September 8

Unstoppable Tomorrows

My dear child, your continued perseverance and unwavering trust in me make you unstoppable. Keep working hard and moving forward. If I am for you, No one can be against you. No man can stop what I've ordained, nor can he separate what I have joined together. Do not let your mind jump away and wander into unknown thoughts about tomorrow or get caught in the snare of the yesterday's past. Today remain present with me. Keeping patient. I have seen your next. I have been to your tomorrows. Everything is in my hands and because you have given me your life and your trust, believe that what I have in store for your life is more than amazing and, oh, so good. Unstoppable tomorrows for you begin today. Remain faithful to me, my child.

> *Being strengthened with all the power according to his glorious might so that you may have great endurance and patience and giving joyful thanks to the Father, who has qualified you to share in the inheritance of his holy people in the kingdom of light.*
> (Colossians 1:11–12, NIV)

> *Blessed is the one who perseveres under trial because, having stood the test, that person will receive the crown of life that the Lord has promised to those who love him.*
> (James 1:12, NIV)

> *Stand firm, and you will win life.*
> (Luke 21:19, NIV)

But thanks be to God, who gives us
the victory through our Lord Jesus Christ.
(1 Corinthians 15:57, ESV)

Prayer: Father God, I ask you to give me rest in my patience and the strength to continue when I grow weary. Remove any thoughts that cause me to worry. Remind me with your loving kindness Lord that you have everything under control. That I do not have to be the fixer. Because you have gone before me and will lead the way, taking care of all the details of my life, and the lives of those around me. I thank you, Lord, for your strength and love, for my unstoppable tomorrows and the peace in today. In Jesus's name, I pray, amen.

September 9

Be Willing

Dear child be willing to be uncomfortable for me. There are situations I will call you too, that will completely take you out of your comfort zone. You may not like speaking in front of large groups of people. Maybe you have always felt more comfortable in one on one conversations. But be willing and ready if that is the very thing, I call you to do. Be ready for whatever I call you to do. Just as I say put on my whole armor each and every morning, with your feet fitted with readiness. Cast off the fear that will pursue you whenever you venture into the unknown. Knowing that I have called you there and that I am with you. You are not alone. Whatever this day holds, however uncomfortable the situation. I will walk with you, be courageous. I will strengthen you, be brave. I will take care of you today and always. I will because I AM.

You did not choose me, but I chose you and appointed you so that you might go bear fruit-fruit that will last, and so that whatever you ask in my name the Father will give you.
(John 15:16, NIV)

He called you to this through our gospel, that you might share in the glory of our Lord Jesus Christ.
(Thessalonians 2:14, NIV)

To this, you were called, because Christ suffered for you, leaving you an example, that you should follow in his steps.
(1 Peter 2:21, NIV)

*But in your hearts honor Christ the
Lord as holy, always being prepared to make
a defense to anyone who asks you for a reason for the hope that is in you; yet do it with
gentleness and respect.*
(1 Peter 3:15, ESV)

Prayer: My Dear God, help me to overcome my fear
when you call me to things that are uncomfortable for me.
Help me to be a light and a blessing to others. Bless my family and friends Lord, that we may all come to know you Lord
as you are our Savior. I thank you, Lord, for the glory of
your salvation, for your love and the grace that you bring.
In Jesus's name, I pray to always find the right things to say,
amen.

September 10

Overflowing Love

Good Morning my child. I am happy when I see you so full of joy. The way you look when you receive kindness from another. The way you get so excited when you notice something from me that was only meant for you. Your heart is so full of my overflowing love. Stay in the moments of my goodness. Not letting any small issues derail you from my path. Do not get ahead of yourself but stay in this present day. No past worries, no future worries. Just this day and all that it holds. Thank me for this day and the grace that my Spirit brings. There is no fear when you stay in my will. Learning my ways and loving others. Perfect love casts out fear and brings forth joy. This day celebrate my perfect love for you. Giving credence to what I say. Give praise and be thankful. Show me how much you love me by the way you live. Walking in my truth. Overflowing with love and kindness for all.

Beloved, let us love one another. For love is from God, and whoever loves has been born of God and knows God.
(1 John 4:7, ESV)

And above all these put on love, which binds everything together in perfect harmony.
(Colossians 3:14, ESV)

Therefore be imitators of God, as beloved children. And walk in love, as

Christ loved us and gave himself up for us,
a fragrant offering and sacrifice to God.
(Ephesians 5:1–2, ESV)

But God shows his love for us in that
while we were still sinners, Christ died for us.
(Romans 5:8, ESV)

Above all keep loving one another
deeply, because love covers over a multitude
of sins.
(1 Peter 4:8, NIV)

Prayer: Father God, thank you for your love. I pray for all my family and friends that we would desire Lord, to walk in your will and seek you and your love with our whole hearts. In Jesus's name, I pray, amen.

September 11

To Speak Without Words

What's wrong my child? There you go again letting the worries of this life weigh you down. I have not asked you to carry any other one's burdens, and yet you do so. This is what it looks like when the tender heart I've placed in you somehow gets filled with guilt and hopelessness. I have said," love thy neighbor as yourself." I've said," if you have anything against another let the person know in private so that you can address the issues." Sometimes that doesn't work. But what matters is you have tried. I see you swimming in circles through the same waters. The same patterns do not get different outcomes. Learn to let go. Not letting go completely but giving them and the worries that accompany them to me. Free yourself up. So that you can live happier and healthier, as this is what I want for your life. When you are happy you shine so bright, creating an example to others of what following me does for your life. It speaks without words saying," Come with me and let's follow God as his ways are so good that they radiate his light of love even from within." It is good when your heart is full of joy. From your heart, you will show others not with words, but with deeds, with the power of my Holy Spirit, and the way you live your life.

And ask the Father, and he will give
you another Helper, to be with you forever.
(John 14:16, ESV)

But the Helper, the Holy Spirit,
whom the Father will send in my name, he
will teach you all things and bring to your
remembrance all that I have said to you.
(John 14:26, ESV)

But when the Helper comes, whom I will send to you from the Father, the Spirit of truth, who proceeds from the Father, he will bear witness about me.
(John 15:26, ESV)

Keep your heart with all vigilance, for from it flow the springs of life.
(Proverbs 4:23, ESV)

Prayer: Jesus my Lord, help me not to repeat patterns that are unhealthy for me. Thank you for the gift of your Holy Spirit within me. Thank you for guiding my ways and my steps. Help me to continue to shine as a light and live the way you want me to live. In Jesus's name, I pray, amen.

September 12

Wrapped in Love

Adversity sets in sometimes. Guard your hearts and your minds with love for me and my words. Earthly circumstances can drag you down, but not if you keep looking up and reaching for me. Rise above the storms, my child. Keep on your assiduous ways. I am speaking to your heart. Always grow with me. You can bear good fruit. Keep planting my good seeds. Just as a parent has the highest dreams for their child and success in their lives, I too have placed dreams into yours. Stay on this gracious and righteous path. Do not be swayed and I will lead you into the accomplishment of your goals. Claim the victory of my plan for your life, by submitting to my will. There is a bright hope for tomorrow and a gift in today. Today is the present and its wrapped with my love.

> *Let me hear in the morning of your steadfast love. For in you I trust. Make me know the way I should go, for to you I lift up my soul.*
> (Psalm 143:8, ESV)

> *I love the Lord, because he has heard my voice and my pleas for mercy. Because he inclined his ear to me, therefore I will call on him as long as I live.*
> (Psalm 116:1–2, ESV)

> *One thing have I asked of the Lord, that I will seek after: that I may dwell in the house of the Lord all the days of my life*

to gaze upon the beauty of the Lord and to
inquire in his temple.
(Psalm 27:4, ESV)

Prayer: Today I come to you Lord, full of joy. I have love and happiness in my life Lord, and I am thankful. I thank you for all my family and friends. Fill them today with your light and love. Thank you for this wonderful day. In Jesus's name, I pray, amen.

September 13

The Good Message

Come with me we shall travel the world and bring to it my good message. The message is my Gospel living and breathing in the pages of my Holy Bible. We have so much to accomplish and you have so much to see. But do not feel pressured to get it all done, as I am with you. I am not held to the standards of earthly time. This path I've chosen for you may not be understood by others as this is your path alone. Do not try to fit into the mold of the world, but instead, display your abilities to be uniquely mine and rightly so. I have heard your prayers and know your dreams about being able to see the world, to venture to places you have never been. I know at times you have felt hopeless as if you could never get there. Do not forget my child who is with you?! Who walks beside you, who lives within you? Your God! I am the one who can move mountains, change the scenery, change seasons, I change lives. I spoke the universe into existence. I formed the heavens and the earth. You need to learn to also take chances. Listen to my voice when I am calling. You may not see everything you dream of, but it is my dream for you that will be realized, and it will be given, according to my will. Come journey with me and we will share my good message together.

God is faithful, who has called you into fellowship with his Son, Jesus Christ our Lord.
(1 Corinthians 1:9, NIV)

And Jesus came and said to them, "All authority in heaven and on earth has been

given to me. Go therefore and make disciples of all nations, baptizing them in the name of the Father and of the Son and of the Holy Spirit, teaching them to observe all that I have commanded you. And behold, I am with you always, to the end of the age."
(Matthew 28:18–20, ESV)

And he said to them, "go into all the world and proclaim the gospel to all creation."
(Mark 16:15, ESV)

Prayer: Today and always give me the courage to follow you, Lord, wherever you call. I pray for all my family and friends, that they may be filled with your Presence. Keep watch over us all Lord, surrounding us with your love and your protection. In Jesus's name, I pray, amen.

September 14

Let Them as I Will Take Care

Do not forget what I have also said, so here is your reminder," There will be people that are disobedient, ungrateful, brutal, arrogant, abusive, people that only think selfishly of themselves." Sometimes you will need to disconnect from them, knowing whatever their suffering I can handle. Keep praying for them. I see you love them, but to love does not join in to cause strife and discord. So when you feel too weak to interact with them, as you are being drawn into arguments, dismiss yourself. These are the times you must love them from a distance and that is okay, my child. Do not drown yourself with the pressure of guilt for not being able to fix them. Only I can do that. Give yourself a break and surrender them completely to me. I know you have been praying, but also know it is my perfect timing that will produce the best outcome for you and the others you are praying for. Trust me, without fail, without doubt, without fear. I will pull them closer when the moment is right. Keep your eyes only on me and thank me with a grateful heart as I take care of your loved ones.

And Mizpah, for he said, "The Lord watch between you and me, when we are out of one another's sight."
(Genesis 31:49, ESV)

Rejoice in hope, be patient in tribulation, be constant in prayer.
(Romans 12:12, ESV)

But I say to you, love your enemies
and pray for those who persecute you.
(Matthew 5:44, ESV)

Continue steadfastly in prayer, being
watchful in it with thanksgiving.
(Colossians 4:2, ESV)

Prayer: Father, I lift my family and friends to you today Lord. You know Lord what they need. I pray to keep my eyes fixed on you. In Jesus's name, I pray, amen.

September 15

Abundance in Life

Sing with me in this day. I fill you up with happiness. Do not try to spend so much time pondering the destination of your life. When you give me a charge over it, you will see that all the details of your journey will fall into place. The goodness of my righteous path will gain momentum in your life. Today we can venture out and enjoy the beauty of nature. Soaking up the awareness that my Spirit brings. I am with you always and I pull you close. Let the light of my love lift you up and give you the gift of my truth and grace. You can live in abundance. Not just monetary as that does not create fullness in spirit. But the abundance of love, health, happiness, and joy. That is true abundance. Smile my child and enjoy this day.

Beloved, I pray that all may go well with you and that you may be in good health, as goes well with your soul.
(Proverbs 14:12, ESV)

Now to him who is able to do far more abundantly than all that we ask or think, according to the power at work within us, to him be glory in the church and in Christ Jesus throughout all generations, forever and ever. Amen.
(Ephesians 3:20–21, ESV)

Both riches and honor come from you, and you rule over all. In your hand are

power and might, and in your hand it is to
make great and give strength to all.
(1 Chronicles 29:12, ESV)

Prayer: Today Father, I thank you for the life you have given me for the leadership I get from following you and I am also thankful Lord to live abundantly. I pray for all this day as well with my soul. In Jesus's name, I pray, amen.

September 16

Well Done

Sometimes my child the day will roll out like a roller-coaster with periods of extreme business and intervals of complete stillness. Days like these have a tendency to keep you on your toes, but also give you moments to reflect. During the busy moments, I see you preoccupied accomplishing your work for the day. It's during the quiet times you will need to have self-control and really hold onto me tightly. As these times make it easy for your mind to wander. Keep your mind focused on me and my goodness so we can keep the enemy and his sneak attacks far from you. Enjoy the day. Even the little chores or tasks that you need to be complete, you can, and once accomplished you will feel a sense of relief. Then I will come to you and say, "Well done my child." Well done…

He giveth power to the faint, and to him who has no might he increases strength.
(Isaiah 40:29, ESV)

But the Lord is faithful. He will establish you and guard you against the evil one.
(2 Thessalonians 3:3, ESV)

Ah, Lord God! It is you who made the heavens and the earth by your great power and by your outstretched arm! Nothing is too hard for you.
(Jeremiah 32:17, ESV)

Prayer: Thank you, Father, for helping me to accomplish my daily tasks and for guarding my mind. I pray that you keep watch and protect my loved ones as well. In Jesus's name, I pray, amen.

September 17

Lift Them Up

Lift your prayers up to me. Lift them high. You are important, as all my children have a job and a place in this life. Ask me to put you in the area you can best serve. I want your best. I want your all. I want your whole heart. The best portions of yourself should be given to me first. Open up to me freely. I know what is in your heart and I know the thoughts within your mind. Let me lead you on my good and gracious paths each and every day. When you feel the weight of the world or the weight of things calling for your attention, be persistent in your search for my peace and lift them up. Be thankful to me in all circumstances. Keep lifting each other up and we will keep on this good fight of faith together.

> *Search me, O God, and know my heart! Try me and know my thoughts! And see if there be any grievous way in me, and lead me in the way everlasting!*
> (Psalm 139:23–24, ESV)

> *Fight the good fight of faith. Take hold of the eternal life to which you were called and about which you made good confession in the presence of many witnesses.*
> (1 Timothy 6:12, ESV)

> *For the Spirit God gave us does not make us timid, but gives us power, love and self-discipline.*
> (2 Timothy 1:7, ASV)

Prayer: Father God, today I lift up all your people in prayer Lord, as you know what each of us needs. I pray Lord, for the strength to accomplish all that I'm called to do. I pray every dream you have placed in my heart may be realized and that you guide me throughout the days and nights. I love you, Father. In Jesus's name, I pray, amen.

September 18

Jesus Leads

I will lead you in my ways. I will give to you my strength and send out others to encourage you when you feel confused or unsure. I will speak to your heart, telling you that you are my child and your life is in my hands. You can relax in peace and journey on with confidence, with me by your side. I know the way seems hard at times, but I have made you strong enough. I will never give you more than you can handle. I am a never-ending supply of everything you need to succeed in this life and become everything I'm calling you to be. Stay faithful and be confident my child. Enjoy this day moment by moment. Spend time with me throughout the day, as we will complete the demands of the day together. I love you, my child. Follow me wherever I lead, and I will call you mine.

No one after lighting a lamp covers it with a jar or puts it under a bed, but puts it on a stand, so that those who enter may see the light.
(Luke 8:16, ESV)

You shall be holy to me, for I the Lord am holy and have separated you from the peoples, that you should be mine.
(Leviticus 20:26, ESV)

And these words that I command you today shall be on your heart. You shall teach them diligently to your children, and shall talk of them when you sit in your house,

*and when you walk by the way, and when
you lie down, and when you rise.*
(Deuteronomy 6:6–7, ESV)

*For I long to see you, that I may impart
to you some spiritual gift to strengthen you,
that is, that we may be mutually encouraged by each other's faith both yours and
mine.*
(Romans 1:11, ESV)

Prayer: I pray this day to stay close to you Lord, that I may shine like a beacon of your love for all to see. I pray you to hold close my family and friends and give them the confidence Lord to know that just as you are with me. You are always with them too. Shower them with your love, grace, and protection. Let them seek you and let you lead. In Jesus's name I pray, amen.

September 19

Stay Hopeful

Quiet your mind my child and stay far from anxiety. Be hopeful in all things good, as I will never let you down. My plans for your life are so much more than you can imagine. Keep walking in grace and truth and find your confidence in faith. As it is your hope in things, I've promised that have assurance without seeing the evidence, just yet. Remain steadfast in prayer. Rejoice in hope, and even affliction as it can strengthen you. Wait on your Lord, but while you wait on me be patient. Finding that things are sweeter when earned. I will uphold you with my right hand and call you out of the mire and the muck of this world. Together we will walk in confidence remaining hopeful in all things I've placed on your heart.

But if we hope for what we do not see, we wait for it with patience.
(Romans 8:25, ESV)

Surely there is a future, and you hope will not be cut off.
(Proverbs 23:18, ESV)

Return to your stronghold, O prisoners of hope; today I declare that I will restore to you double.
(Zechariah 9:12, ESV)

But they who wait on the Lord shall renew their strength; they shall mount up

on wings like eagles; they shall run and not grow weary; they shall walk and not faint.
(Isaiah 40:31, ESV)

Let us hold fast the confession of our hope without wavering, for he who promised is faithful.
(Hebrews 10:23, ESV)

Prayer: Father God help me to stay hopeful when I start to doubt. Lead my mind and give me the assurance I have found in you. I pray for all my family and friends today Lord that you give us patience and surround us with the knowledge of you love. In Jesus's name, I pray, amen.

September 20

Balanced

Busy times will come like a flood and sweep you from your feet if you are not grounded and rooted in my word. Hold onto me, keeping me tight within your grasp when the rush of life comes in. The world will explode around you with all different kinds of situations. Some high tensions and anxiety and some of joy and goodness. Some just a combination of all. During it, all keep me as your center and balance in this day. Hold on my child, even when life gets exciting remember not to get pulled in, but instead allow me to guide you to and through the experiences I give. Do not get discouraged. You are exactly where I would have you be in this moment. Stay balanced my child.

> *For what does it profit a man to gain the whole world and lose his soul.*
> (Mark 8:36, ESV)

> *One person esteems one day as better than another, while another esteems all days alike. Each one should be fully convinced in his own mind.*
> (Romans 14:5, ESV)

> *A false balance is an abomination to the Lord, but a just weight is his delight.*
> (Proverbs 11:1, ESV)

Prayer: Father God I lift us up to you today Lord, that we may find enjoyment even on the most difficult days. I pray you to help us keep our balance. And thank you for your goodness. I also pray for patience Lord and the protection your Spirit brings. In Jesus's name, I pray, amen.

September 21

Good Food Solitude

Let me lead you to places of beauty. Let my Spirit fill within your mind. I long to spend time with you. Be completely comfortable opening up to me and let's talk. I know that you don't understand everything just yet but just keep trusting me, we will get through it all together. I want you to enjoy yourself. During the times of rest that I bring learning to relax. Closing off the busiest part of your mind. Solitude is good food for the soul as you can become more aware of my Presence. I am leading you without your hesitation and that is good, my child. Keep aware of my Presence and keep following where I lead. Stay thankful for the journey and keep your heart open to my love. Make time for moments alone, as a time of reflection and gaining of strength. Find me there in your still moments, as you keep everything in balance, even solitude in proper portions can be good food.

Thy word [is] a lamp unto my feet,
and a light unto my path.
(Psalms 119:105, NUN, KJV)

But when you pray, go into your room
and shut the door and pray to your Father
who is in secret. And your Father who sees
in secret will reward you.
(Matthew 6:6, ESV)

But he would withdraw to desolate
places and pray.
(Luke 5:16, ESV)

Be still, and know that I am God. I
will be exalted among the nations, I will be
exalted on the earth!
(Psalm 46:10, ESV)

Prayer: Father God, please guide me with your Holy Spirit. Fill me up with your love and grace. Guide my family and friends daily Lord, and give us your peaceful joyful Spirit, and the spirit of forgiveness when there is hurt. Let us find you in the stillness and let our hearts sing. In Jesus's name, I pray, amen.

September 22

Health and Longevity

Stay active my dear one, do not let the weight of life drag you down. Just as I am much needed for your life, so is the work of physical activity. When your body becomes sluggish and lazy so does your mind. Keep in step with them both. Walk outside to enjoy the beauty I created. Go for a swim or a run. Get the blood pumping within your veins. The body calls for this activity as it keeps the mind healthy. Do not forget that I designed it to function this way. Many health problems stem from lack of exercise. So go and become healthy in prayer and healthy in activity. I want you to have the longevity you desire, and be healthy in your life...

If we live by the Spirit, let us also keep in step with the Spirit.
(Galatians 5:25, ESV)

For no one ever hated his own flesh, but nourishes and cherishes it, just as Christ does the church.
(Ephesians 5:29, ESV)

Or do you not know that your body is a temple of the Holy Spirit within you, whom you have from God? You are not your own, for you were bought with a price. So glorify God in your body.
(1 Corinthians 6:19–20, ESV)

Prayer: Father God, thank you for today. I pray to you, Lord, please give to me a healthy body, spirit and mind. I pray today that you help me stay active. I pray that you help all of my family and friends stay healthy as well. In Jesus's name, I pray, amen.

September 23

Walk with Certitude

This day my child I will remind you that you do not have to give into fear. You are more than enough. You are beautiful. The distractions of the day will try to pull your focus off me, but you do not have to give in the worldly ways. Spend time with me by praying and satiating your need for my Presence. I can replenish your soul. My good way is to build you up, whereas the worlds way is to pull you in and eventually drag you down. Do not let the world immure you. Stay enshrouded in the light of my love and wrapped in my arms, protected from fear. We can walk confidently with certitude, casting out all doubts and delays. This day my child I call you to a place of victory, it is the victory you have found in me. Keep your head held high as you walk with you, King.

For we walk by faith not by sight.
(2 Corinthians 5:7, KJV)

As ye have therefore received Jesus Christ the Lord, [so] walk ye in him.
(Colossians 2:6, KJV)

For the Lord will be your confidence and will keep your foot from being caught.
(Proverbs 3:26, ESV)

And your ears shall hear a word behind you, saying, "This is the way, walk in it," When you turn to the right or when you turn to the left.
(Isaiah 30:21, ESV)

You shall walk in all the way that the Lord your God has commanded you, that you may live, and that it may go well with you, and that you may live long in the land that you shall possess.
(Deuteronomy 5:33, ESV)

Prayer: Father God, I thank you for this morning and for another beautiful day. I pray for all my family and friends, Lord, that we may stay wrapped in your love today, protected from anxiety and fear. I pray Lord, you to keep us on the path of your good and righteous ways and thank you for the victory. In Jesus's name, I pray, amen.

September 24

The Greatest Is Love

Do not try to stay in the moments of sadness that this life brings, but instead guard your mind and let me lead your thoughts. There are days, my child when you will feel the melancholy sting of life. But just know that it is exactly this, just a moment in time. Thoughts and emotions all bundled together, whether of pleasure or pain are fleeting. Nothing is eternal except my love for you and my promise of eternal life. Focus on these…all the goodness I bring, kindness compassion, gentleness, easiness, joy and especially love. I will lift up your broken heart and repair it with the greatest of my gifts. Today and always dear one I give to you my love. Stay in moments of relaxation and rest till you feel whole once again. Always knowing and always experiencing love from my Spirit to yours. It is me just speaking to your heart.

> *And so we rely on the love God has for us. God is love. Whoever lives in love lives in God, and God in them.*
> (1 John 4:16, ESV)

> *Because your love is better than life, my lips will glorify you. I will praise you as long as I live, and in your name, I will lift up my hands.*
> (Psalm 63:3–4, ESV)

> *Jesus replied, "Anyone who loves me will obey my teaching. My Father will love them, and we will come to them and make our home with them."*
> (John 14:23, ESV)

No one has ever seen God; if we love
one another, God abides in us and his love
is perfected in us.
(1 John 4:12, ESV)

Prayer: Father God, I lift up all my family and friends to you this day Lord. I ask you to bring to us the easiness found in your Spirit and gift us with your loving Presence. Guide us through this day and fill us with the strength of your love. In Jesus's name, I ask and pray, amen.

September 25

You Will Shine

And there will come a day my beloved that the sun will shine again. Many facets of this life enable you to feel the downward pull of life, and then there are the days that you will rise in the morning and sing the song of joy. For no reason that you can perceive. Except to say that today you have been awakened with the truth of my Spirit. As I have whispered to your soul as you slept and effectuated into it, a limitless span of my unending joy. I bring forth my love to you and fill your empty parts. Today may you feel full in spirit and shine with the brightness of a thousand stars... Share my good word and the love I have given with all. May the sun shine today brightly in your soul and may your soul shine brightly with my love... Smile my child.

> *Arise and shine for your light has come. The shining-greatness of the Lord has risen upon you. For see, darkness will cover the earth. Much darkness will cover the people. But the Lord will rise upon you, and his shining—greatness will be seen upon you. Nations will come to your light. And kings will see the shining-greatness of the Lord on you.*
> (Isaiah 60:1–3, NLV)

> *In the same way, let your light shine before others, so that they may see your good works and give glory to your Father in heaven.*
> (Matthew 5:16, ESV)

For God, who said, "Let light shine
out of the darkness," has shone in our hearts
to give the light of the knowledge of the glory
of God in the face of Jesus Christ.
(2 Corinthian 4:6, ESV)

Prayer: Thank you, Father God, for filling me up with your good and perfect Spirit. Today I pray to continue in this good feeling all day through. I pray also for all my family and friends that you enrich their lives with your love and give them the experience of having the best day ever. In Jesus's name, I pray and ask, amen.

September 26

Seek and Learn

Feel empowered today my child. Learn all of my good ways and gather the strength of my Spirit. Read my word and live in the ways I teach. Your walk through this life is developing. And is based on a certainty that when you give your life to me, you are never alone. I know at times you may feel weary, but I have given you the aptitude for the journey. Learn from me becoming wise and insightful. Making you more than a victor in this life. The gifts I bring to you are many, but even on the days of stillness when you seek me, you will learn of what a love pure and true looks like. It can be even more encompassing and empowering than you could ever imagine. Let me surround you today as you keep practicing my ways. I will keep you enshrouded in the light of my love.

> *What you have learned and received and heard and seen in me-practice these things, and the God of peace will be with you.*
> (Philippians 4:9, ESV)

> *But the anointing that you received from him abides in you, and you have no need that anyone should teach you. But as his anointing teaches you about everything, and is true, and is no lie, just as it is taught you, abide in him.*
> (1 John 2:27, ESV)

I will instruct you and teach you in
the way you should go; I will counsel you
with my eye upon you.
(Psalm 32:8, ESV)

Prayer: Father God, I pray you to lead me in your good ways and give me the heart to help others. I seek you all day long, Lord, and it is in the stillness of today that I ask just that you would fill me with your Holy Spirit. Guide my steps and fill my heart. In Jesus's name, I pray, amen.

September 27

Cast Your Burdens

I will make you brave I will call you out of your comfort zone and walk with you. Be kind and giving. Give your first portions to me and see what I will do. When pressures of life are all around, all you can do child is do your best. Let me worry about tomorrow, as today has worries of its own. Call out to me to help you. I am here and I will alleviate and undue stress. Learn my ways and take from my yoke, as I am easy and light. I love you my child with an everlasting love. So put me to the test, and find your trust in me. Ask in my name and you will receive. I have overcome the world and so I can overcome any hurdles that are causing you to stumble. Cast your burdens and give your problems to me with open hands and receive my blessings with an open heart.

Bring the full tithe into the storehouse, that there may be food in my house. And thereby put me to the test, says the Lord of hosts, if I will not open the windows of heaven for you and pour down for you a blessing until there is no more need.
(Malachi 3:10, ESV)

Honor the Lord with your wealth and with the firstfruits of all your produce; then your barns will be filled with plenty, and your vats will be bursting with wine.
(Proverbs 3:9–10, ESV)

Now to him who is able to do far
more abundantly than all we ask or think,
according to the power at work within us.
(Ephesians 3:20, ESV)

Prayer: Father God, I lift my finances up to you today Lord. Please help me always bring to you my best. Lord, sometimes I struggle financially. I trust you, Lord, to help me. I pray to always have enough and some to help others with. I pray for all my family and friends; help bless us in the ways of our money and help us to be good stewards. In your loving name Jesus, I pray and ask and thank you Lord for the victory, amen.

September 28

Trust Him with All

Today my dear child, I will lift your spirit and fill you with my love. I bring to you my grace and quench your thirst for life with my Spirit. We walk together hand in hand through each moment of the day. Bring praise to me, my child. Sometimes in this life, there will be uncertainty. Maybe a financial situation arises. Making it difficult for you to maintain a certain level of stability. So now you are putting all the pressure on yourself. Asking yourself what you can do to make things better for your life, a bit easier for your loved ones. Here is my answer, my child, pray to me, seek me first and trust me… Speak with me about whatever the situation is. I know financial situations can be tough as most people try to keep me and their financial situations separate. And truly it is said, you must not serve money as an idol. Do not let it become your master, or let it pull your attention away from me, as I am your God. But you can trust me within that area of your life too. Keep me as your primary focus. I can help you with all the areas of your life. Even your financial life. I will light the way. Do not be afraid to follow where I lead or to take chances when I call you to do so. It is all about having trust and following me. I will take care of you and your loved ones and we will grow my kingdom together.

For God is not unrighteous to forget your work and the labor of love, which ye have shewed toward his name, in that ye have ministered to the saints, and do minister.
(Hebrews 6:10, KJV)

Blessed is the man who trusts in the Lord. whose trust is in the Lord. He is like a tree planted by the water that sends out its roots by the stream, and does not fear when heat comes, for its leaves remain green, and is not anxious in the year of drought, for it does not cease to bear fruit.
(Jeremiah 17:7–8, ESV)

Beloved, if our heart does not condemn us, we have the confidence before God; and whatever we ask we receive from him, because we keep his commandments and do what pleases him.
(1 John 3:21–22, ESV)

Reader: We all have a season when we fall behind, I just want you to know that God hears our requests and our supplications. He is with us so we should commit our ways to him trusting him, in all areas of our life. Our whole life, even our financial life. I pray for you all, that whatever season you are in, God leads and takes care of you, lighting your way and removing your worries. Filling you with his love, grace, and comfort, amen.

September 29

Grateful Heart

Good morning My child, Today, start out with a grateful heart. I've gone before you, preparing your way. I am leading all my children out of the darkness and bringing them into the light of my ways. I will surround you with like-minded believers who will encourage and strengthen you, as needed for the day. Sing and rejoice when you get to witness someone giving their life to me, being baptized in my Spirit. How beautiful it is to see, as so many are coming home. Keep being an example. Hold fast to your faith, for it is with faith that you will keep fighting the good fight. Do not stop speaking about what you have learned from me and keep sharing with others. Do not be afraid to open up, sharing your testimony in truth. As it may touch someone who walks a similar path. It may even lead them back to me. Be of good courage, my beloved.

> *Wait on the Lord: be of good courage, and he will strengthen thine heart: wait, I say, on the Lord.*
> (Psalms 27:14, KJV)

> *But in your hearts honor Christ the Lord as holy, always being prepared to make a defense to anyone who asks you for a reason for the hope that is in you; yet do it with gentleness and respect.*
> (1 Peter 3:15, ESV)

> *Let him know that whoever brings back a sinner from his wandering will save*

his soul from death and will cover a multi-
tude of sins.
      (James 5:20, ESV)

Prayer: Thank you, Father. I come to you today Lord just as you say with a grateful heart. Thank you for your leading. Thank you for never giving up on us Lord and for the truth that we always have a place with you. I pray for the lost to find their ways back home. I pray for the children who do not know you, Lord, that you would send them a teacher. I pray to be able to be a blessing always to others in my life In Jesus's name, I pray, amen.

September 30

October

Even when you are in the middle of unknown waters, God's love never fails as it will be the place you can rest your feet upon. He offers us firm foundations, in his light we find hope, as we stand upon his promises. His love assures us he is here.

Take a Moment

Take a moment and step back no decisions yet, just wait on me as my timing is always perfect. You do not need to anxiously envision your steps for tomorrow. Have faith and confidence that I have everything under control. We can walk through this day and enjoy it for what it is. You can still remain in the present even while you hold into my promises of a future. Let me open up the way, as I have gone before you. Make sure to follow in my steps and do not try to rush ahead. I know that life can be hard, dear child, and your emotions can run high. But keep in mind that your life is in my hands. And what better place to be then safe within my grasp. Once I take hold of you, you can open up and allow yourself to be completely vulnerable with me. We can take care of past hurts, which will allow you to move forward without the stumbling blocks of yesterday. Once these steps are taken, move ahead. Remaining with your focus hard fixed on things above. Keeping your eyes on me and my path. Follow where I am leading.

> *Wait for the Lord; be strong, and let your heart take courage; and wait for the Lord!*
> (Psalm 27:14, ESV)

> *I can do nothing on my own. As I hear, I judge, and my judgment is just, because I seek not my own will but the will of him who sent me.*
> (John 5:30, ESV)

I will instruct you and teach you in the way you should go; I will counsel you with my eye upon you.
(Psalm 32:8, ESV)

Even as he chose us in him before the foundation of the world, that we should be holy and blameless before him. In love.
(Ephesians 1:4, ESV)

Prayer: Father God, Keep leading me and my loved ones. Make known to us Lord the ways we should go. I thank you for every day of my life and the love and grace that you show. In Jesus's name, I pray, amen.

October 1

The Lord Makes Known

I am the Lord; my powers are untamable. My plans are unstoppable. There is no need to fear. Keep casting all your cares at my feet, feeling confident that they have already been handled. You are on the right path my beloved child. Keeping your eyes fixed on me and the hope of your dreams that I've placed in your heart coming to fruition. As your faith is growing, I am happy. Soon the dreams of what I'm leading you to become I will make known. As you start actuating into the person, I'm fashioning you to be. There is nothing that can stop you if you keep me as the head of your life. No weapon formed against you shall prosper. I am with you and am for you. Leading you into the beautiful journey of your life. Stay faithful, my child, as my promises are coming. I am the Maestro and your life is beautifully orchestrated by me. Hold fast to these truths. Enjoying the song of your life. Staying confident and persevering with faith, always articulating my love.

Call to me and I will answer you, and will tell you great and hidden things that you have not known.
(Jeremiah 33:3, ESV)

For the Lord gives wisdom; from his mouth come knowledge and understanding.
(Proverbs 2:6, ESV)

The precepts of the Lord are right, rejoicing the heart; the commandment of the Lord is pure, enlightening the eyes.
(Psalm 19:8, ESV)

Prayer: Father God, make known your ways in my life. Keep me walking into the journey to which you are calling. Help me keep in step with your Spirit Lord. I pray for all my family and friends Lord that we may all find your good and perfect ways in our lives and that you would bless us and fill us with joy. Help us to find the beauty in our life's song. In Jesus's name, I pray and give thanks. Amen.

October 2

To Show and Shine

Take me, through the day with you. As you will need me, my little precious child. Do not feel ashamed of your feelings of inadequacy or deficiency. Do not try to hide, what you think of as your shortcomings but instead, accept all your faults just as I do. You are human, and being human makes you susceptible to a multitude of sin. No one is perfect in this world. Learn the error of your ways. Grow from the experience and share instead of hiding. As this will become your testimony. Showing others that with me you can overcome the ways of this world. You are perfect in my eyes. I created you to be just the way you are. I have allowed certain experiences in your life to make you grow. And to bring out certain strengths and attributes, as well as your flaws and weaknesses. Sometimes, my child, it is with the flaws and weaknesses that you can draw others even closer, to encourage and light the way in the darkness, bringing them back to me. I will never give you more than you can handle, and you are never truly alone. I am always filling your life with my Presence. So share your story and let it shine my beloved. Walking in the light of my truth.

Whoever conceals his transgressions will not prosper, but he who confesses and forsakes them will obtain mercy.
(Proverbs 28:13, ESV)

But the Scripture imprisoned everything under sin, so that the promise by faith in Jesus Christ might be given to those who believe.
(Galatians 3:22, ESV)

*That is, in Christ God was reconcil-
ing the world to himself, not counting their
trespasses against them, and entrusting to us
the message of reconciliation.*
(2 Corinthians 5:19, ESV)

Prayer: Father God, help me to bravely speak about my shortcomings. Help me to become a light to others who may be making the same mistakes. Help to correct my errors in kindness and with your love. I pray for all my family and all my friends each day. Lord, I lift us all up to learn from your instruction and to live in a way that is pleasing to you. In your name Jesus, I pray, amen.

*Above all, keep loving one another
earnestly, since love covers a multitude of
sin.*
(1 Peter 4:8, ESV)

October 3

A Full Cup

A journey of love… A life created by me. Your cup is not empty. So do not take for granted all the blessings I bring. Always keep a thankful heart. Coming to me with praise and thanks. I love to see my children laughing and dancing in faithfulness, all together they worship me and bring me their praise. I love the celebration of togetherness. To see you exhibit all that I am teaching. Kindness, compassion gentleness, empathy, easiness, encouragement, and love. Also, forgiveness. I do call you to be forgiving when you are wronged. I tell you not to let anger stir within your mind, as it can travel to your heart and bring toxins to your soul. Give the anger away. Cast it off close your eyes and let it go. Pray to me and I will bring your back to the place of calmness, stillness, acceptance, grace, and love. You can rejoice in harmony. Finding my peace as it resonates deep within your soul. Your cup is full. Enjoy it in this day.

If you forgive others their trespasses,
your heavenly Father will also forgive you.
(Matthew 6:14, ESV)

Yours, Lord, is the greatness and the
power and the glory and the majesty and
the splendor, for everything in heaven and
earth is yours. Yours, Lord. Is the kingdom;
you are exalted as head over all.
(1 Chronicles 29:11, NIV)

Sing to God, sing in praise of his
name, extol him who rides on the clouds;

rejoice before him, his name is the Lord. A
father to the fatherless, a defender of wid-
ows, is God in his holy dwelling.
(Psalm 68:4–5, NIV)

Let everything that has breath praise
the Lord! Praise the Lord!
(Psalm 150:6, ESV)

Prayer: Father God, today I praise your name. I lift my family and friends and the people I come in contact with today Lord, I ask that you would give ear to our prayers, Lord, and find favor with us. In Jesus's name, I give thanks and praise, amen.

October 04

Find Your Light

Just breathe today my child. Relax your mind in time for the start of the weeks ending. When you have so much going on nonstop, it can feel like it has been a long couple of months. There are seasons and you know this, but I understand that life itself can be hard to bear sometimes. It is harder to bear when you try to do everything on your own. Other times you can think of the beauty I've created and smile. Share your joy and silliness. I love watching you in those childlike moments when you go back to a time when your heart was pure, and the thoughts of the day were not so consuming. Let me restore you're wellbeing. You should feel happy and relaxed not rushed or pulled. I give you every good and perfect gift. Learn to enjoy and be happy. It takes a while sometimes to find your happiness. To truly find your joy. I can provide that for you. Just be encouraged my child, better days come and go and come again they do. Find your light and shine brightly today.

> *The Lord will guide you always; he will satisfy your needs in a sun-scorched land and strengthen your frame. You will be like a well-watered garden, like a spring whose waters never fail.*
> (Isaiah 58:11, NIV)

> *To shine on those living in darkness and in the shadow of death, to guide our feet into the path of peace.*
> (Luke 1:79, NIV)

*I have no greater joy than to hear that
my children are walking in truth.*
(1 John 1:4, NIV)

*So that by God's will I may come
to you with joy and be refreshed in your
company.*
(Romans 15:32, ESV)

Prayer: Father God, I pray to be happy now. I pray that I can find joy even while waiting for you. I pray to be a blessing to others and that you continue to use me to give you all the glory. I pray for all my family and friends, Lord, that you give them peace while waiting for your guidance. That you make known to them—that it is okay to find peace in daily living because you have provided this journey to us.

In Jesus's loving name, I pray, amen...

October 05

God-Given

When you sit with me and there is only silence within your mind. Do not be sad or feel alone. Be thankful that you are getting a much-needed rest. Do not create worries to fill your thoughts just give these ideas away. Let there be a quiet and a calmness working in your soul. I took charge of your life when you asked me in. I tell you to trust me and to let me guide your, steps, thoughts and all. It is good when you get through the day with lightheartedness and laughter. I know there are many tasks on the list of life that you are compiling for yourself, a lot of things to complete accomplish and learn in order to keep moving forward. But careful my beloved, not to put so much on the list of today's tasks that you get overwhelmed and lose the joy in it all. Sometimes, when my children take on too many things, they actually delay the finished result. As they are pulled in too many directions. Let me guide you and we can accomplish and learn all the tasks on your list. You can do all things because it is I who strengthens you. You have time. I have given you a mind and filled it with knowledge. I can help you organize the now's from the later's. Just keep speaking to me about each step. Don't leave me out of any part of this beautiful journey I have created for you. I am showering you with love and filling you with my Presence. Keep listening as I am speaking to your heart.

But the advocate, the Holy Spirit,
whom the Father will send in my name,
will teach you all things and will remind
you of everything I have said to you.
(John 14:26, NIV)

For everyone who has been born of
God overcomes the world. And in this vic-
tory that has overcome the world, our faith.
(1 John 5:4, ESV)

My son, pay attention to what I say;
turn your ear to my words. Do not let them
out of sight, keep them within your heart.
(Proverbs 4:20–21, NIV)

Your testimonies are my heritage for-
ever, for they are the joy in my heart.
(Psalm 119:111, ESV)

Prayer: Father God, today I pray for discernment. I pray
you to help me prioritize my life Lord, that you help me
to feel peace while I am working so hard to accomplish my
goals. I thank you for everything you have given to me. I pray
for peace and happiness for all today. In Jesus's name, I ask
and pray, amen.

October 06

I Will

I am here to encourage you today my child. I know the journey seems way too ominous at times but remember that I am more than anything that is found solely in the journey. You are more precious to me than anything in this world. I will fill your heart with love and comfort you when you feel weak. I will hold you tightly when you feel alone and enshroud you with the cloak of my Presence when you feel scared. I will laugh with you when you are happy and smile with you when you feel joy. I will rejoice with you when I hear your heart sing. Take comfort my child in knowing, you are with me. Take hold of me. Embracing all my good ways each and every day. Ask me whatever you need and always believe I will…

> *Likewise the Spirit helps us in our weakness. For we do not know what to pray for as we ought, but the Spirit himself intercedes for us with groanings too deep for words.*
> (Romans 8:26, ESV)

> *Until now you have asked nothing in my name. Ask, and you will receive, that your joy may be full.*
> (John 16:24, ESV)

> *And do not grieve the Holy Spirit of God, by whom you were sealed for the day of redemption.*
> (Ephesians 4:30, ESV)

May the God of hope fill you with joy
and peace in believing, so that by the power
of the Holy Spirit you may abound in hope.
(Romans 15:13, ESV)

Prayer: Father God today I come to you weary, with a heavy heart. I lay all of it Lord at your feet. I lift up my loved ones, Lord, the ones who struggle with depression and anxiety. I lift them up high Lord and ask in your precious name Jesus, that you, Father, take hold of their minds and fill their hearts with joy. I love you and I thank you in Jesus's name, I pray, amen.

To my Reader: I know that almost all of us, if not all of us really, who know someone that may suffer from depression or anxiety or both. Perhaps you, yourself suffer. I just wanted you to know that you are not alone. I myself suffer from anxiety and depression at times and I know so many people who do. Don't be afraid to talk about it with someone or talk with the person you know it's affecting it is okay. You will get through it and like they say, "This to shall pass." Pray to the Lord and let him lighten your load.

October 07

Have Faith, Believe

Awaken this day my child, with the feeling of love and joy that I have placed deep within your heart. Bring to this day the knowledge of hope and learn that my good path will prevail. Let go of past hurts be forgiving of them and give them to me, I am your strength. I am the light shining your way out of the darkness. I am the open clear path laid out before you, and I am your love. You are my child and I care deeply for you. I'm encouraging you to give up your ways and walk with me in mine. I am holding your hand and leading you through. When you're feeling lost and full of hopelessness, remember it is nothing compared to the joy that is coming. You just must be patient, have faith, and believe.

> *May the God of hope fill you with all the joy and peace in believing, so that by the power of the Holy Spirit you may abound in hope.*
> (Romans 15:13, ESV)

> *He was still speaking when, behold, a bright cloud overshadowed them, and a voice came from the cloud said, "This is my beloved Son, with whom I am well pleased; listen to him."*
> (Matthew 17:5, ESV)

> *Jesus said to them, "Have you believed because you have seen me? Blessed are those who have not seen and yet believed."*
> (John 20:29, ESV)

Now faith is the assurance of things
hoped for, the conviction of things not seen.
(Hebrews 11:1, ESV)

But for you who fear my name, the
sun of righteousness shall rise with healing
in its wings. You shall go out leaping like
calves from the stall.
(Malachi 4:2, ESV)

Prayer: Father God, I believe in you and all that you are. Please fill my family and friends with this knowledge in love and faith also. May we always find the strength to believe even when life gets tough. Bring us back to your place of joy, in Jesus's name, I ask and pray. Amen.

October 08

I Will Lead; Will You Follow?

I will lead you through your situations in this life. In all situations, I require you to trust me. Even in situations where you have no control. But remember my dear child that I am in control. When the first step that is taken is a step taken with trust in your heart and you can open yourself giving me the situation in prayer. I will tell you, "Do not fear" and to give up the anxiety that accompanies the situation. I am bigger than any problem you face and have unlimited resources to take good care of you. Believe that I am doing just that. As I guide you and surround you with my ever so loving Presence. Be brave little one. Just know that everything will be okay. I have overcome the world have gone before you, to correct the situation. Bringing it back to the place that I have deemed safe for your keeping. Walk in confidence and keep growing in spirit, following in my steps. I love you, my child.

Rejoice always, pray without ceasing, give thanks in all circumstances; for this is the will of God in Christ Jesus for you.
(1 Thessalonians 5:16–18, ESV)

Do not be anxious about anything, but in everything with prayer and supplication with thanksgiving let your requests be made known to God. And the peace of God, which surpasses all understanding, will guard your hearts and your minds in Christ Jesus.
(Philippians 4:6–7, ESV)

You shall serve the Lord your God,
and he will bless your bread and your
water, and I will take sickness away from
among you.
(Exodus 23:25, ESV)

Prayer: Father, help me through my situations when I feel scared and stressed. Thank you, Father, for looking out for my family, friends and me. I open up all my troubles or upcoming situations to you, Lord. I ask you to guide my steps and fill all our lives with your loving grace each and every day. Teach us how to accept what you give in kindness and fill us up with confidence and joy. It is in your loving name Jesus, I pray, amen.

October 09

Called to Joy

Let me strengthen you. Take hold of me this day. Keep learning my good and perfect ways. Reading my word and sharing with others. I know at times you feel like you need to be alone. I would go off by myself too when I was there in the world. Just as I was never truly alone. You are not either, so when you're ready to talk, call out to me and I will be listening. In this world, so many things have gone astray, but take heart and have faith. I am bringing my creation back again to me. Continue to live child, not just merely survive, but live. Embracing all the joy and love I have for you. There are seasons my beloved, and today you are called to joy.

He called you to this through the gospel, that you might share in the glory of our Lord Jesus Christ.
(2 Thessalonians 2:14, NIV)

To make an apt answer is a joy to man, and a word in season, how good it is!
(Proverbs 15:23, ESV)

The Lord your God is in your midst, a mighty one who will save; he will rejoice over you with gladness; he will quiet you by his love; he will exult over you with loud singing.
(Zephaniah 3:17, ESV)

You make known to me the path of
life; in your Presence there is fullness of joy;
at your right hand are pleasures forevermore.
(Psalm 16:11, ESV)

These things I have spoken to you,
that my joy may be in you, and that your
joy may be full.
(John 15:11, ESV)

Prayer: Father God, thank you Lord for calling us to joy! It is a great joy that is found in you. And with that thought, I will simply say thank you, Father God. In Jesus's name, I give thanks and pray, amen.

To my reader,
it is my hope that you will find your
joy in every moment of your life. May all
be well you're you, God Bless.

October 10

You Sow, He Leads

When you feel like your lost in your situation, pray for my guidance to light the way. I can be your compass guiding you across the distant lands. There are times in your life, I know my child that you have been walking aimlessly. You are on your journey so engulfed by the situations and people around you, that when you finally stop... You look up and look around to find that there is nothing familiar in sight. There are no familiar landmarks, that you once used to guide you home. You are somewhere not far, yet you feel lost. I do not want you to fear. Calmly condition yourself to do this...pray to me, ask my Holy Spirit to guide you forward. I am always with you, therefore my dear child you are never truly lost or truly alone. I must lead you here for my good, promoting. I have given you a purpose and fill you with my Spirit. Let my Spirit lead, lightning the way in the darkness. Keep sowing the seeds of my gospel. Your forever home is eternal. As your true home is in Heaven with me. Enjoy the moments of today keeping your faith and the hope that is found in me. You sow and I will lead.

When the cares of my heart are many,
your consolations cheer my soul.
(Psalm 94:19, ESV)

I press on toward the goal to win the
prize for which God has called me heaven-
ward in Christ Jesus.
(Philippians 3:14, NIV)

To this you were called, because Christ
suffered for you, leaving an example, that
you should follow in his steps.
(1 Peter 2:21, NIV)

To my Reader, you are blessed by the
Father. Keep your faith. Knowing that
you are loved.

As always with love,
April

Though you have not seen him, you
love him. Though you do not now see him,
you believe in him and rejoice with joy
that is inexpressible and filled with glory,
obtaining the outcome of your faith, the sal-
vation of your souls.
(1 Peter 1:8–9, ESV)

October 11

Take Delight

Thank me for this day and make time to communicate with me all that is in your mind. There are situations in your heart. You are faithful when you leave them in my care. When you practice bringing your problems to me and can truly leave them. You may start to notice that it frees your mind up to enjoy all your blessings in this life. Start the day off with a positive outlook and know that I am with you. Let your soul feel loved. I will bring to you a new energy and confidence, that you may have felt was missing for quite some time. Just like the seasons, are the seasons of life. Some are sad and others are joyful. As the current one passes, the sky will clear, and the path will seem to open up. Take delight in these times and relish in these loving moments, accepting the gifts I endow to you. There is merriment on the horizon, my child. So take delight in it today.

He changes times and seasons; he removes kings and sets up kings; he gives wisdom to the wise and knowledge to those who have understanding.
(Daniel 2:21, ESV)

Remember not the former things, nor consider the things of old. Behold, I am doing a new thing; now it springs forth, do you not perceive it? I will make a way in the wilderness and rivers in the desert.
(Isaiah 43:18–19, ESV)

And I will make them and the places
all around my hill a blessing, and I will
send down the showers in their season; they
shall be showers of blessing.
(Ezekiel 34:26, ESV)

For everything there is a season, and a
time for every matter under heaven.
(Ecclesiastes 3:1, ESV)

Prayer: Jesus, thank you for bringing me a new season, a season of joy. I pray for all my family and friends that you would help their seasons turn to seasons of joy as well. Thank you for taking all my cares and filling me with the consolation of happiness you bring. In Jesus's name, I pray, amen.

October 12

Skills and Abilities

You can breathe... Today wake up with a feeling of lightness, no heavy burdens weighing down your mind. You have seen so much in your life, so many experiences, some good, and others not so good. These experiences I have used to shape you just like a potter fashioning his clay. I have made you just the way you are now. You are beautiful to me. I will surround you with my love if you let me. Just keep your eyes focused on me and your heart open to my teaching. There are skills that you have learned over the span of your life, skills that I can use for my good promoting. Because you have these certain skills added in combination with the innate abilities you've been given from birth, there is much we can accomplish together. Do not forget my child by sharing the gospel with others, you are essentially helping to promote my Kingdom and leading others to their eternal home, that is found only with me. Feel good about the purpose and what I've chosen you to do. Answer the call that I have put on your heart. Promote my truth and the light of Salvation for all.

I blotted out your transgressions like a cloud and your sins like mist; return to me, for I have redeemed you.
(Isaiah 44:22, ESV)

But grace was given to each one of us according to the measure of Christ's gift.
(Ephesians 4:7, ESV)

To each is given the manifestation of the Spirit for the common good.
(1 Corinthians 12:7, ESV)

*Just so I tell you, there will be more joy
in heaven over one sinner who repents than
over ninety-nine righteous persons who need
no repentance.*
(Luke 15:7, ESV)

Prayer: Father God, thank you for making me who I am today, and for staying with me through it all. I pray for all my family and friends Lord, that you fill them with strength and the light of your promise of Salvation. I pray for each and every one that you would be the focus of our lives. In Jesus's name, I pray, amen.

October 13

His Masterpiece

Thank me in the stillness of the morning. Bring your requests to me at the cusp of the day. Fill the air with the sounds of your praises in the nigh of the evening, and surrender to me the song of your soul the whole day through. You are my child I love so much, with an everlasting love that supersedes even your understanding. I created you and fashioned you with all the characteristics and markings of a masterpiece. And I am pleased to call you my own. My heart sings when I hear you sharing my love with others. As it is love that covers a multitude of sin. I bring you mercy and joy as needed and fill your soul with the strength to persevere. I lavish you with my love and bring grace to you freely. I am your Lord who holds the light of your Salvation. I surround you and enshroud you from the worldly mantras. Protecting your mind from disruptive dismay. I fill you with the Helper, My Holy Spirit who dwells within you. Speaking to your heart, today and always, I lift you up… I raise you up, my child…to love.

> *For by grace you have been saved through faith. And this is not of your own doing; it is the gift of God, not a result of works, so that no one may boast.*
> (Ephesians 2:8–9, ESV)

> *Yours, Lord, is the greatness and the power and the glory and the majesty and the splendor, for everything in heaven and earth is yours. Yours, Lord, is the kingdom; you are exalted as head over all.*
> (1 Chronicles 29:11, NIV)

For you formed my inward parts; you
knitted me together in my mother's womb.
I praise you, for I am fearfully and wonder-
fully made. Wonderful are your works; my
soul knows full well.
(Psalm 139:13–14, ESV)

Prayer: Father God, I shout your praises. There is no other like you. I lift up all my life to you my family and my friends, I ask that you surround us with your love always Lord. In Jesus's name, I pray, amen.

October 14

In the Moments

Rest in the light of my presence little one. Enjoy the beauty, as we journey through the day. Fill your heart with laughter and all my loving ways. Today is my gift of the present and I'm gifting you, my love. Walk in the moments of rest that I bring; in your weakness I will lift you up. Do not rush ahead. Take a single step and follow where I lead. There is an easiness and gentleness in the Spirit I've placed within your heart. So just enjoy these treasured moments. Keep your eyes up fixed on me. Thanking me for this day. As moment by moment, I am with you. Stay encouraged my child. Today may you feel empowered, take all the strength that you need. There is a victory on the horizon. Keep giving your life to me and learning all my peaceful ways, as you may find me time and time again in all your moments.

When the righteous cry for help, the Lord hears and delivers them out of their troubles. The Lord is near to the broken-hearted and saves the crushed in spirit.
(Psalm 34:17–18, ESV)

Now may the Lord himself give you peace at all times in every way. The Lord be with you all.
(2 Thessalonians 3:16, ESV)

The Lord bless you and keep you; the Lord make his face to shine upon you and be gracious unto you; The Lord lift up his countenance upon you and give you peace.
(Numbers 6:24–26, ESV)

Prayer: Father God, may I always find the peace you bring to me. I ask you to watch over all my family and friends be with them in their troubles and keep protecting them. I thank you for everything Lord. In Jesus's name, I pray, amen.

October 15

So Much More

Search your heart to find that there is so much more, that I have placed in you. The closer you are to me the more you will begin to know more of yourself, and you will find hidden talents and capabilities that you never knew you had. I want you to polish all the good gifts I have given and use them for my good. You are always too hard on yourself child but, perfection is not what I desire from you. I only desire to be your God. That you would always place me first above all else and love me with your whole heart and share your love with others. Ease up on your idiosyncrasies, if you let your mind escape you-you will become your own worst critic. Lighten up and accept your abilities without the knowledge of limitations. As I have gifted you with only the best. You can do all things, as it is I who strengthens you. Keep walking in my will and let the possibilities unfold into realities. We are on a good journey together. Don't stop now. Be encouraged, as I will reveal to you so much more.

Now to him who is able to do far more abundantly than all we ask or think. According to the power at work within us.
(Ephesians 3:20, ESV)

A man's gift makes room for him and brings him before the great.
(Proverbs 18:16, ESV)

I can do all things through him that strengthens me.
(Philippians 4:13, ESV)

Call to me and I will answer you, and
will tell you great and hidden things that
you have not known.
(Jeremiah 33:3, ESV)

Prayer: Father God, thank you for leading me. I pray for discernment Lord, that you make your ways known to me so that I may always walk in your will. I ask that you take care of all my loved ones' Lord and guide us gently with your love. Thank you, Lord, for this beautiful day. In Jesus's name, I pray, amen.

October 16

Acts of Kindness

Expect nothing in return for good gestures and acts of kindness. Find the beauty within the private act of generosity. I have created you, my dear one, to be giving and kind, to offer up helping solutions when you see someone in need. It may be as simple as lending an ear to their troubles. Whatever the case may be, when you feel me tugging at your heart, urging you to help I will tell you to listen. My children are to be an example by their actions, not words. It pleases me when I see you exhibiting the love I have given. When you give to others, I fill you with a feeling of correctness as this is the way of living rightly. The way I designed you to be. Take nothing for granted. Enjoy all that I give and be willing to share. Do not let the world tell you that more for yourself is the way to be happy. As selfish desires once obtained leave you empty. Instead, give to others and experience that when you give any bit of yourself to another, your soul becomes full. It is a fullness found in love. Where there is love, you will also find my Spirit as I am your God and I AM love.

Each one must give as he decided in his heart, not reluctantly or under compulsion, for God loves a cheerful giver.
(2 Corinthians 9:7, ESV)

Whoever brings blessing will be enriched, and one who waters will himself be watered.
(Proverbs 11:25, ESV)

If I give away all I have, and deliver
up my body to be burned, but have not love,
I gain nothing.
(1 Corinthians 13:3, ESV)

She opens her mouth with wisdom,
and the teaching of kindness is on her
tongue.
(Proverbs 31:26, ESV)

Note then the kindness and the sever-
ity of God: severity towards those who have
fallen, but God's kindness to you, provided
you continue in his kindness. Otherwise you
too will be cut off.
(Romans 11:22, ESV)

Prayer: Thank you, Father, for this day. Help me Lord to always be a cheerful giver. Fill me with the fullness of your love so that I may have enough to share with others. I pray for all my family and friends that you watch over them and fill them with your joy. In Jesus's name, I pray, amen.

October 17

Warmth and Living Waters

May the day fill you with warmth and the joy you have found in me, so that you can go out and share with others the truth of my ways. I have made you to be a light. Take the warmth of sunshine deep within your soul and radiate it out. Always being thankful for what I have given. Today let my love permeate within you penetrating all the areas of your life. Be joyful my child as today we will share kindness. Encourage others to strive to achieve the best in their lives just as I encourage you. Remind them that I am also for them. My love can reach your deepest parts and can create streams in the deserts of your lives. Take from me my living waters and feel refreshed again. Let my waters wash over you and those around you, as you share in this drink. Your soul can now be full of my warmth and living waters.

Jesus answered her, "If you knew the gift of God, and who it is saying to you, 'Give me a drink,' you would have asked him, and he would have given you the living water."
(John 4:10, ESV)

But whoever drinks of the living water that I give will never be thirsty again. The water that I will give him will become a spring of water welling up to eternal life.
(John 4:14, ESV)

Whoever believes in me, as the Scripture has said,' Out of his heart will flow rivers of living water.
(John 7:38, ESV)

The angel showed me the river of the
water of life, bright as crystal, flowing from
the throne of God and of the Lamb.
(Revelation 2:21, ESV)

Prayer: Father God, thank you for always keeping my spirit quenched. I pray for all my family and friends everyday Lord, that they may also find streams in their deserts and that they know it is you who provides, the living waters. In Jesus's name, I give thanks, amen.

October 18

Unabridged and Complete

Always have hope my child, do not lose your faith. Know my Spirit and all that I bring. Gentleness, kindness, easiness, compassion, empathy, sincerity, peace, patience, love, grace, truth and more. My love for you child, it is eternal and my kingdom reigns eternal as well. I have called you out of the mire and set you apart. There is a fire that I have created in your soul, as you are solid in your seeking of my truth. I whisper to you love songs as the night falls, while you dream deep in your slumber. I speak to you in love tones that only your heart and soul can hear. Feel your unabridged story as it is with me in all my glory and wondrous ways. Feel complete in your faith. A foundation built on me is one that will never fail. Rest in this truth and find comfort.

> *My soul continually remembers it and is bowed down within me. But this I call to mind, and therefore I have hope: The steadfast love of the Lord never ceases; his mercies never come to an end; they are new every morning; great is your faithfulness. "The Lord is my portion," says my soul, "therefore I will hope in him."*
> (Lamentations 3:20–24, ESV)

> *But the fruit of the Spirit is love, joy, peace, patience, kindness, goodness, faithfulness, gentleness self-control, against such things there is no law.*
> (Galatians 5:22–23, ESV)

*Teaching them to observe all that I
have commanded you. And behold, I am
with you always, to the end of the age.*
(Matthew 28:20, ESV)

Prayer: I lift up all my plans to you today Lord. That you may establish my steps and the steps of my loved ones. Lead us always with your kind loving ways. I praise you Lord and thank you for this day. In Jesus's loving name, I pray and give thanks, amen.

October 19

Majestic Absolutions

Distractions from today come in all forms. But keep faithful to my calling and do not be pulled off task. Let me keep the center of your focus. When you do this, you can remain balanced. As your whole life is a walk of majestic absolutions, found within the grace that I have given. All life is beautiful and beautifully purposed. Finding the truth of my irrevocable love for you. Nothing you can do or have done, past, present or future could change the way I love you. When you surrender your life to me and hand over your heart. A new thing I will magnify in you. Stay aware of my purpose, my child, and attuned to the path which I am leading. Pray without ceasing. Rejoicing always and my love will keep lighting the way.

> *Rejoice always, pray without ceasing.*
> *Give thanks in all circumstances; for this is*
> *the will of God in Christ Jesus for you.*
> (1 Thessalonians 5:16–18, ESV)

> *Who saved us and called us to a holy*
> *calling, not because of our works but because*
> *of his own purpose and grace, which he gave*
> *us in Christ Jesus before the ages began.*
> (2 Timothy 1:9, ESV)

> *In him we have obtained an inher-*
> *itance, having been predestined according*
> *to the purpose of him who works all things*
> *according to the counsel of his will.*
> (Ephesians 1:11, ESV)

*Because your steadfast love is better
than life, my lips will praise you. So I will
bless you as long as I live; In your name, I
will lift up my hands.*
(Psalm 63:3–4, ESV)

Prayer: Father God, thank you for your mercy and grace. I surround myself Lord with your love and ask that you surround my family and me with your Holy Presence every day. Direct our steps and fill us, Lord, In Jesus's name, I pray, amen.

October 20

Sullen Sometimes

There are times when you are sullen, and I will direct you to focus on me. Find the joy placed in your spirit. Do not let sadness set in. I want to bring an easiness of rest, as I see that you are tired. Always pushing yourself to do more. Without proper rest, can bring hours of frustration and it will set within your mind. Learn to be good to yourself my child and find the care that comes from me. Every one of my children will at some point experience what the world would call a bad day, but do not let it define you. You are capable of experiencing so much more, goodness and joy. Let these outweigh the weight of the heaviness that anxiety and a busy day can bring. Keep control of your mind and your emotion, by entrusting them in my care. Today just try to find the goodness and the beauty. Be glad in today my child, and let my love lift away any melancholy you feel. Feel the warmth of my assurance and be joyful once again.

But the lord is faithful. He will establish you and guard you against the evil one.
(2 Thessalonians 3:3, ESV)

I have said these things to you, that in me you may have peace. In the world, you will have tribulation. But take heart; I have overcome the world.
(John 16:33, ESV)

And give no opportunity to the devil.
(Ephesians 4:27, ESV)

Prayer: Lord, thank you for guarding my heart and my soul and the same of my loved ones. Fill us up with your Holy presence Lord. Give to us a gentle, peaceful spirit. Guide our every step Lord. This is my prayer today, In Jesus's name, amen.

October 21

His Love

Spend time with me my child and read my word. Do not try to cling to old ways, but instead walk with me on this new path and follow. There is a peace in the day as the sun shines out over the world, the birds sing in the sky. Singing my praise, as even they belong to me. If you feel your foot slip call out to me today and I will place solid ground beneath your feet. With me, you will not fall. Hold tightly to all my good ways and practice them. Share what I have taught you. And speaking of what I am teaching you now. There is always room to learn. Casting off fear, anxiety, sadness, and doubt replacing these with joy, assurance, grace, and love. You will persevere when you walk solidly on the firm foundations found within my word. Reign with victory brought forth and bought by me. As I am with you and have gone before you. No weapon formed against you shall prosper. I will protect you and guide you all of your days. Be thankful and find this joy and the peace of my love forever more. Let your heart sing the song of my praise and relish in this I have given you today and always…my love.

When I thought, "My foot slips," your steadfast love, O Lord, held me up.
(Psalm 94:18, ESV)

I made known to them your name, and I will continue to make it known, that the love with which you have loved me may be in them, and I in them.
(John 17:26, ESV)

One thing have I asked of the Lord,
that I will seek after; that I may dwell in
the house of the Lord all the days of my life,
to gaze upon the beauty of the Lord and to
inquire in his temple.
(Psalm 27:4, ESV)

Prayer: Father God, I lift up my cares to you today Lord, and ask you to be my help. I thank you for my family and friends and ask you for a good day today. It is in Jesus's name, I pray, amen.

October 22

Bask in the Glow

In the morning give thanks. Pray about everything, giving all to me. I have been with you from the beginning. The day cast a light in the morning glow and the warmth of the sun settles on the surface of the earth. Just like the warmth of my Spirit settles on you, filling you with calmness and peace. Let my Spirit lead do not try to force your way ahead or linger too far behind, just keep in step with me. There are times I will ask you to wait in certain situations that you have given to me. There are other times I will require action. Do not worry about getting it wrong. There is nothing you will miss. Trust me during it all and I will help you to retain your peace. When the evening draws near, stay confident and worry-free. Remember my child my plan for your life will always prevail. You are free, to enjoy all the simplicity and blessings that I give. Life is beautiful, enjoy, and bask in the glow of my love…

> *There is nothing better for a person than he should eat and drink and find enjoyment in his toil. This also, I saw, is from the hand of God.*
> (Ecclesiastes 2:24, ESV)

> *The thief comes only to steal and kill and destroy. I came that they may have life and have it abundantly.*
> (John 10:10, ESV)

For I did not receive it from any man,
nor was I taught it, but I received it through
a revelation of Jesus Christ.
(Galatians 1:12, ESV)

Delight in the Lord always; and he
will give you the desires of your heart.
(Psalm 37:4, ESV)

Prayer: Father God I lift up my hands to you. I pray for you to guide every step and to bless my every breath. I give you my all, my love, my heart, my life. I give you my family and friends and ask you to fill them with the guidance and love that only you Lord can bring. In Jesus's name, I give praise and thanks in Jesus's name, amen.

October 23

Freedom from Old

I'm taking you in a new direction. Cast your cares and your hardships, cast them at my feet bring them to the cross and lay them down. Finally, you are learning to be free. Forgiving yourself and others from the ghosts of the past. My love always prevails. Learning to love yourself and the person I've created you to be. "You are beautiful, for you are fearfully and wonderfully made. Your soul knows full well." When your mind finally catches up with all that I have put in your heart you can rejoice. It is like refreshing drops of rain falling onto a dry parched land, quenching the earth. In the same way, my word and my love will quench your soul. My Spirit within guides you and approves you, leading down the path that I have proclaimed. I have set you free from the days of old. Rejoice, my child, rejoice, in your soul.

For freedom Christ has set us free;
stand firm therefore, and do not submit,
again to a yoke of slavery.
(Galatians 5:1, ESV)

Now the Lord is the Spirit, and where
the Spirit of the Lord is, there is freedom.
(2 Corinthians 3:17, ESV)

And you will know the truth, and the
truth will set you free.
(John 8:32, ESV)

So if the Son sets you free, you will be
free indeed.
(John 8:36, ESV)

Prayer: Thank you, Lord, for this day and thank you also for setting us free. I pray to for all of us today Lord that we may walk in your good ways. Learning your good truths. As you bless our steps and guide us filling us with peace and joy. In Jesus's name, I give thanks and pray. Amen.

October 24

Seasoned to Taste

I hear your petitions my child, do not worry. I have not turned a deaf ear. I know you may not see any movement in some situations, but you must learn not only to trust but also to be patient. As everything about my timing is perfect. If my children would have their way, they would have it all at once, without learning and letting me and the lessons of life season them to my good taste. It is when you walk through your hardships that I do the most refining. Keep learning to lean on me in all situations. Do not just pick and choose the ones throughout the day that you feel I would best be suited for. As I AM, your God, and I am suited for them all. I AM the head of your life, So no more worries or fear. Together we can conquer them all. Today be well and feel the calmness of my loving Spirit. This is the season I have called you to taste and see my child, as it is good.

> *Blessed is the man who remains steadfast under trial, for when he has stood the test he will receive the crown of life, which God has promised to those who love him.*
> (James 1:12, ESV)

> *Preach the word; be prepared in season and out of season; correct, rebuke and encourage—with great patience and careful instruction.*
> (2 Timothy 4:2, NIV)

> *I am the Lord, the God of all mankind. Is anything too hard for me?*
> (Jeremiah 32:27, NIV)

The angel of the Lord encamps around
those who fear him, and delivers them. Oh,
taste and see that the Lord is good! Blessed is
the man who takes refuge in him!
(Psalm 34:7–8, ESV)

Prayer: Thank you Lord, for this day. Thank you for working on my behalf in the situations that trouble me and for helping my family and friends. I praise you, Jesus. Help us to be patient and fill us with joy, as you season us to the taste of your good liking. In Jesus's name, I ask and pray. I thank you for the victory, amen.

October 25

The Love Light

There are days when I bring solitude. It is good to have quiet moments, relaxing your mind. This world has a way of pulling my children into circles of business, you hide yourself when you blur your life with your business. You need to slow down my child. I'm calling on you to get to know people, to really let them in. I know the world would have you keep them at a distance. But I will tell you to love thy neighbor just as I love you. People all over the world need me and need to hear my message. Be a beacon of light to them drawing them near and sharing with them my Gospel. Be the salt of the earth. Sharing and encouraging from your heart to theirs. Love them and help them to know me so I can lead them into the light of Salvation. Go out today more than a conqueror. Go out today as a light called love.

Greater love has no one than this, that someone lay down his life for his friends.
(John 15:13, ESV)

We ought always to give thanks to God for you, brothers, as is right, because your faith is growing abundantly, and the love of every one of you for one another is increasing.
(2 Thessalonians 1:3, ESV)

And this commandment we have from him: whoever loves God must also love his brother.
(1 John 4:21, ESV)

> *For what we proclaim is not ourselves,*
> *but Jesus Christ as Lord, with ourselves as*
> *your servants for Jesus' sake. For God, who*
> *said, "Let light shine out of the darkness,"*
> *has shone in our hearts to give the light of*
> *the knowledge of the glory of God in the face*
> *of Jesus Christ.*
> (2 Corinthians 4:5–6, ESV)

Prayer: Father God, always give me eyes to see the best in others. I lift all my family and friends up to you each day. May I always be a light to others Lord and them to me. I give thanks to you this day Lord. In Jesus's name, I pray, amen.

October 26

Surmountable Moments

Be anxious for nothing! Let no one steal your joy or your peace. Keep the worries of the world at bay by keeping focused on me. I will remind you with my Spirit that everything is under my control. I will settle the storm before it begins. I can do anything you ask. But it is my will, which protects you from the selfish ways of the world. Keep focused on things above. This will enable you to remain joyful and persevere through the day. There are so many blessings forming all around you. Will you not open your eyes to see? There are gifts of love I give you in all the surmountable moments. Accept my ways child, fill your life with all kindness, the beauty of my grace wrapped in mercy and grounded in love. Nothing can separate you from the love I give. I AM the King of Kings. I AM your God, your Lord, and I love you, unconditionally and eternally…

That according to the riches of his glory he may grant you to be strengthened with power through his Spirit in your inner being, so that Christ may dwell in your hearts through faith-that you, being rooted and grounded in love.
(Ephesians 3:16–17, ESV)

No, in all these things we are more than conquerors through him who loved us. For I am sure that neither death nor life, nor angels nor rulers nor things present nor things to come, nor powers, nor height nor depth, nor anything else in all creation, will

be able to separate us from the love of God in Christ Jesus our Lord.
    (Romans 8:37–39, ESV)

Humble yourselves, therefore, under the mighty hand of God so that in the proper time he may exalt you, casting all your anxieties on him, because he cares for you.
    (1 Peter 5:6–7, ESV)

Prayer: Father God, I just want to thank you today for your love. Amen.

October 27

Fullness of His Love

Take my Spirit as manifest upon your life. It is a choice you make daily, to trust in me. It is the courage you need to give up your plans for your life an accept my will as your own. There is a blessing that comes along with having faith. It is in response to your faith that you are no longer alone. You have called me into your life and asked me to fill your heart with my great purpose and good ways. It is also a representation of a full tithe of yourself to me. Giving up your will and letting me lead you into mine. I will meet you in the moments. Wherever you are, whether past, present or future. I am here... I will pull you out of the troubles of the past and restore you to the present. Keep bringing me your all, and your life will never be empty. It will be found in the fullness of my love.

In this love of God made manifest among us, that God sent his only Son into the world, so that we might live through him. In this love, not that we loved God but that he loved us and sent his Son to be the propitiation for our sins.
(1 John 4:9–10, ESV)

For the Father himself loves you, because you have loved me and have believed that I came from God.
(John 16:27, ESV)

Love bears all things, believes all things, hopes all things, endures all things.
(1 Corinthians 13:7, ESV)

*And to know the love of Christ that
surpasses knowledge, that you may be filled
with all the fullness of God.*
(Ephesians 3:19, ESV)

Prayer: Thank you for this day Lord. I pray for all my family, friends and I Lord, that you keep our hearts full of your love and kindness. That we may never lose sight of your purpose for our lives, and that we may walk in the confidence of knowing where to walk because you have made the path clear. In Jesus's name, I pray, amen.

October 28

The Easiness of His Love

This day I bring to you easiness and a caress of your spirit. As you may notice that I have been confirming situations to you that you have asked about in prayer. The beauty of these moments is meant to be cherished and remembered, as to stir your spirit and give you peace. I will gift you with what it means to be truly free. Free from burdens, free from worries, and freedom from the world and its ways of turmoil. I will help you to see beauty when none seems evident. I have called you to be a service to love one another and share in the kindness of all of my ways. To help one another and to give of yourself the purpose that I have placed deep within your heart. Take from me my yoke as it is easy and will ease you into the peace of this day. May you always remember child, who it is that I have called you to be. It is within you that my light shines to the world. Forever my child, the easiness of my love is given to you.

And hope does not put us to shame, because God's love has been poured into our hearts through the Holy Spirit who has been given to us.
(Romans 5:5, ESV)

This is how God showed his love among us: He sent his one and only Son into the world that we might live through him. This is love: not that we loved God, but that he loved us and sent his Son as an atoning sacrifice for our sins. Dear friends, since God so loved us, we also ought to love one another.
(1 John 4:9–11, NIV)

Keep yourselves in the love of God,
waiting for the mercy of our Lord Jesus
Christ that leads to eternal life.
(Jude 1:21, ESV)

Prayer: Father God, thank you for your easy loving ways, and providing me with much-needed peace. I pray for all today Lord, that you would just keep leading us within the fullness of love and lifting us up to a place where our spirit can meet yours in all of our moments. I praise your name, Jesus and it is to you, I pray, amen.

October 29

A Moment of Angels

state

A moment to remember. All throughout your life, I have sent angels to direct your steps some to encourage, and others to comfort, some to give hope and others just to watch over. But there are definitely moments to remember. It is in the spaces of the moments that make up a day, a stranger may show up and say just the right thing or shares a long stair and smiles at you. It's just that fleeting feeling for a second, the feeling you feel of being sure this is not of this world. It is a knowing. These are the times you will ponder over on and off whenever the memories come to mind. It is because of your human limitations of thought that I will not allow you to fully understand. One day you will know all the secrets of your heart and of angels and of life but for now, just cherish what I give. Life is a journey and for the faithful, it will be lived with abundant blessings and it will be protected with my steadfast love.

> *For he will command his angels con-*
> *cerning you to guard you in all your ways.*
> (Psalm 91:11, ESV)

> *Let brotherly love continue. Do not*
> *neglect to show hospitality to strangers.*
> *For thereby some have entertained angels*
> *unawares.*
> (Hebrews 13:1–2, ESV)

> *My God sent his angel and shut the*
> *lions' mouths, and they have not harmed*
> *me, because I found blameless before him;*

and also before you, O king, I have done
no harm.
  (Daniel 6:22, ESV)

Behold, I send an angel before you to
guard you on the way and bring you to the
place that I have prepared.
  (Exodus 23:22, ESV)

Prayer: Father God thank you for sending your angels to watch over us. I pray today for continued peace, and for confidence to keep walking where you lead. I pray to always have your angels watching over us. In Jesus's name, amen.

October 30

November

And leaves a green can share the love of the Lord with us too. And nature is so soothing to observe when you are feeling blue.

Faithful Plans of Peace

Step into the peace of my plans for your life. Know nothing is impossible with me. Remember faith includes trusting in the situations to which you have no answers. But I have gone before you and prepared the way for you to which my best serves. I have plans to prosper and not to harm you. My good and perfect ways are far more than you can imagine even for yourself. Also, you must trust that it is in my timing that all will be made right. My light will shine upon the path as you walk one step at a time. Keep your focus on things above and keep your mind on all the good things that I bring. Come to me with your all. Be willing to at times step out of your comfort zone, just follow where I lead. The way before you at times will seem ominous and uncertain but I am surely here, in the confidence of your life. I am the one truth that never changes and all my love for you pours out onto you and your life day after day. Keep faithful my child, you are not alone.

*"For I know the plans I have for you,"
declares the Lord, "plans to prosper and not
to harm you, plans to give you a hope and
a future."*
(Jeremiah 29:11, NIV)

*Trust in the Lord with all your heart,
and do not lean on your own understanding.*
(Proverbs 3:5, ESV)

*The Lord is near to all who call on
him, to all who call on him in truth.*
(Psalm 145:18, ESV)

What you have learned and received
and heard and seen in me-practice these
things, and the God of peace will be with
you.
(Philippians 4:9, ESV)

Prayer: Father thank you for this day and for all the days after. Please watch over all my family and friends and give us your truth to stand upon. We praise you and give you thanks to you for your perfect plans of peace, in Jesus's name, amen.

November 1

A Given Place

Let me lead, do not worry about falling behind, I will always keep you just in step with me, but you must remain focused. I will hold your hand and pull you forward removing all mountains in your way. You are my child I have called to this place found just within today. A place filled with love for others and for kindness and grace. A place where we reach each other's hearts and light up the world. I am giving to you this day a place of mercy. A place you can call your own. Go out into the world with all my glory around you. You are my priceless child. I have made you a warrior and a defender of my truth. I have instilled knowledge in your humility, as you understand no one is more important than the other. It is I who has blessed you with this wisdom. I have given you kind ears to ear and words of calming wisdom to share. I have placed in you an innate gentle nature that soothes even in the midst of the storms. My beloved little child, life is so much clearer once you accept the place I have given. Rejoice and be glad in the light of today. As this is your place and it is given by me.

Do not withhold good from those to whom it is due, when it is in your power to do it.
(Proverbs 3:27, ESV)

Go and learn what this means, 'I desire mercy, and not sacrifice.' For I came not to call the righteous, but sinners.
(Matthew 9:13, ESV)

But I do not account my life of any value nor as precious to myself, if only I may finish my course and the ministry that I received from the Lord Jesus, to testify to the gospel of the grace of God.
(Acts 20:24, ESV)

This also comes from the Lord of hosts; he is wonderful in counsel and excellent in wisdom.
(Isaiah 28:29, ESV)

Prayer: Father God, thank you for giving me the strength and courage to wear my love for you out in the open where everyone can see. I pray to be a blessing to all my family and friends. Thank you for making me the person I have become, and for opening my eyes with your wisdom. I give thanks in Jesus's name, amen.

November 02

You Are Found

I found you there, sitting in the muck and the mire. I picked you up and wiped your tears away. I have given you a purpose of hope and fill you with the light of my loving Presence. I continue with you in your walk daily. I will keep your foot from slipping and set you on solid ground. I AM the firm foundations in which you build. I am beyond the foundations, as I AM your roots. No storm too big for those who are deeply rooted in me. There is a place for you set at my table, so come to me and be fed. Read the living words of the Bible, and let your soul be full. There is much to accomplish and many to share my love with. Go out and be a light, a beacon to others who feel lost. Tell them I love them. No one is too lost or too far removed from me, they can hope when they find me in the moments of their tears. Encourage others, my child, as you know my ways are good. Invite them to find me today. Just as I found you.

You are the light of the world. A town built on a hill cannot be hidden. Neither do people light a lamp and put it under a bowl. Instead they put it on its stand, and it gives light to everyone in the house. In the same way, let your light shine before others, that they may see your good deeds and glorify your Father in heaven.
(Matthew 5:14–16, NIV)

Not only that, but we rejoice in our sufferings, knowing that suffering produces

endurance, and endurance produces char-
acter, and character produces hope.
(Romans 5:3–4, ESV)

And after you have suffered a little
while, the God of all grace, who has called
you to his eternal glory in Christ, will
restore, confirm, strengthen, and establish
you.
(1 Peter 5:10, ESV)

Prayer: Father God, give me the eyes to always see the best in others. And share the love with them. I pray to be an encouragement to all. I pray for all my family and friends this day Lord, that you lead us and give us the ability to remain in your truth of love for all. In Jesus's name, I pray and give thanks. Amen.

November 03

Another Morning of Light

Another morning is here. Time to rise up. I bring to you all the loveliness in this day. Starting off with your thankful heart. Take your time with me this morning and speak to me in prayer. I see you have much on your mind. Just as all my children do, from the time they open their eyes. If they are not careful, they will let their mind find control of them. Keep watchful as not to let any fear or worry creep in. When your mind starts to wander bring your focus back to me. Call out to me aloud if you must. As to snap you out of the worries genre of plays. Create a new playlist when your focus is with me. Think on all the good and precious things I bring daily. Find the sweet spot in your blessings. Take notice of how many there actually are. Let the positive of your life cancel out the negative. Cast the gloomy mood away, finding your smile just within you. My loving, precious, little child I call on you. Another morning light, an essence within today. A brightness resolving the shadows of yesterday and a certainty conquering the unknown of many tomorrows. Let your soul lift, uprising to the occasion that I have called. Enjoy the light of morning the whole day through. Stay in communication with me, and I will keep you balanced, and bring you the victory that's found in me.

> *Devote yourselves to prayer, being watchful and thankful.*
> (Colossians 4:2, NIV)

> *Do not be anxious about anything, but in every situation, by prayer and petition, with thanksgiving present your requests to*

God. And the peace of God, which tran-
scends all understanding, will guard your
hearts and your minds in Christ Jesus.
(Philippians 4:6–7, NIV)

But thanks be to God! He gives us the
victory through our Lord Jesus Christ.
(1 Corinthians 15:57, NIV)

Prayer: Father God, today I bring you all my troubles and my worries. I bring you all my thanks too. I pray for all Lord, that we may find you in every moment of all situations. That we may know that you are watching over and that you are in charge Lord. We have nothing to fear or feel overwhelmed about because you are with us and you have got this. In Jesus's loving name, I pray, amen.

November 04

Special Prayer

Is there something that you are needing? A special prayer placed upon your life. It is in the spaces of time throughout the day and night that I am leading and speaking to your heart. So quiet and calm are these moments. Nothing amidst the faint and somber utterance of a request from your lips traveling up to me, even when you can't find the words. I am here all around you. My Presence holds dear to a home which I have made within you. Holding nothing back from me. It is okay to voice your disappointments, but, do not linger here. Keep the faith, my child, as I am working on the requests made in your heart. Do not give up on the outcome, it will be better than any practiced scenario that you have re-played within your mind. Trust and see the way I will bring the situation out of its lost and wilted way into the full and green garden that is watered with my living waters and fed with my word. There is always time to celebrate, for now just keep counting every blessing, as I know the special prayer whether spoken or not.

Then you will call upon me and come
and pray to me, and I will hear you.
(Jeremiah 29:12, NIV)

And we know that he hears us in
whatever we ask, we know that we have the
requests that we ask of him.
(1 John 5:15, ESV)

Likewise, the Spirit helps us in our
weakness. For we do not know what to

pray for as we ought, but the Spirit himself intercedes for us with groanings too deep for words.

(Romans 8:26, ESV)

I cried to him with my mouth, and high praise was on my tongue. If I had cherished iniquity in my heart, the Lord would not have listened. But truly God has listened; he has attended to the voice of my prayer. Blessed be to God, because he has not rejected my prayer or removed his stead-fast love from me!

(Psalm 66:17–20, ESV)

Prayer: Father God, you know what is on my heart and in my mind, you know my prayers even before I say a word. I thank you for hearing my requests Lord and for working on my behalf and for all the others for whom I pray. I give thanks to the victory that I have found in you, and relish in your love. In Jesus's name, I pray. Amen.

November 05

Newfound Strength

There is a task that I have called you too. it is something to share, it is an ability of talent that was designed just for the person of you. Everyone has gifts, that are all uniquely fitted to just their right character. I do not make mistakes. Do not plan out your steps so rigidly, but instead let me lead as I will establish your ways. I have called you and am bringing you to my good place. My Spirit inside you may shine out like a light drawing others' to the ways of my good news. There is calm on the horizon and a peace in today. A love flourishing inside you and a confidence of new strength. Be brave little one venturing out boldly into the world this day. Bring with you the essence of my Spirit and the newfound strength I have given. As it will be used to overcome, any hardships found within the present moments. Now with your new strength let me guide you into the moments of happiness. Well done my child…

> *And when they had prayed, the place in which they were gathered together was shaken, and they were all filled with the Holy Spirit and continued to speak the word of God with boldness.*
> (Acts 4:31, ESV)

> *The Lord is my strength and my shield; in him my heart trusts, and I am helped; my heart exults with my song I give thanks to him.*
> (Psalm 28:7, ESV)

Whoever speaks, as one who speaks oracles of God; whoever serves, as one who serves by the strength that God supplies-in order that in everything God may be glorified through Jesus Christ. To him belong glory and dominion forever and ever. Amen.
(1 Peter 4:11, ESV)

Yes then, my child, be strengthened by the grace that is in Christ Jesus.
(2 Timothy 2:1, ESV)

Prayer: Father God, I am thankful. I pray that you keep opening the way before me and that you help me Lord to remain brave. I am learning so much and I pray to always see what I am learning through your eyes. I pray for my family and friends and all, that yours Lord, is the loudest voice in our minds. In Jesus's name, I pray and give thanks, amen.

November 06

Why Not Be Joyful

Why do you worry so? Why are you troubled? I have lifted away all the burdens that are heavy on you today and each day that you put your trust in me. I replace your troubles with all the easiness and lightness of my love. When you seek me with your whole heart you will find the love that I have placed inside, not to keep for yourself but to share with the world. When you do this and give to others it creates a deep joy in your life. That is because it is the way I've called all of you to be. Share my heart and my love for others. Be accepting and caring. Always show your empathy and compassion. There is a time to rejoice. For now, be glad in the moments of this day. I'm leading you to rise to this occasion. As it is my will that always prevails. Remain joyful my child, I am with you.

> *By day the Lord commands his steadfast love, and at night his song is with me, a prayer to the God of my life.*
> (Psalm 42:8, ESV)

> *Teach me to do your will. For you are my God! Let your good Spirit lead me on level ground!*
> (Psalm 143:10, ESV)

> *Fear not for I am with you; do not be dismayed, for I am your God; I will strengthen you, I will help you, I will uphold you with my righteous right hand.*
> (Isaiah 41:10, ESV)

Prayer: Father God, I bring you all my worries and anxieties. Mine and those of my family and my friends. I will go out today and walk in the confidence of your love. I pray for your continued guidance Lord. In Jesus's loving name, amen.

November 07

Fullness of Love

When my love meets your life... Oh, how sweet the days and the nights when you know you are surrounded by my love. My love lightens the soul and makes situations that otherwise seem hard, dissipate quickly. When filled with my love you get to experience the truth and the closeness of all life. Nothing else compares to love. Many of my children still have not recognized this as truth. They still toil under the sun. Trying to fill their lives up with achievements and goals. Filling themselves with money and things. But all those will leave you empty without love. As I AM love. And the love that I give brings unity and the balance to live. My purpose for you is filled with love. it is the simple act of giving and receiving. Not one more, than the other. When you love too much and have none in return, it can harden your heart. Loving too little you can become selfish, as this can leave you unfulfilled and empty. But I, your Lord, love you oh so much... I will always give you the love you need to sustain you, lift your soul and carry you through. My grace is sufficient for you this is true, and my love is essential to fully live a complete life. So rejoice in your heart...because my love always prevails.

And over all these put-on love, which
binds them all together in perfect unity.
(Colossians 3:14, NIV)

And if I have prophetic powers, and
understand all mysteries and all knowledge,
and if I have all faith, so as to remove moun-
tains, but I have not love, I am nothing.
(1 Corinthians 13:2, ESV)

See what kind of love the Father has given to us, that we should be called children of God; and so we are. The reason why the world does not know us is that it did not know him.
(1 John 3:1, ESV)

Prayer: Father God, Thank you for your all-encompassing eternal love. I pray you always fill my heart and the hearts of all my family and friends with your love. Let us have your eyes to see the best in people and a heart able to give love freely just as you do. I know we love Lord because you first loved us, and I am grateful. In Jesus's name, I pray and give thanks. Amen.

November 8

Keeping Calm

There are times when your day to day routines may get interrupted by something unforeseen. Everyone has times in their lives that an unforeseen situation may arise, some good and some not so good. It is your response...that can either make or break the situation. Good surprises are heart-warming and fill you with love, which is what I intended for you even in your day to day. As it is love that you should feel always. The not so good surprises require a bit more of you, in those times I will call you to remember you are never alone. I can help you get through any storm that you face no matter the size. Big or small, I am here and bring comfort, peace, and calm. When you remain calm in high-stress situations it is easier, to find a solution. If you allow your mind to run away with you, it can make a bad situation worse. So practice in emergent situations and in all situations eyes up and fixed on me. Let me calm you and help you. So you can be more effective. Always accepting my resolve.

Have I not commanded you? Be strong
and courageous. Do not be frightened, and
do not be dismayed, for the Lord your God
is with you wherever you go.
(Joshua 1:19, ESV)

I sought the Lord, and he answered
me and delivered me from all my fears.
(Psalm 34:4, ESV)

Anxiety in a man's heart weighs him
down, but a good word makes him glad.
(Proverbs 12:25, ESV)

Prayer: Father God, I will keep my eyes fixed on you, and during the unexpected times I will cling to you and your good ways. I pray that you strengthen us and remove anxiety from us Lord. That during stressful times, you give us your peace and deep calm. In Jesus's name, I ask and pray, amen.

November 9

You Will See

When you're upset my little one, I know it's hard to remember that I am still with you. But I am, even if I go unnoticed during most of your trials. I am with you, waiting for you to call on me. It is me whom you can trust to face anything in your life, whether uncertain or not... I am so sorry that at times you have to feel this way. To go through something that hurts your heart, as it hurts mine too. Life is not easy and relationships with other people can be the most challenging aspect of this life. I want you to know that I see when you are doing your best. It's good when you bring your relationships to me. I am working them out. Please be accepting of the outcomes. You know I have wonderful plans for your life and am leading you there. I see you in your patience and want you to know it is not in vain. I do reward my children who stay faithful. I love you, my child. Keep hopeful, stay faithful and in time you will see my good response.

> *Be joyful in hope, patient in affliction, faithful in prayer.*
> (Romans 12:12, NIV)

> *Blessed be the God and Father of our Lord Jesus Christ, the Father of mercies and God of all comfort, who comforts us in our affliction, so that we may be able to comfort those who are in any affliction. With the comfort with which we ourselves are comforted by God.*
> (2 Corinthians 1:3–4, ESV)

Be strong, and let your heart take
courage, all you who wait for the Lord!
(Psalm 31:24, ESV)

Then you will understand what is
right and just and fair-every good path.
(Proverbs 2:9, NIV)

Prayer: Lord, I pray for your good ways to encompass my life and fill me up. That I may have an abundance of happiness and joy and abilities and resources to go to new places and help those in need to give all the glory to you. I want to share your good news with the world. I pray for all my family and friends and people in the world, that you Lord. would lead them to you and keep them happy and safe knowing you are with them. In Jesus's name, I ask and pray. Amen.

November 10

Uncertainty Won't Stay

There are days when you may feel the weight of uncertainty, bringing along fear for the ride. When your mind starts down this road you must remind yourself to stop. Call out to me and pull your focus back to me. The more you do this, it becomes like training. You are learning to control your thoughts instead of them controlling you. This is how I want you to be, my child. As I have not created you to walk in fear and uncertainty... I have created you to be confident in your thoughts and your actions. That you may exemplify my good ways. Therefore, you can walk through the day boldly. Knowing you are my child. And that uncertainty will not stay. It is a peace that I bring to you, found within the moments of the day. The confidence of certainty that you have found in your walk with me brings you a boldness that is unstoppable. Keep your faith strong. Smile then and rejoice for I the Lord your God loves you and is always with you wherever you go.

Let the morning bring me word of your unfailing love, for I have put my trust in you. Show me the way I should go, for to you I entrust my life.
(Psalm 143:8, NIV)

Cast your burden on the Lord, and he will sustain you; he will never permit the righteous to be moved.
(Psalm 55:22, ESV)

*Now faith is the assurance of things
hoped for, the conviction of things not seen.*
(John 21:25, ESV)

*It is the Lord who goes before you. He
will be with you; he will not leave you or
forsake you. Do not fear or be dismayed.*
(Deuteronomy 31:8, ESV)

Prayer: Keep my faith strong Lord, that I may have the ability even in my weakness and sadness to cast off fear, knowing that you have my life in the palm of your hands. Direct my steps, Lord. I pray today that you would watch over and take care of all my family and friends Lord. That whoever seeks your confidence will find it and be strengthened. In Jesus's name, I pray, amen.

To my reader, the word for today is bold. Be bold my friends and know the Lord's plan will always prevail.

November 11

Morning Calls

Morning light calls again. Another start of a beautiful day. Start your day off with a thankful heart as you make the time to spend with me. When you arise in the morning you will find peace in the stillness of the hour. This is a good time to share your heart with me. Make sure to put on my whole armor, so that I may guard you throughout the day. I instill in you; confidence, as with me we can accomplish all that is required. In the situations that have thus far been deemed unfinished, I will bring to you my good resolve, trust my timing, as again it is always perfect. Call on my joy, to fill your heart, pushing off any saddened thoughts or unknowns. Trust in me, again I will remind you. My plans are best. My ways are higher. The destination for the day is flawless and remarkable. It is because you trust in me and have found the faith required to stay in my truth that is now accepted and fully known by you. Trust in affliction, stay hopeful in doubt and confident in love. Patience is truly a virtue my child, practice it when the circumstance calls. Never forget you are loved and be ready when again, morning calls…

> So we can confidently say, "The Lord is my helper; I will not fear; what can man do to me?"
> (Hebrews 13:6, ESV)

> But I will sing of your strength; I will sing of your steadfast love in the morning. For you have been to me a fortress and refuge in the day of my distress.
> (Psalm 59:16, ESV)

Every word of God proves true; he is a shield to those who take refuge in him.
(Proverbs 30:5, ESV)

For the sake of Christ, then, I am content with weaknesses, insults, hardships, persecutions, and calamities. For when I am weak, then I am strong.
(2 Corinthians 12:10, ESV)

Prayer: Father God, I pray for all today that you cover us with your armor Lord. Strengthen us with your love. Walk with us, leading us throughout the day. As we belong to you. In Jesus's name, I pray, amen.

November 12

He Knows Your Heart

Amidst the early morning that carries on throughout the day, here is my love. In every minute of every hour; for all time, my heart sings for you. There is nothing that you can do or have done that will pull my love away from you. I have redeemed you, as you are forgiven. I love you with an everlasting, all-encompassing love. Let then my deep joy that is filled within your soul shine through. Today free yourself by calling out to me and by trusting me with it all. No secrets are kept from me, as it is I who knows even the parts of you that you do not. Do not be afraid or feel unworthy. You are my child and are worth more than the most precious of stones. I see your heart. It is beautiful my child. The kindness that is placed within is a light which shines into the darkness of the day. I have given you the gift of myself, my Holy Spirit within you, to help guide you through. To speak for you when you cannot find the words. Do not worry then that I may have forgotten about things that are important to you. I never forget. I know everything even before a glimpse of the idea sparks within your mind. I know who you are, and I know what you need. I AM your Father and I am leading. Keep hold of my hand. You will find strength in my truth. I speak to your heart daily. Shhh…quiet down then and just listen to my love. My heart is with yours, eternally. Forever, I give to you my mercy, grace, truth, and most importantly my love.

May he grant you your heart's desire
and fulfill all your plans.
(Psalm 20:4, ESV)

Would not God discover this? For he knows the secrets of the heart.
(Psalm 44:21, ESV)

The Lord bless you and keep you; the Lord make his face to shine upon you and be gracious to you; the Lord lift up his countenance upon you and give you peace.
(Numbers 6:24–26, ESV)

Blessed are the pure in heart, for they shall see God.
(Matthew 5:8, ESV)

Prayer: Father God, I rise this morning giving you thanks and praise. Let everything today be under your control. Guide my day and that of all my family and friends. Thank you, Lord, for hearing my prayers and for working them out. Let us walk in confidence today surrounded by your protection and your love.

In Jesus's name, I pray, amen.

November 13

Shield and Strength

Let me be your shield little one. Enshrouding you with my love. Always find your faith as your hope should remain in me. Things in this world may fall short of your worldly expectations. But my truths and words never fail. Let me be your guide. Do not lose your faith, my child. Be vigilant and hold tightly to me good ways. Perseverance doesn't only belong to your idea of strong. For it is my children when they are at their weakest that I am even closer still." I heal the brokenhearted and bind up their wounds." The prayers of my children never fall to the ground I hear every prayer. Ask me to open your eyes and to restore your faith. When you feel your light growing dim, call to me, as I can give you rest. Do not search for empty answers as to why this or when that? Stay faithful in knowing my timing is flawless and perfect. Some things are not meant to be known. It's okay to let these unknowns stay with me. Do not worry about tomorrow for tomorrow has worries of its own. Do not worry about the past as it has already been survived. The only thing that you should carry from the past is the lessons you have learned and practiced in today. Take delight than in the present. Let my love shield you today. Keeping you from the enemy's plots and attacks. I am your rock and your salvation. My steadfast love will always preserve you, as I am your strength and your shield.

He stores up sound wisdom for the upright; he is a shield to those who walk with integrity.
(Proverbs 2:7, ESV)

He will cover you with his pinions,
and under his wings you will find refuge;
his faithfulness is a shield and a buckler.
(Psalm 91:4, ESV)

You have given me the shield of your
salvation, and your right hand supported
me, and your gentleness made me great. You
gave a wide place for my steps under me,
and my feet did not slip.
(Psalm 18:35–36, ESV)

For the sake of Christ, then, I am
content with weaknesses, insults, hardships,
persecutions, and calamities. For when I
am weak, then I am strong.
(2 Corinthians 12:10, ESV)

Prayer: Father God, I lean on you today. I pray you to give us rest and watch over us all, as we start our day. I thank you, Father, and praise your name. Cover us Lord with your armor. In Jesus's name, I pray, amen.

November 14

To my reader; May God always protect you and your family let him always be your shield and fill you with love.

Seeing Beauty

I know in life you may have times when you feel you are at your wit's end. Just know my child that I never give you more than you can handle. I know sometimes the weight at times feels like so much to bear, but I am carrying it with you if you let me. Do not try to do things all on your own as the trouble of the day can become heavy and stagnant. Lift your hands up to me. I am with you. Within the direction of the day, there are many decisions needed to be made, trust that I will lead to the answers as to what is best for you. My child, life is also full of wondrous beauty so don't get stuck in the recesses of your mind. Open your eyes to see the beauty out within the world. There are so many of my creations that my children overlook each day. When you start to feel down go for a walk outside. Really stop and look around. Can you feel the wind upon your skin or the warmth of the sun? Can you hear and see the birds singing in their secret language as they travel from branch to branch? Maybe you see a beautiful butterfly, or brightly colored flowers all enjoying the mid-afternoon. If you make an effort to see them, my child, you will find all the beauty you will need to preserve you through the day. As these are all part of my creations and they are good. Seeing beauty open before you as the day begins. Enjoy it, my child.

I left up my eyes to the hills. From where does my help come? My help comes from the Lord, who made heaven and earth.
(Psalm 121:1–2, ESV)

And I heard every creature in heaven and on earth and under the earth and in the sea, and all that is in them, saying, "To him who sits on the throne and to the Lamb be blessing and honor and glory and might forever and ever!"
(Revelation 5:13, ESV)

For 'In him we live and move and have our being; as even some of your own poets have said, "For we are indeed his offspring.'
(Acts 17:28, ESV)

Prayer: Father God, thank you for your creation. I pray today for eyes to see and really enjoy all the beauty today. I pray for all my family and friends Lord that we would draw closer to you. Thank you for this day that you have created Lord and for everything in it. In Jesus's name, I pray, amen.

November 15

Full of Love

For if you know love bears all things, hopes all things, and believes all things, then why do you doubt? From the moment you opened your eyes in this world, you were given the greatest of gifts. The gift of love. You were even loved before this world, while you were still in your mother's womb, and before you were even formed. You are my beloved child. You are unique and handpicked by me to exist and thrive. I have placed my light inside you, and caused it to shine, by sharing my love with you. Never doubt yourself, my child, as you are one of my most prized. I have called you to different positions and have watched you in your life as you grow. Growing forward still and learning my good ways. I watch you sharing the abilities I have bestowed upon you. I am pleased. I have fashioned you with a tender caring heart. And am leading you not only to share the love with others but to accept it with all graciousness as well. How full then are you? When you let love in, and let it flourish with all the good seeds that exist within your heart? Today I call you to a place of confidence and a place full of all my wondrous love. Don't just learn it my child, but experience it, and share it wherever you go… Smile in this day and be full. Full of love.

Do not be like them, for your Father
knows what you need before you ask.
(Matthew 6:8, ESV)

You are altogether beautiful, my love
there is no flaw in you.
(Song of Songs 4:7, ESV)

See what kind of love the Father has given to us, that we should be called children of God; and so we are. The reason why the world does not know us is that it did not know him.
(1 John 3:1, ESV)

Let brotherly love continue. Do not neglect to show hospitality to strangers, for thereby some have entertained angels unawares.
(Hebrews 13:1–2, ESV)

Prayer: Father God, today I will thank you for your love. Your love not only for myself but the love you to show and give to all of us. I ask you to keep guiding and leading us. I pray you to bring us through whatever situation we are facing with your kindness and your love. In Jesus's name, I pray and give thanks, amen.

November 16

Gratefulness and Thanksgiving

Wake up today and search within your heart for all the goodness to be shown. It is a wonderous and beautiful day. As you spend time with me in prayer, let my love lighten your view of the day and bring joy to all of its happenstances. There is so much to be thankful for. As this is the season of gratefulness and thanksgiving. It is a time to spend with family and good friends. Nourish those relationships, my child, as the closeness of love brings much enjoyment, and brings me closer to the hearts of all. The beauty of giving and receiving serves best when it comes from a place of love and togetherness. I call on all my children to have kind and giving spirits. That no one goes in need when my children are close. I am pleased by the quiet generosity that my children give. Today surround yourself with the lighthearted love and laughter of closeness. As the day comes to its close think back on it and remember all the simple little blessings that make your cup full. I am smiling, as today you share my love with all.

We ought always to give thanks to God for you, brothers, as is right, because your faith is growing abundantly, and the love of every one of you for another is increasing.
(2 Thessalonians 1:3, ESV)

I will give thanks to the Lord with my whole heart; I will recount all of your wonderful deeds.
(Psalm 9:1, ESV)

Let the word of Christ dwell in you richly, teaching and admonishing one another in all wisdom, singing psalms and hymns and spiritual songs, with thankfulness in your heart's to God.
(Colossians 3:16, ESV)

Giving thanks always and for everything to God the Father in the name of our Lord Jesus Christ.
(Ephesians 5:20, ESV)

Therefore let us be grateful for receiving a kingdom that cannot be shaken, and thus let us offer to God acceptable worship, with reverence and awe.
(Hebrews 12:28, ESV)

Prayer: Father God, thank you for good friends and family, I'm grateful Lord for all that you do. Please watch over us today keeping us safe in our travels and fill us with the joy of your love. In Jesus's name, I pray, amen.

November 17

Solidify Your Faith

I am opening the way before you. Do you not perceive the light? Stop letting yourself get carried away, getting pulled back into the troubles of your mind. I will teach you, my child, how to redirect your thoughts. Just keep in close communication with me. When you feel your intemperate emotions starting to call you to attention. Pray to me, call out to me and pull your focus deliberately back to my good center. I can keep the balance of your thoughts calm when you make me the focal point of your day. Always excepting my good view. We can excel in the activities that surround you with perseverance and strength. Hold tightly to my hand my child, as I lead you to keep your trust in me. I only bring you to the situations I know you can handle. And through it all, you will become stronger and more identified in my Spirit. With the light of my good ways shining brightly for others to see. There are unpolished abilities that I am bringing to the surface of your character. As I am shaping and molding you. All for my glory, my child. Keep on my right path and stay joyful. You will find your way solid and grounded by keeping faithful to me. Solidify your faith with love and trust. My mercy will shine upon you, and my grace will reign over you, and my blessings will pour upon you. I love you, my child. Keeping in step with the good fight of faith now and forevermore.

Let your eyes look directly forward,
and your gaze be straight before you.
(Proverbs 4:25, ESV)

Blessed are those who keep his testimonies. Who seek him with their whole heart.
(Psalm 119:2, ESV)

In all your ways acknowledge him, and he will make straight your paths.
(Proverbs 3:6, ESV)

Therefore, as you received Christ Jesus the Lord, so walk in him, rooted and built up in him and established in the faith, just as you were taught, abounding in thanksgiving.
(Colossians 2:6–7, ESV)

Prayer: Father God, I commit my ways before you Lord. I pray for all of my family and friends please keep us in step with you make our paths straight. Trusting your good ways. In Jesus's name, I pray, amen.

November 18

Setback then Step Forward

You will have rough days my child but keep your heart open and eyes wide open. As open is the word for today. Open to blessings, open to love, open to comfort. Be open while still refusing to fear. Casting off fear. I am bigger than anything you face. When you encounter setbacks just know they are just that, setbacks. Meaning you can still move forward. I am with you no need to worry. You are free from the weight of your sin and from death, as I have set you free. We can celebrate this day and everyday hereafter as your faith continues to grow. I bless you my child with an abundance of joy and my good purpose. As you are eager to share. The inspiration exists within finding delight in the promises of my love, and the desire to share, trusting your heart with me. Perseverance can be found in the setback as then it can become a step-forward. Finding victory within each step. Keep moving my child, walking this journey with me, onward and upward.

The Lord said to Moses, "Why do you cry to me? Tell the people of Israel to go forward. Lift up your staff, and stretch out your hand over the sea and divide it, that the people of Israel may go through the sea on dry ground."
(Exodus 14:15–16, ESV)

The Lord our God said to us in Horeb, 'You have stayed long enough at this mountain.
(Deuteronomy 1:6, ESV)

I press on toward the goal for the prize
of the upward call of God in Jesus Christ.
(Philippians 3:14, ESV)

Prayer: Father God, some days are hard for us, so today I pray for strength for all. I ask for strength filled with joy. Make our paths clear Lord that we may know the way you call us to go and give us the courage to walk that way. In Jesus's name, I pray and give thanks, amen.

November 19

Choose the Good

Always choose to see the good in people. I have created you to be together and share my love. I know at times this seems hard as people have different personalities and conflicts of opinions, and of interests. But I haven't made you to all agree, as each one has their own mind, but I bring unity of mind when you engage in sharing my good ways. I have not made you be the judge. No one is blameless, all have sinned, and this is not your place. But I have made you to be a light and to help my children see that even where there is a conflict there can still be love. So make the choice, as it is my way to find the good in all of my children. Be thankful my child to be able to remind them of my presence and of the love I have for them. Share with them my good ways. I will bring peace and ease to any situation the enemy has tried to cause discord. I am the harmony that can set you back on my good path. Keep trusting even when you do not see evidence of me working. Keep hoping even when you feel all hope is lost. Keep loving even when you feel empty. As everything will reveal itself all in my good time. So then find the good in people and find the good in the situations of your life. Knowing that during it all, you are not alone I am with you... As I am your God, I am good, and I AM love.

If anyone serves me, he must follow me; and where I am, there will be my servant also. If anyone serves me, the Father will honor him.
(John 12:26, ESV)

You, my brothers and sisters, were called to be free. But do not use your freedom to indulge the flesh; rather serve one another humbly in love.
(Galatians 5:13, NIV)

Finally, all of you, have unity of mind, sympathy, brotherly love, a tender heart, and a humble mind.
(1 Peter 3:8, ESV)

Prayer: Father God, I will ask you again to help me to always see the good in others, not with my own eyes but with yours. Help me to be the light you have created me to be. I pray for your love to fill our hearts and minds each and every day, and that even where there is a conflict that your love may shine the brightest. In Jesus's loving name, I pray and give thanks, amen.

November 20

Changing Blocks

Don't be sad little one. So many thoughts try to take over your mind. I am the one you should seek first. As when you seek me first and my kingdom all these good things will be added unto you. Cast off the melancholy and the weight as it builds. Like a castle of blocks take it down. Kick it down. Stop building up all the defeat and failure that you are feeling. Replace these with my good blocks. The place where you find my grace, my mercy, my love, my forgiveness, my joy, my peace, my victory and especially my love. There is a path made way through the blocks that together we will find. When you seek me, you will find me, when you seek me with your whole heart. It is my light that you will find leading and guiding with the easiness of my yoke. Let my Spirit create a stillness in you. Confidence, peace, and ease. I am your Creator, your Father, your friend, the lover of your soul. My ways are loving and my timing perfect. Say to me than," Your will, your way, my Lord." Say this and be accepting of all my gracious outcomes. I do not lead you to places of defeat but to victory not just for you but for all. As you are all my children and are loved by me, even with all of your sin. You are forgiven and you are loved. I am with you, I am present, as I am here... Changing the blocks. Removing the blocks with the strength of my love.

The Lord of hosts has sworn; "As I have planned, so shall it be, and as I have purposed, so shall it stand."
(Isaiah 14:24, ESV)

In his hand is the life of every living thing and the breath of all mankind.
(Job 12:10, ESV)

Saying, "Father, if you are willing, remove this cup from me. Nevertheless, not my will, but yours, be done."
(Luke 22:42, ESV)

Prayer: Father God, thank you for your loving leading hand. I ask for your will and not my own. I know your plans are better than I can imagine. I thank you for this day and for all my family and friends I am grateful for everything you have given and hopeful of things that are yet to come. In Jesus's name, I pray giving thanks, amen.

November 21

Hopes and Dreams

Bring to me all your hopes and dreams knowing that I will take care of them. Everything that you hold dear. I hold them, dear, too. I have much to show you and to give to you my child. As I keep you safely tucked in the refuge under my wings. I walk in the day with you. As I am forever holding your hand. Keep letting me lead, as my Spirit guides you to a new place where hopes and dreams can come true. Faith is the assurance of things not seen but is found within the hope of my good promise, as it will be done most assuredly if it is in my will. Knowing the honesty in my promises is the way to which you can truly see the amazing experiences I am bringing. Enjoy the experiences that I give to you now in this present day. There is a place you belong, my child, it is here within the fullness of my love. Keep on hoping. Keep on dreaming, trusting my will and my timing as it is flawless and perfect. This is the way, it is my good way…follow my good path where I light up your steps into the fulfillment of all, that are called your hopes and dreams.

Delight yourself in the Lord, and he will give you the desires of your heart.
(Psalm 37:4, ESV)

For all the promises of God find their Yes in him. That is why it is through him that we utter our Amen to God for his glory.
(2 Corinthians 1:20, ESV)

If you abide in me, and my words abide in you, ask whatever you wish, and

it will be done for you. By this my Father is glorified, that you bear much fruit and so prove to be my disciples.
(John 15:7–8, ESV)

Prayer: Father God, you know what is in my heart, you know all my desires, my hopes, and my dreams, I bring them all to you and ask, giving you thanks for the answers. I pray these devotional finds people and gives them comfort and points them to you. I pray for all of us this day, that we seek you first. Thank you, Father, for the gift and the truth of your promises. In Jesus's loving name, I pray, amen.

November 22

You Are

Let me open your eyes, my child. Even though you are out and about functioning in the world, at times you are not present. Let me bring you peace. I know you need rest from your tender heart and all its battles. The care I have placed in you is well, as it runs deep. It isn't a curse, my child, it is a blessing to care so much for others. It is exactly what I have called you to do. Love them as I love you. This season is a time of togetherness and gratefulness. Being thankful for all that you are and all that you have, and for all that you know, and for what is to come. Relish in the moments of my love. As I offer up the way that truly brings you more than just mere fleeting happiness, more than just emotions found within a moment. A love that is eternal and a purpose that stands forevermore. My purpose and my plan are for all, for everything that I have created. Always for my glory. You are my child, more than any faltered idea of existence. You are more than your mere emotion. You are more than a pawn or puppet as I have given you free will. You are a part of something that is momentous and has great significance for you and those around you. You are a part of my kingdom. You are my ambassador; you are my beloved. You are my child. You are chosen, and you are mine. Come to accept what I'm calling you to do. As you are a light and you are loved.

But overhearing what they said, Jesus said to the ruler of the synagogue, "Do not fear, only believe."
(Mark 5:36, ESV)

And we know that for those who love God all things work together for good, for those who are called according to his purpose.
(Romans 8:28, ESV)

But to all who did receive him, who believed in his name, he gave the right to become children of God.
(John 1:12, ESV)

Prayer: Father God Thank you for loving me. I pray for all= that we always keep praying, hoping, and believing the truth and the strength found in your promises. And that we may always feel your love. In Jesus's name, I pray, amen.

November 23

New Morning

Here in the hours that complete the days and nights, I am here always with you, within you. Guiding you silently as I tug at your heart, It is important to stand firm at times immovable and steadfast. Life can throw many situations at you and some can drag you down causing you to feel stuck in the deep muck and the mire. But I will lift you up and place you on solid ground. Do not be swept away by the wind or the ideas of fleeting interests that pull you this way and that. Stay on the path of my calling and remain solid and grounded. We will cut through all the junk that has taken up your thoughts and wasted time, the precious time I want to spend with you. Let me remove it all. Today make a fresh start as it is a new morning. Fill your mind with goodness and love. This is a season of thanksgiving and gratefulness so find your focus on all these good things. Find the blessings in each moment, no matter how small. Tiny blessings can lead to big surprises. As you will start to see just how much there is to be truly thankful for. There is always a reason to be happy my child, find them and begin on a good note today. Walking in the confidence found within my love. Arise with joy this new morning.

Therefore, if anyone is in Christ, he is a new creation. The old has passed away; behold the new has come.
(2 Corinthians 5:17, ESV)

And I will give them one heart, and a new spirit I will put within them. I will

remove the heart of stone from their flesh
and give them a heart of flesh.
(Ezekiel 11:19, ESV)

Behold, I am doing a new thing; now
it springs forth, do you not perceive it? I will
make a way in the wilderness and rivers in
the desert.
(Isaiah 43:19, ESV)

Let me hear in the morning of your
steadfast love, for in you I trust. Make me
know the way I should go, for to you I lift
up my soul.
(Psalm 143:8, ESV)

Prayer: Father God I look to the heavens, knowing where my help comes from. It comes from you, and I thank you for this new morning and for the new creation that I am. I pray today that you watch over all of us Lord and remind us with kindness of all the blessings that you bring no matter how small. I pray that we feel the fullness of your love and find peace on this day. In Jesus's name, I pray, amen.

November 24

His Good Time

Bring me your troubles and all your situations, I can bring you through. Find confidence when I open up the way revealing to you my deeper truth. You have questions and that is good my child as I am calling you here to the place where you are learning and seeking me more and more. Open yourself up to me each and every day as you give thanks to me for the day and all the treasures it holds. You most certainly have hopes and these I will answer all in my good time. I see the willingness you have to learn more of me, to give your heart to me. You are finding trust in my truth. All stirred up together with all the perfect gifts I bring. In this my good time, I will cover you with grace and wrap you with love. We can walk in today finding peace even among the insecurities that temp your steps. My grace is sufficient for you my child so let me fill the parts you've deemed empty or incomplete. I am the redeemer of your life and will redirect you to what I have designed as right. I make no mistakes. Where you once ventured off of my good path, I will lead you back and make your path straight once again. You will find me when you seek me with your whole heart and here you have found my answer as it is…my love. Finding your faith and the strength of it, all in my good time.

"For I know the plans I have for you,"
declares the Lord, plans to prosper you and
not to harm you, plans to give you hope and
a future.
(Jeremiah 29:11, NIV)

By which he has granted to us his precious and very great promises, so that through them you may become partakers of the divine nature, having escaped from the corruption that is in the world because of sinful desire.
(2 Peter 1:4, ESV)

But the Helper, the Holy Spirit, whom the Father will send in my name, he will teach you all things and bring to your remembrance all that I've said to you.
(John 14:26, ESV)

Prayer: Father God, today I give thanks to you for showing us your ways and your good news. I pray to always be a blessing to others and that you would continue to give me the strength to step out of my comfort zone when I am called to do so. I pray for everyone this day that you would reveal yourself to us all and show us your love. So that we may share your love with others and give them the hope that's found in you. In Jesus's name, I pray, amen.

November 25

His Good Place

Be thankful my child for all I bring. Even the times when my answer is wait, or on occasion, my answer is no. I am the one who knows what is best for your life. Never lose hope but finding it within the truth of my promises and all that I bring. I have plans for you, not to harm you only to prosper you. Bringing a hope for the future. And a fullness of love. You do not need to worry, but through prayer and supplication bring it all to me. I am the truth and the way and the life. Find the light of the day opening up to you when you flow with me in the ways I've designed. Times will come you may feel like your swimming upstream, as the current flows hard pushing against you. Keep me as the head of your life and I will make the way become more natural. And you will find that when you let me guide the current will become calm once again. I bring you to a place where you can rest beside my still waters. Refreshing your soul as you will thirst no more. I take the empty parts and fill them with my words, my purpose and my love. You will never be empty again. I make a way where none is evident. I make ways where you never even had a thought. It is a place for your calling. I bring you to places where you have never even dreamed. These are my good places, as I am the way maker. I take you on my good paths and even though at times there is a wilderness, I lead you through. Enshrouding you with my love and giving you a new place. My good place, a place where victory is found.

For the gifts and the calling of God are irrevocable.
(Romans 11:29, ESV)

*No, in all these things we are more
than conquerors through him who loved us.
For I am sure that neither death nor life,
nor angels nor rulers, nor things present nor
things to come, nor powers, nor height nor
depth, nor anything else in all creation, will
be able to separate us from the love of God
in Christ Jesus our Lord.*
(Romans 8:37–39, ESV)

*You did not choose me, but I chose you
and appointed you so that you might go and
bear fruit-fruit that will last, and so that
whatever you ask in my name the Father
will give you.*
(John 15:26, NIV)

Prayer: Father God, I thank you for this day. I pray that you watch over us all and that you keep our steps on your path so that we may walk with confidence in your will. I also thank you for bringing us to the victory and the fullness of your love. In Jesus's loving name, amen.

November 26

Finding Favor

Here you will find my good favor when you walk the way to which I have called. I will guide you to it and through it and meet you whenever you need me. My Holy Spirit is the Helper and will reveal to you things that you do not know, all in my good time. Keep patient my child as I reveal the truth of my Spirit to you. I will ask you to share these good and precious ways with others in and out of your circle. Find the peace I bring through all the situations you face. As you learn to walk in my steps, keeping the hope that is found in my good assurance. Even though you have not seen. I bring you glimpses of the life I am calling you too, for you to live abundantly and be filled with my deep joy. Finding favor in the moments of this, a life of awakening. Your eyes are opening my child and you are finding peace in my good and perfect gifts. My glory is brought about in all the ways which I show my grace. It is my kingdom you have longed for and I am encouraging you to follow the way as it opens before you. No doubts. You, my child, will find favor in and with me not by your works, but because of my grace and love. All for my glory.

Let the favor of the Lord our God be upon us, and establish the work of our hands upon us; yes, establish the work of our hands!
(Psalm 90:17, ESV)

Let not steadfast love and faithfulness forsake you; bind them around your neck; write them on the tablet of your heart. So

you will find favor and good success in the
sight of God and man.
(Proverbs 3:3–4, ESV)

For by grace you have been saved
through faith. And this is not of your own
doing; It is the gift of God.
(Ephesians 2:8, ESV)

Prayer: Father God, thank you for this day and this morning, I pray that we all find the joy today. I ask also that you keep opening our eyes to see the truths that you have given to us, and for the courage to share these truths. In Jesus's name, I pray, amen.

November 27

Ever-Changing World

Good morning my child, this day let there be a lightness. Sometimes in life, things just happen to flow whether you want them to or not, most certainly there will always be change, as I know many of you are not comfortable with change. Whether it happens suddenly or not. But unlike me and my good plans, the way of the world is constant with change. It is now time to find the goodness in your response to whatever situation unfolds. Some of my children are stubborn. So comfortable in their ways that they dig in their heels refusing to change and making it harder on themselves and those around them to adapt. If you feel something is out of your control, just know that it is okay to let go and bring the situation to me. As I never change. I am the same today, as yesterday, and will forever stand immovable and everlasting. Even into your tomorrows, I remain the same. Trust me to do what is best with your changing situations and let me guide your way. The way may seem unfamiliar and cause you a sense of fear. But I will remind you not to fear, knowing I am with you. Stand bravely in the face of change and uncertainty. Be courageous as you step out onto faith, knowing that I will work it out all for good because you have put your trust in me. Be brave, be bold, be courageous, and you may even find enjoyment in the change. Finding comfort in your steps and the truth of my good ways. It is better for my child to sometimes, embrace the change while holding onto the one who never changes, as you can find refuge in me. Hold fast to the hope that is set before you. As I am leading you into the truth of my promises, and my promises never change.

For I the Lord do not change; therefore
you, O children of Jacob, are not consumed.
(Malachi 3:6, ESV)

God is not man, that he should lie,
or a son of man, that he should change his
mind. He has said, and will he not do it?
Or has he spoken, and will not fulfill it?
(Numbers 23:19, ESV)

So that by two unchangeable things,
in which it is impossible for God to lie, we
who have fled for refuge might have strong
encouragement to hold fast to the hope set
before us.
(Hebrews 6:18, ESV)

Prayer: Very simply today I say, Lord, thank you for being with me and allowing me to hold onto you during it all. I will embrace the change that you bring, and I will try my best Lord to keep in step with your will and your way. I pray to be able to help others along the way. Walking in confidence on your good paths. In Jesus's name, I pray to thank you for the guidance and the victory, you bring. Amen.

November 28

He Makes You Worthy

There are days when you feel less than my child. But this you must surely know; I am for you. I am surrounding you with my love and I forgive you for your wrongs. You are surely worthy of my love my child for so much, as I have designed and called you to greater plans. I created you not to feel less than but to be filled with so much more. There is a light that is shining on the way of my good path. Keep on this path even during times where it may seem a little less evident. Keep your faith and trust strongly rooted in me and my good purpose. Find your steps by holding tightly to me, I will keep your feet planted on solid ground. There is no such thing as perfection in the world. So lighten up on yourself. I am the only perfect way. I am the truth, the way, and the life. I have set a place for you at my good table and have the power to fulfill my good promises. Which I surely will. Believe it and see what the power of your faith found firm will bring. Stand with me, let my immovable joy fill within your heart. I am encouraging you, my child, to walk with me on this journey I have designated just for you. I know everything about you, I will place you in situations that are best for your contribution to my kingdom. No job is more important than the other, as I call all together equally to fulfill my good purpose. Bringing back my creation to my good ways and to me. Remember that you are worthy as I have redeemed you and regard you as so. Persevere my child, and know you are loved.

*So as to walk in a manner worthy
of the Lord, fully pleasing to him, bearing
fruit in every good work and increasing in
the knowledge of God.*
(Colossians 1:10, ESV)

*So we are his workmanship, created
in Christ Jesus for good works, which God
prepared beforehand, that we should walk
in them.*
(Ephesians 2:10, ESV)

*To this end we always pray for you,
that our God may make you worthy of his
calling and may fulfill every resolve for good
and every work of faith by his power.*
(2 Thessalonians 1:11, ESV)

Prayer: Father God, Jesus my Lord, thank you for your sacrifice that now we may be called worthy because you have cleansed us from our sins. I am eternally grateful. I ask and pray today that you keep us in the brightness of your light. That you cast out any darkness that lingers in our lives. I pray to have peace in our hearts and be blessed with joy and the abundance of your love. In Jesus's name, amen.

November 29

Faithful, Abundant Life

I will make possible for you an abundant life. A life that is full of love and enjoyable things. I do not promise a life without struggles or difficulty. But I do promise to always be here with you helping to carry you through. There is sadness in this life but one day my child, there will be no more tears only joy and love. Embrace all the emotions felt in today and allow them to teach you the strength that truly lies within. Today, if all you felt was happiness would you truly appreciate the joy of tomorrow? It is sweeter when allowed to grow and flourish through the hard times. Many of my children only seek me when they are going through difficulty and then I will bring them into the place of my good calling. Where there seems no way, I can make a way using the mountains I have removed to show others the great and Sovern things that can be done when you put your faith and trust in me. I make the impossible possible, so don't lose hope. Never give up my child. Holdfast to my good and mighty ways. Cling tightly to your faith… If you stay steadfast with me, you will soon reap the harvest of the abundant life I give. My will, my way.

And let us not grow weary of doing good, for in due season we will reap, if we do not give up.
(Galatians 6:9, ESV)

But you, take courage! Do not let your hands be weak, for your work shall be rewarded.
(2 Chronicles 15:7, ESV)

And without faith it is impossible to please him, for whoever would draw near to God must believe that he exists and that he rewards those who seek him.
(Hebrews 11:6, ESV)

For nothing is impossible with God.
(Luke 1:37, ESV)

Prayer: Father God, I thank you for this day. I pray to see movement in the current situations of my life and in the lives of those around me. A positive movement, as we hold onto our faith. I put my trust in you Lord and hold tightly to your hand. I follow your good steps and am grateful to you for your guidance, as you always lead us with your love, kindness and good favor. In Jesus's name, I pray and give thanks, amen.

November 30

December

When you choose to follow Jesus, you will become a new creation, your true beauty will be seen, and your heart will rejoice because his love has given you wings.

Called and Chosen

Good morning, my child. Keep up your good pace, as I see you are learning to find the rhythm of your steps in me. Keep your eye on the prize which is what I bring. As it is an eternity with me. Walk with humility, kindness, gentleness, love and all good things. As you are my chosen. I call on you to love one another showing compassion and empathy. Having an understanding and being forgiving when necessary. I have called you to this place and rightly so, as I know you full well. There is a calling I have pulled over your heart and will lead you to the position I have designed for your life. It is my good position. There are no hesitations in the place I have called you too. As I make no mistakes. I will show you your tasks and bring you to them. I do not doubt you, my child, therefore, do not find doubt in yourself. If I have put you in the place of my good calling, I have reason. As I know you can achieve what I am calling you to do by the power of my Holy Spirit that I gifted to you. Be brave little one, find your courage in me. Together we will spread my good news.

> *Now the word of the Lord came to me, saying, "Before I formed you in the womb, I knew you, and before you were born I consecrated you; I appointed you a prophet to the nations."*
> (Jeremiah 1:4–5, ESV)

> *Put on then, as God's chosen ones, holy and beloved, compassionate hearts, kindness, humility, meekness, and patience, bearing with one another and, if one has*

a complaint against another, forgiving each other; as the Lord has forgiven you, so you must also forgive. And above all these put-on love, which binds everything together in perfect harmony.
(Colossians 3:12–14, ESV)

For the gifts and the calling of God are irrevocable.
(Romans 11:29, ESV)

Blessed are the pure in heart, for they shall see God.
(Matthew 5:8, ESV)

Prayer: Father God, I lift my hands to you today and praise you. I pray for the confidence to walk on this path you have chosen for me with no fear. I pray for your strength. I also pray every day, Lord for all my family and friends, surround them with your Presence Lord and your protection. In Jesus's name, I pray, amen.

December 1

Just Ask

There are moments you feel unsure but it's okay, my child. You will find your confidence again. Keep reaching for me. Lifting up to me, your hands and your prayers. I am taking care of and watching over all that you have given to me. Do not let your heart be troubled. Trust in me as I have prepared the way before you. Bringing you to the place of my good keeping. What good does it do to worry? It does no good at all. To waste your precious thoughts on troubles to which you have no control. But think on this…you have given the troubles to me, and if you truly release them, who then is greater than I? As I am the Creator and have everything under my control. I silenced the wind with my words. I parted the Sea so that my people could pass safely. I have done all these wonderous and mighty things for my children. Then why doubt what great things I can do for you? As you are also, my child. I know there are some things that you still have not asked… As I know it is hard to ask for yourself, what you feel you do not deserve. But I know your heart and I know what lies within the places that you haven't even discovered. These wonderous things about yourself that are hidden to you just yet. I will reveal to you not only my truth but, in the truth of your spirit and all that I have known. Just ask…

> *Let not your hearts be troubled.*
> *Believe in God; also believe in me.*
> (John 14:1, ESV)

> *When the Spirit of truth comes, he*
> *will guide you into all truth, for he will not*

speak on his own authority, but whatever
he hears he will speak, and he will declare
to you the things to come.
(John 16:13, ESV)

In that day you will ask nothing of
me. Truly, truly, I say to you, whatever you
ask the Father in my name, he will give it to
you. Until now you have asked nothing in
my name. Ask, and you shall receive, that
your joy may be full.
(John 16:23–24, ESV)

Prayer: Father God, I ask to stay healthy and strong. To persevere with a victory, as I stay walking in your will. I pray to accept the place you call me to daily with joy. I ask for all my family and my friends and myself Lord, a life of joy and abundance. A life that is full of love. I pray to let go of situations Lord where I have no control and ask that you to guide me correctly in the situations where I do. I ask whatever you know in my heart to be good and right and just. In Jesus's loving name I pray, amen.

December 02

With You

Just as the day breaks and the sun cast up its light, I am here with you I never leave you. There will be times when you do not quite feel my Presence…but I am still here. As I will never leave you or forsake you. I am Sovereign over your life, so you do not need to fear. I will bring you to my good plans, as we walk in my will together. There is so much that I can do. As I establish your steps. Helping you with my Spirit to see all the blessings along the way. Where there is love you will feel me once again. There are also times that you must learn to be accepting of my Sovereignty. As my plans are higher and will always triumph, turning all situations that are flawed into the perfect will of my good plans. If I bring you to it, I will bring you through it. Do not let go of my hand. Keep hopeful and joyful always giving thanks. There are times in the stillness, there are times in the desert, there are times in the wilderness, but there are also times in the nourished garden of your life that you must always keep my ways. Letting love and joy prevail. For everything reveals itself, all in my good time. As I am always with you in the moments and through it all.

Teaching them to observe all that I have commanded you. And behold, I am with you always, to the end of the age.
(Matthew 28:20, ESV)

But whoever listens to me will dwell at ease, without dread of disaster.
(Proverbs 1:33, ESV)

He will cover you with his feathers. He will shelter you with his wings. His faithful promises are your armor and protection.
(Psalm 91:4, NIV)

No one has ever seen God; the only God, who is at the Fathers side, he has made known.
(John 1:18, ESV)

Prayer: Father God, thank you for leading this day, and for keeping me in safety under the refuge of your wings. I pray for all today. A day full of confidence and joy. A day of sunshine and gladness. I thank you for your protection of us all, and for never leaving our sides. In Jesus's name, I pray and ask, amen.

December 03

Draw Near to Him

Keep your heart light, finding peace within today. Walking with me on this, my good journey. The way of the day calls you to its beauty, so find it within my good promises, as they open up before you. Do not get discouraged by the people or situations around you, but still draw nearer to me. I draw near to those who long to be with me and spend time with me in prayer and praise. But if the trouble of the day comes and tries to steal your focus, I am patient, as I wait for your attention to become focused once again. Come to me as little children, with your hearts wide open. With humbleness and a thirst for the salvation I bring. I reward my humble children. I offer the gift of Salvation to all. Keep your eyes up and focused on me, holding fast to your faith. Never give up, but instead find your momentum within each good step. The day may try to pull you and push you, causing a rollercoaster of emotion. To remain grounded and balanced always look to me and the constant freedom of my perpetual Sovereignty. Draw near to me my child, come…draw near.

Draw near to God, and he will draw near to you. Cleanse your hands, you sinners, and purify your hearts, you double-minded.
(James 4:8, ESV)

No man shall be able to stand before you all the days of your life. Just as I was with Moses, so I will be with you. I will not leave you or forsake you.
(Joshua 1:5, ESV)

But for me it is good to be near to
God; I have made the Lord God my refuge,
that I may tell of all your works.
(Psalm 73:28, ESV)

Let us with confidence draw near to
the throne of grace, that we may receive
mercy and find grace to help in time of need.
(Hebrews 4:16, ESV)

Prayer: Father God, I look my eyes up to the hills as I know where my help comes from it comes from you Lord. I am thankful. I pray to be near you Lord, and that all my family and friends would draw near to you as well. So that we may all find our refuge in you. I give you thanks Lord and it is in your name Jesus, that I pray, amen.

December 4

Empty Yourself Full

Learn from my good grace. Love is all around not just found within the tiny moments of time, but found all around you, every day. Look and see all the love this life holds. You can find it in the beauty of the natural canvas of all the wonder of nature, in the ashes of unfulfilled plans where my will, brought to life plans far greater than the ones you hoped for yourself. In the moments where the graces of my love touched the hearts of those around you, in the hours to which an unexpected happenstance graced your life with love, in the days, nights and years that make up the story of your life. Every day holds a bit of beauty if you would only open your eyes to see. Some of my children are so stubborn they miss the tiny little nuances of beauty throughout their lives. This I do not want for any of my children. Empty yourself then of earthly wants and desires asking only for my will. This will alleviate any anger or resentment that can happen If things do not go the way you had planned... Then you will be free. Free to focus on all the love and beauty I bring. As my ways are higher than the ways of the world, hold tightly now to the promises I have made. And all will happen in my good time. So empty yourself now, so that you may be filled. As you empty yourself full.

The Lord will fulfill his purpose for me; your steadfast love, O Lord, endures forever. Do not forsake the work of your hands.
(Psalm 138:8, ESV)

But seek first the kingdom of God and his righteousness, and all these things will be added unto you.
(Matthew 6:33, ESV)

And he said to all, "If anyone would come after me, let him deny himself and take up his cross daily and follow me."
(Luke 9:23, ESV)

Therefore, confess your sins to one another and pray for one another, that you may be healed. The prayer of a righteous person has great power as it is working.
(James 5:16, ESV)

Prayer: Father God, I struggle sometimes to give up my plans. Help us to be able to seek you first Lord. Your will, your way. Help us to know the right paths you designed to keep us in your will, and that we may confidently walk in those ways. I ask to always be a blessing to others along the way. In Jesus's name, I give thanks and pray, amen.

December 05

Seek His Truth in All Things

With me all things are possible. There is no failure, no defeat. Only triumph and victory in the ways of my will. Spend time with me in prayer. Knowing that I am caring for you and all things concerning you, brought to me with the gentleness of your tender heart. All things work together for my children who love me. As they are called according to my good purpose. So listen then while in prayer, not just to the echoing of your own voice, but the soothing little nudges of my Holy Spirit within. There are days that feel like forever, as they inch by in ordinary ways, but even in these, you must remain faithful steadfast with me. Allowing me and the light of my Presence to keep you in joy. Walking with you all your days. I bring to you peace in the ways of faith and the hopeful light of tomorrow. There is hope found also in this day, and all the days hereafter. Keep holding tightly to me my child, I am your Lord and I will bring my promises to fruition. Trust me, as I work all things together for good, and in all things, I bring my grace and my truth.

Rather speaking the truth in love, we are to grow up in every way into him who is the head, into Christ.
(Ephesians 4:15, ESV)

Lead me in your truth and teach me, for you are the God of my salvation; For you I wait all the day long.
(Psalm 25:5, ESV)

But the anointing that you received from him abides in you, and you have no need that anyone should teach you. But as his anointing teaches you about everything, and is true, and is no lie-just just as it has taught you, abide in Him.
(1 John 2:27, ESV)

And we know that for those who love God all things work together for good, for those who are called according to his purpose.
(Romans 8:28, ESV)

Prayer: Father God, thank you for the truth of your Spirit, and for working all things together for good. I trust you, Lord. Please continue to lead us daily and keep us strengthened by your love and the good purpose you give. I pray that everyone today will feel peace and calm. In Jesus's name, I ask and pray that this is a good day and thank you for it, amen.

December 06

Trust Have Peace

I am the Messiah, your Lord, your God, and what does that mean to you, my child? If you do not give me your trust and your confidence? If you lack the faith to believe I can do all that I have promised. Then how can you truly follow me? You must trust and believe with your whole heart. Do not try to force your ways upon the situations of the day. Always remember it is I who am your Deliverer and your Savior. I save you from your sin and deliver you from the burdens of this life. With my sacrifice, I have overcome death for you and all who believe in me. I come to you daily and I uphold you with my righteous right hand. I place your feet on a firm foundation. I give you hope for the future and a Sovereign grace for today. Let yourself enjoy this Christmas season and all that it brings, happiness, peace, and goodwill. Keep your helping gentle spirit awake and feeling alive, in the fullness of love. Do not strive for perfection, but instead leave the perfection to me. I can take any situation that arises and bring it back to my good purpose, just follow where I lead. There are places I have gone before you so your spirit can be at ease. As I have been to your tomorrows and am leading you into their good graces. Know that I want nothing more than what is best for you. Keep your hope in me and stay faithful and soon you will have peace once again. Just keep putting your trust in me. I love you, my child. Trust and have peace this day and always…

I have said these things to you, that in me you may have peace. In the world you will have tribulation. But take heart; I have overcome the world.
(John 16:33, ESV)

Truly, truly, I say to you, whoever
hears my words and believes him who sent
me has eternal life. He does not come into
judgment, but has passed from death to life.
(John 5:24, ESV)

What you have learned and received
and heard and seen in me-practice these
things, and the God of peace be with you.
(Philippians 4:9, ESV)

Prayer: Father God, thank you for giving us hope and filling us with love. I pray you to strengthen us in our faith and guide us in our walk daily. Help me to always remember that you Lord, are in charge and keep my worries far from me. I am grateful for this beautiful Christmas season. In Jesus's name, I pray and give thanks, amen.

December 07

He Gives

Good morning my child, today feel the lightheartedness of my love. This season is a time of joy and goodwill. It is a time for giving. A time to celebrate my birth as I came to save you from sin. Before I rose again, on my last day, I endured pain and suffering of unimaginable proportions, but I did it all for you and the love I have for all my children. If you could only remember this daily. That I love you so much, that I took the weight of the world's sins upon my shoulders. I have given you the precious gift of my love, my heart, and eternal life. And for those who believe in me, accept me and follow me, they will have the gift of my Salvation. Sharing with others the truth of my good purpose. I listen to your prayers and help you daily with your fears. I am always with you, as I am the one who loves you eternally. Even though you fall short, I do not condemn you, but instead, I forgive you and bring out the good in all situations. Keep your eye on me and what it means to follow me and my good purpose. When you begin to follow me, I know for some of my children it might be hard to give up the ways of this world. Even some of my most dedicated followers find this hard at times, to remain faithful to me. As the world is always calling and tempting you to give in. But be strong and courageous, for I am the one who gives you strength. I give you the perseverance to continue on this good journey and to keep in step with me. I give to you, a calm and ease of peace found unshakable. It is all because of my truth and love and all that I give. I will sustain you today and always...

Cast your burden on the Lord, and he will sustain you; he will never permit the righteous to be moved.
(Psalm 55:22, ESV)

For God so loved the world, that he gave his only Son, that whoever believes in him should not perish but have eternal life.
(John 3:16, ESV)

I have been crucified with Christ. It is no longer I who live, but Christ who lives in me. And the life I now live in the flesh I live by faith in the Son of God, who loved me and gave himself for me.
(Galatians 2:20, ESV)

Prayer: Father God, thank you for forgiving us of our sins. I pray we always remember that you love us so much Lord, that you sacrificed your Son so that we may live. I ask for guidance and courage while walking in this world and to always remain bold, sharing your good news without hesitations. I love you, Lord with my whole heart. I pray for us all, that we will keep moving forward, growing in our faith, and except the place of your calling in our lives with thankful hearts. In Jesus's name, I pray, amen.

December 08

His Guiding Light of Faith

Oh, my child, be thankful for this day. As I am the Good Shepherd. I bring you mercy and grace all filled with love. I give to you, strength to continue this, the good journey of my purpose. Believe me, my child, I know my own. And have laid down my life for my sheep. No child of mine is too lost to find their way back home. If only they would keep following me and the light of my good path. In this world there is darkness, but I and my faithful bring light. Hold onto my good ways and stay in communication with me, making time for prayer even on the busiest of days. Surround yourself with other followers on the days when you feel a little down. Let them comfort and encourage you, pulling you back to me and my good message. Bringing your focus once again to what is right and just and fair. To what is good and full of faith, hope and love... Where you see no hope, you find no reason to try. This is where you will need your faith, as just a tiny mustard seed of faith can bring about enough hope to last you a lifetime. As your hopes turn into realities of the promises I have made. Keep your hopes aligned with me and my will. No deluded dreams of riches and worldly things. But the deep fulfilling promises of eternity with me in my kingdom. Where there will be no more sadness and no more tears. Only pure in love...in a way you have never known. Do not get drawn into the darkness, my child, just look as I will send a light to guide you home.

Your word is a lamp to my feet and a light to my path.
(Psalm 119:105, ESV)

And without faith it is impossible to please him, for whoever would draw near to God must believe that he exists and that he rewards those who seek him.
(Hebrews 11:6, ESV)

In this you rejoice, though now for a little while, if necessary, you have been grieved by various trials, so that the tested genuineness of your faith-more precious than gold that perishes through it is tested by fire, may be found to result in praise and glory and honor at the revelation of Jesus Christ.
(1 Peter 1:6–7, ESV)

Prayer: Father God, help us to stand confidently on our faith. Protect us from the enemy's lies, as we know he is the father of lies. Help us to discern what is from you, Lord, without confusion, guiding us with your light, making your path clear. So that we may have a confidence that is unshakable. And a strong grounded faith that will keep growing and flourishing. As we put our trust in you. We thank you, Father, for all these things seen and unseen, in Jesus's name I pray, amen.

December 9

Be Vigilant

This present life can be hard my child, yet it also is rewarding. To do what is right, living the way I call offers up a better way. Keep working hard as when you labor, you love. I do not promise an easy life in this the current world, as sin and death had entered in. But I came to the world in sacrifice so that sin and death could no longer lay claim on you. Salvation finds those who call me Lord. And to my faithful children a reward. I do hold the gift of abundant living. As always revealed in my good time. Keep mindful my child, when you live for me that the enemy will try to steal your focus away from me. Be watchful and vigilant, as the enemy is also very clever. He will try to use your own thoughts against you causing you doubts and disbelief. Knowing this, as I am informing you, you can avoid being drawn in by such attacks. Hold even tighter to me, call out to me and I will come to you, enshrouding you with my truth. Protecting you from the darkness with the light of my love.

You keep him in perfect peace whose mind is stayed on you, because he trusts in you.
(Isaiah 26:3, ESV)

Beloved, do not be surprised at the fiery trial when it comes upon you to test you, as though something strange were happening to you.
(1 Peter 4:12, ESV)

*I give them eternal life, and they will
never perish, and no one will snatch them
out of my hand. My Father, who has given
them to me, is greater than all, and no one
is able to snatch them out of the Fathers
hand. I and the Father are one.*
(John 10:28–30, ESV)

Prayer: Father God, I pray for your protection for me
and all my friends and family. I thank you for watching over
us all and for armoring us each and every day with your
Presence. I lift us up to you Lord, that no weapon formed
against us shall prosper. Thank you also for helping us this
day, to find peace and to feel at ease. In Jesus's name, I pray,
amen.

December 10

Jesus the Gift

I am your Good Shepherd and you are my flock. My sheep know my voice and follow where I lead. I send you little nudges using my Holy Spirit which lives in you. But do you not believe? This season you are preparing to celebrate in remembrance, the day of my birth, my coming to earth. My Father sent me to be your Savoir, in the form of a human baby. I came from the womb of a virgin. Born to save the world from sin and death. While I was with you, I walked among you on earth. I told the people of the good message. My faithful listened and followed me. But for others, because of their humanity, they didn't follow me without question. I was loved deeply by my followers and hated with the same intensity by those who felt threatened or didn't understand… But my sheep knew me, and still know me, as I am the Messiah. Even some who did not know me, on my last day before my resurrection, to their hearts I was revealed, and after my crucifixion, their hearts would change, and they would also follow me. I rose again and conquered death for you all. As this is my precious gift. The gift of Salvation and eternal life. A gift of love, to those who believe and call me their Lord. I am a God who forgives, who loves without measure. And you are my children, my beloved, my flock. But you must lose yourself in order to save yourself. Follow me take up your cross daily and commit your ways to me. Losing your will and accepting mine. Being grateful through it all, knowing that my ways are far better. I give the gift of life. As I live, you shall also live, eternally free with me forevermore…

Fear not, little flock, for it is your Fathers good pleasure to give you the kingdom.
(Luke 12:32, ESV)

To him the gatekeeper opens. The sheep hear his voice, and he calls his own sheep by name and leads them out. When he has brought out all his own, he goes before them, and the sheep follow him, for they know his voice.
(John 10:3–4, ESV)

I am the good shepherd. The good shepherd lays down his life for the sheep.
(John 10:11, ESV)

Prayer: Father God, thank you for your precious gift. That you sent your only Son to save us from our sins. I pray to be a blessing to others and that I would know your will, so that I may walk in the path of your choosing. I pray for all today and thank you for the people in my life. In Jesus's name, I pray, amen.

December 11

Take Heart, Enjoy

Cast your mind on things above and in all ways acknowledge me. Seek ye first my kingdom. Keeping your sight pure and focused while remaining rooted in me. There are wide paths and narrow in the way of your life, that you shall remain to follow me. Do not be afraid and turn from me during these most arduous times. But, in these times, I will ask you to trust me even more. Trust me with vigor, wholehearted and complete. Stepping out onto faith, claiming confidence in the day, filled with laughter and love. There will be times of stagnancy, where things may seem to just stop, but know it is for my good purpose and that these times will not last. Finding your steps in me and the foundations of love that I bring. Moving forward with joy once again. No one is happy all the time. As happiness is an emotion, fleeting and changing like the direction of the wind. But take heart, my child, as it is I the Lord who speaks to the wind and it surely obeys. I will bring you a sense of calm and peace again, so that you may enjoy the blessings I bring. Find enjoyment, my child, as it is good. Take heart and enjoy.

His master said to him, "well done, good and faithful servant. You have been faithful over a little; I will set you over much. Enter into the joy of your master."
(Matthew 25:21, ESV)

May the God of hope fill you with all joy and peace in believing, so that by the power of the Holy Spirit you may abound in hope.
(Romans 15:13, ESV)

Also that everyone should eat and drink and take pleasure in all his toil-this is God's gift to man.
(Ecclesiastes 3:13, ESV)

Prayer: Father God, thank you, Lord, for this day help me to find the joy, so that I may be able to share with others, cheerfully your good news. I pray each day for all my family and friends today that this day is light and full of happiness. In Jesus's name, I pray, amen.

December 12

Faithful Steps

Draw near to me my little children, keep steadfast in prayer bringing everything to me. Do not try to hide the parts of your life that you feel I would not approve. There is nothing that I do not know, therefore I call on you and all my children to live in the way that I have deemed as right. I will help you in times of struggle and trouble and celebrate with you in the victory I bring. Remain faithful, my child, always trusting that I am doing what is best for you and know that your next is in my hands. Be thankful for the days I bring rest. Enjoy them and let me replenish your soul so that you do not grow weary. I will quench your thirst with my living waters and feed your soul daily with my words, find your strength by reading your Bible and arming yourself with the life of my good message. Learning to let go of your own ways. Letting me guide your steps, as I will keep you on task. Just keep me close, and I will uphold you. Not causing your foot to slip but placing my firm foundation beneath you, as you keep your eyes up and fixed on things above. This will keep you balanced and in good proportions. Sometimes it seems like you're walking the tightrope of life, but do not fear, as I am with you and will catch you if you fall. Never forget that it is I, your Lord who protects you. So walk through this day without the anxiety and fear. You must have faith to move forward. Trust me, my child, and take your faithful steps…

Keep steady my steps according to your promise, and let no iniquity get dominion over me.
(Psalm 119:133, ESV)

He drew up from the pit of destruction out of the miry bog, and set my feet upon a rock, making my steps secure.
(Psalm 40:2, ESV)

Every place that the sole of your foot will tread upon I have given to you, just as I promised to Moses.
(Joshua 1:3, ESV)

The steps of a man are established by the Lord, when he delights in his way.
(Psalm 37:23, ESV)

Prayer: Thank you, Father God, for your firm foundations, and all the love that you give. I place my trust in you daily. I lift up all my family and friends today. Lord, I ask you to fill our hearts with love. Keep us brave as we take our faithful steps. In Jesus's name, I pray, amen.

December 13

Let Your Heart Be Light

There is so much more child that I will show you. Do not fret over those things in which you have no control. Do not let melancholy find its home in you, as my Holy Spirit lives within you, so there is no room for the dark that sadness brings. Dig deep and grasp with all your might and take hold of your joy, as it is great and placed inside. Stop being so serious weighted and afraid of what the world can do to you. Let me remind you, with me, no weapon formed against you shall prosper. I have gone before you and, in the present, I am here. Stand on the firm foundations of my promises and let your heart be light. There is beauty in this day, waiting for you to take notice. Let this be a day when you take my yoke upon you and feel the weight begin to ease. Surround yourself with love and laughter within these precious moments, spent with family and friends. Let your heart be light, rising as a feather caught within a smooth and gentle wind. Today may you feel easy and unburdened as we walk through this day hand in hand…

Come to me, all who labor and are heavy laden, and I will give you rest. Take my yoke upon you, and learn from me, for I am gentle and lowly in heart, and you will find rest for your souls. For my yoke is easy and my burden is light.
(Matthew 11:28–30, ESV)

For I consider that the sufferings of this present time are not worth comparing with the glory that is to be revealed to us.
(Romans 8:18, ESV)

No weapon formed against thee shall prosper; every tongue that shall rise against thee in judgment thou shalt condemn. This is the heritage of the servants of the Lord, and their righteousness is of me, saith the Lord.
                    (Isaiah 54:17, KJV)

Prayer: Thank you, Father God, for the glory of this day and all the beauty that it brings. I pray you to watch over us all, each and every one, and that you help us to have a day full of the lightness of your love and the fullness of your joy. In Jesus's name, I give thanks and pray, amen.

December 14

You Can Do All Things

In the stillness when you sit and think, there may be times when you wonder, how you can pull through? You feel laden and heavy with burden, and the to-do list grows. But draw from me, my child, as you can do all things with my Spirit...who strengthens you. I will say to the mountain," move" and it moves. I speak to the howling winds of your life, "calm" and the winds calm. I will speak to your heart, "be still...and know that I am God." So be still little one and trust the Lord your God. When you put your trust in me and use the faith that you possess, you will see the most amazing things happen. The impossible with me becomes possible. There is nothing we can't accomplish. The to-do list lessens. The heavyweight begins to ease. And the joy of perseverance leads to the victory of completion. Yes, you can do all things, as you draw from my strength. Therefore, put no limitations on yourself and your good work. Press on knowing that I am with you and am supplying a limitless surge of energy to your soul. I also command the path to open up before you and the skies to cast their light. Making the way clearer to you as you travel and venture on.

I can do all things through Christ who strengthens me.
(Philippians 4:13, ESV)

He gives power to the faint, and to him who has no might he increases strength.
(Isaiah 40:29, ESV)

*But he said to me, "My grace is suffi-
cient for you, for my power is made perfect
in weakness." Therefore I will boast all the
more gladly of my weaknesses, so that the
power of Christ may rest upon me.*
(2 Corinthians 12:9, ESV)

Prayer: Father God, thank you for your love and your strength. I pray you to continue to lead and guide all of us each and every day. I put my trust in you and pray you to continue to grow us up in our faith. We know that with you Lord, nothing is impossible as we set our goals and tackle the daily tasks. We are more than conquerors with you. I praise your name, Jesus, and it is in your name I give thanks and pray, amen.

To my reader: No matter how difficult the circumstance or the situation, you can do all things through Christ who strengthens you. During the times in my life I feel overwhelmed I say it aloud, "I can do all things through Christ who strengthens ME." I put the emphasis on me as a reminder that our Lord works, not only for others but for me also. Sometimes I know we struggle to feel worthy of his help, but he loves us just as much as he does the rest of our faith family. So if you struggle with inferiority or self-worth just know he is for YOU and loves you with the same intensity as he does others. You are worth it because you are His.

December 15

The Cast of Cares

Good morning my beloved, open your eyes...time to rise and shine. Spend your time this morning with me, remaining thankful and opening up to me in genuine prayer. You can be authentic with me, have you not learned? As I can hear your prayers, every word, spoken and even the unspoken that you hold inside. I search your heart and mind and know what is deep within. I can see what you are too afraid to ask. It is as though at times you feel like you deserve less than what I want to give. I see your spirit, so kind, yet troubled by the worries of those around you. It is good to be compassionate, showing them empathy, my child, but do not carry their burdens as your own. Talk to me and cast your cares at my feet. Rest assured in confidence, that I will take care of those you love. For they are also my children and I love them too. Lifting them up when they feel down, wiping the tears away from their eyes. Just the way I do you, and when I have decided that you or they shall learn from the situation no other way. I will bring them peace. There are other times as you will learn that some suffering is for good, as it builds character and strength. Sometimes in your weakness and suffering the true polished spirit emerges, stronger than before. But it is I who knows what is best. I want you to be joyful and full of merriment, sharing your life with others, as you share first my good message. During trials, do you not know where your help comes from? It comes from me. Your Father who cares for you. Your Savor, who washes you of your sin, your Lord who loves you eternally. So cast those cares, my faithful, as always concerning you, I am taking good care...

I the Lord search the heart and examine the mind, to reward each person according to their conduct, according to what their deeds deserve.
(Jeremiah 17:10, NIV)

But as for me, I will look to the Lord; I will wait for the God of my salvation; my God will hear me.
(Micah 7:7, ESV)

Having the eyes of your hearts enlightened, that you may know what is the hope to which he has called you, what riches of his glorious inheritance in the saints.
(Ephesians 1:18, ESV)

Prayer: Father God, I will put my hope and trust in you. I give to you all my cares concerning my loved ones and those around me. I pray continually for your guidance in our lives and I thank you for the victory brought forth by you. I know we are in good hands and am grateful. In Jesus's name, I give thanks and pray, amen.

December 16

Peaceful, Easy Days

There are easy days full of the sunlight that my Presence brings. Clearing up any darkness that previously may have been hanging around. This is my reward, an easy day with no weight or worries. A perfect day where you have found my peace. There are smiles today felt with deep joy. You can share with others my good message and the love that I give. You have held onto me, and I have lightened the thoughts in your mind. As now they can settle on the simplicity that life brings. Breathe my child, take in the fresh air and enjoy the rest I have given, as it is refreshing and cleansing for your soul. There is nature to be appreciated and beauty in this day. I am your Father and all of creation has come from me. Knowing this you should feel unstoppable as you draw your strength from me. Make your way through this day with confidence, that is found within a warriors heart. But slow and gentle should be the tempo. Don't try to rush, take your time today and enjoy the easy, peaceful, days I bring.

You have given me the shield of your salvation, and your right hand supported me, and your gentleness made me great.
(Psalm 18:35, ESV)

Both riches and honor come from you, and you rule over all. In your hand are power and might, and in your hand it is to make great and to give strength to all.
(1 Chronicles 29:12, ESV)

Take my yoke upon you, and learn
from me, for I am gentle and lowly in heart,
and you will find rest for your souls.
(Matthew 11:29, ESV)

Great peace have those who love your
law; nothing can make them stumble.
(Psalm 119:165, ESV)

Prayer: Father God, thank you Lord for your peaceful easy days. I thank you, Father, for the rest that you bring to us all. In Jesus's name, I give thanks and praise, amen.

December 17

Be the Light

Call on me my child, I am here guiding you, protecting you, loving you. I am your Father who wants you to live happily. Living abundantly and full of joy. Trusting the fulfillment of my promises. There is hope when you learn to accept the grace and mercy that I offer, as it brings light to the darkness. Surround yourself with other believers and followers of me and my good message. There is strength in numbers as you can draw from me and from others the power of my Holy Spirit within. I cast out any shadows and bring your life into the light of my Salvation. When you journey out today, just before you step outside, spend time with me in prayer. Put on my whole armor so that you may keep your joy, in the strength of my Spirit. I gift you, child, as I call you my own. Therefore, put no limitations on yourself as you stand with me, finding more strength within each good step. Creating a momentum of victory. Oh, joyous days and glory found here in the perfection of my will. I create a light, so you can be a light and shine it out for all those around you. This is a reminder a light should be seen not hide beneath a box or a cover but put on a stand for all to see. Together we will share and spread the good message of my love. Sharing the gift of Salvation that I offer, and the glory that's found with me. So be the light, my beloved, as It is my good purpose that sets you free.

Again Jesus spoke to them saying, "I am the light of the world. Whoever follows me will not walk in darkness, but will have the light of life."
(John 8:12, ESV)

You are the light of the world. A city set on a hill cannot be hidden. Nor do people light a lamp and put it beneath a basket, but on a stand. And it gives light to all in the house. In the same way, let your light shine before others, so that they may see your good works and give glory to your Father who in is heaven.
(Matthew 5:14–16, ESV)

For at one time you were in darkness, but now you are light in the Lord. Walk as children of light.
(Ephesians 5:8, ESV)

Prayer: Father God, thank you for this day help me to be the light that you are calling me to be. I pray to always be a blessing to others, that they see you in me, Lord. I pray that you watch over us all and keep guiding us filling our hearts and minds with joy that we have found in you. I pray to shine, In Jesus's name, I pray, amen.

December 18

Trust and Believe

Speak to me in the morning, come to me mid-day, bring your requests to me in the evening as my love will point the way. There are so many things vying for your attention trying to pull your focus off of me, but you are stronger than you think and can accomplish more than you know as you stand firm, holding the hand of my promises in truth. I bring you rest when you are weary and when you feel no might I give you strength. You will be like a tree planted by the water if you keep rooted in me. Let all that you do my child, be done in love as it most certainly binds everything together, keeping the song if your life in perfect harmony. Just commit your ways to me, and I will establish your plans. I bring you to hope for a future and the confidence of victory. If you keep your faith solid and fixed on me and my good purpose you will be refreshed and your soul set free, from all the insecurities and uncertainties of this world. Keep walking by faith even when you cannot see the good design of my plans for your life. I want nothing but the best for you. But you must trust and believe.

That according to the riches of his glory he may grant you to be strengthened, with the power through his Spirit in your inner being, so that Christ may dwell in your hearts through faith-that you, being rooted and grounded in love.
(Ephesians 3:16–17, ESV)

Commit your work to the Lord, and your plans will be established.
(Proverbs 16:3, ESV)

For the moment all discipline seems painful rather than pleasant, but later it yields the peaceful fruit of righteousness to those who have been trained by it.
(Hebrews 12:11, ESV)

And above all these put on love, which binds everything together in perfect harmony.
(Colossians 3:14, ESV)

Prayer: Father God, I ask this day for an easy day found in the fullness of your love an easy day where we can be refreshed and full of joy. I pray for us to be surrounded by your loving arms, and thank you for your discipline given in love, for your guidance, and protection. In Jesus's name, I pray, amen.

December 19

Patience: The Gift

Practice having patience my child, I know this can is hard for you. Especially since most of my children have become accustomed to having everything at their fingertips. The world has gotten so much better at throwing distractions at my children, trying to keep them from me and my good purpose. But I am your Lord and I am Sovereign over your life so no distraction or worldly diversion will keep you from the glory of my love. Those who wait on me, when they grow weary, I will renew their strength. I will bring them to the victory of my truth, and they shall walk with confidence and a purpose, all my great design. They will mount up on wings like eagles and soar high above the storms that this life brings. They will not ask for a just recompense for any good gift that they have given, but instead, they will give thanks to the one who enables them to give and remain happy just as well. To you, my children, wait on me happily with joy in your hearts, so that you may rejoice in hope, be patient in afflictions and thankful in the victories brought forth by me as the answers to your prayers. I reward my children who remain faithful. Trust in these good ways you are learning from me. Freely sharing my good news. Practice living the way I have called you to live. And with this…my gift of patience grows your hope, solidifies your faith and your soul will begin to ease. You have heard it said, patience is a virtue, and in fact, it is. As it is a gift from me.

But they who wait for the Lord shall
renew their strength; they shall mount up
with wings like eagles; They shall run and
not be weary; they shall walk and not faint.
(Isaiah 40:31, ESV)

But if we hope for what we do not see,
we wait for it in patience.
(Romans 8:25, ESV)

Therefore the Lord waits to be gracious to you, and therefore he exalts himself to show mercy to you. For the Lord is a God of justice; blessed are all those who wait for him.
(Isaiah 30:18, ESV)

Prayer: Father God, thank you for this good day. I pray to be joyful while waiting, finding hope and remaining faithful to your good plans. I pray for everyone that we can rejoice in our waiting and be thankful for knowing everything is on your time because your timing is perfect. In Jesus's name, I pray and give thanks, amen.

But do not overlook this one fact, beloved, that with the Lord one day is as a thousand years, and a thousand years as one day.
(2 Peter 3:8, ESV)

December 20

His Great Plans

And you know that I have great plans for you my child, even when you cannot make out the steps that lie ahead of you. I am with you leading and guiding. And I know sometimes it is easy to get dismantled, but keep in your mind my power and strength, as I am your God, who brings things together. Binding the pieces of broken hearts, broken relationships, and even broken lives back together with my fierce Sovereignty and the power of my love. when you get broken down by the ways of this world, I will mend you. Filling your empty parts with my unending love. When you pass through dark waters, I will be with you. When you journey through scorched lands I will be by your side. I will never leave you or forsake you, child. Keep your faith and believe that where I am leading is full of my glory. I will give you an abundant life so that you may abound in every good work I call you too. Where I am leading there is peace and great love. Hold tightly to me and keep your feet on my good paths. The journey isn't always easy and at times it is downright hard, but to those who remain faithful and follow me with their whole heart, they will inherit my kingdom. I bring them up and out of the mire, as I use them to lead others to come and follow my teaching. Inviting all my children to come home… to me. Stay faithful as I open up the way. Unfolding for you my great plans.

For I know the plans I have for you,
declares the Lord, plans for welfare and not
for evil, to give you a hope and a future.
(Jeremiah 29:11, ESV)

When you go through deep waters, I will be with you. When you go through rivers of difficulty, you will not drown. When you walk through the fire of oppression, you will not be burned up; The flames will not consume you.
(Isaiah 43:2, NLT)

In him we have obtained an inheritance, having been predestined according to the purpose of him who works all things, according to the counsel of his will.
(Ephesians 1:11, ESV)

Prayer: Father God, this morning I surrender Lord, and give it all to you. Help us to keep our hands off of situations that are not our own. Keep growing us up in our faith and lead our steps as we walk through this day into the fulfillment of your great plans. Remind us, Lord, with your loving kindness that you have everything under control. I praise your name Jesus, and it is in your name, I pray and give thanks, amen.

December 21

Testimony

You are chosen, each and every one, will you not hear what I have called you to do? If you are unsure bring it to me in prayer…the nudging of my Presence will show you the way. Keep growing in your faith by reading my words and learning my good ways. Practice these things daily. When you do these, then the chaos will not find you unaware. Be ready, have your feet fitted with readiness to do and go wherever I call. Be open like a book with your testimony and ready to share. For some, I know this is hard, as people in general, try to keep things private that cause such emotion to stir. But I have given you your testimony, to show others of my glory. Showing them the light of hope that my gift of salvation brings. To show them they are forgiven, and they are loved just as I love you…

Delight yourself in the Lord, and he will give you the desires of your heart.
(Psalm 37:4, ESV)

May the Lord direct your hearts to the love of God and to the steadfastness of Christ.
(2 Thessalonians 3:5, ESV)

Fight the good fight of the faith. Take hold of eternal life to which you were called and about which you made the good confession in the presence of many witnesses.
(Ephesians 4:15, ESV)

My mouth will tell of your righteous acts, of your deeds of salvation all the day, for their number is past my knowledge. With mighty deeds of the Lord God I will come; I will remind them of your righteousness, yours alone. O God, from my youth you have taught me, and I still proclaim your wondrous deeds. So even to old age and gray hairs, O God, do not forsake me, until I proclaim your might to another generation, your power to all those to come.
(Psalm 71:15–18, ESV)

So everyone who acknowledges me before men, I also will acknowledge before my Father who is in heaven.
(Matthew 10:32, ESV)

Prayer: Lord I pray to be bold and share my good testimony that you have given to me. I pray that by sharing more will come to seek you. In Jesus's name, I pray giving thanks and praise, amen.

December 22

Hold Tightly

Take this opportunity to slow down in your mind, my child, as the days will push and pull your thoughts in many different directions. Hold tightly to what I have given, spending time with me in prayer and concentrating on my living words in the Bible. I will restore your strength and give your health all found within my will. Many tasks are at hand my child as this season people everywhere are preparing for the coming day, the celebration of my birth. Take a breath and solidly keep your focus on me. Learning to draw from my strength and in all ways acknowledge me, bringing me your thanks and praise and I will make your crooked paths straight. Whatever pressure you may be feeling, you can cast it off. Let today be what it is and be thankful. Not worrying about tomorrow as tomorrow has worries of its own but living in the moments of the present. Hold tightly to your joy. Hold tightly to my hand. Hold tightly to my ways, and all will get done. Perseverance is the word for today. I have you in the palm of my hands, just hold tight.

For I, the Lord your God, hold your right hand; it is I who say to you, "Fear not, I am the one who helps you."
(Isaiah 41:13, ESV)

You will decide on a matter, and it will be established for you, and light will shine on your ways.
(Job 22:28, ESV)

For to us, a child is born, to us, a son is given; and the government shall be on his shoulder, and his name shall be called Wonderful Counselor, Mighty God, Everlasting Father, Prince of Peace.
(Isaiah 9:6, ESV)

Prayer: Father God, today I bring to you my thoughts… I pray to follow where you lead. Jesus, lead me Lord and guide me. Fill me with your strength. Watch over all my family and friends. Help me to find pleasure in my daily tasks and accomplish them with joy. In Jesus's name, I pray, and I give thanks, amen.

December 23—(2 more days till Christmas! God Bless you all my friends!)

Presence of the King

When you love me, you will keep my commandments as you follow in my steps. You will emulate the nature of my Spirit, creating the light of my glow within you. It is when you live this way that you can truly be a blessing to other people, showing them what my grace and love looks like. Find yourself basking in the glow of all the glorious moments that we get to share. Sit with me a while. I am smiling, as now your heart is full. The Christmas day is almost here, the day when my Father gave his gift to the world. And through this gift, a Son, your Savoir, your Messiah, your Lord, I was sent to save the world. How glorious it is to be in the presence of the King. And you, my child, who spend time with me in prayer, are in the presence of your King every day. How wonderful it should be to know that I, your God am with you. I strengthen you, watch over you, guide you, and love you with an all-encompassing, everlasting and eternal love. I teach you things and show you the way of the light as you walk on my good paths. I build you up when the world tears you down. when you can no longer stand on your own, I pick you up and carry you. And within you, I give to you the gift of my Holy Spirit. The Spirit with whom you can lean on and trust. Yes, my child, you can feel confident knowing that every day of your life you are truly in the presence of your King.

He is the radiance of the glory of God
and the exact imprint of his nature, and
he upholds the universe by the word of his
power. After making purification for sins,

he sat down at the right hand of the Majesty on high.
    (Hebrews 1:3, ESV)

Jesus answered him, "If anyone loves me, he will keep my word, and my father will love him, and we will come to him and make our home with him."
    (John 14:23, ESV)

On his robe and on his thigh he has a name written, King of kings and Lord of lords.
    (Revelation 19:16, ESV)

Prayer: Thank you Jesus, our Lord and our King for remaining present with us. Thank you for loving us. I praise you Lord on this Christmas Eve. I pray for all the people in my life who do not know you, or who know of you, but do not give you the glory for who you really are, that all of them truly come to know you Jesus, the way that I know you. For all of your gentleness guidance and love, I thank you for all of your grace and mercy and kindness. I praise you, Father, and honor your name. In Jesus's name, I praise and pray, amen.

December 24: Christmas Eve: the Bethlehem star—will lead the wise men to our Savior the King of kings.

Merry Christmas Eve!

Merry Christmas

Open your eyes, what do you see? Really look around at this glorious season. All the decor sights and sounds of this Christmas have taken shape. There are love and kindness in the air. This busy season is a time to enjoy all the beautiful characteristics of me, and my nature. As you appreciate humility, kindness, generosity, helpfulness, tenderness, mercy, grace, and love. There is a gentleness that's found within the Christmas season, unlike any other time during the year. It is felt deep within the hearts of all my children, as it is a time of togetherness. Surround yourself with the sights and sounds of love. Perfecting the light that closes out the shadows that try to invade. Practice letting go of past situations and current that are holding you back as you look forward. Moving onward to your new calling. Forgiving others and yourself, as this is the way I will lead you into the abundance of your life. Enjoy the present as my gift. Find honor and beauty in it all... This is truly the season my child, a celebration of me as a gift to the world—Hallelujah, Hallelujah your Savior was born. Merry Christmas my child.

> *But as he considered these things, behold, an angel of the Lord appeared to him in a dream, saying, "Joseph, son of David, do not fear to take Mary as your wife, for that which is conceived in her is from the Holy Spirit."*
> (Matthew 1:20, ESV)

*She will bear a son, and you shall call
his name Jesus, for he will save his people
from their sins.*
(Matthew 1:21, ESV)

*For unto you is born this day in the
city of David a Savoir, who is Christ the
Lord.*
(Luke 2:11, ESV)

*For God so loved the world that, that
he gave his only Son, that whoever believes
in Him should not perish but have eternal
life.*
(John 3:16, ESV)

Prayer: Happy Birthday Jesus! Today may we all gather together and fill this world with your love. I pray you to watch over us all keeping us safe. I lift us up to you Lord, as we celebrate your gift to the world. Jesus, we praise your name. We thank you for this day and all the days of the coming new year, Hallelujah we sing as today is the day our Savoir was born. May we all rejoice. In Jesus's name, I praise. giving thanks and love, amen.

December 25: Merry Christmas. Today is our Lord's birthday. Let there be peace on earth.

Keep Faithfully Following

In light of my Presence, I will speak to your heart and show you great and mighty things that you do not know. I offer you the ways of my good paths, learning to walk beside my still waters while remaining faithful to me through the vast deserts. My words are a lamp unto your feet, as I light up the ways ahead. Keep following me, my child. As with your faithfulness and perseverance, my victory is found. Do not grow weary in doing good. As surely, I will reward your hard work with kindness. Make peace with your shortcomings and let them go so you may begin the upcoming year a new. You have brought much joy to me, my child, as your heart and your actions run concurrently together and are in sync. You have done so much for others trying to share with them a bit of happiness, and the light of my love. Showing them the eternal gift, I offer. Do you not know I see? I see what is in your heart and on your mind, as I am with you always. Keep hoping and dreaming and pursuing. My reward is just for my faithful children if only they shall keep following me.

You shall walk in all the way that the Lord your God has commanded you, that you may live, and that it may go well with you, and that you may live long in the land that you shall possess.
(Deuteronomy 5:33, ESV)

Again Jesus spoke to them, saying, "I am the light of the world. Whoever follows me will not walk in darkness, but will have the light of life."
(John 8:12, ESV)

For this you have been called, because Christ also suffered for you, leaving you an example, so that you might follow in his steps.
(1 Peter 2:21, ESV)

Call to me and I will answer you, and will tell you great and hidden things that you have not known.
(Jeremiah 33:3, ESV)

Prayer: Father God, I pray to always and cheerfully take up my cross and follow you. I ask that the path of your light will be clear to all of my family and friends, myself included and that you protect us all along the way. In Jesus's loving name, I pray, amen.

December 26

Strength and Love

The days ahead, are full of blessings and surprises. But keep your mind on present things and enjoy my good ways. The darkness of the day will finally settle, and a glorious light will radiate down permeating your precious soul. Feel the strength begin to grow as you know you can do all things because I strengthen you. You can enjoy all the moments because of my love. Love is patient, love is kind, love never boasts, love always hopes, always dreams, always pursues, my love doesn't fade or cease. My love is eternal and forever brought forth and given to all my children without condition. Look inside yourself to find the gift of my Holy Spirit the one who helps and leads. Find your footing and enjoy the tiny treasures in this day all full of strength and love.

> *Let not steadfast love and faithfulness forsake you; bind them around your neck; write them on the tablet of your heart. So you will find favor and good success in the sight of God and man.*
> (Proverbs 3:3–4, ESV)

> *Let me hear in the morning of your steadfast love, for in you I trust. Make known the way I should go, for to you I lift up my soul.*
> (Psalm 143:8, ESV)

> *So now faith, hope, and love abide, these three; but the greatest is love.*
> (1 Corinthians 13:13, ESV)

Prayer: Father God, thank you Lord for all your mercy, grace and especially your love. I pay to be thoughtful to others and always emulate your kind nature and loving Spirit. I lift us all up Lord fill us this day with your love. In Jesus's name, I pray, amen.

December 27

Release Them

Learn to release them in my care. Stop trying to fix people who refuse to listen. When they speak in circles about this or that or think that they are still in control, trying to do things their own way, the ways that have not worked thus far. Stop trying to fix them, my child, as I am teaching a good lesson, so I say to you, "Hands off." Let me oversee their molding, keeping your hands off the situation. When you refuse to loosen your grasp, you delay the teaching of their spirit and keep them from growing. There is a time to put away the things of yesterday and learn to walk on my right path. it is a place of truth and it can only be helped when they accept the error of their ways and turn back to me. Learning to admit their faults and surrendering to me. My children who come to me on their knees with emptiness, will not be so likely to resist when I come to them and fill them with all my good and righteous ways. For when you are empty of yourself, you can be full of my Spirit. I can lift them and fill them with love. But first, they must come` to me. Release them so that they may seek me, with an eagerness to learn and a thirst to know me.

Rather, speaking the truth in love, we are to grow up in every way into him who is the head, into Christ.
(Ephesians 4:15, ESV)

The thief comes only to kill and steal and destroy. I came that they may have life and live it abundantly.
(John 10:10, ESV)

He answered, "Whether he is a sinner
I do not know. One thing I do know, that
though I was blind now I see."
(John 9:25, ESV)

Prayer: Father God, please teach me how to release my grasp on my loved ones. I know they need to learn but it is so hard with this tender heart of mine. Help me to know when to step in and when to step out. I lift all of us up to you this day and trust your ways. Teach us how to live the way you want us to Lord. In Jesus's loving name, amen.

If we say we have no sin, we deceive
ourselves, and the truth is not in us.
(1 John 1:8, ESV)

December 28

Love Those around You

This season is a time to celebrate with loved ones. Let joy and love permeate within your hearts and bring your praise to me. We can walk through this day in spite of the difficulty this world has brought to try and discourage. Casting off fear and overcoming doubt. As I am Emmanuel, God with you. Enjoy my Presence and the peace I give. Let my love fill your cup until it runs over, onto the people around you. Share my good message and walk in my steps, following my righteous ways. Always strive to shine your light even on the days when you feel a little dim. My Spirit within you recharging you like a battery will refresh you with an endless power supply. There are honesty and truth found in my nature. Try these things and be honorable and forthcoming to those around you. Do not hold back love as this bind's everything together in harmony. In you, I have made my home and together we can accomplish much. Just look inside yourself to find my Spirit here and ready to help. Where there is love there is hope. Share the good lessons I am teaching, giving freely my love. Try Patience, forgiveness, gentleness, kindness, compassion, humility, and understanding, for this is what it looks like, truly loving those around you.

With all humility and gentleness, with patience, bearing with one another in love.
(Ephesians 4:2, ESV)

Love one another with brotherly affection. Outdo one another showing honor.
(Romans 12:10, ESV)

No one has ever seen God; if we love one another, God abides in us and his love is perfected in us.
(1 John 4:12, ESV)

There is no fear in love, but perfect love casts out fear. For fear has to do with punishment, and whoever fears has not been perfected in love.
(1 John 4:18, ESV)

Prayer: Father God, thank you for this day. Guide my heart always, allowing me to show the people around me what your love looks like. Let them truly feel your Presence and love, working in their lives. I am thankful for you Lord, and all that you give to me daily. Help me to love, the way you love. In Jesus's name, I pray, giving thanks and praise, amen.

December 29

Fix Your Eyes on Things Above

You are mine, my child, I will call you to remember this daily. As the world will tell you, you are many things that you are not. Because you have accepted me and my good purpose, I have restored you. You lack nothing because it is I, who am in you, making my home in the sweet dwelling place of your heart. Stand firm and confident when the dark one comes to you and says," you are nothing, you're a failure. You have no clue what you're doing." You simply stand firm and say to the deception, not my truth! Your truth is mine, my child, as I am your Lord. Walk on the good paths of my promises and learn to stand up for yourself. Do not cave into the pressures and the lies that are thrown into your mind. If you need my strength to conquer the lies, I say to you, "take it." I have endless strength for you and the love to grow your spirit up in faith. Call out to me, Jesus, and I will stay and make the lies dissolve, turning them into nothing. Sending them back to the one who will try to deceive you. My Spirit knows the clever lies and will not cave to the obtrusive attacks, and you, my child must not either. Do not for one-minute feed into the duplicitous strikes. Your mind should be kept on the one who loves you, so keep your eyes up focused on things above. Keep your eyes on me. Keep your thoughts full of truth and light. See yourself through my eyes and not on those deceitful lies of the false one. Ask me to clear your mind and to purify your thoughts with my love. Yes, my child, just keep your mind focused on me, and all else will follow. Fix your eyes on things above... I love you, my child.

Fixing our eyes on Jesus, the pioneer
and the perfecter of our faith, for the joy set

before him he endured the cross, scorning its
shame, and sat down at the right hand at
the throne of God.
(Hebrews 12:2, NIV)

Set your mind on things that are
above, not on things that are on earth.
(Colossians 3:2, ESV)

But the wisdom from above is first
pure, then peaceable, gentle, open to rea-
son, full of mercy and good fruits, impartial
and sincere. And a harvest of righteousness
is sown in peace by those who make peace.
(James 3:17–18, ESV)

Prayer: Father God, thank you for this day. I pray to be strengthened by your Spirit daily. I pray that on days I feel unsure or doubtful that you would come to me and remind that I am your child, so I can be the light to others and remind them that they belong to you too. I pray to be strengthened in my faith with your loving kindness. In Jesus's name, I pray, amen.

December 30

Experience and Share

Start off your day with a thankful heart and together we can grow up your faith in love. A love for others, a love for your circumstances, a love for your life, a love for yourself and most importantly a love for me. Where there is love there most certainly is hope. A new year is approaching, and the excitement starts to stir, as many will make new year resolutions. They will be hopeful of good change. To my children, I say be happy in the new year. Be happy all year long. Show kindness and love always. Stay positive, remain joyful and hopeful. Be the light that I have called you to be. Share my good news with others. Help lead those in darkness out into the light of my love. Show them what faith looks like, and that with my love, there will always be hope. I love all my children and will bless them abundantly as they follow in my steps. These words I want you to call to mind daily, and bring them into action; Faith, Love, Patience, Hope, Kindness, and Peace, all these good things exist for all my children. In the new year and always, all throughout their lives these good things and good works for all my beloved children to live, to dream, to experience and share...

And I will give them one heart, and a new spirit I will put within them. I will remove the heart of stone from there flesh and give them a heart of flesh.
(Ezekiel 11:19, ESV)

And let us consider how to stir up one another to love and good works, not neglecting to meet together, as is the habit of some,

*but encouraging one another, and all the
more as you see the Day drawing near.*
(Hebrews 10:24–25, ESV)

*In the same way, let your light shine
before others, so that they may see your
good works and give glory to your Father
in heaven.*
(Mathew 5:16, ESV)

Prayer: Father God, I lift this new year up to you Lord,
I ask that you bring peace, love, kindness, joy, abundance
and of all your goodness and grace. Fill this year with your
wonderful blessings for all your children, Lord. And always
to you, Lord Jesus be the glory forever and ever, in Jesus's
name I pray, amen.

Happy New Year's Eve! Be safe and have fun.

God Bless us all in this next year and all the years to
come. In Jesus's name, amen.

December 31

Prayers, Reflections of the Past Year, and Upcoming Hopes for the Next

_____

_____

_____

_____

_____

_____

_____

_____

_____

_____

_____

_____

_____

_____

_____

_____

_____

_____

_____

_____

_____

_____

_____

_____

_____

_____

_____

_____

Afterword

During this entire journey, I have learned so much as the Lord opened his good path to me. Here is my honestly, I am still seeking him. Every day, I choose to let him lead. He doesn't pull or force his will upon me. He guides me with his easy gentleness and fills me with love for all of us, all his children and all his creation. I am still in awe. He has given me this ability to write. I have no formal training, no degrees, nothing by worldly standards that makes me outshine from any other person on this earth. So this to me has been a pretty amazing journey. And although I don't have the worldly recognition of papers or degrees, I do have what is most important and that is a great love for my Father in heaven, and a great desire to please him above all else. I have a love for people and want to help everyone come to know Jesus. It is what he has placed inside me. He was here all along. Even during the times, I chose to push him back. Even during my lost times, I let go of his hand, he forgave me, he forgives me still. He loves me unconditionally and has called me to write this to share with others. Letting you into the privacy of our conversations, something all can relate to. He sends me hearts in the shapes and forms of everything from a leaf on a tree, a stain on the ground, a rock, a piece of wood, a cloud, even a shadow casting its shade. He has been sending me these God winks for quite some time now, and I never understood exactly why? Except now I'm realizing this was all part of his plan to get my attention to do what he has been calling me to do. And while he leads me, he shows me that I am on the right track, and that he is leading me to do something good. Something he has called me to do. I feel him, he speaks to my heart. He gave me the title for this devotional as I was searching for a title and suddenly, I realized by him sending me hearts and by our time together, Then came with the thought" Speaking to the Heart" it came to me so suddenly as if out of nowhere and with intensity. I would call it, a true epiphany, a genuine lightbulb moment. I am grateful to Jesus that he uses me for his glory and not my own. This is all for his glory. If you haven't found him yet I encourage you to keep seeking. You will find him when you search for him with your whole heart. I believe if we sit back in stillness, we can all hear him, maybe not audibly but hear him in the tender whispers within ourselves, speaking to our hearts. If you invite him in, his Holy Spirit will make his home in you and guide you leading you to his great calling. Just let him in and watch what he does.

This is mine to share, a small part of my testimony of what Jesus can do with anyone. He turns the ordinary into extraordinary. I hope you enjoyed this devotional and that it pointed you to Him. Keep reading your Bible, fill your life up with his living words. You are worth it, nothing you've done could ever separate you from His love. Thank you for allowing me to share this year long journey with you. I pray these words to find you always, God loves you...unconditionally.

May God bless you and strengthen you. As always with love, April <3

> Now may the God of peace who brought again from the dead our Lord Jesus, the great shepherd of the sheep, by the blood of the eternal covenant, equip you with everything good that you may do his will, working in us that which is pleasing

in his sight, through Jesus Christ, to whom
be the glory forever and ever. Amen.
(Hebrews 13:20–21, ESV)

Bibliography

The Holy Bible (English Standard Version, New International Version, King James Version)

Regarding Art reference: Kintsugi found on page dated for use of information (Wikipedia free encyclopedia/ *My Modern Met*. 2017-04-25. Retrieved 2017-07-12.)

Reference: "Amazing Grace," hymn, written by John Newton (1779)

Reference: *Bringing in the Sheaves* written by Knowles Shaw (1874)

About the Author

April Suzanne Yarber is a newly published first-time author who has felt inspired her whole life to write. "There was always an internal tugging," she says. And a long while later, the Lord began showing her His love in a tangible way. As she began seeing heart-shaped objects, that she has taken pictures of and collected over the years. She is a single mother of 2 beautiful daughters. She has been working at a hospital for 14 years and loves helping people. She has a love for people and feels compassion for everybody. She wants to see everybody excel and succeed in life. To see them overcome their struggles and live their dreams. She has great empathy for all people but has a soft spot for people who are having difficulties. She is a cancer survivor, so she knows firsthand how precious life is. She has been through so much in her life. Let's just say her life hasn't been easy. But the Lord placed in her a big heart and he grew in her a big faith. Where he taught her to believe in herself for who she is. He showed her how to love herself the way that he loves her. She wants to share the love of Jesus with the world and desires everyone to be saved… But also, she would like people to build their faith in the Lord and know that nothing is unattainable to those who work hard and believe.

And if you believe in the Lord then you will learn to believe in yourself, because he is with you. He loves you and he cares for YOU.

CPSIA information can be obtained
at www.ICGtesting.com
Printed in the USA
FFHW011124230919
55137410-60862FF